CW00696924

The Politics of Unease
in the Plays of John Fletcher

The Politics of Unease
in the
Plays of John Fletcher

GORDON McMULLAN

For Sue —
And nary a mention of
The Nice Valour in the
entire volume…

Gordon

THE UNIVERSITY OF MASSACHUSETTS PRESS

AMHERST

Copyright © 1994 by
The University of Massachusetts Press
All rights reserved
Printed in the United States of America
LC 93-28554
ISBN 0–87023–892–2
Designed by Susan Bishop
Set in Linotron Garamond No. 3 by Keystone Typesetting, Inc.
Printed and bound by Thomson-Shore, Inc.

Library of Congress Cataloging-in-Publication Data
McMullan, Gordon, 1962–
The politics of unease in the plays of John Fletcher / Gordon McMullan.
p.   cm. — (Massachusetts studies in early modern culture)
Includes bibliographical references and index.
ISBN 0–87023–892–2 (alk. paper)
1. Fletcher, John, 1579–1625—Political and social views.
2. Politics and literature—England—History—17th century.
3. Political plays, English—History and criticism.
I. Title.   II. Series.
PR2517.P6M35   1994   93–28554
822'.3—dc20   CIP

British Library Cataloguing in Publication Data are available.

This book is dedicated to my mother, Muriel McMullan,
and to the memory of my father, Alexander McMullan, who died
while it was being written, and without whose love and belief
it would never have been possible.

CONTENTS

Preface   ix

ONE
Parentage and Patronage   1

TWO
"This is a pretty Riot / It may
grow to a rape"   37

THREE
The Reason in Treason   85

FOUR
Collaboration   132

FIVE
"Strange carded cunningnesse"   156

SIX
Discovery   197

CODA
"Strange bifronted posture"   257

APPENDIX 1
Family Trees of Beaumont, Fletcher,
Huntingdon   263

APPENDIX 2
Chronology for the Plays of John Fletcher
and His Collaborators   267

Textual Note   271

Notes   275

Bibliography   313

Index   333

PREFACE

A visit to the Cinque Port of Rye, Sussex, where John Fletcher was born, is a very different experience from a trip to Stratford-upon-Avon and in many ways a more agreeable one. There are no signposts proclaiming this to be "Fletcher country" and no placards directing you to his birthplace, the former vicarage, a modest building located a few yards below the splendid parish church. Fletcher's father was "minister of the word of God in Rye" in the 1570s, and the vicarage is now the "Fletcher's House" lunch and tea rooms. The frontage of the house was altered in the eighteenth and nineteenth centuries, but the interior remains relatively unspoiled, with a display of "some of the oldest window glass in England," and a small sign outside tells you about Fletcher, who is characterized mainly as a collaborator with Francis Beaumont and, inevitably, a friend of William Shakespeare's. Rye is in fact better known now for Lamb House, where Henry James wrote some of his novels, than it is for producing Shakespeare's successor at the Globe.*

The fifty-four plays in which Fletcher was involved form the single most substantial canon of dramatic work to come down to us from the English Renaissance. Yet they remain almost wholly unexplored by critics. The simplest aim of this study is to redress this critical imbalance by opening up the canon to those who have not previously wished to approach it, and to propose that a knowledge of Fletcher's plays is essential to an understanding of Renaissance drama as a whole. Fletcher occupies a curious position among Renaissance playwrights, managing to be at once central and marginal. He is central for three reasons: he wrote three plays with Shakespeare (two of which are extant), he succeeded Shakespeare as the chief playwright of the King's Company, and he exerted a substantial generic influence over drama for decades both before and

---

*I am grateful to Adam Steinhouse for mentioning a reference he had seen to "Fletcher's House" in the relevant *Let's Go* guide.

after the shutdown of the theaters in the 1640s and 1650s. At the same time, he is almost entirely overshadowed culturally and historically by the phenomenon of Shakespeare, as the long-running arguments over the authorship of *Henry VIII* and *The Two Noble Kinsmen* amply testify. What is clear above all is that Fletcher is always seen in his relationships with other playwrights, as the sign outside the Rye tearooms suggests.

Yet Fletcher's importance goes far beyond his subordination to others: his particular dramaturgy shaped the work of writers such as Massinger and Shirley and, later, the bulk of Restoration playwrights. Along the way—perhaps as soon as 1634, with the appropriation of *The Faithful Shepherdess* to the cultural conditions of the court of Henrietta Maria—his characteristic tone of irony and unease was misplaced, or perhaps displaced. Yet without recognizing the role and origins of that unease in Fletcher's drama of the 1610s and 1620s, a crucial part of the construction of Jacobean drama is lost to the critic. Fletcher wrote ironic, collaborative, tragicomic drama in a range of forms: the plays all share the duality embedded in each of these terms. Interpretively, they are remarkably complex, premised upon cultural, political, and sexual matrices which create a distinct unease in audience and critic alike. They are remarkably difficult to locate, too, in terms of the professional practice involved in their construction, being almost invariably the unfinished, almost casual product of at least two writers. Generically, they are self-contradictory and elusive, creating and created by a form—tragicomedy—which had never (and still has never) established itself in any clear and definitive way.

In this study I have attempted to find appropriate ways of reading a group of plays which, in terms of their politics, their generic complexities, and their collaborative mode of production, appear to defy standard critical practices. I begin with context and narrative, and I wish to explain the logic of this at the start. I do not intend to suggest that the particular contexts I examine are the only ones within which it is possible to read Fletcher's plays. The information provided is certainly not to be regarded as the definitive key to the historical meaning of the plays: the histories offered are, after all, textual, and as much subject to interpretation and occupation as the plays. Rather, it provides a basis—a set of historicized starting points—for literary analysis. Thus I suggest that knowledge of Fletcher's own family context and the family and milieu contexts of his patrons, the fifth earl and countess of Huntingdon, is of tangible value in ordering and analyzing the many plays in which Fletcher had a hand. This location grounds certain issues repeatedly broached in an apparently dislocated series of plays. "Dis-location" might in fact usefully describe a necessary twofold maneuver in analyzing Fletcher's work. I refer to a process by which the plays are both located in certain contexts requiring a rejection of the centralizing tendency of criticism of Renaissance texts over the last twenty years and relocated in a literary history which privileges neither courtly nor tragic absolutes, but instead looks to multiple allegiances, multiple generic inputs, and multiple authorships, aiming to delineate the negotiation of conflicting loyalties apparent in the plays.

To begin with, I specify the particular environments within which Fletcher was brought up, briefly considering the households and attitudes of his grandfather, father, and uncle, and I account as far as possible both for his origins as a playwright and for his acquaintance with the young Francis Beaumont. I have dealt at some length with the Huntingdons, both because they remained Fletcher's patrons throughout his career and because they serve as a test case for approaches to "country" matters in the 1610s and 1620s. In the process, and in order to provide adequate contextualization for a reading of two of Fletcher's early solo plays, I have incorporated a narrative of certain events in the year 1607 in which the earl of Huntingdon was substantially involved and which set the tone for Fletcher's reading of the country throughout his career. I trust that a more detailed description of these events than is usually offered in criticism of, for example, Shakespeare's *Coriolanus,* will be of interest in itself, but the logic of the narrative is both to provide a basis for a local reading of the plays and to offer a narrative alternative to the strategy of the literary anecdote made familiar by recent historicist critics.

I have also dealt with the critical problem of collaborative writing, looking for an appropriate way to analyze a canon consisting in large part of texts which are the product of joint writing, and arguing for the necessity of detailed textual information for adequate literary criticism. I have analyzed playwright-patron relations in the context of the Fletcher canon, demonstrating not only the predominant role of the countess, rather than the earl, in matters of patronage at Ashby, the Huntingdons' seat, but also the modulation of shared interests between writer and patron. I argue that while their shared experience of Protestantism will have provided an essential point of contact between Fletcher and the earl, their attitudes—both to the management of the country and to colonial venture—could at times diverge, particularly since Fletcher's audiences would have had a quite different view on these matters from that of his patrons. I am thus equally interested in the ramifications of influence (in collaborative as well as patronage relations), in the possibility of agency within the broader context of a dependent relationship, and in the necessary negotiations undertaken by a writer whose sources of patronage and funding came simultaneously from very different quarters. Above all, my aim has been to provide a coherent analysis of Fletcher's political plays, spending a relatively high proportion of my time on those solo and collaborative plays written in the second half of his career which are rarely, if ever, discussed in criticism of "Beaumont-and-Fletcher." Fletcher's plays and contexts are largely uncharted territories, and I trust that the detailed examination of dramatic texts offered in the latter part of the book will both balance and benefit from the particularity of contextualization and localization provided at the outset.

THIS STUDY is a revised version of my Oxford D. Phil. thesis of the same title, submitted in 1991. I am grateful to the British Academy for funding my doctoral work, and to Wadham College and the Bodleian Library for providing a magnificent environment for that work. I am also grateful to St. Peter's College for providing me with the means for a further year of study. I would like to thank the Leave Committee and the Department of English Literature of the University of Newcastle upon Tyne for providing a timely term's sabbatical leave as I was completing the revisions.

Many people encouraged, influenced, and instructed me prior to and during the writing of the thesis, and I am especially grateful to Danny Anderson, G. Douglas Atkins, Francis Barker, David Bergeron, Martin Butler, Helen Cooper, Terry Eagleton, Jonathan Hope, David Johnson, Emrys Jones, James Knowles, David Lindley, Annabel Patterson, Michael Pincombe, John Pitcher, Robin

Robbins, Frank Romany, Nigel Smith, and Mark Williams. I also wish to thank the following for their suggestions and comments: A. R. Braunmuller, Donald Foster, Judith Hawley, Dennis Kay, Kathleen McLuskie, Nigel Mapp, and Suzanne Trill. Arthur Kinney, general editor of Massachusetts Studies in Early Modern Culture, and Bruce Wilcox, director of the University of Massachusetts Press, have both been tremendously positive and generous.

Gratitude for support, belief, and irony is due to various friends on the Wirral, in Oxford, and in Newcastle—in particular to Karl McHorton, Clare Tarplee, Gill Plain, and James McKinna—as well as to Jo for holding the torch in Cranbrook Church, to J. Fletcher (no relation) for good company at Coleorton and Ashby, and to Marzena Polak.

By far my greatest debt is to David Norbrook, who supervised the thesis in exemplary fashion, and who has been a good and supportive friend. His scholarship, thoughtfulness, and modesty are to be envied and emulated. He is of course not to be held responsible for any errors of judgment which remain in the book.

ONE

Parentage and Patronage

I

I t must have been about the time of John Fletcher's birth on 20 December 1579 that his grandfather, Richard Fletcher senior, gave to the martyrologist John Foxe the disturbingly detailed account of the burning of Christopher Wade, which first appears in the 1583 edition of the *Acts and Monuments*.[1] As this connection might suggest, the future playwright was born into an ecclesiastical family with strong Protestant credentials, and the martyrdom of Wade clearly remained a vivid memory and a symbol of the Protestant struggle for Richard senior for the rest of his life. It seems to have had a profound effect too upon Richard junior, the playwright's father and future bishop of London, who was just twelve when he witnessed the burning. Fletcher senior had known Foxe since their ordination together in 1550: relating the events of Wade's death to him will have served not only to commemorate the martyr but also to remind Fletcher's more outspoken parishioners of his experiences as a Protestant under the Marian persecution. The account is particularly vivid, and is notable in ensuring that we hear in Wade's dying words a defense of Edwardine prayer-book Protestantism rather than Puritan nonconformism.

It was also in the same year as the playwright's birth that the churchwardens of Cranbrook in Kent returned the formal complaint against his grandfather that Patrick Collinson uses as the starting point for a discussion of Wealden popular Protestantism in his collection *Godly People*. Richard senior had been vicar of Cranbrook since his arrival there from nearby Frittenden in October 1561. Born in Yorkshire, *honestis parentibus* (according to the memorial plaque erected in Cranbrook Church by his sons Richard and Giles), he had been sent to Cambridge, which was established from then on as the Fletcher family university. He married his wife

Joan around 1540, and within three years, on 28 September 1543, their first son, Richard, was born. They were probably settled in Kent by this time. Langdale, the biographer of Phineas Fletcher, the playwright's cousin and a "Spenserian" poet, claims that Richard senior then "went off on an embassy to the Sophi of Persia," though there is no evidence for this.[2] Persia or no Persia, he was established in an unspecified capacity in Watford, Hertfordshire, by 26 November 1546, when his second son, Giles, was born. As the inscription in Cranbrook Church proudly states, it was Nicholas Ridley, later martyred, who conferred holy orders on Fletcher and Foxe "before the high altar at St. Paul's, according to the rite, manner, and form of the Church of England lately published and enjoined" on 24 June 1550.[3] Richard thus became one of the first English Reformation ministers. He was ordained at Fulham, again by Ridley, later in the year, on 9 November, becoming vicar of Bishop's Stortford in June 1551, but was forcibly removed in 1555, the year of Ridley's martyrdom, presumably (as Collinson observes) as a married priest.[4] The Cranbrook inscription claims, perhaps unsurprisingly, that Fletcher was imprisoned for persistent Protestantism during Mary's reign, though this clashes with Collinson's conjecture that "as a staunch Edwardine Protestant he may have evaded the Marian persecution by concealing himself in the close, wooded country of the Weald" (Collinson 404–5). He undoubtedly suffered under Mary, but he cannot have been in prison in July 1555 at least, since it was then that he witnessed the death of Wade.

With the accession of Elizabeth in 1558, Fletcher's fortunes, along with those of English Protestants generally, looked up. He was admitted to the church at Cranbrook on the resignation of the Marian vicar in October 1561. As Collinson observes, "[u]ntil this date there had probably been no experience of a genuine Protestant ministry in the parish, and not much experience of a resident vicar" (Collinson 406), though, in common with other centers of the clothing trade in Kent, Cranbrook was known for its tendency to be nonconformist. It was at this time one of the most populous parishes in Kent, with approximately fifteen hundred communicants. Richard Fletcher became a substantial figure in parish life, "appearing constantly in the act books of the archdeacon's court as the moving force behind the detection of sexual crimes and other

Portrait of John Fletcher in 1647. By permission of the British Library.

3

transgressions, publishing sentences of excommunication and more occasionally certifying the due performance of penance" (Collinson 399). On 16 November 1562 his eldest son, Richard, aged nineteen, was admitted pensioner to Trinity College, Cambridge, was made a Scholar of the college a year later, and received his B.A. probably before April 1566.

Richard Fletcher senior's career in Cranbrook was not entirely an easy one. He appears to have been an energetic vicar of a large and unruly parish, who, despite his impeccable Protestant history, nonetheless had occasional trouble with radical Protestants and schismatics. Collinson observes that his practice in the church of St. Dunstan was firmly Protestant without being Puritan, pointing out that "[b]efore Fletcher's arrival, the rood-loft had been taken down and the altars removed (in accordance with the Injunctions), and a great quantity of Catholic ornaments and furniture sold or otherwise disposed of." He adds that "[i]n Fletcher's first year there was payment to the painter 'for blottynge owt of the ymagrye in the glass wyndowes'" (Collinson 407). On the other hand, Fletcher was clearly by this time a client of Archbishop Parker (Richard junior was made one of Parker's Norfolk Fellows at Corpus Christi, Cambridge, in 1569, which, bearing in mind that the Fletchers had no recorded connection with the country, can only have been the product of direct patronage), and became a pluralist thanks to Parker's gift of his collation to the relatively lucrative, nearby rectory of Smarden in 1566.

Parker's ecclesiastical influence can perhaps be seen in certain features of church practice in Cranbrook—the wearing of the surplice, for example, and the receiving of communion in the kneeling position—which must have been unpopular with nonconformist elements in the parish. The need to maintain a balance between conformable Protestantism and uncompromising Puritanism in Cranbrook perhaps explains the apparent embodiment of this balance in preaching arrangements. Between 1575 and 1585, Fletcher employed in succession three unofficial curates of overtly Puritan sympathies. He clearly had need of assistance in his pastoral duties in such a large parish, and Collinson suggests that financial pressure may have obliged him to listen to the suggestions of the "godly" in the parish in naming his curate-preacher assistants. This arrangement, however, produced certain frictions, which came to a head in 1579, the year of John Fletcher's birth, in a clash between the two Richard Fletchers and the Puritan party in the parish, an argument which hinged on accusations of schismatism made by Fletcher senior against certain of his parishioners. The lawsuit which resulted eventually faded away, but both Fletchers, Richard junior in particular, had by this time made plain their distance from the radical Puritans.

Their staunch Protestantism was, however, not in doubt. Richard Fletcher junior had followed his father to Cambridge, taking his B.A. in 1566. Three years later, he proceeded to his M.A. and took up the Norfolk Fellowship at Bene't College (Corpus Christi). In 1572 he traveled with one Thomas Staller to Oxford, where they were both incorporated M.A. of the University on 15 June.[5] Staller had become a member of Corpus Christi in 1562 and gained a fellowship in 1567, also under Parker's patronage. The archbishop a little later "took him into his Family in the capacity of one of his Domestick Chaplains" (Masters 374) despite the fact that Staller was in trouble over a question of "suspected books" in 1568. The problem seems to have been his involvement in objections to Elizabeth's order that Latin prayers be introduced in college chapels. Protestant dislike of this seems to have been particularly marked at Corpus, where several fellows (presumably including Staller) stormed out of Chapel during a reading by the Master, giving their opinion that "*Latin Service was the Pope's Dreggs*" (Masters 106n). Richard Fletcher is thus connected with one variety of forthright Protestantism at this stage, and is privy to arguments over the proper nature of the English Reformed Church.[6]

Later in the year, on 30 September, he was named Prebend of Islington in St. Paul's, this time by courtesy of the patronage of Archbishop Parker's son, Matthew. Masters suggests that Matthew Parker "probably had the Patronage of that Turn made over to him by Bp *Grindal,* in order to carry on his Father's Scheme of annexing Prebends to the Fellowships he had founded" (Masters 285). Thus Fletcher held this office in conjunction with his fellowship, remaining in Cambridge, and became president of Bene't College "upon Mr. *Norgate*'s promotion to the Mastership the year following," in which office he "acquitted himself with credit" (Masters 285).[7] He did not long retain the position, however, since in 1573 he married Elizabeth Holland at Cranbrook, and was therefore obliged to give up his fellowship. He seems briefly to have acted as assistant to his father in Cranbrook between May 1573 and his engagement as "minister of the word of God" at Rye, Sussex, in September 1574.[8]

John Fletcher was born in the vicarage at Rye, which lies some fifteen miles southeast of Cranbrook. In the sixteenth century the two towns shared not only close trade and social connections but also a strong independent tradition in matters of religion. The trading links were, according to Graham Mayhew, facilitated by the use of barges and lighters along the Rother which was navigable as far as Bodiam (Mayhew 78). From there, pack animals would have been used to the Wealden towns and as far as London. Apart from its primary role as a supplier of fish to the London markets, Rye exported timber from the Kent forests around Cranbrook and Tenterden, and imported dyestuffs and other commodities for the clothiers there (Mayhew 60; 237–38). The seven or so years of John Fletcher's father's ministry at Rye marked the tail end of a period of unsurpassed prosperity and independence for the port. In the 1540s it had been the predominant trading center of Sussex. By the beginning of the seventeenth century, its harbor was silting up fast, and its trade and fishing fleets, as well as its population, had reduced accordingly. But in 1574, the year in which Richard Fletcher junior became minister there, Rye was thriving. The town's internal government and self-opinion reflected both this prosperity and its status as a Cinque Port, which by and large exempted it from the jurisdiction of Sussex and Kent magistrates. Rye saw itself as a semi-autonomous "commonweal," and solved many of its more serious problems with individuals by the simple expedient of banishment. This tendency toward autonomy in matters of local government seems to have been reflected in a nonconformist cast of mind in matters theological. Rye was the first Sussex town fully to embrace Protestantism, and during Mary's reign openly opposed her government, electing Protestant mayors and M.P.s and even refusing to acknowledge a forced loan in 1557 (Mayhew 51). Religious influences upon Rye prior to the influx of Huguenot refugees in the 1570s seem to have been twofold, due on the one hand to its trade links with the Netherlands, especially Antwerp, which for many years before the English Reformation had been a refuge for Protestants (including, for exam-

6

ple, Tyndale), and on the other to its proximity to the Lollard towns of the Kentish Weald, amongst which Cranbrook appears to have been prominent.

There was a certain congruence, then, in the appointment of a Cranbrook man to the church at Rye, and there must have been a reasonable continuity of approach on the younger Richard Fletcher's part. Although he began as "minister" rather than vicar of Rye, Richard occupied the vicarage, a stone's throw from the church door, and he appears to have been financially comfortable. Relations between the town and its absentee vicars were either nonexistent or hostile, and it is a measure of the seriousness with which the authorities viewed Protestant doctrine and preaching that they employed resident ministers and preachers throughout the sixteenth century. The general sense is that the town preferred its ministers to be strongly Protestant yet not outright nonconformists; sectarianism and radical forms of Puritanism were not easily tolerated (see Mayhew 79). Despite his later pluralism and the accusations of unscrupulousness that characterize descriptions of the way Richard Fletcher behaved in the various offices to which he ascended over the next two decades, he seems to have developed at Rye an essential Calvinism that never left him. Some of his tasks around this time were grim enough: it is more than likely that his immediate response to his father's request for help in his ecclesiastical dispute at Cranbrook in the summer of 1579 was prompted by the desire to escape from the infected air of Rye for a few weeks, since the period from July 1579 to October 1580 marked the town's worst-ever outbreak of plague. Preventive measures taken included marking the houses of victims with a cross, the provision of fresh water every two days to each house, and, after September 1579, payment to women for viewing and sacking the dead bodies and tending the sick, as well as for killing any stray dogs found within the town walls; but the deaths of 813 parishioners in the period must have presented an appalling task for Fletcher and his curates. Thus on 20 December 1579, when John Fletcher was born, his father was undoubtedly busier than he had ever been.[9]

Richard Fletcher stayed at the Cinque Port until 1581 when he became chaplain-in-ordinary to Queen Elizabeth herself. There is no evidence to explain this sudden and dramatic rise in his fortunes. One can only assume that he had maintained and cultivated connections made in his Cambridge days. Apparently, Archbishop Whitgift recommended Fletcher for the deanery of Windsor, but the queen chose to make him dean of Peterborough on the death of the incumbent in 1583. It would seem that he gave up the living of Rye at this time and that his family moved to Richard senior's house at Cranbrook, presumably because of the unsettled nature of his career at this stage. Elizabeth Fletcher, Richard's wife, had given birth to five children at Rye and produced four more at Cranbrook. As his uncle Giles's family appears also to have been resident at Cranbrook at this time, John was brought up at least for a while as the immediate contemporary of his cousin Phineas, the future "Spenserian" poet.

During his time as dean of Peterborough, Richard Fletcher had attended the execution of Mary, Queen of Scots, as her chaplain and has apparently been particularly vindictive in his exhortations to her to renounce her Roman Catholicism in the moments before her death.[10] This uncharacteristic vehemence may have stemmed from his experience of watching the burning of Wade as a child: it may also of course (more simply) have been a conscious career move. He became bishop of Bristol in 1589, and then in 1593 transferred to the rather more lucrative see of Worcester. Two years after this, he achieved what must long have been his goal, becoming bishop of London on 10 January 1595.[11] As things turned out, however, he did not long enjoy his new office in peace. His first actions as bishop seem to confirm that, despite his enthusiasm for the court and the accusations of time-serving frequently leveled against him in church histories, his form of Anglicanism had not changed beyond recognition since his days at Rye. A debate over aspects of the Calvinist doctrine of predestination had begun in Cambridge in 1595. Certain senior dons consulted with Archbishop Whitgift, and in due course came up with the Lambeth Articles, nine propositions which emphasized the compatability of the Thirty-nine Articles of the Church of England with Calvinist theology.[12] Though they were never officially adopted, the Lambeth Articles demonstrate how Calvinistic the archbishop—no Puritan himself—believed the Church of England to be at the close of the sixteenth century. According to Sir John Harington's unkind epitaph, Fletcher "could preach well and could speak boldly, and yet keep *decorum*. He knew what pleased the Queen, and would adventure on that though that offended others."[13]

Yet Fletcher's touch seems to have begun to fail him as soon as he settled properly in London. His involvement as bishop-elect of London in the drawing-up of the Lambeth Articles seems to have irritated Elizabeth. But it was not a theological matter per se which lost Richard Fletcher the royal favor he had so long sought and maintained. He had not been in office a month when he remarried. His new wife was Lady Mary Baker, widow of Sir Richard Baker of Sissingherst in Kent, who had died less than a year earlier.[14] A combination of factors in regard to this marriage served to enrage the queen. She had never appreciated clerical marriage at the best of times, and for a bishop to remarry in apparent haste so soon after his elevation to office was more than she cared to bear. Moreover, Lady Baker came with something of a reputation which the gossip, inevitably associated with the marriage, only served to heighten, "this being indeed a marriage that was talked of at least nine dayes" (Harington 27). Thomas Fuller is at his pettiest with regard to Mary Fletcher. "He married," we are told, "a Lady of this county [Kent], who [her first husband] commendeth for very virtuous, which if so, the more happy she in herself, though unhappy that the world did not believe it."[15] A satire on the marriage in the form of Marprelate verses ascribed in recent years to Sir John Davies suggests that they may "devide the name of Fletcher: / He my Llord F, and she my Lady Letcher."[16] Elizabeth's rage at the match was such that she refused Fletcher access to herself or the court and, on 23 February, had him suspended from his episcopal duties.[17] Masters comments that "[h]er wonted Favour therefore was turned into Displeasure (which yet some rather suspect to have been owing to Abuses in his Courts and Offices)" (Masters 286–87), yet, despite Fletcher's tarnished record up to this point, he could hardly have done much damage in the bare month since he had taken office. Whatever the actual cause, Fletcher was firmly out of favor, and he never regained his position in the queen's sight. It was something like six months before she allowed him to return to his duties as bishop, and it seems she never revoked his banishment from her presence.[18] On 7 January 1596 he wrote to the Lord Treasurer asking him to intercede with the queen on his behalf, and saying:

Yt is now a yere within a weeke or two since I haue sene her Majesty, which to me hath semed a longer tyme then a whole *seculum,* it being the especiall cumfort seculer that ever I conceyved to haue lived in hir highnes gratious aspect and favour now xx^ty yeres past. Your Lordship was the honorable meanes of the fyrst recovery of that hir Majestys good favour to the libertye of my function, and if it please your Lordship to add therunto your honorable mediation to hir Majesty to let hir vnderstande my most humble sute to do my dutye and service in hir presence, and, if not farther, yet to see hir Majesty, I shall hould my self most bound to your Lordships kindenes.[19]

We do not know what response Cecil received from the queen nor whether he even attempted any intercession on Fletcher's behalf. In the event, Bishop Fletcher was dead before any return to favor could be effected. Fuller assumes a direct connection between the death and the bishop's disgrace:

Sure I am that Queen Elizabeth (who hardly held the second matches of Bishops excusable) accounted his marriage a trespasse on his gravity, whereupon he fell into her deep displeasure. Hereof the Bishop was sadly sensible, and seeking to lose his sorrow in a mist of smoak, died of the immoderate taking thereof. (Fuller, *Worthies* [*Kent*]: 73)

Harington's version assumes that there was in fact a successful intervention on Fletcher's behalf, but describes a curiously sudden death:

[C]ertain it is that (the Queen being pacified, and hee in great jollity, with his faire Lady and her Carpets and Cushions in his bed-chamber) he died suddenly, taking Tobacco in his chaire, saying to his man that stood by him, whom he loved very well, 'Oh boy, I die!' (Harington 28)

In his *Church-History,* Fuller is only a little less cruel, saying that the bishop was

one of a comely person, and goodly presence, (qualities not to be *cast away* in a *Bishop,* though a *Bishop* not to be *chosen* for them,) he lov'd to ride *the great horse,* and had much skill in managing thereof, condemned for very proud, (such his natural stately garb) by such as knew him not, and commended for humility by those acquainted with him, he lost the *Queens favour* because of his second unhappy match, and died suddainly, more of grief then any other disease.[20]

Whatever the actual cause of Bishop Fletcher's death, the salient fact for his family was that he died heavily in debt. It was up to

Richard's younger brother Giles to deal both with the debts and with the bishop's many children.

2

At the time of the death of his father, the young John Fletcher was probably still at Cambridge. It would appear that he had gone up to Bene't College (now Corpus Christi), his father's old college, at the early age of eleven in late 1591. Bentley finds various John Fletchers in the registers of Oxford and Cambridge colleges, but believes the most likely candidate to be a "John Fletcher of London," admitted pensioner to Bene't College on 15 October 1591. Matriculation at such an early age was by no means unusual in the late sixteenth century. Francis Beaumont went up to Broadgates Hall (now Pembroke College), Oxford, at the same age six years later in the company of his two elder brothers Henry and John. As Bentley observes, Bishop Fletcher obviously had many connections with the college, and when supplicating for the bishopric claimed to live most of the time in London, "so that the John Fletcher of London entered at Corpus Christi in 1591 might plausibly be assumed to be his son."[21] Fletcher was not of course the first Bene't College man to turn to writing plays. The plaque in Corpus Christi which now commemorates Fletcher's years at the college subordinates his name to that of Christopher Marlowe, who matriculated there a decade earlier.

The events of the years between John Fletcher's (presumed) proceeding M.A. in 1598 and his first appearance as a playwright in about 1607 are entirely undocumented. The last confirmed reference to his Cambridge career is his becoming Bible clerk, reading the lessons in college chapel, in 1593, "as if," as Gayley observes, "destined for holy orders."[22] This, on the face of it, would seem logical for the child of an overwhelmingly ecclesiastical family. His elder brother Nathaniel had just taken his B.A. at Queen's and would proceed through college life to a career in the church. His uncle William Atkinson was a preacher. His cousin Phineas would go into the church and remain fierily Protestant all his life, as did his uncle Giles. His father had been made bishop of Worcester at the beginning of the year, and was clearly still on the way up. Everything would seem to point to a clerical career for

John. Yet the next recorded trace of John Fletcher is as junior collaborator in the writing of a satiric comedy called *The Woman Hater* with Francis Beaumont, a younger man who had already made himself known (and not through legal study) at Gray's Inn.[23] *The Woman Hater* dates probably from early in 1606: there are thus at least eight years unaccounted for in Fletcher's early life. Lawrence Wallis fancifully suggests that some time after his father's death John "may well have travelled on the continent in the entourage of his uncle, Dr. Giles Fletcher, the diplomat," and adds that "[i]t is also possible that this gentleman found the young man useful to him as a secretary, or else used his influence to place him in a similar position elsewhere."[24] Yet it is also possible that he did nothing of the sort, since it was at this time that John's elder brother Nathaniel was involved in a legal dispute with Giles senior. Unless this row was patched up with remarkable speed, Nathaniel, for one, must have made his way without his uncle's patronage, since by 1604 he had become chaplain to the self-consciously Protestant ambassador to Venice, Sir Henry Wotton, whose consummate abilities as a spy master and whose grand schemes for conversion to Protestantism of the Venetian state are abundantly clear in his extant letters.[25] By 1604, Giles Fletcher was anyway far too tainted with the memory of the Essex affair to be of much use as a patron for his extended family. He had tried for years to secure Cecil patronage and had consistently failed to do so. In June 1596, with his financial position destabilized by the sudden death of his brother and the consequent introduction of the bishop's eight children into their uncle's household, he turned to the earl of Essex instead. As Lloyd Berry observes, Giles Fletcher had "three qualities which would particularly recommend him to Essex. He was a zealous Protestant, a man of letters, and Remembrancer of London—a position which had much influence over the people of the city."[26] As things turned out, of course, this was not an auspicious move. He was committed to private custody after the abortive rebellion of 1601 and was obliged to defend his connections with Essex before the Privy Council. His defense was successful, and he retained the position of Remembrancer until 1605 when he finally surrendered it to Cecil pressure.[27] After his accession, King James rehabilitated several of those implicated in the Essex rebellion, including Southampton, but Giles Fletcher seems to have remained under the shadow of Essex for the rest of his life, and would have been of little use as a patron either for his own or for his brother's children.

Direct family influence thus seems highly unlikely to have been the immediate means of introducing John Fletcher to theatrical circles. There are, however, two clues upon which it is possible to base educated guesses about John Fletcher's movements in this liminal phase of his life. Both, in a sense, are contained in the circumstances of *The Woman Hater,* the first play in which we have evidence of his involvement as a writer. There is certainly no suggestion at all that Fletcher, like, say, Shakespeare or Jonson, trod the boards before beginning writing. He undoubtedly worked very closely with the King's Company Players from 1609 onwards, and he clearly had a gift for stage composition and a facility for writing from the start. But his writing for the stage was not, as far as we can ascertain, the result of personal experience as an actor.

The first circumstantial clue to the route he may have taken into the theater, I would suggest, is the company for which *The Woman Hater* was written. The play is the only work Beaumont and Fletcher seem to have done for the Children of St. Paul's.[28] Both playwrights established an early connection with another children's company, the Children of the Queen's Revels, which they maintained for a time even once they were writing regularly for the King's company. But they apparently began playwriting for the schoolboys of Paul's. The choir school (the part of St. Paul's responsible for dramatic performance) had appointed a new master in about 1600, a man named Edward Pearce, who clearly had a strong interest in drama.[29] The headmaster of Paul's at this time was Richard Mulcaster, born in 1531 and educated at Eton when Nicholas Udall was headmaster there. Mulcaster's *D.N.B.* entry suggests that "[f]rom Udall he may have caught some tincture of the severity he afterwards himself showed as schoolmaster, as well as his fondness for dramatic composition."[30] He went to Oxford, moving from there to London, where he rapidly made his name as a teacher with fairly avant-garde educational views. When the Merchant Taylors school was founded in 1561, he was appointed its first headmaster. He stayed at Merchant Taylors until 1586, during which time he brought his boys to Court for performances on more than one occasion. There was, however, a brief, but, for our purposes, significant, hiatus in his career as a teacher. He retired temporarily from teaching on 1 April 1590, and became for a while vicar of Cranbrook.[31] Six years later, at the age of sixty-six, he returned to teaching, becoming high master of St. Paul's, where he stayed until 1608. His pupils at Paul's "frequently performed masks, interludes, and the like before Elizabeth and the court," and it would appear that he encouraged Edward Pearce's interest in promoting drama at the school (*D.N.B.* XIII: 1172). There is thus a Cranbrook connection with the Paul's boys, offering the possibility that Fletcher may have begun writing for the company by way of his grandfather's reputation and his strong family connections in general in the Wealden town.

The second clue to be gleaned from the writing of *The Woman Hater,* simply enough, is in his connection with his first collaborator Francis Beaumont, since the origins of Fletcher's friendship with the aristocratic younger playwright must also be considered in tandem with his patronage relations with the fifth earl and countess of Huntingdon. Fletcher seems to have been more fortunate than either his father or his uncle in developing and sustaining stable relations with patrons. Philip Massinger, Fletcher's later collaborator, provides the first evidence of the Huntingdon patronage. His "Copie of a Letter written vpon occasion to the Earle of Pembrooke Lo: Chamberlaine" contains the following lines:

> I know
> That Iohnson much of what he has does owe
> To you and to your familie, and is neuer
> Slow to professe it, nor had Fletcher euer
> Such Reputation, and credit wonne
> But by his honord Patron, Huntington[.]
> Vnimitable Spencer n'ere had been
> Soe famous for his matchlesse *Fairie Queene*
> Had he not found a Sydney to preferr
> His plaine way in his *Shepheards Calender*
> . . . These are Presidents
> I cite with reverence.[32]

At a later date Massinger also sought the patronage of Katherine Stanhope, wife of Philip Lord Stanhope, future earl of Chesterfield, by dedicating *The Duke of Milan* to her in 1623. Edwards and Gibson point out that Massinger would presumably have felt encouraged to address Lady Katherine in part because she was the "sister of Fletcher's patron, the Earl of Huntingdon."[33] Fletcher was certainly part of the fifth earl's milieu by 1609, when he published *The Faithful Shepherdess* with dedicatory verses to Sir Walter Aston and Sir William Skipwith, both habitués of the castle of Ashby-de-la-Zouche, the Huntingdons' seat in Leicestershire. Also, the Beaumont-Hastings connections in Leicestershire and Northamptonshire are such that it is more than tempting to assume either that Beaumont introduced Fletcher to the earl or that the earl brought the two aspiring writers together. R. C. Rowland prefers to assume that the Huntingdon connection came first.[34] I would tend to agree. Perhaps part of Massinger's implication in "The Copy of a Letter" is the earl's responsibility for bringing together the two collaborators in the first place.

Certainly, there can be little doubt that Francis Beaumont and Henry Hastings, fifth earl of Huntingdon, were acquainted almost from birth. The fifth earl was close politically, geographically, and personally to Beaumont's cousin, Sir Thomas Beaumont of Coleorton. Francis's grandfather had married Elizabeth, daughter of Sir William Hastings, uncle of the first earl, thus resolving decades of feuding between the comparatively recently arrived Beaumonts and the firmly entrenched Hastingses.[35] Francis and the fifth earl were thus not-too-distant cousins, were exactly the same age, had been near neighbors in their youth (Ashby is about an hour's walk from Francis's childhood home at Grace-Dieu), and were contemporaries at Oxford and the Inns of Court, where Beaumont was clearly something of a personality. Moreover, Huntingdon was a member of Gray's Inn, which has always maintained a close connection with the Inner Temple, the inn to which Beaumont belonged: the connection of the two Inns of Court is perhaps most succinctly underlined by the 1613 *Masque of the Inner Temple and Gray's Inn,* written by Beaumont for the wedding of Princess Elizabeth and Frederick, the elector palatine. Despite these connections, we have no evidence of the circumstances in which Fletcher met either Beaumont or Huntingdon. Critics have generally assumed, though without firm evidence, that Beaumont's verse epistle to Ben Jonson, written, according to the 1647 folio, "before he and Master *Fletcher* came to *London,* with two of the precedent Comedies, then not finisht, which deferred their merry meetings at the Mermaid," was written from the Beaumont home at Grace-Dieu, now occupied by Sir John Beaumont since the death of his father, where the playwrights would occasionally (at least according to legend) retire to write.[36] If this is so, it is entirely possible (to judge at least from the verse letter Fletcher wrote to Elizabeth, countess of Huntingdon, in about 1620, in which it is quite clear that Fletcher was by that time a longstanding regular at Ashby)[37] that Beaumont and Fletcher could have spent time there on their travels northward. There is evidence in the form of a letter dated 26 January 1618 of a polite relationship at that time between Francis's brother Sir John Beaumont and the fifth earl.[38] On the whole, though, Huntingdon seems to have had more connections with the Coleorton and Stoughton branches of the Beaumont family than with the Grace-Dieu line of which Francis was a part.

It is also difficult to know what connection, if any, there might have been between the Huntingdon circles based around Ashby and the Mermaid circle in London. There is certainly no evidence of a relationship between Ben Jonson and the Huntingdons. Jonson and the fifth earl would have been highly unlikely to see eye to eye in matters of either religion or politics. Yet Michael Drayton, for one, a leading light at the Mermaid, seems to have had at least peripheral connections with the Ashby grouping, with both Sir Walter Aston, his chief patron, and the Beaumonts, his close friends. John Beaumont had published his mock heroic "Metamorphosis of Tobacco" in 1602 (not an auspicious move, considering the next monarch's sensitivity on the subject of smoking) with a dedicatory verse by Drayton as well as a brief prefatory verse by his younger brother.[39] Later in the year, John responded to Francis's gesture with a prefatory verse to the latter's "Salmacis and Hermaphroditus." It would seem probable that John Beaumont was well enough connected with the Mermaid circle by 1602 to introduce his brother to the group at some time between then and 1607, when both Francis and his new friend John Fletcher penned commendatory verses for Jonson's *Volpone*. And Richard Brome's prefatory verse in the 1647 folio arguably serves to confirm the implicit suggestion that Fletcher was, at least briefly, considered a son of Ben: "*Most knowing* Johnson (*proud to call him* Sonne) / *In friendly Envy swore, He had outdone / His very* Selfe."[40]

If the fifth earl and countess did bring together the two collaborators and introduce Fletcher into his circle at Ashby, it would certainly not have been the beginning either of Fletcher-Hastings connections or of Hastings patronage of the drama. Richard Fletcher and the third earl had both been involved in the imprisonment and execution of Mary, Queen of Scots, who had been held temporarily at Ashby. The third earl (Henry Hastings's great-uncle) had for some years patronized his own acting company, and the third countess developed a reputation for patronage of religious works by nonconformists. The fourth earl also maintained a company of actors. This was disbanded under the fifth earl, yet the Hastings milieu was still responsive to a theatrical aesthetic. This is clear enough from the nature of the festivities produced for the visit of Alice, the dowager countess of Derby, the fifth countess's mother, to Ashby castle in 1607, which included a masque by Sir William Skipwith and a dramatic entertainment by John Marston.[41] Marston wrote several plays for the Paul's boys toward the close of that company's career, and therefore, presumably could have been someone to introduce Fletcher, by way of the Huntingdons, to Paul's.[42] Mulcaster, high master of St. Paul's, would, as has been suggested already, know and perhaps feel indebted to the name of Fletcher from his time at Cranbrook. Moreover, the chief Paul's boys playwrights, including George Chapman (who was certainly a friend of Fletcher's by 1609, when he wrote a commendatory verse for *The Faithful Shepherdess*) and Thomas Middleton as well as Marston, were notable for their uncourtly political allegiances. It would, after all, be no advantage in Hastings circles at that time to have aspirations to position at court.

The second, and principal, witness to the playwright's friendship with the earl and countess is a verse letter by Fletcher to the fifth countess. This provides evidence of a close and relaxed (while nonetheless respectful) relationship between patron and playwright as well as a clear, shared political understanding. Dating probably from as late in his career as 1620, the letter suggests a long-standing friendship.[43] I shall quote the text of the letter in full:

> "To the excelent and
> best Lady the Countess
> Of Huntingdon."
>
> There ys not any Sculler of our Tyme
> inventing nowe; more misbegott wth ryme

Then I am at this Instant: But 'tys so
that I must write. yett hange mee If I knowe
of what; or to what End: ffor that maine sinne
of my fforgetfulness (best of yo^{r}kinne)
I knowe yo^u haue forgeuen; for I am sure,
Yo^u are too good to Lett yor anger dure;
and so that subiect's Lost. Saye then I strive
extreamely to commend yo^u; Some doe thrive
by those vaine gloryes, Butt they knowe whoe neede
such commendations; (as I knowe that creede
I take from; by addition) Lett mee then
write something (Madame) lyke those honest men
that haue no busines; Something that affordes
some savor to the wrighter. Knights, and Lords
praye by yor Leaues, I will not treate of yo^u
Ye are too teachy: nor whether ytt bee true
wee shall haue warrs wth Spaine: (I wolde wee might:)
nor whoe shall daunce i'th *maske;* nor whoe shall write
those braue things done: nor summe up the Expence;
nor whether ytt bee paid for ten yeere hence.
All theise I overpasse; and come att Length
Out of myne owne dexterytie, and strength
to wish my selfe at *Ashby:* There I am sure
I should have Brawne, and Brackett, wch indure
Longer then twentie Tryumphs; and good Swan,
able to choake Th'ambition of a churchman,
and Pyes *cum privilegio,* wthoute sinne
forbydding all to Make 'um, but *Ralph Goodwin:*
And yo^u O Ladie I should see agen,
ther's all my maine End: yo^u that Euery man,
and every ayre breaths' well of, yo^u that styll
Lyke *Eue* before the fall must bee unyll.
and though yo^u haue the power to doe amis
ye haue the apple still to knowe what 'tys,
yo^u I should see I saye, That of my all
service, and prayers, are originall.

Roome for a Little prose. lyke a Lenvoy; There were certaine Bookes
Maddame that Sr Thomas *Beamont* mencioned, and (as hee told mee) ffor
yor Ladiship wch shall bee shortely sent downe, and some other to attend
them. I am sure you will doe my seruice to my Lord: so I commytt you to
yor (s) Closett. [*maddame*] All at yor noble service.   John fletcher.[44]

Portrait of Elizabeth Hastings, countess of Huntingdon, by Von Somer. Courtesy National Portrait Gallery, London.

This letter is important as the firmest evidence we have of the closeness of the relationship, personal and political, that Fletcher had with the Huntingdons. Moreover, it gives us both a very clear picture of the attitudes and aims of the Huntingdon milieu and several examples of Fletcher's habitual literary strategies.

Fletcher's strategy in the letter to the countess is simple. He claims not to be doing what in fact he does, in the tradition of *occupatio*. He begins by denigrating his own ability, at the moment of composition, to write anything of value. He knows a letter is overdue, but he does not know what he can write of substance. He knows too the conventions of such a letter: that he ought probably to offer praise to his respected patron. Yet (having already referred to the countess as "best of yor kinne," and "too good to Lett yor anger dure"), he announces that he will not indulge in such praise, that he will in fact avoid unnecessary flattery and the consequent platonic movement to encomium. He echoes in his tone the last recorded words of his uncle Giles, with whom he found a home after his father's sudden death, as recorded by John's cousin Phineas Fletcher in his *Father's Testament:*

My Son had I followed the course of this World, and would either have given, or taken bribes, I might (happily) have made you rich, but now must leave you nothing but your education, which (I bless God) is such, as I am well assured you chuse rather that I should dye in peace, then your selves live in plenty. But know certainly, that I your weak, and dying Father leave you to an everliving, and All-sufficient Father, and in him a never fading inheritance; who will not suffer you to want any good thing, who hath been my God, and will be the God of my seed.[45]

In the same way, John Fletcher implies a contrast between those writers who will unashamedly indulge in the "Vaine gloryes" of courtly flattery in order to "thrive"; and the good, bluff Protestant writer: "Butt they knowe whoe neede / such commendations; (as I knowe that creede / I take from; by addition)." He announces, then, that he will proceed as if he were not a client writing for a favor to a patron: "Lett mee then / write something (Madame) lyke those honest men / that haue no busines," that is, "Something that affordes / some savor to the wrighter." The letter now switches key slightly as Fletcher turns his attention to what he will not discuss, namely, matters to do with the court. In the process, he gives a succinct opinion of such matters. He says he will not treat of "Knights, and Lords" because they are "too teachy" (presumably, "tetchy"). He gives instead a "country" view of court interests and activities. He disparages the perennial rumors of war with Spain, implying simply that he wishes the uncertainty would stop and England would exercise her power as a Protestant nation. He criticizes too the court masque (the form he and Beaumont had recognized years before to be "tied to rules / Of flatterie")[46] and makes sarcastic reference to the "expence" of the entertainment, "nor whether ytt bee paid for ten yeere hence." This, I will suggest, is analogous to the numerous occasions in his drama where he makes plain both the collaborative, dependent nature of rule and the means of production of courtly display.

In the wake of these critical remarks, he moves on, in what is effectively the third section of the letter, by way of three lines of descending cadence ("All theise I overpasse; and come att Length/ Out of myne owne dexterytie, and strength / to wish my selfe at *Ashby*") to the subject that will "afforde [ ] / some savor to the wrighter," namely his patrons' country seat at Ashby-de-la-Zouche. He compares the wholesome yet by no means parsimonious delights of country cuisine with the unwholesome excesses of court (presumably the idea of "dexterytie, and strength" contrasting with courtly dependence and weakness), and opposes the endurance of country living to the temporary pleasures of the court. At Ashby he is sure he could "have Brawne, and Brackett, wch indure / Longer then twentie Tryumphs." Each item of food mentioned operates as part of a political critique: he writes of "good Swan, / able to choake Th'ambition of a churchman," and of "Pyes *cum privilegio,* wthoute sinne forbydding all to Make 'um, but Ralph Goodwin." Goodwin, we know from the Hastings accounts, was indeed the Huntingdons' cook at the time; the "*cum privilegio*" is presumably both a deflating reference to courtly monopolies and a quiet reminder of the Huntingdons' royal blood.[47] Once he has set the tone with these political-culinary references, he proceeds to the platonic praise of his patroness he claimed earlier he was avoiding. In the context of the country idyll he has drawn to contrast with the tasteless activities of the court, he can now speak of the countess without accusation of dishonest flattery. Even so, the terms he uses are so hyperbolic that they seem almost blasphemous. He says that she "[l]yke *Eve* before the fall must be unyll," thus reappropriating Marian theology to a country-Protestant end. He concludes the verse part of the letter in a manner which is fully aware of the dangers of praise and flattery, yet which manages to praise and flatter quite adequately. We are left with a strong impression of Fletcher's intimacy with the Huntingdon household and of the countess's strong position within the household, as well as of the governing attitude at Ashby toward James's court.

Something of the aversion of the earl and countess for matters courtly (evident in the Hastings papers from the earl's numerous excuses for nonappearance) is apparent in a letter of warning sent by his cousin the bishop of Bath and Wells in 1613. The king has voiced the expectation that Huntingdon will for once be present at court for the wedding of Princess Elizabeth and the elector palatine. The Bishop points out that

It should seeme ther hath ben more indeavor used to drawe your Lo^P to London at this solemnity than I supposed could have bene for now his Maty seemes to be desierous to have your Lo^P there and my La: to, and thinkes he hath spared your Lo^P a great while. For his Majesty sayeth, if ever you will come you will come now It is the mariadge of the Kings only Daughter he sayeth and if that be not occasion enough he knowes not what is Yet if your Lo^{P}s owne health will not serve, I suppose my La: her presence heere will supply the want of your Lo^{P}s absence But if your Lo^P thinketh it not fitt to send my La: and stay behind Yf I mighte advise I would wishe your Lo^P to come, since I see the kinge so desierous of your presence and so loath to want any honor his Lords may doe him at this time Your Lo^P may use the matter as well as you may but all will not be well I see unless your Lo^P be heere.[48]

The inference is fairly plain ("for his Majesty sayeth, if ever you will come, you will come now") that this overtly Protestant wedding—the alliance of an English princess with the most promising Protestant prince in continental Europe—should be enough of an incentive to bring this descendant of Elizabeth's "Puritan earl" to London.[49] But it would seem that the fifth earl was uninclined even to attend these celebrations, a reaction at odds with even the most implacable of Jacobethans in the *annus mirabilis* of 1613. It is certainly no coincidence that James, who had always been aware and wary of the Huntingdons' distant claim to the throne, turned up at Ashby just a year later for a prolonged visit which appears to have been designed primarily to bankrupt the estate. As Philip Finkelpearl points out, "[w]ithin the Hastings family it was felt that King James paid long visits to Ashby out of a malign urge to impoverish a potential rival of the Stuarts."[50] James Knowles has suggested that there is a marked change of tone in the lifestyle of the Huntingdons around the time of this letter, a change due chiefly to the massive debts that they had to cope with from then on, which had been building up over decades and which were badly exacerbated by repeated lengthy visits from the king.[51] It is quite clear that extended visits by the king on progress were an unofficial royal weapon to be used against some of his less obviously loyal country nobility. In a manner similar perhaps to some of the "Spenserian" poets, then, the Huntingdons' disaffection from court, nurtured by family tradition, was sustained not so much by fundamental ideological differences as by financial problems and a sense of deliberate neglect or ruin. The debts which had become obvious in 1613 or thereabout certainly continued to plague the earl for years: much later, in 1626, the earl writes to Marlborough, Charles's Lord Treasurer, explaining his inability to respond to the latest request for money from the king:

My Lo, all my lands as yor Lp knowes are in extent to his Ma;^{tie} for my Ancestores debt, my lande entayled three of my yonger Children unprovided for, and my self in many Thousand pounds debte, & the land that I have reserved for the payment therof being but sufficient for that end; therfore I hope by yor Lps favourable informacon unto his Matie of theis my reasons I shalbe excused fro[m] lending seing I cannot do it unless I take it up upon use and plunge my self further into debt.[52]

It would seem that Charles simply extended the treatment his father had meted out to the earl. Certainly, the fifth earl had little to be grateful for to either James or Charles, and his distaste for court life becomes increasingly apparent in his correspondence. In a letter of 1627 to his younger son Henry, the earl offers a little sage advice:

I should be sorry that yo^u should like a Courte life too well for it is but *splendida miseria* & Sr Walter Mildmay a great Courtier and Counsellour of State in queene Elizabeths tyme in a little booke of his hath this sayinge (Know the Courte but spend not thy tyme there) & I can say in my owne experience that have tasted of all the waters that have issued from honest delights that noe life for the good of the soule, of the bodie & estate, are answeareable to a Cuntrie life.[53]

This "Cuntrie life" to which the earl refers is in many ways key to literary representations of the political alternatives to James's extravagant absolutism. It is by way of religious matters, of attitudes to hospitality and to duty, of relations between landlord and retainer, that the "honesty" on which Ashby and other similar aristocratic households prided themselves is defined: this ethos finds dramatic expression in Fletcher's plays throughout his career.

Huntingdon clearly disagreed with the king on questions of practical religion. He had, after all, been brought up by his uncle, the "Puritan" third earl. Among the Hastings papers there is a 1613 letter in which reference is made to the earl's habit of supporting nonconformist ministers. The minister in question that year was Arthur Hildersham, a distant relative of Huntingdon, who had been first brought in by the third earl, became vicar of Ashby-de-la-Zouche in 1593, was deprived of office in 1605, and was subsequently suspended from his duties by the High Commission in the year of the letter from Archbishop Abbot. Abbot apologizes for the brevity of his note (pleading overwork) and then continues:

[Y]our L[p]. must take heed how you appeere to moove for any of those ministers, who have bene silenced for not conforming themselves unto the orders of the Churche. For I see no hope or expectation that any of them will bee tollerated to preache upon any pretence whatsoever, unlesse they do subscribe, as by the Canon they are directed. And therefore if m[r] Hildersham bee resolved to maintaine the peace of the Churche, and to testify it by his subscription, we shall bee most glad to receive him: but if hee still refuse, hee is assured to sustaine the indignation of his Ma[ty], if hee offer to preache; for hee is a person, whom his Highnesse hath particularly in observation.[54]

Two years after this, Hildersham was imprisoned for refusing an "ex officio" oath. At the time of his first deprivation in 1605, Huntingdon, Sir Thomas Cave, and Sir William Skipwith had signed a letter supporting Hildersham and other deprived Leicestershire ministers. It has even been suggested that Hildersham was in fact the fifth earl's personal secretary at the time of his deprivation.[55] Certainly he remained Huntingdon's chaplain for many years, and the third earl's legacy in religious and other matters, as exemplified by Hildersham, seems to have provided the general ethos of the household throughout the period.[56] It should nonetheless be recognized that local loyalties appear to have transcended nominal religious affiliations: several local families—the Beaumonts and the Treshams, to name only two—had recusant members. This in itself seems not to have been a block to membership (if that is the word) of the Ashby milieu. Attitudes to literature and to performance were clearly not "puritanical." As we have seen, the fourth earl had maintained an acting company, and, though this was disbanded under the fifth earl, literary and dramatic patronage, at least with the introduction of the new countess into the household, remained strong. Moreover, active patronage, both literary and political, seems much of the time to have had its source in the countess rather than the earl.[57] Amongst the Hastings papers there is a fine letter, dated 30 October 1616, from Sir Thomas Roe, the diplomat and explorer, addressed to the countess from India. In this letter, Roe thanks her for unspecified patronage in the past which she has been "so noble as to forget." He insists in expressing his gratitude: "You once undertook to put me into action, but God would not you should have any obligation to those who were not worthy of it. [Y]our noble design to do me a courtesy was so free, so undeserved, that I will never forget that I owe your Ladyship more than I am or ever shall be."[58] In describing his experiences in India, Roe refers to courtly "wickedness" in a manner which can only assume a like opinion on the subject (and which suggests why Roe was almost permanently employed in missions to distant parts of the world), and this serves in a way as a companion piece to Fletcher's rather more intimate verse letter to the lady. He expresses his regret at being far away from her ladyship, who, he says, has been good to him beyond the call of duty. Writing from the court of the "Great Mogul," Jehangir Khan, he tells her:

There is nothing in this new world that is like you. But if I let go the consideration of fine things, and meditate upon goodness or virtue, I may well say I walk with your Antipodes: you have all in you, more than the books and religion of these.

And he adds wryly that the Indians "have craft enough to be as wicked as any in our court, and in all the wisdom of the Devil

they are excellently learned. So that I am like to profit well." For
Philip Finkelpearl to dismiss Roe simply as a "literary camp fol-
lower" is substantially to underestimate his standing and personal
strengths.[59] He had received his knighthood from James in 1605,
and gravitated first toward Prince Henry, who sent him on his first
New World voyage, and then after the prince's death, toward
Princess Elizabeth. He remained her staunch supporter throughout his life, seeking diplomatic means for the restoration of the
Palatinate; she would address him as "Honest Tom" in correspondence. He was involved in extensive travels and embassies, spending much of his life abroad in one capacity or another and writing extensive journals of his travels. When in England, he was a
vocal member of Parliament. He was married to Eleanor, daughter
of Sir Thomas Cave, an appropriately country-Protestant match
between two families connected with the Huntingdons.[60] And he
was clearly a Christmas regular at Ashby: there is a postscript to
the letter in which he writes, "I will presume to offer my service to
my Lord; for whom I will be stored with discourse for two Christ-
mases, to talk out candles and fires and all patience" (56).

A letter of Sir John Holles to the fourth earl in February 1603
provides some insight into the respective characters of the fifth earl
and the countess.[61] Holles observes that the earl "hath sent hither
to the court my Lord Hastings your grandchild with address that
he either be about the King or Prince," but suggests that young
Hastings is both "somewhat too old and grave for the Prince and
too young and raw for the King." Holles goes on to outline the
pitfalls of courtly life and to suggest foreign travel as a better
means to educate the future earl. Holles skates just this side of the
tactless, explaining that he recommends travel for the young man
"for, to speak as I think, he hath already too much water in his wine
and needs rather the sunshine than the shade." Holles is of course
irritatingly unspecific, but we are left with a strong sense that the
future fifth earl does not at this stage have the "touch and metal the
court requires." His tone when describing the young Elizabeth
Hastings suggests a marked contrast of character: she is a "forward
spirit" who demonstrates "many good hopes of honour and for the
present beyond her years a well governed carriage." Thus one
comes away from the letter with a sense of the future earl's naïveté
and the future countess's presence of mind. The earl himself was in

later years clear enough about his wife's strengths. In the same letter in which he gave his son advice about staying away from court, he chided him for a liaison with a grand but unspecified courtly lady. His objections to this woman serve as an oblique characterization of the fifth countess. "Yo^r mother," he writes, "hath such a judicious conceit & masculine understandinge that that would gravell another woman wch wth great facility shee can dispatch." Clearly, the earl considers his son's potential mistress to be several notches below the countess:

sure shee must bee a great woman great in bulke, great in riches, great in rancke that thinkes her selfe but little inferioure to my wife, & I am sure a verie great one if shee have that ability in her & have the Predominant understandinge of yor mother wch this demonstra[b]lie showes shee hath not, for an Eagle soares soe high that she lookes not to her feet & an understandinge minde cannot discend soe lowe as to thinke of Carpetts or anie thinge under her feet, and if yor mother like as Travellers y^t lie in Innes manie tymes should lie in a bare roome soe good & sweet a disposicon in soe well shapt & formed a bodie is a ritcher furniture than if the roome were ceiled wth the purest gould of Ophir. [62]

The earl was clearly not impressed, and we are left with a very strong impression of the fifth countess's "masculine understandinge."

In this regard it is also perhaps worth comparing Fletcher's verse letter with other poems written to or for the countess. There are two poems by John Donne addressed "To the Countess of Huntingdon." Donne first met her during his time as the lord keeper's secretary at York House before his clandestine marriage to Anne More abruptly lost him his ties with the Egerton household. Elizabeth Stanley was about thirteen when she became Egerton's ward; despite her youth, she was married to Henry Hastings shortly afterward. Her acquaintance with Donne at this time must therefore have been brief: they became reacquainted much later via Sir Henry Goodyer. [63] Neither of Donne's extant poems to the countess has been dated with conviction, though John Yoklavich is clearly right to object to the suggestion that "That unripe side of earth," probably the earlier of the two, was written as early as Donne's voyage to the Azores in 1597. The countess, after all, would have been only ten at that time, and the tone of the poem most inappropriate. Both poems address her as above the moral and spiritual level of most women, as somehow defying by her nature the low status usually accorded to women. Virtue, Donne claims rhetorically, has merely "gilded" men, but the countess is Virtue herself.[64] In the earlier poem, he compares his own relation to New World natives with the countess's relation to him: "as they do / Seem sick to me, just so must I to you."[65] The New World context of the poem, including his reference to "the tempest of a frown," is interesting both in light of the fifth earl's increasing interest in the Virginia Company around this time and in view of the language of Sir Thomas Roe's letter to the countess.[66] In both poems, the countess is described as a woman of rare, almost divine, purity: "You are a perfectness," Donne tells her, "so curious hit, / That youngest flatteries do scandal it."

Thomas Pestell's "Verses of ye Countess of Huntington" are in many ways parallel both to Donne's poems and to Fletcher's verse letter: it is tempting even to wonder if "[th]at Poett" referred to by Pestell in the poem is in fact Fletcher himself. Pestell begins with a similar strategy to that adopted by Fletcher, opening with a denial that he has the wit to write. There is a similar tone, not exactly antigovernmental or anticlerical but perhaps a little wry about the institutions of both, about his denial of an ecclesiastical remedy for the loss of wit he has described:

> [T]o mend this the State hath yet noe plott,
> Noe Nor the Lawe, the Church releives vs not;
> . . . Our Church in tyme of Warr, a Litanie
> hae's wth Collects for peace, & when tis drye
> for raine, but look yf you Can finde in it
> A prayer to help againste the drought of witt
> for fires, & wracks wee geather; witt once gon:
> there is nor Collect, nor Collection. (9–10; 13–18)[67]

After this preamble, however, Pestell begins to praise the countess openly while yet declaring her presence paradoxically detrimental to his art:

> [W]hen I, or preach, or praye,
> Or reade before her, or wou'd some thinge saye
> What to another might prove eloquence
> To her w^{t}h verie much adoe is sence. (45–48)

He moves from this to hyperbolical praise phrased in a manner which might seem rather odd for a consciously Protestant vicar:

> The Sun putts out all lesser fires;
> And I doe thinck (tho this maye bee gaynsayd)
> That next to God, & his bright Mother mayde;
> I shall doe reverence to her in Heaven. (58–61)

And he carries on praising her saintly virtues:

> Shee that haes such a soule, & such a face,
> whose Conversation is in stead of grace
> Whose good workes are soe full; yf anie shee
> bee sav'd for merritt; shee is sure to bee. (67–70)

Both here and in Fletcher's verseletter, then, the countess is compared with Mary as part of a poetic tribute to her virtues. As we have seen, in the particular circumstances of the Ashby circle, such apparent catholicisms are occasionally to be expected: the term "Puritan," appropriate perhaps for the third earl, is not an accurate term to use in describing the quality of the fifth earl's brand of "country Protestantism."[68] Pestell's poem even seems to imply that the fifth countess sponsored a morris dance and suggests a direct correlation between pastimes and poetry:

> But whether the fresh season of the yeare
> . . . Or Change of aire, or wine, or beinge one
> Y^t parted w^th [th]att Poett late, and tooke
> th'infection soe or whether I did looke
> too fervently vpon thy morris daunce,
> And soe the same vnruly Muse (perchance)
> That inspirde them, (as sure some Muse it was)
> hae's enterd mee, to make mee playe the asse;
> I knowe not but at my retorne I finde
> My penn to verses fatally enclinde. (21, 26–34)

This verse allows for distinctions to be made between a "puritan" minister like Pestell and "Puritan" attitudes. The customary assumption about Puritans is that they were vehemently opposed to sports and pastimes, yet here is a militant Protestant minister happily equating his own inspiration to write verse with the "vnruly Muse" of a morris dance.[69] It is quite clear that Ashby Protestantism is as far from the cliché of "puritanism" as it is from the ethos of courtly life.

Perhaps the clearest sense of this comes out of the "Antimask" to "A maske presented on Candlemas nighte at Coleoverton."[70] This was a masque given by Sir Thomas Beaumont at his house at

Coleorton, a village not far from the Huntingdons' seat at Ashby, in honor of the marriage of Sir William Seymour and Lady Frances Devereux, sister of the earl of Essex, in 1618. Its authorship remains anonymous, though Fletcher and Pestell have both been suggested as candidates.[71] Though thematically at variance with the masque proper, the antimasque provides a sense of the ethos of the marriage. Puck, "yᵉ Cuntrie Sprit, steals in softlie," but is tricked almost immediately by his old friend Bob, "yᵉ Buttrie Spirit." In a spirit of good humor, nonetheless, Puck cries "welcome to Leicestershire againe" (p. 329, ll. 9–10), but hears bad news. "All over England," he is told, hospitality has come "[d]owne and arise it never shall" (p. 329, l. 15). The problem is one of misconception. The overzealous have rejected generous country hospitality as ungodly behavior, equating "good ffellowship" and "feasting" with the errors of Papism, and "Countrie mirth and pastime" with the error of Pontius Pilate (p. 329, ll. 19–20). These spoilsports are characterized as a "new Sect" of "Puritans and Pettifoggers" who are as hypocritical as they are miserly: "trulie, if ere they drink, Drunk 'tis with Ale and in Private" (p. 329, ll. 24–25). These people are equated in Puck's mind with James's *nouveaux riches:* "nowe everie hinde is growne a gentleman; gentlemen, knightes, barrons & Barronetts, Boy. & then my madam, dropt out o'th Dung Cart, or whose Father's sheepe ha ffarted her into a Ladiship, must ha four horsess, one more than Phoebus" (p. 329, ll. 30–34). The destructive extravagance of these people—"Th'hard arable Land shal be converted into loose gownes, & the Medowes flie up in Petticootes" (p. 330, ll. 1–3)— is compared to the generosity of the established country aristocracy. Yet the old aristocracy is facing difficult times: "This robs both buttrie and kitchinge" (p. 330, l. 3), says Bob, and Puck affirms that "thers not nine shillings left in little Brittan" (p. 330, ll. 15–16). But Bob rallies, and turns to praise of the masque's sponsors and participants. "[T]hers store of gold left yet, boy," he cries, "& a few good fellowes in this corner of the Contrie," and he introduces the Earls of Huntingdon and Essex and Coleorton's own Beaumonts: "Her's honest Harrie of Ashbie, Bonny Bob of Lichfield, besides a brace of my bully Beaumonts" (330, ll. 18–20).

The particular curiosity of this masque lies in its juxtaposition of an emphasis on country hospitality and generosity with an apparently radical analysis of gender relations. When the masque proper commences, an alter appears, inscribed *"Jovia Hospitali Sacrum"* (331, 17), before which Favonius, the West Wind, praises what he calls "[t]h'hospitable sacrifice" and ushers in "[s]ix brave virtues masculine" to dance in honor of Lady Frances, the masque's "child of light." Led by Sir Vere Dux (an anagram of Devereux, the earl of Essex's family name), a series of masquers appears, all with obviously Spenserian names: Sir Arthur, Sir Sapient, Sir Artegall, Sir Guyon, and Sir Calidore, representative, as in *The Faerie Queene,* of key virtues—Valour, Wisdom, Justice, Temperance, and Courtesy. Suddenly, the scenery moves aside to reveal six women masquers, female counterparts to the "virtues masculine," presided over by the goddess Iris and intent on showing "yᵉ precedencie of female vertue" (334, 16). "Be not blind," they sing to the women present,

> But know your strength & your own Vertues see
> which in everie Several grace
> of the mind, or of the face,
> Gives women right to have Prioritie.
> Brave Amazonian Dames
> Made no count of Mankind but
> for a fitt to be at the Rutt.
> free fier gives the brightest flames;
> Menns overawing tames
> And Pedantlike our active Spirits smother.
> Learne, Virgins, to live free;
> Alass, would it might bee,
> weomen could live & lie with one another! (334,30–42).

This vehement if wistful feminist separation is negotiated into a "dance together" in which "[t]he male & the female graces / Tread in . . . equal paces" (335, 38–39), and the accompanying song instructs both sexes in appropriate gender relations:

> Learne, women, to forsake
> Your coynes, scorne, and proud disdaine;
> Men mach, tho not exceed you,
> Tis Jove, hath thus agreed you;
> And let Men warning take:
> All strife with women is in Vaine. (336, 1–6)

In conclusion, intimations of separatism are supplanted by the male masque's assertion that in a society without recognition of sexual difference, gender identity would be lost: "Women ciphers are, and want / Mixture of well-figur'd men[.] / Themselves un-significant, / Joynd they have a mening then" (335, 26–29).

The masque is thus a curious affair: it is both a glorification of the established country aristocratic households exemplified by the Huntingdons of Ashby and the Beaumonts of Coleorton and an assertion of equality between the sexes that suggests a certain degree of feminocentrism in the households in question. In view of the masque's swipes at James's court and the political interests of the dancers, this emphasis on the unexpected power of women no doubt harks back to the days of Queen Elizabeth. This assumed inheritance is reinforced by the Spenserian references: the masque represents an extension of perceived Spenserian politics (in the wake of the Sidney patronage noted by Massinger in the "Copie of a Letter") into and by privately commissioned dramatic enter-tainment in a self-consciously Protestant, provincial setting. The masque thus carefully situates Coleorton (and, by implication, Ashby) in respect both to Protestant sects and to Puritans, to the court and to those representative of the new peers and landowners created by James, and to James himself. The Beaumonts and the Huntingdons are quite clearly not "puritans": they are firmly Prot-estant aristocrats rooted in a country ethos which sees itself as threatened by the behavior of London and the court. Moreover, the ethos of these estates readily acknowledges the collaborative role of male and female in society, as well as the possibility of power and virtue for select aristocratic women.

Even if this country-house masque was not (as has been sug-gested) written by John Fletcher, it nonetheless signals its con-nections with London and the stage. The introduction of Iris and the masque of Spenserian knights refers to and partially inverts *The Masque of the Inner Temple and Gray's Inn,* Francis Beaumont's masque for the wedding of Princess Elizabeth and the elector palatine some five years earlier. The allusion is a complex one, both calling to mind and questioning the nature of royal masques, and reminding the participants of 1613, the year in which for a brief while it looked as if James's policies might turn toward militant Protestant interests. At the same time, the masque reminds the members of its audience of their own family and milieu connec-tions with the London stage, reworking aspects of the Inner Temple masque at least in part (one would presume) as a tribute to Sir Thomas Beaumont's cousin Francis, who had died at the age of thirty only two years earlier, and thus, of course, also calling to mind Beaumont's collaborator and friend (and the Huntingdons' client) Fletcher.

3

Massinger, in the "Copie of a Letter," makes little distinction between patronage of poetry and patronage of drama in his assessment of the necessary, dependent relations involved in literary production. Spenser, Jonson, Fletcher, and their relations with aristocratic promoters, are all precedents Massinger cites "with reverence." Several aspects of these relations can be gleaned from these few lines. The model (ostensibly, at least) appears to be one of preferment rather than financial support or dependence. It is Sidney's promotion of Spenser in his *Apology for Poetry* which Massinger names as key to that poet's place in the Jacobean canon. At the same time, the language used of the two dramatists, Jonson and Fletcher—"owe" ("Iohnson much of what he has does owe / To you and to your familie") and "credit" ("nor had Fletcher euer / Such Reputation, and credit wonne")—ambivalently implies a certain financial element in the transaction. But the kinds of patronage appropriate to a writer of poems on the one hand and a writer of public theater plays on the other must differ. After all, dramatists—especially King's company dramatists—had three domains of patronage available to them: the king, the paying audience, and the nobility or gentry.[72] The audience, by way of the theater company or entrepreneur, provided (most of the time, at least, though popular theater playwrights such as Dekker were rarely out of debt) a living for the dramatist, thereby freeing him from the closer relationship of necessity forced upon the poet. With theater funding, then, and with the regular assurance of royal support, a playwright of Jonson's or Fletcher's status was not inherently bound to seek a particular aristocratic or city patron.

Yet quite clearly the dramatists often did seek such external patrons, carrying out additional commissions from city pageants to private entertainments and court masques, and hoping in exceptional cases (though generally without the urgency of the poets) for preferment at court to some post which might enable the leisure required for literary production. Fletcher, unlike his father, appears to have had no courtly ambitions at all, and if he did have such ambitions, he picked the wrong aristocratic patrons. Yet he did sustain a patronage relationship beyond the obligatory domains (the court and the audience) of King's company funding, and this relationship in various ways informs his work throughout his career.

One complicating factor in any analysis of a dramatic patronage relationship such as that between Fletcher and the Huntingdons is its dependence upon a certain degree of silence. Where, with poetry, the patronage relationship is expressed overtly in a dedication or series of dedications, with drama the relationship is generally far less obvious. Fletcher's dedication of the published text of *The Faithful Shepherdess* to three members of the gentry with literary interests, and Massinger's dedication of *The Duke of Milan* to Katherine Stanhope are exceptions (and the publication of *The Faithful Shepherdess* came about only because of the play's initial failure in performance): dramatic dedications are rare.[73] A nondramatic poem such as Æmilia Lanyer's *Salve Deus Rex Iudæorum* makes its patronage relations plain for all to see, providing dedicatory verses to a range of women patrons and making overt reference to the principal patron, the countess of Cumberland, and her relatives and circle. But when a public theater dramatist receives patronage, the acknowledgment is mostly silence. One way of reading between the lines of King's company plays such as Shakespeare's is to seek implicit reference to the company's own royal patron, but beyond court-centred analysis, silences—the spaces between the lines—are more difficult to fathom.

Fletcher's plays are also King's company plays, yet their sustained attitude to royalty and absolutism suggests a problem with such court-centred readings. Without the "external" evidence of his verse letter to the countess, and without Massinger's verses, it would be impossible to infer Huntingdon patronage for Fletcher's plays. Yet with that external evidence, dramatic threads can be traced and connections made. Not that the threads of drama always lead to the same conclusions, as is made clear enough in recent debates over the involvement of the earl of Pembroke and the duke of Buckingham in the scandal of Middleton's *A Game at Chess*. In

Fletcher's case, however, a number of symmetries are apparent between the country-based, feminocentric, uncourtly environment cultivated by the Huntingdons at Ashby and the politics of the plays, which are cynical of court and assertions of absolutism, and are fascinated both with negotiations of city and country and with issues of gender, in particular with female dominance and agency. In this context, the Coleorton masque—whether by Fletcher or not—offers a dramatic bridge between the milieu and the plays.

It is thus important to see Fletcher's dramatic work as in various ways the product of negotiation between the ethos of the aristocratic, Protestant country household and of life in London and at court. In order to demonstrate this, I shall proceed with a detailed historical narrative of events which took place at the beginning both of Fletcher's writing career and of his acquaintance with the earl and countess of Huntingdon. By means of this narrative, I hope to provide an adequate basis for a local reading of the drama. "Local reading," as elaborated by Leah Marcus, has the advantage for materialist or historicist critics of Shakespeare of "turning us away—temporarily at least—from a Shakespeare who can be perceived as self-cohesive and universal."[74] On these grounds, localization would seem the only way forward for Fletcher criticism, which has, after all, never labored under such misapprehensions. It is difficult to think of a less "self-cohesive" author than Fletcher, always paired (or halved) with Beaumont in the passing reference, fragmented across fifty or so mostly collaborative plays, considered in fewer critical books than have been devoted to even the least popular of Shakespeare's plays. But a local reading of Fletcher has still further relevance and importance in questioning one of the givens of Shakespeare (and therefore of Renaissance drama) criticism over the last decade or so, namely the centrality of London to interpretation of the theater. Obviously, the plays we discuss were acted in London; one of their key localizing factors is the Bankside and its environment. The "place of the stage," as Steven Mullaney has eloquently shown, was (in various ways) London and its liberties, and interpretation of Shakespeare's plays—performed at court, at the Blackfriars, and at the Globe—must acknowledge this location. The plays can be seen in this light to articulate local tensions between Bankside and Whitehall, Liberties and City. Analysis of Fletcher's work must also fall within this remit: his role as Shakespeare's King's company successor requires it. Yet, in analysis of Fletcher's plays, there is a further necessary localization, which I have already begun by detailing his parentage and patronage. Marcus briefly discusses, but also to some extent deflects, this further localization as she mentions the danger of the "local" being associated "with a kind of retrograde regionalism" (36), with what is generally written off from the "centers" of culture as the "provincial." Yet it is useful to recall the tale told of Lord Dainton who, when asked for the umpteenth time how it felt to return to Oxford from the provinces, said that he had thoroughly enjoyed the transition from the provincial to the parochial. There is a danger that, in locating the meanings of English Renaissance plays firmly and only in London, critics are in danger of succumbing to a kind of parochialism. Even American critics, who ought to be free from certain British cultural allegiances and prejudices, seem to be guilty of this: Marcus, for example, concludes her book on "local reading" with a substantial section entitled "London." Yet London was not the only local context for drama. We have only fragmentary evidence of the effect of provincial tours on the repertoire of companies such as the King's Men, yet such tours did take place with regularity. Personal and patronage relations with England beyond London, even if only briefly acknowledged, must become part of the matrix of meaning of the plays.

"Location" does not simply imply location of performance, and Fletcher's plays thus provide a test case for local reading. Performed in London, yet emanating in part from a cultural milieu with firm roots in the East Midlands, in Leicestershire, and in Northamptonshire, and written by a playwright born and brought up in Sussex and then translated to London, these plays take much of their meaning from tensions not simply between City and Liberties, but between London and the counties, city and country. Philip Finkelpearl has begun this process of Fletcherian localization, but his analysis retains certain problematic historicist assumptions about "court and country": I hope, in a postrevisionist context, to acknowledge and benefit from the local, detailed preoccupations of revisionist historiography while retaining an urge for the larger picture.[75]

TWO

"This is a pretty Riot / It may grow to a rape"

They be such curious things / that they care not for Kings, / And dare
let them knowe it.[1]

I

By the time Henry Hastings, fifth earl of Huntingdon, had
reached the town of Leicester on Friday 5 June 1607, he must
have been perfectly aware of the problems he faced. The previous
night he and his company had lodged in Northampton, after a six-
hour delay at Dunstable to await fresh horses. On Friday morning
he set out across the disturbed county toward the Leicestershire
border and in the process must have passed through or near the
centers of revolt. Arriving in Leicester he found little to encourage
him, took overall command, and began to mobilize the county's
forces. The earl was only twenty-one, the same age as his distant
cousin the dramatist Francis Beaumont, when, in his capacity as
lord lieutenant of Leicestershire, he was commanded by King
James to travel north and deal with the Midlands Revolt of 1607.
A couple of years earlier, in November 1605, he had received a
series of vivid accounts from his uncle John, first lord Harington,
of the pursuit and capture of the Gunpowder conspirators near
Coventry.[2] And, though inexperienced, he seems to have taken
swift enough action to gain control of the unsettling situation he
found in his lieutenancy, though not without coming under a
certain level of criticism from London for alleged leniency to the
rebels.

The immediate problems of 1607 had begun in earnest toward
the end of May, but the causes of unrest went back much further
than that. Fifteen ninety-six and ninety-seven had seen the worst

Map from William Burton's *Description of Leicestershire* (1622)

harvest in the Midlands in living memory, as well as an abortive insurrection in Oxfordshire, and though crops recovered in the years that followed there remained nonetheless a scarcity of grain. Prices rose steadily, chiefly as a result of widespread poverty which forced the poor to make do with oats and other less nutritious cereals rather than wheat and corn. Demand fell, and prices rose still further. The harsh winter of 1606–7 led to a poor harvest, and it must have been grimly apparent to the poor of the Midlands in early summer 1607 that hard times were upon them. John Martin emphasizes widespread concern over the grain supply as the primary cause of the insurrection that ensued.[3] Three features of the 1607 revolt stand out. One is that the troubles constituted considerably more than a series of unconnected enclosure riots and are best seen, in Martin's words, as "a consciously organized movement of protest in the areas affected" (Martin 174).[4] The second is that the riots were almost entirely free from violence against persons. The third, perhaps surprising, feature is that the organizers appear to have been somewhat better educated than might be expected.

Some of them were literate. There is extant a manuscript exhortation from "The Diggers of Warwickshire to all other Diggers" in which the "poore Deluers & Day labourers" hope for a response from the king to their demands. The motivation is quite clearly lack of corn:

Louing Freinds & Subjects all under one renowned Prince, for whom we pray longe to continue in his most Royall estate to the subuerting of all those Subjects of what degree soeuer y^t haue or would depriue his most true harted Com[m]unalty both from life and lyvinge. Wee, as members of ye whole, doe feele ye smart of these incroaching Tirants, wch would grinde our flesh upon ye whetstone of pouerty, & make our loyall hearts to faint wth breathing, so y^t they may dwell by themselues in ye midst of theyr Hearde of fatt weathers. It is not unknowne unto yo^{r}selues ye reason why these mercyless men doe resist wth force agst our good intents. It is not for ye good of our most gracious Sou[er]aigne, whom we pray God y^t longe he may reygne amongst us; neyther for ye benefitt of ye Communalty, but onely for theyr owne priuate gaine; for there is none of y^{em} but doe tast ye sweetness of our wantes. They haue depopulated & ouerthrown whole Townes, & made thereof Sheep pastures nothing profitable for our Com[m]onwealth. For ye com[m]on Fields being layd open would yeeld us much com[m]odity, besides ye increase of Corne, on wch standes our life. But if it should please God to wthdrawe his blessing in not prospering ye fruites of ye Earth but one yeare (wch God forbidd) there

would a worse & more fearfull dearth happen then did in K. Ed: y^e
seconds tyme, when people were forced to eat Catts & Doggs flesh, &
women to eate theyr owne children. Much more wee could giue you to
understand, but wee are perswaded y^t you your selues feele a part of our
grieuances, & therfore need not open ye matter any plainer. But if you
happen to shew your force & might ag^st us, wee for our partes neither
respect life nor lyuinge; for better it were in such case wee manfully dye,
then hereafter to be pined to death for want of y^t wch these deuouring
Encroachers doe serue theyr fatt Hogges & Sheep withall. . . .[5]

As this shows, the question of inadequate corn supplies was part
and parcel of a larger question in the minds of the poor, that of
rights to common land, focused by the rapidly growing problem of
enclosure.[6] According to Martin, the 1607 Midlands Revolt is
"central to an understanding of the relationship of agrarian transformation to peasant revolt in the transitional period in England,"
and comprises "the last concerted effort by the peasantry to halt
those changes" (161). Stow lists the levelers' grievances: "The
preuention of further depopulation, the encrease and continuance
of tillage to relieue their wiues and children, and chiefly because
it had beene credibly reported vnto them by many, that of very late
yeeres, there were three hundred and forty Townes decayed and
depopulated."[7] The insurrection was organized in such a way as to
concentrate action in conspicuously depopulated areas rather than
simply to provoke isolated riots in less significant places. Thus
many of the rioters traveled fifteen or more miles away from their
own troubled parishes to level hedges on the land of the most
notorious Midlands enclosers such as Thomas Tresham of Newton
and John Quarles, who owned the old Devereux land at Cotesbach
but who controlled it from London.[8]

The riots that comprised the revolt of 1607 followed a basic
pattern, often extending over several days, since the destruction of
miles of hedgerow was no mean task even for large numbers of
levelers. Enclosing hedges were planted on mounds: rioters tore
down the hedges and threw them into the ditches left when the
mounds were created. They then set fire to the uprooted hedges
and buried them by leveling the mounds back into the ditches.
This process often took place against a background of annual
religious festivals—in the case of the 1607 revolt, May Day and
Trinity Sunday. Each riot itself seems to have been something of a
ritual, as rioters processed through villages, with a popular leader

41

on horseback at their head, to the tune of pipe and tabor and often the clamor of church bells.[9] The marchers were accompanied in the general air of festivity by representatives of the whole peasant community—women, children, old people—and they carried spades and mattocks as well as more overt weaponry.[10]

In the months leading up to May 1607, there had been a sense of increasing unrest in the Midlands counties, a level of unease reflected in a series of Star Chamber cases for that year. May Day festivities seem to have coalesced this sense of unease and heralded sporadic enclosure riots in Northamptonshire. As the month progressed, rioting grew more frequent, resulting in expressions of nervousness from the Privy Council. The government seems generally to have been anxious not to overreact, lest a heavy-handed response provoke outright rebellion. But by late May it was apparent that firmer action was required. Rioting was spreading from Northamptonshire to Warwickshire and Leicestershire and showed no sign of flagging. On 30 May James issued a proclamation to suppress enclosure riots with armed militia, and the country gentry were ordered to mobilize.[11] It was becoming apparent to the justices of Leicestershire that the rebellious field workers had begun to receive assistance from the townspeople of Leicester. Martin suggests that far more than the recorded seventy-one townspeople went out to join the rebels.[12] The county authorities ordered that Leicester's gates be closed, but a substantial number of people left town that night, ostensibly to prepare for Trinity Sunday festivities the next day. In fact, they traveled to key loci for enclosure protest. Five thousand people gathered at Cotesbach, and began to level hedges.

Cotesbach had been owned for 150 years by the Devereux family, but the earl of Essex, in substantial debt, had sold it to Sir Thomas Sherley, the treasurer for war, in 1591. Five years later Sherley "sold it to a London merchant named John Quarles, who destroyed the old order before he finished with it."[13] Quarles increased rents dramatically, on the principle that "[i]f the tenants would not renew their leases on terms more profitable to the lord, then he, in order to recoup himself, would enclose the manor" (Parker 59). The tenants had resisted enclosure at every stage and had even at one stage unsuccessfully petitioned the king for relief from enforced depopulation.[14] The revolt provided another way of focusing attention on their plight. Quarles family members appear to have been unrepentant enclosers. Sir Thomas Parry wrote to the fifth earl in June 1613 on behalf of George Quarles, who had petitioned to delay the opening-up of an enclosure called the Thwaites which the commoners of Leicester forest have claimed until the due legal process is complete. And around 1620, a "Mr. Quarles of Enderby" is accused of "destroying certain coppices in the forest of Leicester" (HMC *Hastings* IV:204).

In fury at the participation of townspeople in country riots, the county authorities ordered the mayor of Leicester to act, and he belatedly sent out a company to bring back those of his people who had taken part. The involvement of townsfolk in righting country grievances clearly disturbed the authorities. Writing to the earl of Huntingdon on 12 June, the lords of the Council asked him to take special note of "Townsmen, whether they be Artificers or others, as did put themselves into this Rebellion among the Countrey people." The Council was of the opinion that these townspeople had "more heynouslie offended then some others, in respect they had lesse pretence of greevance, having little or nothing to do wth Enclosures, and yet ministring most healp by numbers of men, weapons, and other meanes of assistance."[15]

Rioters were thus coming not only from the fields but from bordering woods and towns, and a sense of coherent organization developed. The first week in June saw sustained rioting over a wide area, including much of the three counties of Northamptonshire, Leicestershire, and Warwickshire. The revolt finally reached a head on 8 June at Thomas Tresham's enclosures at Newton, Northamptonshire, with an onslaught on a thousand-strong gathering of levelers by an official force, which comprised the retainers and servants of the most prominent gentry of the counties, since the county militia appeared inadequate to the task. The levelers stubbornly refused to desist, and the gentry force, led by Sir Edward Montagu and Sir Anthony Mildmay, charged them.[16] The battle looked uncertain for a moment, but the second charge succeeded in routing the rebels. Approximately fifty of the rioters were killed in the rout, and several of those captured were hanged and quartered.[17] This battle was the only major confrontation of the revolt and it marked the effective end of organized disorder, though isolated rioting carried on throughout June as far afield as Bedfordshire, Worcestershire, and Oxfordshire. But the government hold on the counties was tight by then, and confidence was such by mid-July that the authorities began to organize commissions of inquiry into the causes of the revolt.

On 3 June, King James had written to the earl of Huntingdon informing him that the sheriff of Leicester, Sir William Skipwith, and the local JPs were sufficiently concerned with the activities of the "disordered persons" in the area that they wished to have a "person of eminent degree amongst them from whom they might receive an uniform direction."[18] James was fairly unequivocal about the treatment he expected his lieutenant to mete out, though bloodshed was to be tempered with pragmatic mercy:

Although we can be content that for sparing of blood some special persons should be made example to others, yet in the case of any resistance you are to use the force of our county and the assistance of our subjects to invade, destroy and disperse them. Yet if you find the resistance likely to be such as the subduing of them will cost too much blood, we can be content that you publish by proclamation in our name that if they shall acknowledge their offence and submit themselves to our mercy, they shall have pardon for their lives, excepting only such as shall be found to have been the first movers and inciters of others to this rebellion.[19]

The Privy Council sent Sir Josias Bodley with the earl "as a man of experience and knowledge in the wars."[20] Bodley had served both in the Netherlands and in Ireland, and his detailed survey of the Ulster plantation forms part of the Hastings papers.[21] When Huntingdon and Bodley arrived in Leicester they found that several of the rebels had been taken. The JPs had determined to send three of the prisoners down to London for questioning, but in consultation with Huntingdon it was decided to send only one, "the chiefest leader and director of the rebellious company," whom we learn from the Council's reply of 9 June to be John Reynolds, perhaps better known as "Captain Pouch" and generally considered to be the ringleader of the revolt.[22] The logic of sending only one man was determined partly "in regard of the simplicity of the other two" and partly "in respect of the dangerous passage through Northamptonshire" (193). This suggests that the earl had had a fairly alarming journey from Northampton to Leicester on the Friday morning, a sense which is compounded by the fact that he sent Reynolds to London under the charge of his cousin, Sir Henry Hastings, presumably with a fairly substantial company. Huntingdon nonetheless assured Salisbury in his letter that Leicestershire was "very quiet" and that he expected it to remain so in view of his mobilizing activities. On arrival in Leicester he had ordered a gibbet to be set up in the marketplace and a considerable quantity of gunpowder and ammunition to be kept, guarded, in the town hall. To prevent further supportive sorties from Leicester itself, he had a substantial watch placed on the town's gates.

The Council in the meantime had begun investigations into the depopulation grievances seen to be the primary cause of the revolt and sent Huntingdon a preliminary list of alleged depopulators. The earl replied on 7 June with modifications to the Council's list, sending one of the offenders, Sir Thomas Humfrye, to London. He pointed out that one of the chief enclosers, John Quarles, "being a Londoner[,] has no abode in this county," but added that Quarles had indeed "depopulated the manor of Cosbich [Cosby], which is the only place in all the county cast down."[23] It is clear that in face of the Council's promptness in compiling a list of depopulators, Huntingdon was keen to ensure that "no depopulation shall lie undiscovered," adding that he "perswade[s him]self that this has been the chief motive of these rebellious assemblies." No mention, predictably enough, is made of rising corn prices and starvation.

Despite Huntingdon's earlier assurances to the Council, the county was by no means quiet. On the Saturday morning there was a substantial and "tumultuous" assembly of would-be levelers at Welham, and Huntingdon was obliged to ride out to disperse them, taking several of the leaders into custody. The Council's response when informed of this encounter sounded to the earl like criticism of his actions so far. They expressed the king's gratitude both to the earl and to the "justices of the peace and gentlemen of that Countie" who had dealt with the early stages of the uprising. "Nevertheless," they continued:

because wee do perceive, that both in that Countie and the next (where these riotous and rebellious people have assembled), it sufficeth not that they be once dispersed, neither doth the present dispersion give as-surance of quiett, and their obedience, (they being eftsoones readie to reassemble themselves, and to give new workes, as soone as ever they finde the authoritie and force that is to represse them a little remooved), wee thinke it verie needefull to lett yor Lp: know, that wch his Matie now findeth to be most necessarie, namelie, that some example must be made of severe punishment and iust revenge upon their disobedience and disloialtie, by the losse of the lives of some few of them, when, and wheresoever they shalbe found any more in such rebellious mannere assembled, be their number greater or lesse. ffor if upon their departure, they shalbe still suffered to goe wth impunitie, and consequentlie wth boldnes to renew their attempts, . . . what can ensue heerof but a dishono^r to his Matie, a most unworthy storme to the State, and contynuall toile [&] restlesse labo^r to yor Lp: and the rest of the gentlemen of the Countrey. . . . And therefore somewhat must be done sharpelie, and if it had bin done before there had bin neede of lesse labour now: wth sharpnes in verie deede, wilbe the truest waie of clemencie, because if they be forborne, they will runn headlong more and more into daungere. . . . W^ch would be prevented by the example of some few, that might iustlie in the act of their disobedience suffer the paine of death due to them; W^ch yor Lp: had neede well consider and take care of, if yo^u looke that either yor selves shall have an ende of the troble and businesse there, or we heere.[24]

Their letter of 12 June continued in the same vein, urging the earl to provide a "rodd for sharpe and present punishment."[25] Huntingdon was stung into providing a detailed self-justification:

Before my cominge to the place where I heard they weare assembled. they were all gone, havinge done little or nothinge, whereupon I sent some of my horsemen several ways and of that number could take not above viiij or x^en persons, wch were very poore creatures yet neverthelesse I caused ij or iij of them to be brought noe tree being near unto a wyndmylne, where I comanded halters to be put about there neckes. Finding them so penitent for there fault and submittinge themselves unto his ma.^ts mercye [I] held it fit to spare their executione for that time, intendinge if the least stir had agayne risen to have put to death some of them before my goinge forthe. and to have delt verye sharply wth others I had taken though they hadd yielded. Never since that time hathe there beene I thanck God the least assemblinge of these badd persons. so that I think yor L.^ps maye assure yo^rselves of no further disobedience in this countrye.[26]

This last may well have appeared true by the time of the earl's reply on the 14th, but on the Monday morning after the Welham encounter, the townspeople of Leicester made a gesture of solidarity with the imprisoned levelers which cannot have cheered Huntingdon. It was raining hard and few people were about when a group consisting of the beadle, the jailer, his underkeeper, one of his prisoners, and a number of boys tore down the gibbet Huntingdon had had erected in the square. The mayor tried in vain to persuade his people to rebuild the scaffold, and in the end the remains were shifted to a nearby yard out of fear that "the same shoulde be stoulne or cut in peeces" (Martin 171). In face of the mayor's apparent inability to have the scaffold rebuilt, Huntingdon peremptorily removed him from office and placed him under arrest.[27]

However, by the time he wrote to the Council from his home at Ashby-de-la-Zouche on 14 June, Huntingdon had control of both town and county, and there seems to have been no further complaint from London. In the same letter in which they criticized him, the Council had informed the earl that the king had decided to institute a commission of oyer and terminer to consider the causes of the insurrection and that they were already anxious to investigate those "in fault for enclosures, or depopulations." Their next letter to Huntingdon introduced the judges with whom he would be associated on the commission.[28] By 29 June, the earl wrote from Ashby that the situation was sufficiently quiet that he had felt able to dismiss his forces, and he noted the care with which the judges had performed their duties. Several executions, including that of John Reynolds, followed the Northampton trial. But according to Roger Manning, "[a]lthough Sir Edward Coke and the royal judges had laid it down in 1597 that conspiracy to commit treason constituted high treason and that all conspirators were to be regarded as principals, the defendants in the Northampton trial were dealt with under the three categories of high treason, felony-riot, and misdemeanor-riot—despite the fact that Sir Edward Coke, now chief justice of the Court of Common Pleas, was the presiding judge" (Manning 233–34). As Huntingdon noted in his letter of 29 June, by no means were all the levelers convicted of either treason or felony. The general sense is that the legal authorities were much more lenient in their treatment of the 1607 levelers than they had been in dealing with those responsible for the short-lived Oxfordshire rebellion of 1596.[29] The outcome of the commission of oyer and terminer thus suggests that the authorities, while determined to be ruthless with insurrection, recognized the real grievances which had led to the revolt. Indeed, as the letter of 5 June suggests, the government seems to have recognized the problem of enclosure and depopulation from the beginning of the risings.[30] Toward the end of July, the Council ordered Huntingdon to select six "disinterested gentlemen of Leicestershire" for a commission of inquiry into the practice of enclosure in the county.[31] This was followed, on 24 July, by a royal proclamation of pardon to any of the levelers who made submission before Michaelmas.[32]

The authorities appeared content to acknowledge the fault of the enclosing gentry and to concede that, though rebellion itself was unacceptable, the rebels had genuine grievances and that the rebellion was caused primarily by fear of famine. This reading of the situation is underlined by a sermon preached later in June at Northampton by Robert Wilkinson. Wilkinson deliberately suggested in his sermon that enclosure was not the sole grievance. The congregation to whom the sermon was preached included the earl of Exeter, the earl of Huntingdon's opposite number as lord lieutenant of Northamptonshire, and the other commissioners for the county, presumably including Huntingdon himself. Wilkinson, as chaplain to Exeter and a client of his extended family, was a logical choice of preacher. [33] The sermon was published before the year was out, with a dedication to Exeter, and the title page of the published text featured an etching of a wheat sheaf. In his epistle dedicatory, Wilkinson plays on Exeter's coat of arms, which features "a sheafe supported with Lyons," to appeal on behalf of the poor to the lord lieutenant that he "strongly . . . maintaine the cause of *corne* & of *bread*," and points out in the process that "iudgement looketh both wayes: and therfore as it chastiseth the offendor, so it represseth him likewise, by whose couetousnes & cruelty the offence cometh." [34] As Annabel Patterson has recently noted in an essay on the connections between *Coriolanus* and the Midlands Revolt in her *Shakespeare and the Popular Voice,* what is of particular interest about Wilkinson's sermon is that it "intends for itself a mediatorial status." [35] "It is true," writes Wilkinson in the epistle dedicatory,

that we are fallen into tempestuous and troublesome times, wherein the excessive couetousnesse of some hath caused extreame want to other, and that want not well disgested hath riotted to the hazard of all; yea and by these stormes we are cast among the rocks, even two the most dangerous rocks of estate, Oppression of the mighty, and Rebellion of the manie, by mischiefe wherof many florishing kingdomes and countries have miscarried, and so had we in this vndoubtedly, had not God by your good indeauors preuented it. (A3ʳ–A3ᵛ)

He follows this carefully balanced analysis with a similarly balanced plea to the earl of Exeter: "[W]e are bold to intreat you, that as you haue bin meanes for the due execution of iustice vpon the rebellious, so likewise (as opportunity shall serue) to promote the cause & cōplaints of the expelled, halfe pined, and distressed poore, that they rebell no more" (A4ʳ).

Wilkinson's text for his sermon is Matthew 4.4: "But hee answering sayde: It is written, Man shall not liue by bread onely, but by euery word that proceedeth out of the mouth of GOD" (B1ʳ). And, in an astonishing feat of political-theological troping, he outlines an overt analogy between the levelers and Christ, Northamptonshire and the wilderness:

[F]or the diuel finding Christ of late, first fasting, & then hungry in a desolate & barren wildernesse where nothing was to be had, aduiseth him not to looke vp to heauē, (frō whence in extreme want all help is to be waited for) but rather to take the way that was next at hand, & by a new kind of Alchimy, of stones to make himselfe bread, & vnto this Christ answereth him with the text I haue read, *man liueth not by bread onely, &c.* and there is nothing in this whole story so sutable, or so aptly speaking to the occasion & season of the time as this; for it is said before, that *Christ fasted,* meaning a religious fast, as few do now; and it is said likewise, that he was hungry, and no maruell, for he was in a place, where was neither bred nor corn, as may be now; & it is said likewise, that *thē the tempter came,* that is, the Diuell came, as all the world seeth he is vp and abroad now; & some he tempteth to turne bread into stones, that is, to decay the plenty of the earth, as many rich & greedy minded mē do now; & some he tempteth to turne stones into bread, that is, to vse vnlawful means for their own releife, as the mad & rebelious multitude doth now; but in this verse Christ sheweth a bettet [*sic*] way for mens reliefe, that is, by resting thēselues in the pleasure & prouidence of God, which is for all men an apt & godly answer, to such a diuilish & vngodlie temptation. (B1ᵛ–B2ʳ)

As Patterson suggests, Wilkinson offers a "remarkably materialist exegesis" (139) of his text: "That *man liueth by bread,* is inferred out of the very text; for euen where he saith, *Not by bread onely,* it followeth of necessitie, that amongst other meanes, yet by bread for one. . ." (C2ᵛ), and he moves on to overt discussion of "this depopulation" (C4ʳ), asking "is it not . . . vnnaturall (thinke ye) to see a man put out, to put in a beast, and men turned out to bring in sheepe, whereas God created the earth for men, and not for sheepe" (C3ᵛ). He is well into his stride by this point, and carries on:

[I]t is time, yea high time to speake of this, the text of it already being written in bloud; and no maruell if they which feele it, runne madde and wild vpon it, since wee which but see it are so much amazed at it; for a stranger which coasteth these countries, and findeth heere and there so many thousands and thousands of sheepe, & *nihil humani generis,* in so

49

many miles not a thing like a Man, might take vp a wonder, & say with himselfe; what? hath there bin some sorceresse, or some *Circe* heere that hath transformed men into beasts? (C3ᵛ)

Wilkinson acknowledges that rebellion against authority is a far greater evil than any oppression that may trigger such rebellion, yet he continues his onslaught against the depopulators, employing the familiar body metaphor for the state which inevitably brings to mind the awkward and incongruent tale told by Menenius Agrippa to the rioters at the beginning of *Coriolanus:*

I know ye thinke it horrible, that (as in this late Rebellion) Mechanicall men are come to beard Magistrates; and it is horrible indeede, *Euen the vile* (as *Esay* saith) *to presume against the honorable. Esa. 3.5.* But as it is an ill foote that kicketh at the head, and an ill hand that beateth it, so is it an ill head that wisheth the hand cut off, or deuiseth a way how to haue fewer fingers on the hand. . . . [T]o haue all parts peopled in due proportio is the glory, beauty & strength of the land, and hee that crosseth this, though he rise not in Rebellion to open disturbance, yet he is worse then a forraine inuador, and professed enemy of the land, for such a one, though hee come to kill vp the people, yet he doth it by open hostility, & of such there be wayes to beware: But these *Anthropophagi,* these deuourers of men vnder a name of right and property, doe the verye same thing. (C4ᵛ–D1ʳ)

Wilkinson extends this metaphor of the body still further a few pages later:

[F]or the belly sayth that bread must be had, and the soule subscribeth, that bread must be had too; and though reason may perswade and authoritie command, and Preachers may exhort with obedience and patience to sustaine the want of bread, yet for all that, *Venter non habet aures,* in case of extreame hunger men will not be perswaded, but they will haue bread. (D3ʳ)

At this point, however, the preacher clearly feels obliged to return rather abruptly to the spiritual aspects of his text—an eloquent disjunction—and he exhorts his listeners to consider "whence arise conspiracyes, riottes, and damnable rebellions; not from want of bread, but through want of faith" (E3ʳ). "Therefore," he says, "if yee will haue bread, conspire not in mutinies, but conspire in mutuall prayers; roote not vp harmelesse hedges, nor rend vp the bowells of the earth; but looke vp to heauen from whence yee shall haue bread" (E3ᵛ).

For Wilkinson, the insurmountable problem of revolt is its momentum. The original aims of a revolt might be almost justified, but they are invariably lost in the process of insurrection. He unwittingly echoes the tone of James's letter to Huntingdon by instructing him to repair to his lieutenancy, in which the king writes of the rioters, "using the colour of laying open grounds unlawfully enclosed" (HMC *Hastings* IV:192), to cover more seditious intents:

[L]et men set what pretence & colour they will, yet this hath bin from time to time the cōmon proceeding of popular mutinies; first to murmure vpon some iust cause, as the *Isralites* did at *Moses* when he brought them where was neither water to drinke, nor bread to eat. *Ex.* 15. 24 & *Ex.* 16.3. Afterward when they had both to eate & to drinke, yet (Nū. 11.) they murmured, not for wāt, but for wantōnes. . . . But *Nōb.* 14, their murmuring came to that, that they would change the state, they would put off Moses, and haue an other to guide them. (F2ʳ)

Wilkinson then describes the gradual escalation of the motivations for revolt in 1607 until they had moved well beyond redress of limited grievances into an open challenge to the state:

For marke, I beseech ye, the course of this creeping conspiracie, first they begā in the night, as checkt with feare & conscience of a crime, but afterward they cāe forth in the broad day, as flesht and hartened on by him who is euermore the maister of rebellion; first vpon discharge they yeeld to depart, as retaining still some reuerence of authority, but afterward they outstand the discharge, right as *S. Iude* saith, *Despising authority. Iud.* 8. First, like *Adams* sonnes they come forth with shouels and spades, like simple men to reduce the earth to her ancient and natiue tilladge, but afterward they come forth like *Tubal-kains* sonnes, armed with swords and weapons of yron; & they turned not as *Micah* saith, *their swords into spades,* but cleane contrary, spades into swords, or rather as the Iewes Nehem. 4. though in a different quarrell, they come with weapons in one hand, and working tooles in another, to professe themselues as ready to fight as to work. First they professe nothing, but to throwe downe enclosures, though that were indeed no part of common powre; but afterward they will reckon for other matters, They will accompt with Clergie men, and counsell is giuen to kill vp Gentlemen, and they will leuel all states as they leuelled bankes and ditches: and some of them boasted, that now they hoped to worke no more; the sword & the gallows making them true Prophets, and some of them in plaine termes, they thought that now the law was downe, as in times of common vproare, both ciuill and diuine law and all goe downe. . . . And therfore though it bee an easie matter to begin a commotion, yet is it no easie matter to stay it. (F2ʳ–F3ʳ)

That Wilkinson thus openly discusses the possibility that local protest can easily threaten the political system is remarkable, considering the sermon's context. Yet there is an ambivalence about the sermon, which it makes little effort to resolve, that on the one hand exhorts the landlord "not to rack, but so to rate his tenant that he may liue, not miserably, for so it were better to die" (D2ʳ) and that flays the practices of enclosure and depopulation, yet that on the other concludes with plain encouragement to Christian patience in face of acknowledged grievance. As Patterson observes, this ambivalence is characterized by certain "essentially *literary* strategies by which Wilkinson invokes sympathy for the insurgents even as he delegitimates their intervention" (140). The sermon is no model, however, for a reading which requires the containment to be in some way equivalent to the subversion. Wilkinson's radical analysis of the revolt develops by way of a series of *conscious* ambivalences which only partly subsume political action to theological patience, and one is left in very little doubt as to the locus of the preacher's sympathies. As Patterson observes, Wilkinson's occasional lapse into the first person plural suggests his only partially sublimated acknowledgment of the motivation to intervene despite his theological awareness of the requirement for patience in adversity: "we are come to banding . . . & now at last we are come to flat resisting" (F1ʳ).

It is taken for granted in the criticism that Shakespeare's motivation in beginning *Coriolanus* with a plebeian corn revolt resided at least in part with the events of 1607. E. C. Pettet was the first to draw attention to the probability that the Midlands Revolt is a subtextual presence in the play.[36] He points out that Shakespeare modifies the variety of reasons for the plebeian revolt given by Plutarch in the source-text, and concentrates solely on the question of grain, which, as Pettet observes, he "entwines with the fear of Coriolanus's absolutist temper" (37). He goes on to suggest that "something had given fresh significance and sense of urgency to old ideas of political philosophy that even Shakespeare himself may have come to regard as platitudes" (37). The poet was thus "re-stating" these platitudes, "both for his own satisfaction and the good of his audience, with a sharpened sense of social consciousness" (37). As this last formulation might suggest, Pettet opts for a conservative reading of Shakespeare's politics:

we can dismiss these changes [to the source-material] as mere chance. But they make more sense if we regard them as, to a large extent, the natural reactions of a man of substance to a recent mob rising in his country. Whether or not Shakespeare had been shocked or alarmed by the 1607 rising is anyone's guess; but it is fairly certain that he must have been hardened and confirmed in what had always been his consistent attitude to the mob. (39)

Biographical assumptions of this sort may explain in part why critics with conscious political motivations have been oddly inconsistent in their recognition of the importance of the 1607 revolt to a reading of *Coriolanus*. In his brief account of the play in *Radical Tragedy*, for example, Jonathan Dollimore perhaps surprisingly fails to mention the revolt at all.[37] He does mention "dearth" as an underlying cause of some of the play's debates, and even refers in passing to the abortive Oxfordshire rising of 1596, yet does not situate his analysis in the specific political events of 1607. Annabel Patterson, however, has, as I have mentioned, recently returned to the question of the relationship of *Coriolanus* to the 1607 revolt. She demonstrates the development of the "belly" metaphor in political debate after 1607, quoting from the earl of Northampton's version of the tale given at a conference in autumn 1610 and suggesting that "this speech confirms the intuition that Shakespeare's version of the body fable comes late in the discursive formation begun by the Midlands Rising and ending, in February 1611, with the collapse of the Great Contract and the dissolution of parliament" (145). This observation is a diluted version of Patterson's argument in an earlier paper, in which she suggests a date of composition of *Coriolanus* as late as the summer of 1610, a full two years after the date assigned by Wells and Taylor.[38] Such a claim is, however, unnecessary, since even without assigning such a late date to *Coriolanus* it is nonetheless impossible to ignore the interaction of the events of 1607 and the production of the play. Shakespeare seems to have returned quite deliberately to the arena of "history" in *Coriolanus*, but in doing so he pushes beyond the concerns of his earlier "history plays" in order to offer an entire dramatic structure which can represent the problem of the permissible extent of popular power. Previous Roman plays had already provided a focus on versions of enclosure ("I'll set a bourn how far to be beloved," says Cleopatra, flirting with Antony, whose denial of boundaries rapidly encloses him),[39] but the effect of opening

Coriolanus with a scene drawn directly from immediate and disturbing events is clearly quite different. Patterson points out, partly in order to defend her argument about the play, that enclosure was not the sole cause of the 1607 revolt, and that dearth of grain was a substantial secondary cause. This is undoubtedly true, as Wilkinson's sermon alone would attest, yet it would be inappropriate to infer from this that Shakespeare was unaware that enclosure was the chief stated cause of the revolt.[40] It is no coincidence that he has Sicinius use the language of resistance to enclosure in his denunciation of Coriolanus as a "viper / That would *depopulate* the city and / Be every man himself."[41]

It has thus been recognized for nearly forty years that Shakespeare wrote *Coriolanus* with the Midlands Revolt in mind. Shakespeare is, however, not the only playwright in the period to write in response to the troublesome events of 1607. At least two other dramatists seem, by way of their patronage and milieu connections, to have been much more closely aware of the local effects of the revolts. The playwrights in question are Marston and Fletcher, both of whom at different times came under the patronage of the Huntingdons. It has been suggested recently that Marston's *Entertainment at Ashby,* written in 1607 for celebrations organized by the fifth earl for his mother-in-law, Alice, dowager countess of Derby, may have been written in at least partial response to the troubles of that year, with its opening unease about dangers and tempests only just averted.[42] Fletcher would have been arguably still more aware of the aftermath of the revolt than either Shakespeare or Marston. The riots seem likely to have preceded his first visits to Ashby by only a matter of months or perhaps even weeks. He appears to have been a regular there from around this time, and his plays repeatedly examine political questions of the kind foregrounded by the revolt, questions first broached in print by Wilkinson's sermon. It is as if this context of unrest, on what may well have been Fletcher's first visit to the Midlands, made him always a little uneasy about the politics of the land. For every country idyll that his plays set up in contrast to life at court, there is a concomitant possibility of violence and insurrection in the fields and trees.

The vivid memory of the events of May and June 1607 was to stay sharply in the minds of Leicestershire and Northamptonshire locals, peasant and landlord alike. "[T]he rising of the hedge-breakers" is still clearly a concern of the earl's some two years later when he is discussing appropriate quantities of gunpowder to be stored in the county.[43] And it was during the 1607 Revolt that the resonant terms "digger" and "leveller" passed into common usage in the context of hedge-breaking and with the broader, more radical political connotations acknowledged by Wilkinson. Patterson claims that, in *Coriolanus,* Shakespeare is searching for a way to represent the possibility of voicing the unspeakable (a voicing partly, if briefly, achieved by Wilkinson's sermon), namely that the people could have the political consciousness to connect the immediate injustice of corn shortages to the imbalances of unrepresentative government. I argue that in several of his plays, Fletcher seeks ways to explore the complexities of government in the context of local unease and unrest, representing the possibility that mismanagement of the ramifications of changing property relations could lead to serious destabilization in the country. It is the direct relation of threat in the counties to the stability of property relations in London that marks Fletcher's particular mediatory politics and perhaps best characterizes him as a London playwright with country patronage and allegiances. It is thus important to locate a reading of several of Fletcher's early plays in the events of 1607 in order to provide a localized base from which to develop a sense of the ideological motivations for the many insurrections and rejections of tyranny or failed paternalism in Fletcher's plays.

2

The Faithful Shepherdess, Fletcher's first solo play, written within a year of the events of May and June 1607, is also the first of his plays to represent the dangerous potential of popular unrest. The play failed miserably on the Jacobean stage, and Fletcher takes revenge on the audience in his petulant preface to the published play entitled "To the Reader," a short piece of prose regularly quoted out of context by critics eager for a snap definition of Renaissance tragicomedy. It is of course a critical minefield to attempt to separate an "original" intention in the process of writing a stage play from an intimated intention in the process of its subsequent publication, especially after failure in performance. Yet it has been the critical fate of *The Faithful Shepherdess* to have become a barely remembered adjunct to its own self-presentation at the time of publication. An examination of the prefatory material and the text of the play reveals that the publication apparatus constitutes a complex, conscious politicization of the play text itself and of the genre it represents, a psychological contextualizing that opens a series of questions which remain prevalent in Fletcher's drama right up to his death.

It has been suggested that, because of his family and patronage connections, it might be appropriate to think of Fletcher as a "Spenserian" playwright.[44] This, very simply, would entail seeing in his plays viewpoints congruent with the work of a broad range of nondramatic poets, including the playwright's uncle Giles and his near-contemporary cousins Phineas and Giles Jr. as well as younger writers such as William Browne and George Wither. The grouping also includes Michael Drayton and, in the broadest definition, Samuel Daniel.[45] These poets are perhaps best seen as a group connected not primarily on ideological grounds but simply by virtue of being out of favor with, and therefore at odds with, King James's court. They shared a dislike of Ben Jonson and envied the increasing favor shown him by the king. Daniel and Drayton in particular, disgruntled by the continuation of the "regnum Cecilianum" after 1603 and by their sustained failure to secure courtly patronage, maintained a hostile stance both to Jonson and to James. These poets, along with Giles Fletcher and his sons and perhaps even Fulke Greville, could, according to David Norbrook, "almost be described as constituting a poetic 'opposition'" (198), though it is useful to register the "almost" here. Their most notable shared poetic technique was the use of the political symbolism of pastoral which they had self-consciously inherited from Sidney and Spenser. Spenser had regularly criticized Burghley and Cecil, and this provided the younger poets, disillusioned with the first few years of James's reign, with a sense of political continuity.

It took until the crisis years of 1612–14, when Jacobethan hopes of the young and militant Prince Henry and the marriage of Princess Elizabeth and Frederick the elector palatine were both raised and dashed, for these poets to develop their form of political pastoral in a consciously Protestant, even apocalyptic, manner, but the seeds of this development can be seen nonetheless in, for example, Drayton's *Pastorals* of 1606. That the pastoral was a fundamentally political form had been made clear by Puttenham in his *Arte of English Poesie,* in which he claimed that "the Poet deuised the *Eglogue* long after the other *drammatick* poems, not of

56

purpose to counterfait or represent the rusticall manner of loues and communication: but vnder the vaile of homely persons, and in rude speeches to insinuate and glance at greater matters."[46] As Louis Adrian Montrose observes, "Puttenham suggestively describes a verbal complex that is literally pastoral in form, pervasively amorous in content, and intrinsically political in purpose."[47] And Drayton's preface "To the Reader of his Pastorals," added to the reprinting of his *Poemes Lyrick and Pastorall* in the 1619 edition of his poems, echoes these concerns. "The subject of Pastorals," he writes, "as the language of it ought to be poor, silly, & of the coursest Woofe in appearance. Neverthelesse, the most High, and most Noble Matters of the World may bee shaddowed in them, and for certaine sometimes are."[48] Drayton's attitude seems to have been typical of the "Spenserian" poets.

Philip Finkelpearl has suggested that it was possibly "only Fletcher's union with Beaumont" (an interestingly ambiguous turn of phrase) that "saved us [*sic*] from companion pieces to Giles Fletcher's *Christ's Victory and Triumph* and Phineas Fletcher's *Purple Island*," but this is both to make light of the chronology of Spenserian development and to ignore simple dating evidence for the first two Beaumont and Fletcher collaborations, *The Woman Hater* and *Cupid's Revenge*.[49] It also implies a shared theological dogmatism for which there is very little evidence in John Fletcher's plays, and against which his position as effectively the only secular member of a family of clerics might well be a witness. We have, after all, no evidence of a relationship between John and his cousins after Giles senior's death, and relations before that seem to have collapsed chiefly into financial backbiting. I would suggest that, while it is essential to recognize the ways in which Fletcher's dramatic project shares political impetus and, at least to begin with, literary strategy, with the various Spenserians, to refer to John Fletcher unequivocally as a "Spenserian playwright" is to oversimplify the development of his writing and to ignore some of the fundamental distinctions between poetry and drama in the early seventeenth century. Yet Finkelpearl is right nonetheless, I think, in seeing in *The Faithful Shepherdess* the beginnings of what might have been a pastoral project congruent with that of the Spenserians. Fletcher does appear to imply in his dedicatory verse to Sir Walter Aston that he looked in due course to produce a poetic work in the Spenserian mold, following the "pastoral-to-epic" pattern mapped by Spenser from *The Shepheardes Calender* to *The Faerie Queene*. "[W]hen I sing againe," he writes, "as who can tell / My next devotion to that holy well, / Your goodnesse to the muses shall be all, / Able to make a worke Heroycall."[50] This project, if it be such, never came to fruition, and may simply have been wishful thinking in the context of the audience's reception of *The Faithful Shepherdess*. It was, after all, the tastes of the London theatrical audience that curtailed Fletcher's earliest experiment in writing something which might be considered "[b]oth a Poeme and a play," and which stung the young playwright into writing an elaborate response.

The most important feature of Fletcher's "To the Reader" is not, as has generally been assumed, the poker-faced observation that "[a] tragie-comedie is not so called in respect of mirth and killing, but in respect it wants deaths, which is inough to make it no tragedie, yet brings some neere it, which is inough to make it no comedie," but rather his irritable comment that the ignorant audience "missing whitsun ales, creame, wassel and morris dances, began to be angry" (497, ll. 20–23; 7–8). This is the first, undeveloped reaction in Fletcher's writing to the question of popular festivity, and, though his response changed markedly over the next decade in ways I shall explore below, it premises a certain unease which remained more or less constant in his representations of the country. He quite deliberately fails to incorporate whitsun ales and morris dances into his pastoral because he is categorically not writing about the common people. As far as he is concerned, the form of pastoral is about something else entirely, and he has made the error of assuming too much knowledge on the part of the audience. "If you be not reasonably assurde of your knowledge in this kinde of Poeme," he begins, "lay downe the booke or read this, which I would wish had bene the prologue" (497, ll. 1–3). He offers two conflicting definitions of the play's form, "pastorall Tragie-comedie," with a consciously obfuscating sarcasm. The people, he claims, "having ever had a singular guift in defining," have "concluded [it] to be a play of country hired Shepheards, . . . sometimes laughing together, and sometimes killing one another." But this arbitrary definition is hopelessly wrong as far as the writer is concerned. The play, he tells us, is not "a play of country hired Shepheards," but a *representation* of shepheards and shepheardesses, with their actions and passions, which must be such as may agree with their natures, at least not exceeding former fictions, and vulgar traditions: they are not to be adorn'd with any art, but such improper ones as nature is said to bestow, as singing and Poetry, or such as experience may teach them, as the vertues of hearbs, and fountaines: the ordinary course of the Sun, moone, and starres, and such like.[51]

This is of course enragingly uninformative, and is an early example of the ironic double strategy we observed in Fletcher's letter to the countess of Huntingdon—both writing about a topic and not writing about it. Yet there are two crucial terms appearing twice in the passage which both require and defy coherent interpretation. The first, as I have suggested by italicizing, is that favorite word of the New Historicism, "representation"; the second is "hired."

The Faithful Shepherdess, according to Fletcher, is not "a play of" but "a representation of" shepherds. He glosses this by differentiating between the "hired Shepheards" of the limited popular imagination and his own shepherds who—in line, he claims, with precedents classical and contemporary, presumably including Sidney—are "the *owners* of flockes and not hyerlings" (497, ll. 19–20; my italics), thus allowing them the right to political autonomy.[52] At this point, he breaks back to tantalizing genre-definition without further glossing the essential shift in property relations which he claims differentiates his "pastorall Tragie-comedie" from that of others. We are left with a sense that some level of class appropriation has been made in the process of defining the genre. And I would suggest that the only way to understand the differentiations outlined in this passage is by relation to the rest of the publication apparatus.

It is significant that *The Faithful Shepherdess* is the only play which Fletcher saw through to publication, the only play for which he demonstrated any interest in the presentation of the printed product: unusually for a dramatic text in this period, it comes complete with a set of dedicatory verses. Hoy comments that "[c]opy for Q1 must have been, if not the author's own manuscript, then a carefully prepared transcript of this" (486), and adds that "[t]he care that went into the preparation of printer's copy was matched by the care expended on it by Compositor *A* who began the job of setting it in type" (486), though he admits that *A*'s fellow compositors do not seem to have been quite such precision-ists. Nonetheless, the object of this care would thus seem to be more than a simple stage play. It is, as Chapman points out in his commendatory verse, "both a Poeme and a play," and is quite clearly to be taken seriously as a work of literary value rather than just an entertainment.

Fletcher and his various commenders specifically oppose the play's intrinsic worth to its rejection at the hands of the "multi-tude." I use the term "multitude" advisedly: Beaumont and Chap-man use the exact word; Field, Jonson, and Fletcher himself em-ploy correlative terms. The play's failure in performance seems to have taken on an odd significance for the way in which the published article is presented, which, in the context, seems to merge political with literary unease. Field fears "the monster" who "clap[s] his thousand hands, / And drown[s] the sceane with his confused cry" (490, ll. 33–34). Beaumont writes disparagingly of the "multitudes . . . whose judgements goes / Headlong" (491, ll. 27–28) according to theatrical fashion. Jonson condemns, among other culprits, the "many-headed *Bench,* that sits / Upon the Life, and Death of *Playes*" (492, ll. 1–2). Chapman echoes Fletcher's critique in "To the Reader," suggesting that if he had simply written "a thing / That every Cobler to his patch might sing: / A rout of nifles (like the multitude) / With no one limme of any art indude" (493, ll. 15–18), then he would have had praise. Fletcher, in his dedicatory poem to Sir Walter Aston, expresses his contempt for "the common prate / Of common people" (493, ll. 4–5), and describes, resonantly, how his play

> Had falne for ever prest downe by the rude
> That like a torrent which the moist south feedes,
> Drowne's both before him the ripe corne and weedes:
> Had not the saving sence of better men
> Redeem'd it from corruption. (493–94, ll. 8–12)

For Fletcher at this juncture, there is little difference between the mass actions of the multitude and the kind of destructive weather conditions that Titania in *A Midsummer Night's Dream* had de-scribed as the tangible result of her arguments with Oberon. Fletcher's "pastorall Tragie-comedie," written a little over a year after the Midlands Revolt of 1607, is in many ways a conscious reworking not only, as Finkelpearl has suggested, of Spenser's

Shepheardes Calender, but also of *A Midsummer Night's Dream,* and in that sense alone it signals its own relationship to a context of dearth and unrest. It has long been acknowledged that Titania's speech on the dislocation of the seasons is a topical reference to the foul weather that stretched effectively from March 1594 to the summer of 1596. The immediate effect was flooding and consistently poor harvests—the 1596–97 harvest was the worst in the Tudor and early Stuart period—and the long-term effect a massive increase in the price of grain from 1594 to 1598.[53] Titania speaks of fogs "which, falling in the land, / Hath every pelting river made so proud / That they have overborne their continents." And she expands on the problems this has caused:

> The ox hath therefore stretched his yoke in vain,
> The ploughman lost his sweat, and the green corn
> Hath rotted ere his youth attained a beard;
> The fold stands empty in the drownèd field,
> And crows are fatted with the murrain flock.
> The nine men's morris is filled up with mud,
> And the quaint mazes in the wanton green
> For lack of tread are undistinguishable.
> . . . [T]he spring, the summer,
> The childing autumn, angry winter change
> Their wonted liveries; and the mazèd world,
> By their increase, now knows not which is which.[54]

Titania's speech is a description of the altered elemental, and therefore human, conditions that have resulted from her dispute with her husband. No political critique is implied. The problems are not the result of poor government: they are beyond human control. The passage is silent about the recent abortive but nonetheless disturbing Oxfordshire uprising of 1596.[55] But the equivalent problems within the natural scheme of things in Fletcher's pastoral are social, not supernatural, and they form a discursive response to the political events of 1607. Chapman, in his prefatory verse, subtly registers the possible causes of the "common torrent" that Fletcher has described. "Your poeme," he says,

> Renews the golden world; and holds through all
> The holy lawes of homely pastorall;
> Where flowers, and founts, and Nimphs, and semi-Gods,
> And all the Graces finde their old abods:
> Where forrests flourish but in endless verse;

And meddowes, nothing fit for purchasers:
This Iron age that eates it selfe, will never
Bite at your golden world; that others, ever
Lov'd as it selfe: then like your Booke do you
Live in ould peace: and for that praise allow. (493, ll. 20–30)

This passage is characterized by a highly resonant nostalgia which appears inescapably Spenserian in its longing for a prior order. In Fletcher's arcadia, "meddowes" are "nothing fit for purchasers" and this "Iron age . . . eates itselfe": an apparent reference to the adverse effect that Fletcher's circle considers enclosure and land rationalization to have had in the country.[56]

It is thus useful to read the introductory verses to *The Faithful Shepherdess* in the awareness that they participate in the discursive wake of the causes and events of the 1607 revolt. It is as if, by an odd psychological shift, the fate of *The Faithful Shepherdess* at the hands of its audience is viewed as the product of the same kind of destructive momentum that Wilkinson feared in rebellion. It is hardly surprising, then, that Fletcher wishes to emphasize that the locus of his representation of an arcadian realm is not with the "hyerlings" but with "the owners of flockes." Thus we can recognize that the "golden world," that Chapman suggests Fletcher renews, finds its location neither with the common people nor with the court but with the kind of people—"the owners of flockes"— to whom he dedicated the published play. The names and connections of Sir William Skipwith and Sir Walter Aston, two of the dedicatees of the published version of *The Faithful Shepherdess,* suggest both a context for the play in the events of 1607 and a conscious relationship with at least one of the poets known as the Spenserians.

Sir Walter Aston is perhaps best known as Michael Drayton's chief patron. The First Part of *Poly-Olbion*—Drayton's *Faerie Queene,* an immense glorification of England in the form of a poetic chorography—was published in mid–1612, though the only dated title page is of the second edition of 1613. The volume is dedicated, resonantly, to Prince Henry, who is called—with unforeseen irony since Henry was to die within months of the poem's publication—Britain's "best hope, and the world's delight," and pictured in chivalric pose upon the frontispiece. But Drayton acknowledges his own particular long-standing patron in his prefatory "To the Generall Reader":

[W]hat ever is herein that tastes of a free spirit, I thankfully confesse it to proceed from the continuall bounty of my truly Noble friend Sir *Walter Aston;* which hath given me the best of those howres, whose leasure hath effected this which I now publish.[57]

This is by no means the first place in which Drayton acknowledged Aston's patronage. In 1602 he dedicated an edition of *Englands Heroicall Epistles* to Aston, and the following year dedicated his *Barons Warres,* the rewritten and politicized *Mortimeriados* of 1596, to Aston. The *Barons Warres* also, of course, included a prefatory verse by John Beaumont, as did the 1604 *Moses in a Map of his Miracles.* The list of Drayton dedications to Aston is apparently endless, including *The Owle* (1604), a vicious satire on Cecil and the court, *Poemes Lyrick and Pastorall* (1606), similarly critical of James's court, and *The Legend of Great Cromwell* (1607 and 1609). Drayton also dedicated the 1619 folio edition of his poetry—nostalgically and pointedly called "the works of that Mayden Reigne, in the Spring of our Acquaintance" (Hebel II:2)—to Aston, thus broadcasting clear Jacobethan allegiances at a time of increased national awareness of events in Europe. Drayton's patron was an intimate of the Ashby circle, a connection which is underlined by the ascription of the three surviving copies of John Donne's "Letter to the Countesse of Huntingdon" to "S^r wal: Ashton."[58] It is no surprise, then, that Fletcher should have become acquainted with Aston by 1608.

Drayton was also close to the Beaumonts.[59] John Beaumont—who, as a recusant who lost substantial lands to a Scottish courtier in 1607, had every reason to share Drayton's opposition to the court—had dedicated his *Metamorphosis of Tobacco* to his "loving Friend" Drayton in 1602.[60] Drayton's response included a stanza of the Eighth Eglogue of his 1606 *Pastorals* which he locates in Charnwood Forest near Gracedieu and in which he praises John and Francis Beaumont together with their sister Elizabeth:

> Then that dear Nymph that in the Muses joyes,
> That in wild *Charnwood* with her Flocks doth goe,
> MIRTILLA, Sister to those hopefull Boyes,
> My loved THIRSIS, and sweet PALMEO:
> > That oft to *Soar* the Southerne Shepheards bring,
> > Of whose cleere waters they divinely sing.[61]

The Beaumonts in fact also form one of the most obvious links between Aston and Sir William Skipwith, the second dedicatee of

ful Shepherdess, who died in 1610, not long after the
[perform]on of the play.[62] John Beaumont's elegy for Skipwith
[died] in 1629 in the posthumous collection *Bosworth Field,*
[w]as put together by his son. There are other links between
Aston and Skipwith. Aston wrote several poems in the style of
Donne (who of course had connections with Elizabeth Stanley
before she became countess of Huntingdon), including an elegy for
Prince Henry which appears in a surviving manuscript with the
"manifestly incorrect heading 'An Elegie on the Death of my neuer
enough lamented master King Charles the first,' [and] is attributed to 'Henry Skipw[th]:' " (Kay 206). Henry was, as we have seen,
Sir William Skipwith's son, a well-known royalist in the forties.
William had been elected second knight of the shire in 1601 with
the support of the fourth earl of Huntingdon, and, as sheriff of
Leicester at the time of the 1607 revolts, was involved with the
fifth earl in the suppression of the levelers. He was a minor poet,
praised by Fuller for *impresa* "neither so apparent that every rustic
might understand them, nor so obscure that they needed an Oedi-
pus to interpret them" (*Worthies* i. 584), and several of his poems
appear in manuscript collections alongside those of the Beaumonts
and other connected writers, including Thomas Pestell.[63] He was
also, of course, author of the masque performed that year at Ashby
for the dowager countess of Derby along with Marston's *Entertainment,* and a known supporter, with the fifth earl of Huntingdon
and others of the Hastings circle, of deprived Protestant ministers
in the Leicestershire area. He was even the Huntingdons' next-door
neighbor at their Leicester townhouse.

The identity of the third dedicatee of *The Faithful Shepherdess,* Sir
Robert Townsend, suggests peripheral connections between the
Mermaid circle in London and the Ashby milieu in the East Mid-
lands. This dedication might seem at first sight to contradict the
other two by foregrounding a London context for the play, since
Townsend is best known as an early patron of Ben Jonson, who
dedicated a copy of *Sejanus* to him. But his social connections lo-
cate him as a mediatory figure between the Mermaid and Ashby.[64]
He had been knighted in relevant company in 1603. On 11 May,
King James was on the last leg of his progress from Edinburgh to
London, and on departing from Theobalds he knighted a substantial batch of gentlemen including Townsend, along with Sir Henry

Hastings, Sir Robert Cotton, Sir Walter Mildmay, Sir Edwin Sandys, and Sir Thomas Beaumont.[65] Townsend thus arguably provides a coherent link between country and city. In the event, however, the city audience was not to react as Fletcher might have hoped to his political pastoral.

The Faithful Shepherdess is a political play. The sexual ventures that motivate the action of the play are circumscribed by suggestions of a real, specific world beyond arcadia. Perigot and Amoret set the tone for this in their opening conversation:

> *Amoret:*   Speake, I give
> Thee freedome Shepheard, and thy tongue be still
> The same it ever was: as free from ill
> As he whose conversation never knew
> The court or cittie: be thou ever true.
> *Perigot:* When I fall off from my affection,
> Or mingle my cleane thoughts with foule desires,
> First let our great God cease to keepe my flockes,
> That being left alone without a guard,
> The woolfe, or winters rage, sommers great heat,
> And want of water, rots: or what to us
> Of ill is yet unknowne, fall speedily,
> And in their generall ruine let me goe. (I. ii. 45–57)

The quality of life in Fletcher's arcadia is premised on its difference from "court or cittie." Yet the country is subject to real threats, predators, and natural ills, each of which is related to a sense of moral and theological well-being. Where, in *A Midsummer Night's Dream,* natural disasters are the result of divine backbiting, here they are the direct product of human failure. And Amarillis's description of the Sullen Shepherd reinforces the possibility of unease in this "golden" world. "There is a Shepheard dwels / Downe by the More," she says,

> whose life hath ever showne
> More sullen discontent then *Saturnes* browe
>   . . . whose nye starved flockes
> Are alwaies scabby, and infect all sheepe
> They feede withall. (I. ii. 193–95; 204–6)

The world outside arcadia is potentially threatening, too. The Priest's warning to the shepherds reinforces Perigot's sense of unease:

[L]et your dogs lye loose without,
Least the Woolfe come as a scout
From the mountaine, and ere day
Beare a Lambe or Kid away:
Or the crafty theevish Foxe,
Breake upon your selves from these,
Be not too secure in ease,
Let one eie his watches keepe,
Whilst the tother eie doth sleepe. (II. i. 19–28)

These terms are familiar from Protestant polemic—perhaps most immediately from Spenser's *Shepheardes Calender*—and the apocalyptic New Testament injunctions to spiritual watchfulness echoed in this passage offer a context for the almost Calvinistic internalizing of politics effected in the course of the play. Daphnis, trying to control his own passions, inverts the body metaphor with which we are familiar from both Menenius and Wilkinson, and discusses his desires by way of a distinctly political trope:

I charge you all my vaines
Through which the blood and spirit take their way,
Locke up your disobedient heats, and stay
Those mutinous desires, that else would growe
To strong rebellion. (II. iv. 16–20)

Sexual politics and state politics appear indistinguishable for the shepherds: they share both a specific context in 1607 and a general context in political philosophy.

At the beginning of the final act, the Priest and the Old Shepherd awake to find that none of the younger shepherds has spent the night indoors. The Old Shepherd points out that

[N]ot a swayne,
This night hath knowne his lodging, heere; or layne,
Within these cotes: the woods or some neere towne,
That is a neighbour to the bordering downe,
Hath drawne them thether, bout some lusty sport,
Or spiced wassal Boule, to which resort,
All the young men and maydes of many a coate,
Whilst the Trim Minstrell strikes his merry note.
(V. i. 24–31)

Here, then, is the "wassal Boule" that Fletcher specifically rejects in "To the Reader," and it is quite clear that such country sports are viewed negatively. The Priest sighs, "God pardon sinne," adding: "[S]howe me the way that leades, / To any of their haunts" (V. i. 32–33). In the context, it is important to recall that many of the rebellious townspeople of Leicester made their way to Cotesbach on the eve of Trinity Sunday 1607 ostensibly in preparation for the rural festivities that would mark the day: festivity and revolt are thus closely linked. When the Priest and the Old Shepherd over-hear the Sullen Shepherd's admission of his misdeeds, they step forward, and, again, the Priest's words seem to partake of a broader politics. "Monster stay," he says,

> Thou . . . art like a canker to the state,
> Thou livest and brethest in, eating with debate,
> Through every honest bosome, forcing still,
> The vaynes of any men, may serve thy will
> (V. iii. 132–36)

—thereby providing an overtly political context both for the earlier suggestion that the Sullen Shepherd's flockes "infect all sheepe / They feede withall" and for Daphnis's injunction to his "vaines" not to be rebellious.

Toward the end of the play, the Priest and the Old Shepherd, effectively the governors of the play's arcadia, repair to Clorin's cabin for a judgment. They are happy to submit themselves to the virgin priestess that Clorin seems by now to have become. Philip Finkelpearl has recently extended James Yoch's analysis of the play to suggest that the absent god Pan is to be identified with King James. The political effect of the transfer of power is thus highly charged, since figures representative of both spiritual and secular power in the play defer to a virgin for an appropriate solution to the country's ills, a thoroughly Jacobethan literary strategy recalling the mythologized norms of the reign of Eliz-abeth.[66] Clorin asks the Priest, whom her Satyr has determined by way of his (again Biblically echoed) flame-test to be "full of blisse" (V. v. 74), why he has sought her cabin. He gives a dignified reply:

> First honourd virgin to behold thy face,
> Where all good dwells, that is: next for to try
> The trueth of late report, was given to mee:
> Those sheepheards that have met with foule mischance,
> Through much neglect, and more ill governance,

> Whether the wounds they have may yet endure
> The open ayre, or stay a longer cure:
> And lastly what the doome may be, shall light
> Upon those guilty wretches, through whose spight
> All this confusion fell. For to this place,
> Thou holy mayden have I brought the race,
> Of these offenders, who have freely tolde,
> Both why, and by what meanes, they gave this bold
> Attempt upon their lives. (V. v. 76–89)

"Much neglect, and more ill governance" might be self-condemnation, but it sounds much more like condemnation of a higher government we have not heard about. The overall political structures of the state are, after all, left deliberately vague. Either way, however, there is a clear shift to the question of political responsibility.

Clorin's response is Calvinistic enough. She peremptorily orders the culprits to be ejected from the land, and the Priest reports that "the swaine / In whom such heate, and blacke rebellions raigne / Hath undergone your sentence" (V. v. 127–29), though he has kept Amarillis back and asks Clorin to forgive her as she is penitent. The scene closes with a dual blessing from Clorin and the Priest. The Priest blesses the shepherds' "after labours, and the Land, / You feede your flockes upon" (V. v. 195–96). Clorin begins with a blessing for Amarillis, and goes on to outline the proper behavior of true shepherds:

> Yonge sheepheardesse now, ye are brought againe
> To virgin state, be so, and so remaine
> To thy last day, unlesse the faithfull love
> Of some good sheepeheard force thee to remove,
> Then labour to be true to him, and live
> As such a one, that ever strives to give
> A blessed memory to after Time:
> Be famous for your good, not for your crime.
> Now holy man, I offer up againe
> These patients full of health, and free from paine:
> Keepe them from after ills, be ever neere
> Unto their actions: teach them how to cleare
> The tedeous way they passe through, from suspect:
> Keepe them from wrong in others, or neglect
> Of duety in them selves, correct the bloud,
> With thrifty bitts and laboure: let the flood,

Or the next neighbouring springe give remedy
To greedy thirst, and travaile, not the tree
That hanges with wanton clusters: let not wine,
Unlesse in sacrifice or rights devine,
Be ever knowen of shepheards: have a care,
Thou man of holy life, now do not spare
Their faults through much remissnes, nor forget
To cherish him, whose many paynes and sweat,
Hath given increase, and added to the downes.
Sort all your Shepheards from the lazie clownes,
That feede their heafers in the budded Broomes,
Teach the young maydens strickness that the grooms
May ever feare to tempt their blowing youth,
Banish all complement but single truth,
From every tongue, and every Shepheards heart,
Let them use perswading, but no Art:
Thus holy Priest, I wish to thee and these,
All the best goods and comforts that may please
                              (V.v. 158–91).

Virginity is glorified. Courtly discourse is eschewed. All is drawn within a religious frame. As the play closes, we are given one more hint of contextual specificity. The Satyr—who now appears, appropriately enough, a transitional figure between Puck and Ariel—asks,

Shall I stray,
In the middle Ayre and staye,
The Sayling Racke or nimbly take,
Hold by the Moone, and gently make
Suite to the pale Queene of the night,
For a Beame to give thee light? (V. v. 244–49)

and concludes by promising that at her request he "will daunce / . . . Faster then the Windmill sayles" (V. v. 263, 267), a last reminder of the mechanics of actual rural life, the processes of turning corn into bread. Furthermore, his description of Clorin seems inescapably to equate her with the lost Virgin Queen:

Thou devinest, fayrest, brightest,
Thou most powerfull mayd, and whitest,
Thou most vertuous, and most blessed,
Eyes of Starrs and Golden Tressed,
Like *Apollo*. . . . (V. v. 238–42)

69

Even the sexually ambiguous reference to hair like Apollo reminds us of the queen who claimed to have the body of a woman but the heart and stomach of a king. If Finkelpearl is right in suggesting that we see the absent Pan as a version of King James, then James's own sexual ambiguity becomes the subject of satire. And the general point is clear enough: any poem, or play, which celebrates the memory of Elizabeth's reign as clearly as does *The Faithful Shepherdess* is already an indictment of aspects of James's reign. Moreover, if the allegory of the play is allowed to retain a certain multivalence, it is perhaps possible to see implicit praise both of the countess of Huntingdon and of her mother, the dowager countess of Derby, as well as of the absent Virgin Queen, in the person of Clorin.

I would thus suggest that *The Faithful Shepherdess* is involved both in the discursive negotiations that mark the aftermath of the 1607 revolt and in the development of the form of specifically *political* pastoral that was the hallmark of Spenserian poetry under James. The "pastorall Tragie-comedie" of *The Faithful Shepherdess* is thus anything but a "courtly" form. It makes an ironic comment (though not an "unsubtilizing" one)[67] on the Italianate influence in English pastoral as well as on negotiating "country," or perhaps better, "county" affairs upon the London stage. For both of these reasons it becomes entirely understandable why a London audience relatively unconcerned with such matters should reject the play.

3

In a recent essay on Jacobean chorography and cartography, Richard Helgerson focuses on an unlikely simile in the first Song of Michael Drayton's *Poly-Olbion*.[68] Drayton begins his lengthy *"Chorograph-ical* Description of *Tracts, Riuers, Mountaines, Forests,* and other Parts of this renowned *Isle* of *Great Britaine"* with a journey through Cornwall and Devon. Toward the close of the first Song, he describes how the Ex gathers smaller streams as it makes its way to its own confluence with the river Dert:

> As all assist the *Ex,* so *Ex* consumeth these;
> Like some unthriftie youth, depending on the Court,
> To winne an idle name, that keepes a needless port,
> And raising his old rent, exacts his Farmers store
> The Land-lord to enrich, the Tenants wondrous poore,
> Who having lent him theirs, he then consumes his owne,

That with most vaine expense upon the Prince is throwne,
So these, the lesser Brooks, unto the greater pay;
The greater, they againe spend all upon the Sea.[69]

This is a sufficiently far-fetched comparison to invite a closer political reading, and the concerns of this passage perhaps provide both
an analogue to John Fletcher's concerns in his 1614 play *Wit
Without Money* and a further point of entry into the degree of his
sympathy with Spenserian attitudes. The motivation for Fletcher's
discussions of problems of the land would appear to reside within a
broader consideration of the politics of inheritance which stems at
least in part from his curiosity about the tenets of romance as a
dramatic genre. *Wit Without Money*, perhaps his first solo play after
Beaumont's marriage and retirement from playwriting, and which
analyzes a similar inheritance problem to that outlined in Drayton's poem, can again be read in light of the increased awareness of
the broader political ramifications of popular insurrection that was
brought about in the wake of the 1607 revolt.

That the fifth earl of Huntingdon should have had to face the
inherent problems of country government in the events of 1607
seems in a sense ironic, since he was, after all, no absentee landlord, and since, as his response to the events of the revolt suggests,
he was not in favor of the tendency to enclose and depopulate. He
must, however, have turned a blind eye or two, since by no means
do all of his circle of acquaintance seem to have been wholly
sympathetic to their tenantry. On 15 June, the day after the earl
wrote to the Privy Council defending himself against their crit-
icisms and assuring them that there would be "no further disobedience" in Leicestershire, there were enclosure riots at Grace-Dieu,
Sir John Beaumont's seat. The site of the dissolved monastery of
Grace-Dieu had originally been purchased by the first earl of Huntingdon and had been bought later by the Beaumonts, whom
Martin describes bluntly as "well-known Leicestershire enclosers"
(187). As we have seen, the Beaumonts were—with the Treshams,
the most notorious enclosers in the region—also known for persistent recusancy, yet their political and social connections seem,
oddly enough, to have been preeminently Protestant, even militant Protestant, in credential. Nonetheless, religious dislikes
clearly aggravated enclosure disputes. Trouble in Belton, the parish to which Grace-Dieu belonged, was incited by the constable,

William Burrows, whose aim was to reclaim common rights removed by the Beaumonts forty years earlier. Sir John's servants tried to dissuade the levelers and were arrested as alehouse rogues by the constable. When the case came before Star Chamber, Burrows and his accomplices argued that Beaumont, as an indicted recusant, was "presumed to be excommunicated and outlawed and thus disabled from bringing suits at law" (Manning 102). Sixteen hundred and seven was clearly not John Beaumont's year: his indictment in May was followed on 22 September, as we have seen, by the confiscation of substantial quantities of his land.

The collateral branch of Beaumonts at nearby Coleorton was, by contrast, unwaveringly Protestant. Although we can assume that Sir Thomas Beaumont would have had little sympathy for troubles brought on his cousins by reason of their recusancy, and although we know from his letter to the countess that Fletcher was still on good terms with Sir Thomas as late as 1620 or thereabouts, one suspects nonetheless that a play such as *Wit Without Money* would possibly not have been written if the partnership of Beaumont and Fletcher had still been in existence in 1614 (unless of course Francis Beaumont's wry sense of humor extended further than might be expected), since the Treshams and the Grace-Dieu Beaumonts, at least, might in a sense be seen as a kind of conglomerate role model for the problems examined in the play.[70] Perhaps more pertinently, though, the particular problem raised by John Quarles's habits of enclosure and his status as intruding Londoner are quite distinctly voiced at the most dangerous moment of the play.

As *Wit Without Money* opens, Valentine, despite his status as an elder brother, has rejected his patrimony and made the decision to live by "wit," a term that in Fletcher's hands, as Martin Butler has registered, begins to lose the generally pejorative connotations it has in Middleton's writing but which has yet to develop as a necessary attribute for members of a particular London social grouping.[71] Valentine is characterized in the *dramatis personae* as *"a Gallant that will not bee perswaded to keepe his estate."* He has decided to deny both inheritance and duty. He has, according to his uncle, developed a naïve utopianism—"if you but talk of states / He cannot be brought now he has spent his owne, / To thinke there's inheritance, or meanes, / But all a common riches"—which his creditor, the Merchant, unsurprisingly considers "something dangerous."[72] His uncle describes with heavy sarcasm how Valentine will allow

> [n]o Gentleman that has estate to use it
> In keeping house, or followers, for those wayes
> He cries against, for eating sins, dull surfets,
> Cramming of serving men, mustering of beggers,
> Maintaining hospitals for Kites, and curs,
> Grounding their fat faithes upon old Countrey proverbes,
> God blesse the founders; these he would have vented
> Into more manly uses, Wit and carriage,
> And never thinkes of state, or meanes, the ground workes:
> Holding it monstrous, men should feed their bodies,
> And starve their understandings. (I. i. 12–22)

His notion of wit serves, as Butler has noted, to convert "his sense of displacement into aggression" (159). And if his uncle and creditor are disturbed by his behavior, his tenants are furious, since they rely wholly on such structures of mutual dependence.

Lance, the tenants' spokesman, *a Faulkoner, and an ancient servant to* Vallentines *Father,*" describes the way things used to be until the death of Valentine senior: "His Father kept good meate, good drinke, good fellowes, / Good hawkes, good hounds, and bid his neighbours welcome; / Kept him too, and supplyed his prodigality, / Yet kept his state still" (I. i. 69–72). "Must wee turne Tennants now," they ask,

> After we have lived under the race of Gentry,
> And maintaind good yeomantry, to some of the City,
> To a great shoulder of Mutton, and a Custard,
> And have our state turned into Cabbidge Gardens,
> Must it be so? (I. i. 72–77)

Valentine pays little heed to his tenants' rejection of city control over the country. He argues fiercely when they beg him to return things to normal "[f]or [their] poore childrens sake." His contempt for the tenants appears boundless. "Who bid you get um?" he asks cruelly:

> Have you not thrashing worke enough, but children
> Must be bangd out oth' sheafe too? other men
> With all their delicates, and healthfull diets,
> Can get but winde egges: you with a clove of garlicke,

A peece of cheese would breake a saw, and sowre milk,
Can mount like Stallions, and I must maintain these tumblers.

(I. i. 90–96)

Lance flares up, and voices an argument of mutual, collaborative
duty:

You ought to maintaine us, wee have maintained
You, and when you slept provided for you;
Who bought the silke you weare? I thinke our labours;
Reckon, youle find it so: who found your horses
Perpetuall pots of ale, maintain'd your Tavernes,
And who extold you in the halfe crowne boxes,
Where you might sit and muster all the beauties?
Wee had no hand in these, no, we are puppies:
Your tennants base vexations. (I. i. 97–105)

Lance continues to evoke the mutual loss that Valentine's denial of
state will cause, and he does so in highly resonant terms:

Had you Land, and honest men to serve your purposes,
Honest, and faithfull, and will you run away from um,
Betray your selfe, and your poore tribe to misery;
Morgage all us, like old cloakes; where will you hunt next?
You had a thousand acres, faire and open:
The Kings bench is enclosed, thers no good riding,
The Counter is full of thornes and brakes, take heed sir,
And bogges, youle quickly finde what broth they're made of.
       . . . They say yare a fine Gentleman,
And of excellent judgment, they report you have a wit;
Keepe your selfe out oth raine and take your Cloake with you,
Which by interpretation is your state, sir,
Or I shall thinke your fame belyed you, you have money
And may have meanes. (I. i. 106–19)

The confused language of Lance's argument is of particular interest
in the context of the Midlands Revolt some seven years earlier,
since he conflates the inevitable result of city (and therefore purely
financially motivated) control over the land—enclosure, in the
sense of both depopulation and imprisonment—with the failure
of legal measures to contain the problem. Thus, "[t]he Kings
bench," the name both of a debtors' prison and of a court which
from time to time imposed fines upon enclosers, is itself "enclosed."[73] The free passage through life that Valentine thinks wit

74

will provide him will simply take him into uncultivated, depopulated areas which will soon entangle and incarcerate him. The most interesting feature of this representation of the tenant's voice is its equation of loss for tenant and landlord alike. Thus the tenants may be mortgaged "like old cloakes," yet the lord is advised to "take [his] Cloake with" him, "[w]hich by interpretation is [his] state."

Lance and Valentine continue to bandy both technical term and interpretation. In Act II Valentine refers to the falconer slightingly as "old Coppihold," to which Lance replies: "My hearts good freehold sir, and so youle find it" (II. iv. 11, 12). But in Act I Valentine rejects Lance's main outburst mercilessly, and in so doing reveals the extent of his rejection of patrimony. "Your Fathers Worship, would have used us better," the tenants point out, to which Valentine's reply is: "My Fathers worship, was a foole" (I. i. 129–30). Lance is of course shocked by this, and Valentine's uncle, too, is taken aback. But Valentine makes no apology for his inversion of the respect for family and inheritance which his position requires. Instead, he explains his singlemindedness in saying why he thinks his father was a "foole":

> I meane besotted to his state,
> He had never left mee the misery of so much meanes else,
> Which till I sold was a meere meagrome to me:
> If you will talke, turne out these tennants,
> They are as killing to my nature Uncle,
> As water to a feaver. (I. i. 132–37)

Remarkably, facing this utter rejection, the tenants remain determined to resist: "We will goe, / But it is like Rammes to come again the stronger, / And you shall keepe your state" (I. i. 137–39), perhaps the first hint of the dangerous power that resides with the tenants.

Once the tenants have gone, Valentine describes his fear of the responsibilities of inheritance, and concludes with a manifesto which, centuries later, Herman Melville slightly reworked as the epigraph for a short story in *The Encantadas:*

> How bravely now I live, how jocund, how neare
> The first inheritance, without feares, how free
> From title troubles. (I. i. 153–55)[74]

His uncle laughs at his desire for freedom from responsibility, pointing out that he will be free from means, too. Valentine replies with an appealing passion which I would suggest offers a framework for argument absolutely typical of Fletcherian writing. Fletcher repeatedly examines versions of utopia, brief alternative realms that cannot exist in the face of the imperatives of practical living. Whether through the picaresque gentleman, as here, or through, for example, assertive and dominant women, he offers glimpses of possible new worlds which are much more appealing than the pragmatics that indicate how impossible they are.

He had previously most fully explored this question in the character of Lurcher in *The Night-Walker,* written a couple of years before *Wit Without Money* in 1611.[75] Lurcher's motivation as a highwayman is overtly political, as he explains to his acquaintance Jack Wildbrain. For Lurcher, "stealing is [t]he best inheritance." Wildbrain disagrees: "Not in my opinion, / Thou hadst five hundred pound a year." But Lurcher replies simply:

> 'Tis gone,
> Prethee no more on't, have I not told thee,
> And oftentimes, nature made all men equal,
> Her distribution to each child alike;
> Till labour came and thrust a new Will in,
> Which I allow not: till men won a priviledge
> By that they call endeavour, which indeed
> Is nothing but a lawful Cosenage,
> An allowed way to cheat, why should my neigh[bou]r
> That hath no more soul than his Horse-keeper,
> Nor bounteous faculties above a Broom-man,
> Have forty thousand pounds, and I four groats;
> Why should he keep it?
>   . . . Why should that Scrivener,
> That ne'er writ reason in his life, nor anything
> That time e'ver gloried in, that never knew
> How to keep any courtesie conceal'd,
> But *Noverint Universi* must proclaim it,
> Purchase perpetually, and I a rascal:
> Consider this, why should that mouldy Cobler
> Marry his daughter to a wealthy Merchant,
> And give five thousand pounds, is this good justice?
> Because he has a tougher constitution;

Can feed upon old Songs, and to save his money,
Therefore must I go beg?[76]

Valentine's reply to his uncle's gibe about means retains the optimism of his manifesto and echoes Lurcher's "communism":

> Why all good men's my meanes, my wits my plow,
> The Townes my stock, Tavernes my standing house,
> And all the world knowes theres no want; all Gentlemen
> That love society, love me; all purses
> That wit and pleasure opens, are my Tennants;
> Every mans clothes fit me, the next faire lodging
> Is but my next remove, and when I please
> To be more eminent, and take the aire,
> A peece is levied, and a Coach prepared,
> And I goe I care not whether, what neede state here?
>
> (I. i. 156–65)

His uncle simply asks if these means will last. Valentine replies:

> Far longer then your jerkin, and weare fairer,
> Should I take ought of you, tis true, I begd now,
> Or which is worse then that, I stole a kindnesse,
> And which is worst of all, I lost my way int. (I. i. 167–70)

And he goes on to reject the very enclosure which his tenants are
convinced will in fact be the result, perhaps paradoxically, of his
behavior.

What he dreams of is a kind of psychological common land in
which wit will be the only means, a radical, genuinely utopian
vision akin to that of Gonzalo ("All things in common nature
should produce / Without sweat or endeavour"):[77]

> Your mindes enclosed, nothing lies open nobly,
> Your very thoughts are hindes that worke on nothing
> But daily sweate, and trouble: were my way
> So full of dirt as this, tis true I'd shift it;
> Are my acquaintance Grasiers? but sir, know
> No man that I am allyed too, in my living,
> But makes it equal, whether his owne use,
> Or my necessity pull first, nor is this forc'd,
> But the meere quallity and poysure of goodnesse,
> And doe you thinke I venter nothing equall?

> . . . Whats my knowledge Uncle,
> Ist not worth money? whats my understanding,
> My travell, reading, wit, all these digested,
> My daily making men, some to speake,
> That too much flegme had frozen up, some other
> That spoke too much to hold their peace, and put
> Their tongues to pensions, some to weare their clothes,
> And some to keepe um, these are nothing Uncle;
> Besides these wayes, to teach the way of nature,
> A manly love, community to all
> That are deservers, not examining
> How much, or whats done for them, tis wicked
> And such a one like you, chewes his thoughts double,
> Making um onely food for his repentance. (I. i. 156–94)

Proof of the practicality of this arrangement is given by the arrival of small gifts of clothes and money from some of Valentine's acquaintances, and in face of his uncle's continued cynicism, Valentine gives reasons for his distaste for "state" which amount to a kind of antipastoral, a satire on the actual rather than the ideal activities of landlords. "Are not these ways," he asks, after his uncle has scoffed at his plans,

> as honest as persecuting
> The starved inheritance, with musty Corne,
> The very rats were afine to run away from,
> Or selling rotten wood by the pound, like spices,
> Which Gentlemen doe after burne byth ounces?
> Doe not I know your way of feeding beasts,
> With graines, and windy stuffe, to blow up butchers?
> Your racking pastures, that have eaten up
> As many singing Shepherds, and their issues,
> As *Andeluria* breedes?[78] these are authentique,
> I tell you sir, I would not change wayes with you,
> Unlesse it were to sell your state, that houre,
> And if it were possible to spend it then too. (I. i. 203–15)

Reacting to this tirade, which of course glances bitterly at the effects of enclosure and depopulation ("Your racking pastures . . . have eaten up / . . . many singing shepherds, and their issues"),[79] his uncle loses his temper and snaps: "[S]ince you are grown / Such a strange enemy, to all that fits you, / Give mee leave to make your brothers fortune" (I. i. 217–18), to which Valentine responds, infuriatingly, with a continued assumption of the equation of wit and means: "My brother and myselfe, will runne one fortune," he says, "He has wit at will, the world has meanes[;] hee shall live / Without this trick of state[. W]e are heires both, / And all the world before us."[80]

It is of course the simple fact of living in London which allows for this vision of survival by wit rather than responsibility. *Wit Without Money* thus demonstrates an unresolved ambivalence toward London. The city both allows for and undermines Valentine's utopian hopes, providing the social milieu within which it is possible to survive without inheritance and by wit, and producing the inexorable acquisitiveness of the Merchant. This unease about the effects of city life can perhaps best be seen in the reaction of Lady Hartwell and her waiting-woman, Luce, to the changed character of the household fool, Shorthose, whose witty remarks come thick and fast now that he is a citizen. Luce confronts him with this change:

> You have gleand since you came to *London:* in the Countrey *Shorthose,*
> You were an arrant foole, a dull cold coxcombe,
> Here every Taverne teaches you, the pint pot
> Has so belaboured you with wit, your brave acquaintance
> That gives you ale, so fortified your mazard,
> That now theres no talking to you. (II. iii. 27–32)

This clearly reflects on Valentine's new-found sense of possibilities in the environment of the city.

The way in which Fletcher's romantic comedies and tragicomedies represent a negotiation of the conflicting loyalties expressed in *Wit Without Money* is clear too in *The Scornful Lady,* a mainly Fletcher play of mid–1613 which probably serves as a final marker of the Beaumont and Fletcher partnership, since it appears to be the last play to receive its final form at Beaumont's hands, their usual practice in collaboration, and it is in many ways a rehearsal for Fletcher's concerns a year later in *Wit Without Money.*[81] The opening debate illustrates the motivations—a minefield of inheritance, responsibility, and sexuality—of Elder Loveless, Younger Loveless, and Savil, the steward, respectively:

Elder Loveless: Brother, is your last hope past, to mollify Morecraft's heart about your mortgage?

Younger Loveless: Hopelessly past. I have presented the usurer with a richer draught than ever Cleopatra swallowed; he hath sucked in ten thousand pounds worth of my land more than he paid for, at a gulp, without trumpets.
Elder Loveless: I have as hard a task to perform in this house.
Younger Loveless: Faith, mine was to make an usurer honest, or to lose my land.
Elder Loveless: And mine is to persuade a passionate woman, or to leave the land. . . . I fear I shall begin my unfortunate journey this night, though the darkness of the night, and the roughness of the waters, might easily dissuade an unwilling man.
Savil: Sir, your father's old friends hold it the sounder course for your body and estate, to stay at home, and marry and propagate, and govern in your country, than to travel for diseases, and return following the court in a night-cap, and die without issue. (I. i. 1–18)

In the present context, it is Savil who is of most interest. He is by no means presented in a wholly favorable light, but the very stuffiness of his reminders of inherited duty informs the play's equivocations, its struggles between the necessity of responsibility and the attractions of life by wit in the city, and he foreshadows *Wit Without Money*'s concern with the effects of city control over the country. He points out what will happen if the mortgage to Morecraft be forfeit. "Sir," he begs the Younger Loveless, "for my old master's sake, let my farm be excepted: / If I become his tenant, I am undone, / My children beggars, and my wife God knows what" (II. iii. 126–28). Later he asks, "What shall become of my poore familie? they are no sheepe, and they must keepe themselves" (III. ii. 42–44).

After the primarily sexual motivations of the central acts, Act V scene ii of *Wit Without Money* returns its gaze to the problems of the land. Valentine, his younger brother Francisco, and Lance the chief tenant have been drinking together. Lance is still furious with his master for mortgaging his land and endangering the tenants, and he becomes aggressive in his drunkenness. The drunken struggle receives a wry ongoing commentary in carnivalized language. Lance voices his annoyance in oddly chivalric terms, and the response he receives takes the form of a kind of mock romance. Yet beneath the humor of the romance terminology lies more than a hint of political danger, which perhaps drives Valentine toward a change of heart and also offers a way to keep his creditors away before he has reclaimed his responsibilities. Lance is belligerently drunk: "Now could I fight, / And fight with thee," he cries to which Valentine replies, initially delighted: "With me thou man of *Memphis?*" (V. ii. 4b–5). The dialogue continues:

> *Lance:* But that thou art mine owne naturall master,
> Yet my sacke saies thou art no man, thou art
> A Pagan, and pawnest thy land, which a noble cause—
> *Vallentine:* No armes, no armes, good Lancelet,
> Deare *Lance,* no fighting here, we will have Lands boy,
> Livings, and Titles, thou shalt be a Viceroy,
> Hang fighting, hang't tis out of fashion.
> *Lance:* I would faine labour you into your lands againe,
> Goe too, it is behoovefull.
> *Francisco:*   Fie Lance, fie.
> *Lance:* I must beate some body, and why not my Master,
> Before a stranger? charity and beating
> Begins at home. . . .
> For looke you if you will not take your Morgage
> Againe, here doe I lie *Saint George,* and so forth.
> *Vallentine:* And here doe I *St. George,* bestride the Dragon,
> Thus with my Lance.
> *Lance:*   I sting, I sting with my taile.
> *Vallentine:* Doe you so, doe you so Sir, I shall taile you presently.
> *Francisco:* By no meanes, doe not hurt him.
> *Vallentine:*   Take his Nellson,
> And now rise, thou maiden Knight of *Malligo,*
> Lace on thy helmet of inchanted sacke,
> And charge againe. (V. ii. 6–17, 22–30)

"I play no more, you abuse me," concludes Lance, and departs, yet the effect of the mock battle has not been entirely lost on Valentine, who is suddenly aware of the danger of turning loyal tenants into masterless men: "This rogue, if he had beene sober," he says, "sure had beaten me, / Is the most tettish knave" (V. ii. 35–36). We have already seen that a strategy of doing-and-undoing is characteristic of Fletcher. Here, the exploration of the politics of unrest comes by way of an examination of the politics of genre, a simultaneous manipulation and mockery of the possibilities of romance as a generic vehicle for conflict.

When the Merchant comes to claim the land, Valentine unexpectedly defies him, and the language he uses would seem to indicate that he has learned from Lance's potential violence the dangers inherent in denial of responsibility and in transferring power over the country to the wrong hands. The danger of the world-upside-down he has helped create, the world of mortgaged lands and absentee landlords, informs his speech in response to the Merchant's claim. One cannot help thinking of John Quarles, the "London merchant . . . who destroyed the old order [at Cotesbach] before he finished with it" and whose land was a particular target in 1607. Valentine points out that any direct effort on the city's part to change the ways of the country will inevitably result in civil disobedience, disorder, and outright revolt: "Goe take possession," he says, menacingly, "and be sure you hold it, / Hold fast with both hands,"

> . . . for there be those hounds uncoupled,
> Will ring you such a knell[. G]oe downe in glory,
> And march upon my Land, and cry alls mine;
> Cry as the devil did, and be the devill,
> Mark what an eccho followes[. B]uild fine Marchpanes,
> To entertaine Sir Silkworme and his Lady,
> And pull the Chappell downe, to raise a Chamber
> For Mistris Silverpin, to lay her belly in[.]
> Marke what an Earthquake comes, then foolish Merchant[.]
> My tennants are no subjects, they obey nothing,
> And they are people too, never Christned,
> They know no law, nor conscience, theile devoure thee[ ]
> Within three dayes[. N]o bit nor memory
> Of what thou wert, no not the wart upon thy nose there,
> Shall be ere heard of more, goe take possession,
> And bring thy children downe, to rost like rabbits,
> They love young toasts, and butter, *Bowbell* suckers;
> As they love mischiefe, and hate law, they are Canibals:
> Bringe downe thy kindred too, that be not fruitfull,
> There be those Mandrakes, that will mollifie um,
> Goe take possession. (V. ii. 62–84)[82]

This chilling speech stuns the listeners. It marks a remarkably explicit rejection by the country of London control, metaphored in contempt for the spoiled offspring of pampered citizens and the religious and political attitudes of the city.[83] It marks also Valentine's recognition of the violent potential his denial of responsibility has unleashed. And he is now suddenly prepared to capitalize upon the fear this induces to delay his creditors. Valentine's uncle attempts to make the best of this speech, recognizing that it marks a U-turn in Valentine's attitude ["Hees halfe drunke sure, / And yet I like this unwillingness to loose it, / This looking backe" (V. ii. 85–87)], but the Merchant sees the danger in it, calling his debtor's behavior "harsh and strange" (V. ii. 88).

Valentine's lengthy outburst embodies all of the center's fears of the periphery, of the centrifugal dangers implicit in the rural status quo, and should be read in light of the events of 1607. A change such as the Merchant's takeover of the land—and the structural, social, and religious alterations that will imply—will bring with it a world-upside-down, a physical revolt. The "hounds uncoupled" will "march upon [the] land": they will "Cry as the devil did, and be the devill." The courtier ("Sir Silkworme"), with his unrural religious views, who will "pull the Chappell downe," will start a civil "Earthquake." There is an explicit denial of rural self-fashioning as centric subjects. Country people become equated with savages, with the characteristics popularly attributed to the Irish and the native Americans. These tenants are "no subjects, they obey nothing, / And are people too, never christned, / They know no law, nor conscience" (V. ii. 72–74). For the Merchant to "goe take possession" (a tag mockingly repeated) will invoke the marginal nature of the otherwise peaceful tenants: the large-scale equivalent of an angry Lance. And this explicit identification with the New World marginal is picked up by the Uncle and the Merchant in the immediate aftermath of Valentine's speech. The Merchant attempts recuperation via bravado: "Cannibals," he splutters, "[I]f ever I come to view his regements, / If faire termes may be had—" (V. ii. 90–91), but Valentine's uncle interrupts him:

> Hee tels you true sir;
> They are a bunch of the most boystrous rascalls
> Disorder ever made, let um be mad once,
> The power of the whole Country cannot coole um,
> Be patient but a while. (V. ii. 91–94)

Patience does indeed pay off, since in the last scene the political and sexual plots combine in Valentine's marriage and rejection of his utopian ideals. Yet Valentine's "Goe take possession" speech and the responses of his uncle and creditor underline the substantial danger inherent in changes to the rural status quo. Intrusion by the city will inevitably lead to an awakening of local feeling which will itself, as was made abundantly clear in 1607, inevitably lead beyond remedy to outright rebellion.

Wilkinson's fear, expressed in his sermon, of the momentum of revolution receives its analogue both directly in Valentine's speech and indirectly in the play's correspondent sexual conclusion, a conclusion which moves the play unerringly towards a typically Fletcherian form of tragicomedy, defined by the tension required to achieve a positive outcome. When Valentine's younger brother Francisco meets in the street the widow's sister Isabella, whom he knows to be in love with him, he decides to press home his advantage. Isabella, amazed by the sudden momentum of his passion, registers a fear congruent to the play's political unease: "This is a pretty Riot," she remarks nervously, "It may grow to a rape" (V. iii. 39–40). And Francisco's reply—"Doe you like that better? / I can ravish you an hundred times, and never hurt you" (V. iii. 40–41)—seems hardly designed to inspire her with confidence. As the play closes, Valentine pays off the mortgage on his land, announcing that "everything shall be in joynt again" (V. v. 48). There is a strong sense, characteristic of Fletcherian drama, that riots and rapes have only been narrowly and uneasily avoided.

THREE

The Reason in Treason

I

In the fourth act of Fletcher's *Women Pleased* the clown Soto enters carrying the text of a proclamation, which he is trying, slowly and painstakingly, to read:

> That it is, that it is, what's this word now? this is a plaguy word, that it is, *r.e.a.* that it is, reason, by your leave, Master *Soto,* by your leave, you are too quick, Sir,
> Ther's a strange par'lous *T.* before the reason,
> A very tall *T.* which makes the word *High Treason.* (IV. i. 19–23)

The clown's interpretive abilities perhaps leave a little to be desired, particularly in the context of the struggles of the play's protagonist, Silvio, to find the correct interpretation for a riddle he is obliged to answer. Yet Silvio wants to learn about meanings, and Soto the clown is learning the tricks of multiple meaning that letters can play. Soto's achievement in word-piecing is in a sense the exact opposite of that of the Venetian inquisitors mocked by the Black Knight in Thomas Middleton's satirical play *A Game at Chess* a few years later in 1624: the inquisitors, he claims, "came all spectacled / To pick out syllables out of the dung of treason / As children pick out cherry-stones, yet found none / But what they made themselves with ends of letters."[1] Soto may in fact be piecing together "ends of letters" but he finds not that he has to make up meanings but that the arbitrary effects of spelling and reading generate new and dangerous meanings. For what Soto sees quite clearly is the reason in treason.

Both treason and unease about the arbitrary meanings words can have are the keynotes of a tale Thomas Fuller tells about Fletcher's role in the writing of a play:

Meeting once in a tavern, to contrive the rude draught of a Tragedy, Fletcher undertook *to kill the King* therein; whose words being overheard by a listener (though his Loyalty not to be blamed herein), he was accused of High Treason, till, the mistake soon appearing, that the plot was onely against a Dramatick and Scenical King, all wound off in merriment.[2]

Whether the anecdote is true or not is in a sense irrelevant, since it suggests an unease highly significant for a discussion of the politics of Fletcher's plays. Since Fuller's anecdote is framed with discussion of the partnership of Beaumont and Fletcher, one must assume that the meeting was with Beaumont. Determining the plot of the play becomes plotting because it has become a collaborative effort, the product of teamwork. And the play in question sounds like *The Maid's Tragedy,* perhaps the two playwrights' best-known collaborative work. There is an eavesdropper in the tavern, the sort already pilloried by Beaumont and Fletcher in their first collaboration *The Woman Hater,* the preface of which demands that "[i]f there bee any lurking amongst you in corners, with Table bookes, who have some hope to find fit matter to feede his ——— mallice on, let them claspe them up, and slinke away, or stay and be converted."[3] In the play proper Count Valore, brother to the female protagonist Oriana, mocks an informer who "thinks to discover as much out of the talke of drunkards in Taphouses" and who brings "informations, pick'd out of broken wordes in mens common talke, which with his malitious misapplication, hee hopes will seeme dangerous" (I. iii. 172–77), a prediction of the events Fuller describes (or perhaps indeed the origins of the tale).

In any event, in the anecdote, some figure expressive of sovereign authority (a constable, say) is presumably called by the informer. When the truth is discovered—that the only plotting was simply "dramatic and scenical" plotting—there is much "merriment," and everything is fine. A false alarm. Yet why tell the tale in the first place? The absence of a genuine signified for the words *"to kill the King,"* the exact phrase "High Treason," and the general idea of confusion over the generative and therefore politically dangerous nature of words all provide a mirror for Soto's word-fumblings. Soto, at first anyway, reads too little, not too much, into (or from) his words. But, playing with ends of letters, he generates a genuinely provocative political reading. There is a similar uneasy doubleness of meaning in the way Fuller tells his tale. Why, for example, is the coyly parenthetical "(though his Loyalty not to be blamed herein)" placed where it is in the containing sentence? Is the subject of the parenthetical clause Fletcher or the eavesdropper? Fletcher, presumably. But if this is the case, one is left with exactly the opposite feeling: that if eavesdroppers were present to listen in on Fletcher's plotting, maybe there was something suspect about his "Loyalty." After all, Thomas Fuller, writing at the moment of Restoration and the reopening of the theatres, could hardly be unaware either of the reality of regicide or of the direct relationship between politics and theater.

"Merriment" is nonetheless possible because "the plot was onely against a *Dramatick* and *Scenical* King" (my italics) and thus outside the laws of treason. Yet the very edginess of Fuller's tale blurs the boundaries of politics and theater in such a way as at least partially to belie the conclusion drawn. And both Fuller and Soto in their different ways voice a political and theatrical unease which underlines the logic of state censorship of dramatic texts in Jacobean England. We know that Sir George Buc, master of the Revels, reading Fletcher and Massinger's collaborative *Tragedy of Sir John Van Olden Barnavelt* in his capacity as censor, found the divide between "Dramatick and Scenical" politics and the real thing to be decidedly blurred, and we are peculiarly fortunate to have his comments on an extant manuscript. When Buc scores out a scene and writes in the margin "I like not this: Neith^r do I think y^t the pr[ince] was thus disgracefully vsed," we are left with a distinct impression that the play is the thing.[4] And it was, after all, only a few years before overworked Buc lost his reason entirely.

2

For an analysis of the politics of Fletcher's plays, the collaborative work with Massinger is more important than that with Beaumont because these collaborations come from later in his career, when he had established his own professional and political preferences, and because they generally display evidence that Fletcher was the dominant partner in the writing process. As a result, the bulk of this book concentrates on plays which postdate Beaumont's retirement and death. To interpret the later plays, however, it is essential to have a working knowledge of the ways in which the early collaboration with Beaumont oriented Fletcher's later work and to plot the development of Fletcherian politics across the collaborative partnerships. Buc, in censoring *Sir John Van Olden Barnavelt* in 1619, complained with particular vehemence about the scene in which the prince of Orange finds himself barred from entering the parliament building until his counselors have reached a decision about the matter they are discussing. The effect of a scene of this nature, particularly in a play about a well-known republican leader, is both to foreground the possibility of subjects' autonomy and agency in face of absolutist claims and to offer an example of what I will call the politics of collaboration in Fletcher's work.[5]

Princes had in fact been "disgracefully used" in plays in which Fletcher was involved from the very beginning of his career. The possibility that a sovereign may be politically naive or fallible and that the subject may have the right to defy a sovereign seen behaving in an unprincely manner and to expect acknowledgment in the processes of government is repeatedly examined in the early Beaumont and Fletcher collaborations. As examples I shall refer to the two plays mentioned in the discussion of Fuller's tale about Fletcher's plotting—*The Woman Hater* and *The Maid's Tragedy*—both of which are in fact chiefly the work of Beaumont and which broach political questions that remained Fletcher's preoccupations during and after his collaboration with the young aristocrat.

The Woman Hater, the first such collaboration, opens with a prologue presenting an immediate correlation between political provocation and the genre of tragicomedy which was to be sustained in Fletcher's solo and collaborative work all his life.[6] "I dare not call it Comedie, or Tragedie," announces the prologue, " 'tis perfectly neither: A Play it is, which was meant to make you laugh" (Bowers I: 157). And he goes on disingenuously:

[Y]ou shall not find in it the ordinarie and over-worne trade of jeasting at Lordes and Courtiers, and Citizens, without taxation of any particular or new vice by them found out, but at the persons of them: such, he that made this, thinkes vile; and for his owne part vowes, That hee did never thinke, but that a Lord borne might bee a wise man, and a Courtier an honest man. (Bowers I:157)

Such arch and ironic comment is, of course, nothing less than an invitation to listen for the very criticism the prologue denies. At the same time, both prologue and play proper mock the subtle interpreter. Much mirth is extracted from the schemings of the two intelligencers in the play, who eavesdrop on conversations with the avowed intent of gleaning information about treason and plots, and who provide a perfect vehicle for satire on the spy network the Cecils had created in the preceding decade or so with the help of the Bacons. Once they settle on a victim, there is little he can say that will not be willfully misread. "[L]et him speak wisely, and plainely, and as hidden as a can, or I shall crush him," says one of the spies, "a shall not scape charracters, though a speake Babel" (III. ii. 5–6).

The Woman Hater belongs to a dramatic fashion—the disguised ruler play—which flourished briefly in the immediate wake of James's accession, and as such it not only consciously echoes Shakespeare's early foray into tragicomedy, *Measure for Measure,* but also reflects the equivocal attitude to kingship and sovereignty felt in many of these plays and perhaps particularly in *Measure for Measure.* The opening scene of *The Woman Hater* quite clearly mocks the motivations of Shakespeare's Duke Vincentio. Dawn has not yet broken in Milan when its duke rises in secret. He mischievously sets about asking his courtiers why they think he has got them up so early. They answer in various generically self-conscious ways. Lucio thinks the duke is probably "[a]bout some waightie State plot." Arrigo holds that he aims "to cure / Some strange corruptions in the common wealth." But the duke scorns these dutiful replies, and asks a further coy question to the puzzlement of his counselors:

> *Duke:* Y'are well conceited of your selves, to thinke
> I choose you out to beare me company
> In such affaires and businesse of state:
> But am I not a patterne for all Princes,
> That breake my softe sleepe for my subjects good?
> Am I not carefull? very provident?
> *Lucio:* Your grace is carefull.
> *Arrigo:*   Very provident.
> *Duke:* Nay knew you how my serious working plots,
> Concerne the whole estates of all my subjects,

I, and their lives; then, *Lucio* thou wouldst sweare,
I were a loving Prince. (I. i. 13–23)

We immediately recall the unconvincing stance of Vincentio in *Measure for Measure* and his attempts to seem omniscient, apparently supported by Angelo's shocked and mystified comment ("I perceive your grace, like power divine, / Hath looked upon my passes") at the close of the play.[7]

There is a further mocking echo of Shakespeare's tragicomedy in the last line of the quoted exchange, which is glossed a few lines later. The courtiers are still determined to find out the real reason that the duke is up so early. Lucio tries again: "I thinke your grace / Intendes to walke the publique streetes disguised, / To see the streetes disorders." But the duke simply says: "It is not so." Arrigo has a second attempt: "You secretly will crosse some other states, / That doe conspire against you." To which the duke replies, amused: "Waightier farre." At which point he relents and tells them the true reason. He breaks his sleep, he says, "to see a wench." He has thus allowed the courtiers to run the gamut of political and generic possibilities (paralleling the assumptions of both the intelligencers and those members of the audience who are doing their best to find political allegory in the play) before undercutting their appropriately sovereign logic with the simple facts. One cannot help remembering Vincentio again, when he hastily dismisses the friar's natural assumption that he has gone into disguise because of a love affair ["No, holy father, throw away that thought. / Believe not that the dribbling dart of love / Can pierce a complete bosom" (I. iii. 1–3)] and when he suddenly and awkwardly asks Isabella to marry him in the last scene.[8] At the close of *The Woman Hater,* the duke chooses a similarly arbitrary moment to ask out of the blue: "Best of all comforts; may I take this hand, / And call it mine?" to which Oriana replies equivocally, "I am your Graces handmaid," and again later: "My Lord, I am your subject, you may command me, / Provided still, your thoughts be faire and good" (V. iv. 86–87; 90–91).

We are left with a sense of unease about *The Woman Hater's* self-conscious representation of sovereignty which is by no means resolved in the course of events. Only a few lines after the opening exchange, there is an awkward conversation, quite remarkable for its political cynicism, between the duke and Lucio about the nature of the court and of court favoritism. Once it has been established that the duke is awake for sexual rather than political ends, the two parallel plots of the play are rather arbitrarily introduced in the motif of a seafood delicacy, the umbrana's head. We hear of Gondarino, the eponymous misogynist, and of Lazarillo, an obsessive gourmand. Noting Arrigo's description of Lazarillo as a "Courtier," the duke waxes philosophical about court structures:

> *Duke:* A Courtier cal'st thou him?
> Beleeve me *Lucio,* there be many such
> About our Court, respected, as they thinke,
> Even by our selfe; with thee I will be plaine:
> We Princes do use, to prefer many for nothing, and to take particular and
> free knowledge, almost in the nature of acquaintance of many; whome
> we do use only for our pleasures, and do give largely to numberes; more
> out of pollicy, to be thought liberall, and by that meanes to make the
> people strive to deserve our love; then to reward any particular desert of
> theirs, to whome we give; and doo suffer our selves to heere Flatterers,
> more for recreation then for love of it, though we sildome hate it:
> And yet we know all these, and when we please,
> Can touch the wheele, and turne their names about.
> (I. i. 59–72)

Lucio comments wryly that he "wonder[s] they that know their states so well, / Should fancie such base slaves" (I. i. 73–74a), and in response the duke opens the *arcana imperii* a little further, asking coyly: "Do'st not thou thinke, if thou wert Duke of *Millaine,* / Thou shouldst be flattered?" (I. i. 75–76), and, to Lucio's stalwart reply of "I knowe my Lord, I would not" (I. i. 76), he says:

Why so thought I till I was Duke, I thought I should have left me no more Flatterers, then there are now plaine-dealers; and yet for all this my resolution, I am most palpably flattered: the poore man may loathe covetousnes and flattery; but Fortune will alter the minde when the winde turnes: there may well be a little conflict, but it will drive the byllowes before it. (I. i. 77–82)

In the wake of this cynical admission of the perils of rule, he switches abruptly back to high-flown language in verse ("see fair *Thetis* hath undon the bares / To *Phebus* teame"), and concludes by invoking Erycina to "inspire / Her [i.e. his wench's] heart with love, or lessen my desire" (I. i. 91–92). This carnal, material, all-too-human duke appears decidedly other than "[v]ery provident."

The very beginnings of the collaboration of Beaumont and Fletcher thus both reflect the established attitudes of the milieu to which Beaumont belonged and to which Fletcher had recently been introduced and set up the essential political veins which Fletcher would work for twelve years after his partner's retirement from writing. *The Maid's Tragedy,* the subject of Fuller's anecdote about collaborative plotting and perhaps the most widely read of the plays in which Fletcher was involved, shares a certain degree of political unease with the first of the collaborations. In the opening moments of the play, the king's brother Lysippus asks a gentleman named Strato what he thinks of masques such as the one planned for that night. Strato replies that he thinks it will be "[a]s well as masks can be," and he glosses this by saying that the problem with masques is that "they must commend their King, and speake in praise / Of the assembly, blesse the Bride and Bridegroome, / In person of some god." They are, he says bluntly, "tied to rules / Of flatterie."[9] The conversation breaks off as the general, Melantius, enters (though he also disparages masques a little later as "soft and silken wars"), but the tone of cynicism about the court and its attitudes has been set for the entire play. Strato's interlocutor is nonetheless happy to promote royal absolutism, claiming that "[t]he breath of kings is like the breath of gods" in its capacity to demand and receive obedience.[10] We discover of course in Act II that the play's king is decidedly less than godlike in his long-term sexual liaison with Evadne and his arranging for her to marry an unsuspecting Amintor as a cover for the continuation of their affair.

The discovery that he has been tricked by the king leaves Amintor, with his conventional sense of loyalty, psychologically compromised. "[L]et me know the man that wrongs me so," he demands of her on the wedding night, "That I may cut his body into motes, / And scatter it before the northern wind." Evadne coolly tells him that he dare not strike the man in question, to which Amintor blusters: "[I]f his body were a poisonous plant / That it were death to touch, I have a soul / Will throw me on him." She initially resists identifying the culprit, but finally, exasperated by his naïveté, tells him " 'tis the King." At this Amintor abruptly changes his tune. "[T]hou has nam'd a word, that wipes away / All

THE REASON IN TREASON

thoughts revengeful! In that sacred word, 'The King,' there lies a terror: what frail man / Dares lift his hand against it?" (II. i. 307–10). Yet the anguish of the internal debate this situation provokes in the loyal Amintor is deeply disturbing. And when Amintor calls him "tyrant," the King is forced to remind him of royal prerogative:

> *King:* Draw not thy sword; thou know'st I cannot fear
> A subject's hand; but thou shalt feel the weight
> Of this, if thou dost rage.
> *Amintor:* The weight of that!
> If you have any worth, for heaven's sake, think
> I fear not swords; for, as you are mere man,
> I dare as easily kill you for this deed,
> As you dare think to do it. But there is
> Divinity about you, that strikes dead
> My rising passions. (III. i. 232–40)

The question of divinity thus simultaneously calls for and denies revenge upon the king. When Melantius, brother to Evadne and friend to Amintor, discovers the crime, however, he feels no such equivocation, crying:

> Dost thou not feel, 'mongst all those, one brave anger,
> That breaks out nobly and directs thine arm
> To kill this base king?
> *Evadne:* All the gods forbid it!
> *Amintor:* No, all the gods require it;
> They are dishonour'd in him. (IV. i. 142–46)

So he forces her to promise to kill the king. She does so, and the play ends in a mass of casual slaughter, bequeathing a bleak moral which does little to redeem the forbid / require imperative. It is left to Lysippus to speak the trite but inescapable concluding aphorism: "[O]n lustful kings / Unlook'd-for sudden deaths from Heaven are sent; / But curs'd is he that is their instrument" (V. iv. 293–95).

These words are of course politically dangerous, and Sir George Buc apparently felt obliged to censor certain words and phrases in *The Maid's Tragedy* when it came before him. The 1622 second quarto of the play appears to have been based upon a different manuscript from the first quarto of three years earlier, and it is reasonable to infer from this that the new lines in the 1622 quarto were originally lines which had been excised at Buc's request back in 1610. As Janet Clare points out, perhaps the most notable omission from the 1619 quarto is the description given by Amintor of Evadne after she has killed the king. "[T]o augment my woe," he says, "You now are present, stained with a king's blood / Violently shed" (V. iii. 145–47). Buc must have felt that to permit such a spectacular reminder of the mortality of kings would be a dereliction of his duty.[11]

The earliest Beaumont and Fletcher collaboration in which it is possible to establish distinct scenes as the work of Fletcher alone is the oddly antiplatonic tragedy *Cupid's Revenge,* which dates probably from late 1607, thus preceding the writing of *The Faithful Shepherdess* by a matter of months.[12] The play provides, in one of the Fletcher scenes, the first of several popular coups d'état in the canon, a moment which is perhaps the most unnerving representation of political unrest in the early plays. In face of the duke's senility and his intent to execute the popular prince, the citizens decide to rebel:

> His Houre was come
> To lose his life, he ready for the stroke,
> Nobly, and full of Saint-like patience,
> Went with his Guard: which when the people saw,
> Compassion first went out, mingled with teares,
> That bred desires, and whispers to each other,
> To doe some worthy kindnes for the Prince.
> And ere they understood well how to doe,
> Fury stept in, and taught them what to doe,
> Thrusting on every hand to rescue him,
> As a white innocent: then flew the rore
> Through all the streetes, of *Save him, save him, save him;*
> And as they cryde, they did; for catching up
> Such sudden weapons as their madnesse shew them,
> In short, they beat the Guard, and took him from em,
> And now march with him like a royall Army. (IV. iv. 43–58)

The passage is equivocal about the actions of the citizens, yet the status of the prince in the play and the overt echoes of Foxean martyrology in the description of his fortitude in the face of imminent execution suggest that the revolt, though disturbing, is in some way justified. Nonetheless, the transformation of a mob of citizens into something akin to a "royall Army" is startling in the context of the events in the Midlands only a few months before the play was produced. Already, Fletcher's sense of the possibilities of political unrest can be seen to outweigh Beaumont's aristocratic humor at the expense of the possibility of political collaboration between rulers and common people.

Unrest and the desire for involvement in the political process are not by any means solely the preserve of the common people in Fletcher's plays. The most serious moral dilemmas in the early plays are those suffered by well-meaning statesmen faced with overt tyranny. Like Shakespeare, Fletcher wrote a series of "Roman" plays which broach key questions about the nature of politics and of political personalities. Fletcher's Rome, however, comments much more frankly upon the state of Jacobean England than does Shakespeare's, and thus perhaps suggests some of the ways in which Fletcher's work remains congruent with that of the Spenserians after the failure of the project which was to have begun with *The Faithful Shepherdess*. When the eponymous protagonist of Fletcher's *Bonduca*, a solo play written around 1612, gives her opinion of Rome from the ramparts of her fortress, it is difficult to avoid hearing the voice of the English Reformation in her glorification of the "chaste and simple puritie" of the Britons:

> If *Rome* be earthly, why should any knee
> With bending adoration worship her?
> She's vitious; and your partiall selves confesse,
> Aspires the height of all impietie:
> Therefore 'tis fitter I should reverence
> The thatched houses where the Britains dwell
> In carelesse mirth, where the blest houshold gods
> See nought but chaste and simple puritie.
> 'Tis not high power that makes a place divine,
> Nor that the men from gods derive their line.
> But sacred thoughts in holy bosoms stor'd,
> Make people noble, and the place ador'd. [13]

Fletcher's metaphoric geography is characteristically protean: in *Valentinian,* a solo tragedy written around the same time as *Bonduca,* he presents a Rome whose instabilities can all too easily be equated with those of Jacobean England.

The central and by now familiar problem of *Valentinian* is the level of loyalty owed by virtuous courtiers to a corrupt king and court. Maximus asks "Why is this Emperor, this man we honor, / This God that ought to be / . . . why is this Author of us . . . / Thus led away, thus vainly led away?[14] Aecius's reply retains a dangerous ambivalence: "[S]ay he be an ill Prince, are we therefore / Fit fires to purge him?" (I. iii. 89–90). A political situation is presented in which loyal and virtuous subjects such as Aecius and his captains are left sufficiently frustrated and aggrieved that they argue and fight amongst themselves, and it becomes very difficult not to see in the Rome of *Valentinian* a correlative of Jacobean England seen from the point of view of militant Protestantism as a nation rotting from inaction. The adaptation of a song from *Valentinian* to mourn the death of James's eldest son, Prince Henry, in November 1612 (an adaptation which fixes the *terminus ad quem* of the play) suggests that the play's political relevance was indeed apparent to its audience.

Certainly, it is difficult not to relate the frustrations expressed in the play to the contemporary political context, particularly to James's persistent self-glorification as *rex pacificus,* a stance seen by English militant Protestants as a thoroughgoing failure to address the joint problem of Spain and Roman Catholicism in continental Europe. Aecius, loyal general to Valentinian, tells the emperor of his soldiers' frustration at inaction. They complain that

> weapons
> And bodyes that were made for shining brasse,
> Are both unedg'd and old with ease, and women;
> And then they cry agen, where are the *Germaines,*
> Linde with hot *Spain,* or *Gallia?* bring 'em on,
> And let the son of war, steel'd *Mithridates,*
> Lead up his winged *Parthians* like a storme,
> Hiding the face of Heaven with showres of arrowes;
> Yet we dare fight like *Romanes;* then as Souldiers
> Tyr'd with a weary march, they tell their wounds,
> Even weeping ripe they were no more nor deeper,
> And glory in those scarrs that make 'em lovely,
> And sitting where a Campe was, like sad Pilgrims
> They reckon up the times, and living labours
> Of *Julius* or *Germanicus,* and wonder
> That *Rome,* whose turrets once were topt with honours,

> Can now forget the Custome of her conquests:
> And then they blame your Grace, and say, who leads us,
> Shall we Stand here like Statues? were our Fathers
> The Sonnes of lazie *Moores*, our Princes *Persians*,
> Nothing but silkes, and softnesse? curses on 'em
> That first taught *Nero* wantonnesse, and bloud,
> *Tiberius* doubts, *Caligula* all vices;
> For from the spring of these, succeeding Princes—
> Thus they talk Sir. (I. iii. 183–208)

Aecius adds his own statement:

> Let not this body,
> That has lookd bravely in his bloud for *Cesar*,
> And covetous of wounds, and for your safety,
> After the scape of Swords, Speares, Slings, and Arrows,
> (Gainst which my beaten body was mine Armour)
> The Seas, and thirstie deserts, now be purchase
> For Slaves, and base Informers. (I. iii. 227–33)

The emperor even admits that, up to a point, Aecius's words have affected him: "The honesty of this *Aecius*, / Who is indeed the Bullwark of the Empire, / Has div'd . . . deep into me" (I. iii. 244–46).

The cashiering of Pontius ("an honest . . . Captaine," according to the dramatis personae) maps the narrow line in the play between treason and reason. The scene opens as Aecius, in a rage, pursues Pontius, claiming that he has "pluck[ed] the Souldiers to sedition . . . / And sow[n] Rebellion in 'em" (II. iii. 5–7). Maximus, who is not entirely sure where his own loyalties lie, parts them and tries to calm Aecius. Maximus asks the general to explain his fury. Aecius rages:

> Did I not take him preaching to the Souldiers
> How lazily they liv'd, and what dishonours
> It was to serve a Prince so full of woman?
> Those were his very words, friend. (II. iii. 25–28)

Maximus's reply is significant in face of the similarity of the complaints that he has already voiced to Aecius and Aecius to the emperor himself:

> These, *Aecius*,
> Though they were rashly spoke, which was an errour
> (A great one *Pontius*) yet from him that hungers

> For warres, and brave imployment, might be pardond.
> The heart, and harbourd thoughts of ill, make Traytors,
> Not spleeny speeches. (II. iii. 28–33)

Nonetheless, Aecius says he will cashier Pontius, who asks for a right of reply, and says:

> Tis true I told the Souldier, whom we serv'd,
> And then bewaild, we had an Emperour
> Led from us by the flourishes of Fencers;
> I blam'd him too for women. . . .
> And like enough I blest him then as Souldiers
> Will doe sometimes: Tis true I told 'em too,
> We lay at home, to show our Country
> We durst goe naked, durst want meate, and mony,
> And when the Slave drinkes Wine, we durst be thirstie:
> I told 'em this too, that the Trees and Roots
> Were our best pay-masters; the Charity
> Of longing women, that had bought our bodies,
> Our beds, fires, Taylers, Nurses: Nay I told 'em,
> (For you shall heare the greatest sin, I said Sir)
> By that time there be wars agen, our bodies
> Laden with scarres, and aches, and ill lodgings,
> Heates, and perpetuall wants, were fitter praires,
> And certaine graves, the cope the foe on crutches:
> Tis likely too, I counselld 'em to turne
> Their Warlike pikes to plough-shares, their sure Targets
> And Swords hatcht with the bloud of many Nations,
> To Spades, and pruning Knives, for those get mony,
> Their warlike Eagles, into Dawes, or Starlings,
> To give an *Ave Cesar* as he passes,
> And be rewarded with a thousand dragma's,
> For thus we get but yeeres and beets. (II. iii. 60–63, 64–85)

He continues with a plea:

> My Lord, I did not wooe 'em from the Empire,
> Nor bid 'em turne their daring steel gainst *Caesar,*
> The Gods for ever hate me, if that motion
> Were part of me: Give me but imployment, Sir,
> And way to live, and where you hold me vicious,
> Bred up in mutiny, my Sword shall tell ye,
> (And if you please, that place I held, maintaine it,
> Gainst the most daring foes of *Rome*) I am honest,

A lover of my Country, one that holds
His life no longer his, then kept for *Caesar.*
Weight not (I thus low on my knee beseech you)
What my rude tongue discovered, t'was my want,
No other part of *Pontius:* you have seen me,
And you my Lord, doe something for my Country,
And both beheld the wounds I gave and took,
Not like a backward Traytor. (II. iii. 88–103)

This defense is to no avail. It is enough to Aecius that the errant captain has "[d]are[d] talke of but neere sedition," and he strips him of command. The audience, however, cannot help but hear the voice of reason in Pontius's plea.

3

Two events of 1612 and 1613 mark a watershed in English Protestant politics (and therefore poetics) in the period: the death of Prince Henry, and the marriage of James's only daughter Princess Elizabeth to Frederick, the elector palatine, whose ejection from his newly acquired kingdom of Bohemia six years later would set the Thirty Years' War in motion. Both occasions, funeral and wedding, required public poetry which allowed for the involvement of those generally excluded from James's sphere.

Prince Henry's court had attracted and financed a large number of persons disaffected for one reason or another from the king. The prince was known to have a much more militant cast of mind than his father, and was looked to as the future hope of English militant Protestantism. He appears, as we have seen, in chivalric garb on the frontispiece to Drayton's *Poly-Olbion,* which the poet had quite deliberately dedicated to the young prince rather than to James, who would have been the more logical dedicatee of a work of such epic pretensions. Henry was known to prefer the kind of military entertainment, such as the barriers, which James disliked, and he became the focus of a developing cult of chivalry. He undoubtedly patronized artists and poets in a way his father never did (often appreciating them for the very features that James disliked), and his advisers, the earl of Arundel among them, were men of considerably greater cultural and aesthetic achievement than those generally to be found at James's court. Most important of all, the young prince was known to combine his love of the arts and of matters military with an ardent Protestantism. He was looked to by the more militant of English Protestants as the figure who would replace James's excess and pacifism with a degree of courtly austerity combined with a thoroughgoing hostility to Spain, and who would in due course be the catalyst for European Protestant union and apocalyptic dreams.

Henry was enthusiastic about his sister's impending marriage to the elector palatine, since that alliance promised well for European Protestant union against the omnipresent threat of Spain. Frederick was the most vehemently Calvinist of the continental princes and was a popular figure in England. His match with the resonantly named Elizabeth, combined with the developing signs of militancy in Henry, seemed to English Protestants to present boundless possibilities for advancement of the Protestant cause both at home and on the continent. Henry himself was apparently involved in planning the entertainments for the wedding.[15] This may be one reason for the identities of the masque writers for the occasion: the main masques were written exceptionally not by Jonson (who was conveniently abroad at the time) but by Thomas Campion, George Chapman, and Francis Beaumont. Campion was a client of the Howards and a year later wrote a masque for the wedding of the earl of Somerset: his 1613 masque was commissioned by the king as an ideologically acceptable replacement for the abortive *Masque of Truth*.[16]

Campion's masque was performed on 14 February, the day of the wedding, followed by Chapman's on the fifteenth and Beaumont's on the twentieth (the latter postponed, to the frustration of its sponsors, Gray's Inn and the Inner Temple, from the sixteenth). There is no documented connection between Beaumont and Henry, but Chapman was known to be close to the prince and shared a fascination for things French with him. And as we have seen, Beaumont and Chapman had connections with various Spenserian poets and generally with those distrustful of James and his court. One might expect that, given the unique circumstances, their entertainments might take the opportunity to make a conscious step away from established norms in order to develop a new orientation for the court masque. It is a testimony to the strength and pervasiveness of the Jonsonian masque that, though the masques for the wedding of February 1613 exhibit certain qualities alien to Jonson's work, they are still clearly dependent upon the masque form he had worked out with Inigo Jones. Indeed, there is a continuity in staging, despite Chapman's mockery in his masque of the predictable inclusion of huge artificial rocks in the sets, since Jones and Chapman were partners in creating the first of the two inn-of-court masques.[17] Yet the political premises of the masques were far from anything Jonson had produced. Prince Henry's influence, even in death, can be seen in each of the masques performed, not just in the traces of the canceled *Masque of Truth*.

Beaumont's contribution, *The Masque of the Inner Temple and Gray's Inn*, was the last of the masques put on for the wedding, and it thrust both of its sponsoring inns of court deeply into debt. It celebrated the marriage of the rivers Thames and Rhine, and involved an elaborate "voyage by water" before the actual performance, "[t]he gentlemen Maskers being placed by themselves in the Kings royall barge with the rich furniture of state, and adorned with a great number of lights placed in such order as might make best shew."[18] This was as far as proceedings got on the night of the sixteenth, primarily because "the King was so wearied and sleepie with sitting up almost two whole nights before, that he had no edge to yt, [and] could last no longer."[19] The masquers, "much discouraged, and out of countenance," had to start all over again on the night of the twentieth, though they were treated by James to a grand dinner the next evening in recompence.

Once the river journey is accomplished, the masque begins with the appearance of Mercury and Iris, messengers respectively for Jupiter and Juno, who are come to "doe honour to the Mariage of the two famous Rivers *Thamesis* and *Rhene*" (127). Mercury contrives a dance of Naiades and Hyades which Iris criticises as "[a] livelesse dance, which of one sexe consists" (131). He responds by first introducing four Cupids and then a group of partly living statues, "in token that the Match should be blessed both with Love and Riches" (127), who together dance the first antimasque. Iris, "for her part in scorne of this high flying devise, and in token that the Match shall likewise be blessed with the love of the Common People," brings on a "May-daunce or Rurall daunce" (127). This second antimasque, comprising a May Lord and Lady, "A Countrey

Clowne, or Shepheard" and a "Countrey Wench," as well as male
and female baboons and other rural figures, formed "a confusion, or
commixture of all such persons as are naturall and proper for
Countrey sports" (127). In the wake of this dance, the masque
proper begins. A traverse is drawn to reveal a military scene, the
camp of fifteen Olympian knights which is adorned with "rich
Armour and Militarie furniture" (135), a residual element presumably of Prince Henry's influence on the proceedings prior to his
untimely death. After a priests' song, the knights "take their
Ladies to daunce with them Galliards, Durets, Corantoes, &c. and
lead them to their places" (137), and the masque closes with a final
grand dance, in which the knights "put on their Swords and Belts"
(138). There can have been no mistaking the glorification of Protestant militarism that this masque represented.

Beaumont was not alone in accommodating his poetics to the
unique context of 1612–13, and to the promise of a new era of
Protestant gain. Even Fletcher, writing with Shakespeare in *Henry
VIII*, participated in the process, penning the grand prophecy
spoken by Cranmer which closes the play on a triumphant and
forward-looking note.[20] James is represented as the divinely appointed successor to Queen Elizabeth, and as such, implicitly, the
inheritor of her stalwart Protestantism:

> This royal infant—heaven still move about her—
> Though in her cradle, yet now promises
> Upon this land a thousand thousand blessings
> Which time shall bring to ripeness. She shall be—
> But few now living can behold that goodness—
> A pattern to all princes living with her,
> And all that shall succeed. Saba was never
> More covetous of wisdom and fair virtue
> Than this pure soul shall be. All princely graces
> That mould up such a mighty piece as this is,
> With all the virtues that attend the good,
> Shall still be doubled on her. Truth shall nurse her,
> Holy and heavenly thoughts still counsel her.
> She shall be loved and feared. Her own shall bless her;
> Her foes shake like a field of beaten corn,
> And hang their heads with sorrow. Good grows with her.
> In her days every man shall eat in safety
> Under his own vine what he plants, and sing
> The merry songs of peace to all his neighbours.

God shall be truly known, and those about her
From her shall read the perfect ways of honour,
And by those claim their greatness, not by blood.
Nor shall this speace sleep with her, but, as when
The bird of wonder dies—the maiden phoenix—
Her ashes new create another heir
As great in admiration as herself,
So shall she leave her blessèdness to one,
When heaven shall call her from this cloud of darkness,
Who from the sacred ashes of her honour
Shall star-like rise as great in fame as she was,
And so stand fixed. Peace, plenty, love, truth, terror,
That were the servants to this chosen infant,
Shall then be his, and, like a vine, grow to him.
Wherever the bright sun of heaven shall shine,
His honour and the greatness of his name
Shall be, and make new nations. He shall flourish,
And like a mountain cedar reach his branches
To all the plains about him. Our children's children
Shall see this, and bless heaven.[21]

Protestant triumphalism is implicit in every word of this speech.
Elizabeth's "perfect ways of honour" will validate the belief voiced
by Bonduca that " 'Tis not high power that makes a place divine, / Nor that the men from gods derive their line. / But sacred
thoughts in holy bosoms stor'd."[22] Thus James's mantle as Elizabeth's true successor depends upon his fulfilling what she had
begun, and the projects outlined, including the making of "new
nations," a clear reference to English ventures in the New World,
are those previously associated with Henry's court, not James's. For
a brief while, even the most disgruntled of James's subjects were
united in their joy at the marriage and in the apparent political
prospects it offered.

Yet even in *Henry VIII* there are seeds of unease. The penulti-
mate scene (also Fletcher's) offers a response to Beaumont's celebration of the "love of the Common People" in his masque by emphasizing the negative side of popular "confusion." The palace porters,
it turns out, can scarcely contain the restive energy of the crowd
which flocks to see the newborn Elizabeth. The Porter's Man points
out the impossibility of stopping the crowd:

'Tis as much impossible,
Unless we sweep 'em from the door with cannons,

To scatter 'em as 'tis to make 'em sleep
On May-day morning—which will never be.
We may as well push against Paul's as stir 'em,
(V. iii. 12–16)

and when the Lord Chamberlain appears and orders them to make sure there is room "for the ladies / When they pass back from the christening" (V. iii. 72–73), the Porter tries to explain his predicament. "We are but men," he says, "and what so many may do, / Not being torn a-pieces, we have done," adding that "[a]n army cannot rule 'em" (V. iii. 74–76). In the space of two brief scenes, we have seen both Cranmer's great prophecy of Elizabeth and James and the festive fury of an overenthusiastic and barely contained mob: the effect of this juxtaposition, if not exactly self-canceling, is nonetheless unsettling.

Furthermore, Cranmer's resort to the metaphor of the phoenix in the course of his prophecy seems more than a little contrived in its attempt to paper over the cracks of succession. In his subsequent speech he acknowledges that there will be no direct heir: "she must die— / she must, the saints must have her—yet a virgin, / A most unspotted lily shall she pass / To th' ground, and all the world shall mourn her" (V. iv. 59–62). And we have just seen the birth of yet another daughter to a king desperate for sons somewhat cynically dramatized a few minutes earlier in one of Shakespeare's scenes. An old woman bursts in on the king to tell him of the birth. "Now by thy looks / I guess the message," he cries, "Is the Queen delivered? / Say, 'Ay, and of a boy'" (V. i. 162–64), to which the woman gives an awkward and curiously androgynous reply: "Ay, ay, my liege, / And of a lovely boy. The God of heaven / Both now and ever bless her! 'Tis a girl / Promises boys hereafter," she tells him, adding hopefully, " '[t]is as like you / As cherry is to cherry" (V. i. 164–67; 169–70). Henry responds abruptly by telling a courtier to "[g]ive her an hundred marks" (V. i. 171), and goes to see the queen. We have little verbal sense of the king's emotion on hearing of the birth of a daughter, but the old woman was clearly looking for a more effusive reaction. "An hundred marks?" she asks angrily, "By this light, I'll ha' more. . . . Said I for this the girl was like to him? I'll / Have more, or else unsay't" (V. i. 172, 175–76), hardly a reverent attitude to a royal birth.

Within a few years Fletcher was to offer a series of wry glances at his own behavior and that of Chapman and Beaumont over the illusory glories of 1613. His criticism of Chapman's wedding masque, the *Memorable Maske of . . . the Middle Temple and Lyncolns Inne,* appears in "The Triumph of Time," the closing section of *Four Plays,* an unusual dramatic showpiece written in collaboration with Nathan Field probably late in 1613, and involves a thorough critique of Chapman's glorification of the motivations for the colonization of Virginia: I shall discuss this in detail in a later chapter. Fletcher's inclusion of part of Beaumont's masque in *The Two Noble Kinsmen* is arguably part of the same process. The play's radical tragicomic conclusion of simultaneous death and marriage, most clearly voiced in Palamon's concluding paradox—"That we should things desire which doe cost us / The losse of our desire; That naught could buy / Deare love, but losse of deare love"—would seem peculiarly appropriate to the events of 1612–13.[23] It is difficult to avoid wondering why Fletcher incorporated the "rurall daunce" of Beaumont's masque into his play. Wells and Taylor point out that the dance had been a great success with James, who had demanded an encore, and suggest simply that "the King's Men—some of whom may have taken part in the masque—decided to exploit its success by incorporating it in a play written soon afterwards."[24] This may well be true, but the obvious connection of Beaumont with Fletcher, whose scene it is, demands closer investigation.

I would suggest that Fletcher is poking mild fun at his erstwhile collaborator by including the dance in a context of rural buffoonery in which the schoolmaster's incompetent narrative becomes a burlesque version of the published description of the masque:

> The body of our sport, of no small study,
> I first appear, though rude, and raw, and muddy,
> To speak, before thy noble grace, this tenor
> At whose great feet I offer up my penner.
> The next, this Lord of May and Lady bright;
> The Chambermaid and Servingman, by night
> That seek out silent hanging; then mine Host
> And his fat Spouse, that welcomes, to their cost,
> The gallèd traveller, and with a beck'ning
> Informs the tapster to inflame the reck'ning;

Then the beest-eating Clown; and next, the Fool;
The babion with long tail and eke long tool,
Cum multis aliis that make a dance—
Say 'ay,' and all shall presently advance. (III. v. 123–36)

Thus each of Beaumont's dancers—"A Pedant, May Lord, May
Lady, Servingman, Chambermaid, A Country Clown, or Shepherd, Country Wench, An Host, Hostess, A He-Baboon, She-
Baboon, A He-Fool, She-Fool, ushering them in"—receives a
downgraded counterpart in the parts played by the morris dancers,
carnivalized by the Schoolmaster's appalling half-rhymes and details such as the baboon's "long tool."[25]

Fletcher even seems to have mocked his own involvement as
well as that of his friends in the political consensus of 1613. There
is a hint of self-criticism in his attack on Chapman's masque in *Four
Plays* when Anthropos, alternately the representative man and
representative monarch of "The Triumph of Time," asks Jupiter to
"[r]aise from his ruines once more this sunk Cedar," an overt
and surely highly dangerous reference to Cranmer's description of
James as "a mountain cedar [who will] reach his branches / To all
the plains about him."[26] This was arguably not the only self-
critical and politically dangerous reference that Fletcher made to
the speech he had given Cranmer in 1613. As Alexander Dyce
pointed out long ago, some nine years later in *Beggars' Bush*
Fletcher seems to have harked back to the same moment from
Henry VIII in a further parody of Cranmer's words about James.[27]

Beggars' Bush, first performed at Christmas 1622 but possibly
written at an earlier date, is in part, as Martin Butler has observed, a literary source for later country plays such as Massinger's
The Guardian and Suckling's *The Goblins*.[28] Indeed, Massinger
either collaborated in or revised *Beggars' Bush*: it would seem that
he learned ways of representing the politics of the country from
Fletcher.[29] The location of the play is the Bush itself, outside
London, and this geographically marginal location allows for the
presentation of an alternative social and political structure.[30] Outside the city, the beggars create for themselves a self-contained
realm, free from state burdens. Clause, alias Gerrard, father to the
rightful earl of Flanders, is to be crowned king of the beggars'
commonwealth, and his friend Higgen makes a coronation speech
which is a curious celebration of anarchy and reversal:

This is the beard, the bush, or bushy-beard,
Under whose gold and silver raigne 'twas said
So many ages since, we all should smile.
No impositions, taxes, grievances,
Knots in a State, and whips unto the Subject,
Lye lurking in this beard, but all kem'd out:
If now, the Beard be such, what is the Prince
That owes the Beard? a Father; no, a Grandfather;
Nay the great Grand-father of you his people.
He will not force away your hens, your bacon,
When you have ventur'd hard for't, nor take from you
The fattest of your puddings: under him
Each man shall eate his own stolne eggs, and butter,
In his owne shade, or sun-shine, and enjoy
His owne deare Dell, Doxy, or Mort, at night
In his own straw, with his owne shirt, or sheet,
That he hath filch'd that day. [31]

The beggars' desire to be free from "impositions, taxes, grievances" and from "whips unto the subject" must surely have made for awkward moments at court during the 1622 performance.

Yet the political effect of the speech is complex: it is a strange blend of the circumscribed utopian hopes of Shakespeare's Gonzalo and genuine possibilities for a life of liberty away from court and state. Quite clearly, there are elements in the beggars' realm that would have been highly appealing to the audience—the paternalistic abundance of the commonwealth as well as its freedom from taxes—yet this positive political resonance is counteracted by the careful way in which we are reminded of the provenance of the beggars' possessions: references to 'stolne eggs, and butter," and the "shirt, or sheet, / That he hath filch'd that day," as well as later admissions that

> there is a table [that] . . . enjoyns 'em
> Be perfect in their crutches, their fain'd plaisters,
> And their torne pas-ports, with the ways to stammer,
> And to be dumb, and deafe, and blind, and lame,
> There, all the halting paces are set downe,
> I'th learned language (II. i. 131–37)

would be guaranteed to alienate the sympathies of most of the audience. In fact, the beggars are more analogous here to the wasteful courtiers of the earlier plays than to the hardworking inhabitants of the countryside.[32] More to the point, as Dyce and others have observed, the promise that "[e]ach man shall eate his own stolne eggs, and butter, / In his own shade, or sun-shine" (117–8) is quite clearly a parody of Cranmer's Old Testament-inspired prophecy in *Henry VIII* that "[i]n her days every man shall eat in safety / Under his own vine what he plants, and sing / The merry songs of peace to all his neighbours" (V. iv. 33–35). To parody such an overt and biblically based reference to James's pacifism in this way at any time, particularly after 1613, would seem a risky venture, yet it appears a wry glance by Fletcher (assuming the scene is his) at his own participation in the festivities of that year. These and subsequent events in *Beggars' Bush* only serve to amplify its satirical aspects: the entire scene is a satire on rituals of coronation and concludes with a song celebrating the "*Beggars Holli-day*":

> *At the Crowning of our King,*
> *Thus we ever dance and sing.*
> *In the world looke out and see:*
> *Where so happy a Prince as he?*
> *Where the Nation live so free,*
> *And so merry as do we?*
> *Be it peace, or be it war,*
> *Here at liberty we are,*
> *And enjoy our ease and rest;*
> *To the field we are not prest;*
> *Nor are called into the Towne,*
> *To be troubled with the Gowne.*
> *Hang all Officers we cry,*
> *And the Magistrate too, by;*
> *When the Subsidie's encreast,*
> *We are not a penny ceast. (II. i. 145–60)*

If the audience still had sympathies with the beggars at the start of this song, one suspects that they would have become decidedly uncomfortable by the end. The beggars' realm depends upon a complete rejection of the responsibility of one part of the commonwealth for the rest: it is a fierce satire both of James's pacifism and of the tendency of the court to ignore political signals from the rest of the country.

PHYLASTER.

Or, Loue lyes a Bleeding.

Acted at the Globe by his Maiesties Seruants.

Written by ⎨ *Francis Baymont* and *Iohn Fletcher.* ⎬ Gent.

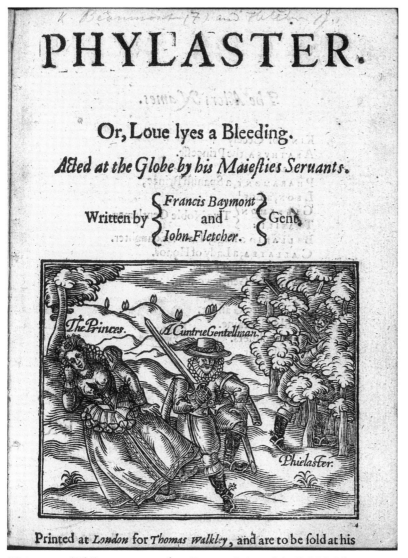

Printed at *London* for *Thomas Walkley*, and are to be fold at his

Title page of *Philaster* quarto, 1620. By permission of the British Library.

4

It is essential to view Fletcher's politics of the countryside in the contexts of his patronage relations with the Huntingdons and of broader questions regarding gradually changing attitudes toward the country in the 1610s and 1620s. The connection with Ashby allows a specific context for political analysis, but it must be remembered that that context changed and developed in the two decades of Fletcher's career. One curious correlative of that development involves the changing face of *Philaster,* the play which was the first major success for the partnership of Beaumont and Fletcher. I use the term "changing face" because it is an illustration of the action rather than the action itself which provides the initial puzzle. The 1620 quarto bears a title page illustration which appears to offer a re- (or mis-) reading of the action of one scene of the play. This change arguably reveals a shift in audience expectation and in the ethos surrounding the play.

Both the original subtitle of *Philaster—Love lyes a-bleeding—* and the illustration in question focus immediate attention upon the two brief and apparently inexplicable scenes in which Philaster wounds in rapid succession two women who love him. In the first of these scenes, his violence is defused by the arrival of a country person who professes ignorance of courtly ways and is characterized vocally as a rustic. In response to Arathusa's masochistic dismissal ("What ill-bred man art thou, to intrude thy selfe / Upon our private sports, our recreations?" she demands of him), he replies in honest, disarming, local prose: "God uds me, I understand you not; but I know the rogue has hurt you," and he turns to face Philaster, saying, "I know not your rethoricke, but I can lay it on if you touch the woman."[33] He proceeds to fight with Philaster, and they wound each other before Philaster flees. The situation, then, is clear enough: a prince who is admirable in other ways but who has lapsed into a kind of derangement, in which he is intent upon stabbing the true princess, is stopped from doing so at the eleventh hour by a doughty yokel. The illustration which faced the buyer of Thomas Walkley's 1620 quarto of *Philaster,* however, differs from this in significant detail.[34] It comprises three figures from the scene in question: Arathusa, the countryman, and Philaster. The setting is the countryside: in the distance are tree-capped hills, grass grows at the protagonists' feet. To the left of the picture is the wounded Arathusa, "[t]he Prince[s]," ornately-dressed in lace and ruff but with her breasts exposed. She has a gaping wound in her right breast and she is swooning on a grassy slope. To the right is "Phielaster," with drawn sword, lurking spurred and hatted in a clump of bushes, heading away from the scene but looking back. So far, then, the illustration is a true representation of the action in the text. At the center of the illustration, however, is a figure tagged as "A Cuntrie Gentellman," who, far from wearing a yokel's rags, is better dressed than Philaster—surcoated, booted, spurred, and with drawn, ornately hilted sword—standing in a position of staunch defense of the wounded princess.[35] This presents a curious problem for a reading of the politics of *Philaster*.

Philip Finkelpearl dismisses the illustration as an irrelevance. He considers it misleading, because it shows the countryman "dressed as a gentleman and even labels him 'A Cuntrie Gentellman.' " "This dignifies him too much," he continues, "and hence diminishes the humiliation the prince himself acknowledges having suffered by being outfought by someone variously described as 'a meane man,' 'ill bred,' a 'Boore,' and a mere 'Fellow'; his lowerclass speech confirms that."[36] In this reading, Finkelpearl follows Robert K. Turner's arguments in his edition of *Philaster*.[37] Turner also notes the differences between the representations of the country man in the two quartos of 1620 and 1622. His entrance in the 1620 text is given the stage direction "Enter a Countrey Gallant," thereby roughly matching the title page illustration's "Gentellman," whereas in the second quarto of 1622 he is labeled as a "Countrey Fellow," and one or two small changes in the dialogue emphasize his low social status. Turner points out the textual superiority of the later quarto, maintaining that where the 1620 text was set up "from a truly miserable manuscript," the 1622 quarto seems to have been based on "either the prompt-book or authorial fair copy or a transcript of one of them."[38] He offers the suggestion that the "elevation in rank" given by the first quarto to the country person is the result of a mistaken inference from the fact that he must carry a sword in order to fight Philaster. Turner's evidence, combined with the pervasively rustic nature of the country person's language in both quartos, makes it clear that of the two quartos, the 1622 version is the much more authoritative text.

Walkley explained his decision to reissue the play in 1622 in a preface, and the metaphor he uses draws our attention yet again to the scenes of wounding. "Courteous reader," he begins, "Philaster and Arathusa his love have lain so long a-bleeding, by reason of some dangerous and gaping wounds which they received in the first impression, that it is wondered how they could go abroad so long or travel so far as they have done." And he points out that "they were hurt neither by me nor the printer," yet without identifying the culprit.[39] It seems safe, however, to assume that it was the censor who was responsible for the "gaping wounds," and that Walkley had in the meantime come across an uncensored manuscript.[40] It thus remains difficult to ignore the changing treatment of the countryman. There is enough evidence in the two extant quartos to show that there was an attempt to change the nature of the scene by modifying the status of the character who saves Arathusa from the frantic Philaster. In this context, it is perhaps useful to recall (as the audience of 1620 would presumably readily do), the moment of Oswald's death in Shakespeare's *King Lear,* when Edgar's superiority in rank despite his disguise as Poor Tom is given its correlative in his victory over Goneril's unscrupulous steward.[41] There, a country yokel, characterized as such by a rural accent, turns out to be a gentleman in disguise, defending his father against a vicious courtier. In the case of *Philaster,* particularly for the readership in 1620, this might well provide a subtle resonance to the intrusion of the countryman into the "private sports" and "recreations" of royalty.[42]

I would suggest, in fact, that the readership of Walkley's quarto would have seen an overt reference to contemporary politics in the title page illustration. The equation of the royal body with the state had been a political commonplace for decades, and the immediate context in 1620 provides an obvious parallel to the situation in the illustration. The previous year had seen continental Europe slide toward the struggle that was to become the Thirty Years' War: the opening gambit was the ejection of the recently elected king of Bohemia from his realm by Spanish Hapsburg forces in July 1620. The Bohemian king was Frederick of the Palatinate, the most prominent Protestant leader in Europe, whose marriage to Princess Elizabeth had been the subject of the 1613 festivities. Their fate was sealed when Frederick's army was routed by the

Spaniards at the battle of the White Mountain on 8 November 1620. Thus an English princess was suddenly thrust into exile by what seemed to English Protestants to be the first moves of a counter-reformation that might in due course attempt to make its way across the Channel. James's response was halfhearted: he had little desire for war with Spain, and his preferred way of solving the European crisis over the next few years was to seek a peace-making dynastic connection with Spain's royal family. Indeed, he had already infuriated his more militant subjects the previous year by pressing ahead with the project for a Banqueting House in White-hall as a suitable setting for masques to celebrate a future union of the Stuart and Hapsburg lines. And English Protestants were predictably unimpressed by James's failure to go to the aid of his exiled daughter.

The political situation in 1620 thus provides a resonant context for the first quarto publication of *Philaster,* and perhaps explains the changes embodied in the title page illustration. Where a prince is apparently intent on destroying a loyal princess, it is a country gentleman who intervenes, driving away the offender and placing himself between the princess and the sword. It would be difficult to miss the implication that it is only in the country that the excesses and errors of court could be put right. It would be unreasonable to infer from this particular piece of evidence that Fletcher himself was in some way responsible for such a reading of *Philaster.* But the illustration does suggest something of the political stance and attitudes of those likely to purchase his plays and the way in which dramatic texts can develop without the involvement of the author. Janet Clare observes that *Philaster* is "a good example of a text which acquired greater political significance after its composition."[43] The play's anti-Spanish sentiment, apparent enough to its first audiences when Dion points out that "the King labors to bring in the power of a forraigne Nation, to awe his owne with," and presumably equally clear to the censor in the first place, must have taken on increasing significance for audiences by the beginning of the 1620s.[44] Thomas Walkley seems to have been quick to realize the increasing relevance of the play to contemporary events, putting out first of all the censored text with his own political embellishments and then printing an authoritative text when he found one.[45]

As we have seen, many of the plays in which Fletcher was involved, from the early collaborations with Beaumont onward, would have made entertaining watching or reading for those who viewed court life somewhat askance, and it is perhaps useful to recall the political attitudes he expressed, most probably in 1620, in his verse letter to the countess of Huntingdon: he disparages knights, lords, and masques, and claims not to be interested "whether ytt bee true / wee shall haue warrs wth Spaine," while nonetheless adding in coy parentheses "(I wolde wee might)." His views in the letter are those of an English Protestant unhappy with aspects of the court's behavior. And many of his plays, as we have seen, reflect these views. Yet in focusing on this reading of Fletcher's political outlook as well as on his dramatic examinations of the politics of the country, I do not wish to invoke the simple, dated polarization of court and country or to suggest that there were factions in the Parliament of 1621 that already constituted some kind of coherent opposition or country party.[46] For one thing, as I hope has already become apparent, Fletcher is as much concerned in his plays with the responsibilities of the country aristocracy to their own tenants and retainers as he is with the relations of the court to provincial peers and gentry.

Nonetheless, in Fletcher's plays we can see certain embryonic structures upon which later dramatizations of political upheaval would build. Martin Butler has suggested, for example, as I have mentioned, that *Beggars' Bush* underpins several of the country plays of the 1630s. This is hardly surprising: the pervasiveness of Fletcher's style on the whole of the drama from his death to the closing of the theaters makes it inevitable that his stamp will be apparent on a substantial proportion of the specifically political plays written in that period. But the self-consciousness of the country as a political entity developed only gradually and unevenly across the 1620s, and the drama in many ways followed suit. In *Philaster,* text and illustration, we can see traces of how the play might have been seen at first performance as critical of aspects of James's policies and how its apparent political relevance grew over the subsequent decade. The 1620 and 1622 quartos in different ways demonstrate responses to the continuing and developing political engagement of Fletcher's play. Thus in the re-presentation of *Philaster* for the readership of the twenties we can see the dramatic and political processes which underpinned the dramatizations of crisis that Martin Butler and others have described in the 1630s.

5

The by-play between yokel and country gentleman in the *Philaster* quartos received something of a dramatic correlative three years later in *The Maid in the Mill*. Written in collaboration with Rowley, this play invokes the persistent themes of Fletcher's representation of political relations in the countryside, seeing the country as a locus of both threat and potential enlightenment and calm, examining the difficult question of revels and sports, and emphasizing the aggrieved individual's right to point out failures of responsibility in government. Florimel, fifteen-year-old daughter to Franio, the local miller, is snatched away from country revels by Gerasto to satisfy the desires of the lord of the manor, Count Otrante. Franio turns up at the house of Count Julio, the sponsor of the revels, to express his rage. The masque had been given by the locals in honor of the house of Julio: now, as far as Franio is concerned, this very "house hath injur'd" him.[47] Furious at Franio's outburst, Julio asks him contemptuously where he was brought up, but the miller's persistence turns his contempt to unease: "Obstreperous Carle, / If thy throats tempest could o'erturn my house, / What satisfaction were it for thy child?" (III. i, p. 30). Perhaps aware of the implications of Julio's "if," Franio presses on, emphasizing not their difference in status but their common humanity:

> Were yours the loss,
> Had you a Daughter stoln, perhaps be-whor'd,
> (For to what other end should come the thief?)
> You'ld play the Miller then, be loud and high.
> But being not a sorrow of your own,
> You have no help nor pity for another. (III. i, p. 30)

Astonishingly, the leveling subtext of this argument finds an instant correlative in Julio's anguished recollection of his own lost daughter:

> Oh, thou hast op'd a Sluce was long shut up,
> And let a floud of grief in; a buried grief

Thy voice hath wak'd again: a grief as old
As likely 'tis thy child is; friend, I tell thee,
I did once lose a Daughter. . . .
Franio: But was she stolen from you?
Julio: Yes, by devouring thieves, from whom cannot
Ever return a satisfaction:
The wild beasts had her in her swathing clothes.

(III. i, p. 30)

The country thus serves a dual role here: as the venue for theft and intended rape, and also as a locus for a certain leveling of assumed hierarchical differences.

Once Julio has wandered off to grieve quietly alone, Franio's rebelliousness resurfaces. His wife arrives to announce that she has located Florimel. Presumably in view of Julio's presence, she whispers in his ear that the girl is held at Otrante's house. Furious at this attempt at a kind of latter-day *droit de seigneur,* Franio dangerously redefines "Landlord" as "Lord of my Lands, / But not my Cattle" and threatens to sell his mill in order to buy a huge cannon (a "Roaring Meg"): "I'll batter down his house," he rages, "and make a Stewes on't" (III. i, p. 31). Despite his wife's attempts to calm him, he threatens considerable violence: "If she be the *Counts* whore, the whore's *Count* / Shall pay for it" (III. i, p. 31). By his master's actions, the miller has become masterless and has taken on the destructive potential of masterlessness.

In the midst of this dangerous talk, we learn that the king is passing through the locality on progress, and Franio and his wife determine to present him with a supplication. There is some confusion when Franio initially presents his plea to a foolish tailor who is desperate to be a courtier. This enables the king, when he arrives, to distance himself from courtly vices:

Because I am homely
Clad, in no glitt'ring suit, I am not look'd on:
Ye fools that wear gay cloaths, love to [be] gap'd at,
What are you better when your end calls on you?
Will gold preserve ye from the grave? or jewels?
Get golden Minds, and fling away your Trappings
Unto your bodies, minister warm raiments,
Wholsome and good; glitter within and spare not:
Let my [C]ourt have rich souls, their suits I weigh not.

(III. i, p. 35)

Having established his credentials with the audience, the king turns to Franio and asks him his request, and is suitably appalled at the charge against Otrante. A courtier asks if the miller is mad, prompting the first of a series of breathtakingly dangerous speeches from Franio in which he comes close to voicing the frustrations of a restless populace:

> No, no, my lord;
> I am in my wits, I am a labouring man,
> And we have seldome leisure to run mad,
> We have other business to employ our heads in,
> We have little Wit to lose too: if we complain,
> And if a heavie lo[r]d lie on [our] shoulders,
> Worse than a sack of Meal, and oppress our poverties,
> We are mad streight, and whop'd, and ty'd in fetters,
> Able to make a horse mad, as you use us,
> You are mad for nothing, and no man dare proclaim it,
> In you a wildnes is a noble trick,
> And cherish'd in ye, and all men must love it:
> Oppressions of all sorts, sit like new clothes,
> Neatly and handsomely upon your Lordships:
> And if we kick when you honors spur us,
> We are Knaves and Jades, and ready for the Justice.
> I am a true Miller. (III. i, p. 36)

The king is astonished by this outburst but is advised by one of his courtiers that Franio "is reputed for a good man / An honest and substantial fellow." Nonetheless, after a brief aside ("He speaks sence, / And to the point"), the king demands, "Must every Peasant / Upon a saucy Will affront great Lords! / All fellows (Miller?)."

This spurs Franio to still greater heights of bitter class-conscious eloquence:

> I have my reward, Sir,
> I was told one greatness would protect another,
> As beams support their fellows; now I find it:
> If't please your Grace to have me hang'd, I am ready,
> 'Tis but a Miller, and a Thief dispa[t]ch'd:
> Though I steal bread, I steal no flesh to tempt me.
> I have a wife, and't please him to have her too,
> With all my heart; 'twill make my charge the less, Sir,
> She'll hold him play awhile: I have a boy too,

> He's able to instruct his Honors hogs,
> Or rub his horse-heels: when it please his Lordship
> He may [make] him his slave too, or his bawd:
> The boy is well bred, can exhort his Sister:
> For me, the Prison, or the Pillory,
> To lose my [goods], and have mine ears cropt off;
> Whipt like a Top, and have a paper stuck before me.
> For abominable honesty to his own Daughter,
> I can endure, Sir: the Miller has a stout heart,
> [T]ough as his Toal-pin. (III. i, pp. 36–37)

Finally, when the king tells him to be absolutely sure he is right, he simply points out that even kings can suffer the same as millers (something he has learned, presumably, from Julio's hidden grief): "Your Grace may have a Daughter, think of that, Sir, / She may be fair, and she may be abused too, / A King is not exempted from these cases / Stolen from your loving care—" (III. i, p. 37). This frankness is the only way out of a situation brought on by aristocratic disrespect for duty. Otrante and Gerasto are obviously flouting their responsibilities by trying to rape Florimell. More to the point, the venue they choose for the kidnapping suggests a further dereliction of duty in respect to country festivity. Julio had cautioned the aristocrats to treat the sports not critically but appreciatively:

> Here are sports (*Dons*)
> That you must look on with a loving eye,
> And without Censure, 'less it be giving
> My countrey neighbours loves their yearly offerings
> That must not be refus'd; though't be more pain
> To the Spectator, then the painful Actor,
> 'Twill not abide no more test than the tinsel
> We clad our Masks in for an hours wearing,
> Or the Livery Lace sometimes on the cloaks
> Of a great *Don*'s Followers: I speake no further
> Than our own Countrey, Sir. (II. ii, p. 21)

There are, here and elsewhere in Fletcher's writing, certain obligations toward their countryfolk that the aristocrats must observe. Regulation of these obligations is, however, a serious problem.

In a speech before Star Chamber in 1616, King James revealed a series of worries about the uncontrollability of the country. In his

speech, he attempts to regulate the country, both to remind aristocrats such as Huntingdon, with their roots in the counties, of their
duty to the court and to force back to the country those loyal gentry
(and, for that matter, the less loyal ones, too) who would be of far
more value to the king there as regulators and controllers than they
are in London. In the speech James addresses several of the key
problems:

And now out of my owne mouth I declare vnto you, (which being in this
place, is equall to a Proclamation, which I intend likewise shortly hereafter to haue publikely proclaimed,) that the Courtiers, Citizens, and
Lawyers, and those that belong vnto them, and others as haue Pleas in
Terme time, are onely necessary persons to remaine about this Citie;
others must get them into the Countrey; For beside the hauing of the
countrey desolate, when the Gentrie dwell thus in *London,* diuers other
mischiefes arise vpon it: First, if insurrections should fall out (as was
lately seene by the *Leuellers* gathering together) what order can bee taken
with it, when the country is vnfurnished of Gentlemen to take order
with it? Next, the poore want reliefe for fault of the Gentlemens hospi-
talitie at home: Thirdly, my seruice is neglected, and the good gouern-
ment of the countrey for lacke of the principall Gentlemens presence, in
seeing to their owne businesse at home. Therefore as euery fish liues in
his owne place, some in the fresh, some in the salt, some in the mud: so
let euery one liue in his owne place, some at Court, some in the Citie,
some in the Countrey; especially at Festivall times, as Christmas and
Easter, and the rest.[48]

This speech serves as a revealing essay in Jacobean provincial
government and methods of containing possible and actual unrest.
Above all, James is concerned about the possibility of insurrection
in the country, quoting the "leveling" events of 1607 as his example, and speaks of the neglected needs of "the poore," not, it is
fairly obvious, out of philanthropic concern, but because without
the social control of private charity, there would be distinct danger
of revolt. Yet he makes remarkably little effort to mollify the very
people upon whom he relies for enforcement of provincial government. His aquatic metaphor, equating those who live in the country with fish which live in mud, seems unlikely to endear him to
the countrymen.

It is particularly interesting that in this speech, and shortly after
he has made reference to the Midlands revolt levelers, James ac-

knowledges that the need for provincial control is greatest at "Festivall times, as Christmas and Easter, and the rest." We have seen in the events of 1607 specific proof of the liberties that could be taken at holiday time: the rural riots began on May Day 1607 and came to a head on Trinity Sunday with the collaboration of townspeople whose excuse to move out into the countryside was their preparations for the festival. Festivity and sports in many ways provided a weathervane for stable relations between ruler and ruled in the countryside of Jacobean England. James was well aware of this, and in 1618, two years after his Star Chamber speech, he issued a royal proclamation on the subject that became known as *The Book of Sports* and was the subject of debate for many years. *The Book of Sports,* as Leah Marcus's book *The Politics of Mirth* has usefully demonstrated, was an attempt to incorporate marginal festivity under the sovereign gaze by giving royal sanction, to the fury of the godly, to various kinds of Sunday and holiday sports and pastimes such as morris dancing. As Marcus puts it,

[b]y placing their official stamp of approval on the old pastimes, James and [with the re-issue of the proclamation] Charles I attempted to extend royal power into an area of ambivalence and instability, to channel the equivocal status of popular festival into what we can perhaps call an official "paradox of state"—a condition of happy ambiguity in which the license and lawlessness associated with the customs could be interpreted as submission to authority.[49]

Part of the political process which included *The Book of Sports* was a new emphasis, focused on what Marcus calls "the new idealization of pastoral in the masque," on the age-old customs and honesty of the country which were to be embodied in "a return to the ancient simplicities of the countryside at the expense of urban sophistication" (70). But the ancient simplicities required surveillance, and in his Star Chamber speech—effectively, as he observes, a royal proclamation—James is ensuring his control over the landlords.

James issued *The Book of Sports* in the face of strong Puritan opposition to such activities as a way to bolster popular support for the Church of England. Radical Puritans specifically objected to the conjunction of church services and festive pastimes, regarding the latter as pagan practices diametrically opposed to any form of Christian worship, and therefore savoring of popery.[50] Such objections had been most overtly stated during Elizabeth's reign in the Marprelate pamphlets; yet the queen's response to Sunday pastimes had always been somewhat ambivalent. James, and subsequently Charles when he reissued *The Book of Sports,* jettisoned this ambivalence in their attempts to rewrite festive activities as a spectacular link between sovereignty and popular community. Thus *The Book of Sports* prescribed a series of acceptable pastimes which could legitimately follow Sunday service:

[A]s for Our good peoples lawfull Recreation, Our pleasure likewise is, That after the end of Diuine Seruice, Our good people be not disturbed, letted, or discouraged from any lawfull Recreation; Such as dauncing, either men or women, Archery for men, leaping, vaulting, or any other such harmelesse Recreation, nor from hauing of May-Games, Whitson Ales, and Morris-dances, and the setting vp of Maypoles and other sports therewith vsed, so as the same be had in due and conuenient time, without impediment or neglect of diuine Seruice.[51]

Thus for James, country festivity, sanctioned and therefore simultaneously censored, ensured the creation of a link with the court: in some way the legalizing of sports by the king contained their more anarchic potentiality.

As Marcus notes, the assumptions of *The Book of Sports* about the effects of festive activity seem to parallel certain nineteenth- and twentieth-century anthropological theories of the psychological politics of carnival, seeing such moments of contained cultural inversion simply as a steam valve built into society. From this viewpoint, the brief, temporary anarchy that expresses itself in carnival forms releases the tensions and pressures within society which might well lead to full-fledged insurrection if unchecked or unreleased. Thus, for James, country sports and pastimes, with their carnivalesque inverted worlds and playful floutings of authority, could be turned in an ostensible paradox into a control on the marginal activities of the people rather than an opportunity for lawlessness. Court poets of James's reign celebrated this inversion of the inversions and capitalized upon its further advantages. As Marcus points out, Jonson's *Love Restored,* for example, which predates *The Book of Sports* but belongs to the ideological process that led toward it, "establishes delight in such sport as an honest and praiseworthy trait ingrained in country folk and demonstrates an essential kinship between country pastimes and more lavish festivities at court," providing by turn a neat way to legitimate courtly excess by implicating popular festivity along with it.[52] Marcus quotes Lucy Hutchinson to suggest that those Puritans who hated the old pastimes were well aware of what James was doing in *The Book of Sports:*

The court itself under James she termed a "nursery of lust and intemperance" which insinuated its own nature into the countryside through James's sponsorship of public games: "To keepe the people in their deplorable security till vengeance overtook them, they were entertain'd with masks, stage playes, and sorts of ruder sports. Then began Murther, incest, Adultery, drunkennesse, swearing, fornication, and all sort of ribaldry to be no conceal'd but countenanced vices, favour'd wherever they were privately practis'd because they held such conformity with the Court example."[53]

For Hutchinson, there is little moral difference between "masks" and "sorts of ruder sports": in a strange way, she acknowledges James's theory of festive containment even while detesting the results.

The catalyst for later Fletcherian representation of the complexities of government in the country, as has already been apparent in several of the plays in which he was involved—from Theseus's tactful praise of the dire country masque in *The Two Noble Kinsmen* to Julio's exhortation to his fellow-aristocrats to "look on with a loving eye, / And without censure" at country sports in *The Maid in the Mill*—was his long-standing interest in the politics of festivity. He takes issue, I would suggest, with the belief that the manifestations of carnival could be contained in such a way that they would act as a steam valve and thereby paradoxically (for all their apparent flouting of authority) reinforce sovereignty. His position seems to be embodied in an emphasis on the *incongruity* of court requirements and country festivity: quite the opposite statement from that expressed by king and Puritan and dramatized by Ben Jonson. Where, for example, Jonson's response in the masque is to ensure that the antimasque is quelled, demonstrating the ease with which authority can reassert control over festive anarchy, Fletcher's response is to suggest that carnival is always likely to be unresponsive to authority, and that a process of negotiation in the country will be essential to successful government. From Fletcher's mature pen, carnival occasions provide a base from which he can question certain strategies of state in the context of the country. Ironically, his criticism takes as its vehicle a celebration of sports which the king himself has sanctioned.

It is not until 1618 and the publication of *The Book of Sports* that Fletcher's attitude to festivity becomes consistent. We have seen the genuine fears embodied in semi-humorous reports of riotous crowds in *Henry VIII* and *Wit Without Money,* and it is worth dwelling upon two scenes from early solo plays to develop a sense of the unease in Fletcher's dramatizations of carnival from the beginning of his career. The scenes in question come from *The Woman's Prize* and *Monsieur Thomas,* two solo plays from 1611 or thereabouts.[54] In *Monsieur Thomas,* Launcelot gleefully describes a scene of riot:

> O the noyse,
> The noyse we made. . . .
> A fellow rayling out of a loophole there,
> And his mouth stopt with durt. . . .
> The gentleman himselfe, yong Master *Thomas,*
> Invirond with his furious Mermidons,
> The fiery Fidler, and my selfe; now singing,
> Now beating at the doore, there parlying,
> Courting at that window, at the other scalling,
> And all these several noyses to two Trenchers,
> Strung with a bottome of browne thred. . . .
> Nor here sir,
> Gave we the frolicke over: though at length
> We quit the Ladies Skonce on composition
> But to the silent streetes we turn'd our furies:
> A sleeping watchman here we stole the shooes from,
> There made a noyse, at which he wakes, and followes:
> The streetes are durty, takes a Queene-hithe cold,
> Hard cheese, and that choakes him o' Monday next:
> Windowes, and signes we sent to *Erebus;*
> When having let the pigs loose in out parishes,
> O the brave cry we made as high as Algate!
> Downe comes a Constable, and the Sow his Sister
> Most trayterously tramples upon Authority,
> There a whole stand of rug gownes rowted mainly

And the Kings peace put to flight: a purblind pig here
Runs me his head into the Admiral's Lanthorne,
Out goes the light, and all turnes to confusion:
A Potter rises, to enquire this passion,
A Boare imbost takes sanctuary in his shop,
When twenty dogs rush after, we still cheering:
Down goes the pots, and pipkins, down the pudding pans,
The creame bols cry revenge here, there the candlesticks.

(IV. ii. 17–20, 22–54)

There is something almost lyrical about the description of the riot—"to the silent streetes we turn'd our furies"—yet that fury sees "the Kings peace put to flight," and behind the "cheering" and the vengeful "creame bols" lies a certain "trayterous[ ] trampl[ing] upon Authority."

There is a description of a similar scene in *The Woman's Prize,* Fletcher's mock sequel to *The Taming of the Shrew,* given by Petruchio's servants Jaques and Pedro. Describing the arrival of the Regiment of Women, Jaques expresses his genuine fear of them in carnivalesque terms, introducing a series of double-entendres and misogynistic metaphors into his narrative. "Arme, arme, out with your weapons," he cries, "For all the women in the Kingdom's on ye: / They swarm like waspes, and nothing can destroy 'em," and he and Pedro take it in turns to provide a rather disjointed description of the scene:

Pedro: There are more women, marching hitherward,
In rescue of my Mistris, then ere turn'd taile
At Sturbridge Faire; and I believe, as fiery.
Jaques: The forlorn-hope's led by a Tanners wife,
I know her by her hide; a desperate woman:
She flead her husband in her youth, and made
Raynes of his hide to ride the Parish, her plackett
Lookes like the straights of Gibraltar, still wider
Downe to the gulphe, all sun-burnt Barbary
Lyes in her breech; take 'em all together,
They are a genealogy of Jennets, gotten
And born thus, by the boysterous breath of husbands;
They serve sure, and are swift to catch occasion,
(I meane their foes, or husbands) by the fore-locks,
And there they hang like favours; cry they can,
But more for Noble spight, then feare: and crying

124

Like the old Gyants that were foes to Heaven,
They heave ye stoole on stoole, and fling main Potlids
Like massie rocks, dart ladles, tossing Irons,
And tongs like Thunderbolts, till overlayd,
They fall beneath the waight; yet still aspiring
At those Emperious Codsheads, that would tame 'em.
There's nere a one of these, the worst and weakest,
(Choose where you will) but dare attempt the raysing
Against the soveraigne peace of Puritans,
A May-pole, and a Morris, maugre mainly
Their zeale, and Dudgeon-daggers: and yet more,
Dares plant a stand of battring Ale against 'em,
And drinke 'em out o'th Parish. . . .
Pedro: There's one brought in the Beares against the Cannons
Of two church-wardens, made it good, and fought 'em
& in the churchyard after even song.
Jaques: Another, to her everlasting fame, erected
Two Ale-houses of ease: the quarter sessions
Running against her roundly; in which businesse
Two of the disannullers lost their night-caps:
A third stood excommunicate by the cudgell.
The Cunstable, to her eternall glory,
Drunke hard, and was converted, and the victor.
Pedro: Then are they victualed with pies and puddings,
(The trappings of good stomacks) noble Ale
the true defendor, Sawsages, and smoak'd ones,
If need be, such as serve for Pikes; and Porke,
(Better the Jewes never hated:) here and there
A bottle of Metheglin, a stout Britaine
That will stand to 'em; what else they want, they war for.
(II. iv. 33–35, 39–85)

Jaques's description of the "raysing" of the Maypole offers a fragmented sense of attitudes toward festive activities in the decade
prior to *The Book of Sports.* Such behaviour is seen both to spite
Puritans and to subvert constables, local figures of sovereign authority.[55] These narratives attempt by way of the grotesque humor
of the carnivalesque to contain the genuine threat they describe,
yet, for all their mirth, they remain too vivid to contain fully the
danger of the anarchic behavior they describe. They suggest a
radical ambivalence in Fletcher's dramatic portrayal of carnival
which he does not successfully resolve until 1618, when he brings

together his conflicting responses to *The Book of Sports* in his romantic tragicomedy, *Women Pleased*.

Women Pleased is an uneven play which focuses upon the romantic concerns of interpretation and magic. Textual evidence would suggest that the version of the play printed in the 1647 Folio may well be a revision of an earlier play either by Fletcher himself or by an unknown dramatist.[56] The version we have, for various reasons, however, "must be considered as of a play in the repertory of the King's Men in 1619–23."[57] Revision post–1618—in the wake of *The Book of Sports*—is a distinct possibility, especially considering the thematic concerns, the oddness and apparent arbitrariness of act 4, scene 1 of the play, the scene which most clearly responds to *The Book of Sports*. In this scene we are pitched directly into a pastoral world, and it is difficult to read or interpret the action outside the immediate context of the *Book of Sports* controversy. The protagonist Silvio has been wandering, seeking a valid interpretation of the riddle he has been set. "What labour and what travell have I runne through?" he asks, frustrated,

> And through what Cities to absolve this Riddle?
> Diviners, Dreamers, Schoolemen, deep Magitians,
> All have I tride, and all give severall meanings,
> And from all hope of future happiness,
> To this place am I come at length, the country,
> The people simple, plaine, and harmlesse witty,
> Whose honest labours Heaven rewards with plenty
> Of Corne, Wine, Oyle, which they againe, as thankfull,
> To their new Cropps, new pastimes celebrate,
> And crowne their joyfull harvests with new voyces;
> By a rich farmer here I am entertain'd,
> And rank't among the number of his Servants,
> Not guessing what I am, but what he would have me,
> Here may be so much wit (though much I feare it)
> To undo this knotty question; and would to heaven
> My fortunes had been hatch'd with theirs, as innocent,
> And never knowne a pitch above their plainnesse.[58]

Seeking a single, full interpretation of his "knotty question" rather than the uncertainties of "severall meanings," Silvio has had to abandon the learning of cities and look for enlightenment in the simplicities of the country. And his straightforward eulogy of the "plainnesse" of the country specifically relates the "honest . . .

plainnesse" of country folk to their harvest "pastimes." As he is wondering if these people will be able, despite their lack of sophistication, to solve his riddle for him, the buffoon Soto comes in, as we have seen, trying to decipher some writing which turns out to be a proclamation on his life, the proclamation that offers him a glimpse of the "reason" in "treason."

No longer simply Claudio's servant, Soto turns out to be the son of the "rich farmer" whose servant the disguised Silvio has become. The city order of master and servant is thus instantly inverted. Soto rebukes the "melancholly" Silvio for being "unmorriss'd" at carnival time, and reminds him of the respect due to him at this festive time. "[A]m not I here, / My fathers eldest Son," he asks, "[a] better man than my father by far, Lord of this Harvest, Sir, / And shall a man of my place want attendance?" (34–37). He observes that Silvio's failure to respect the inverted rules of carnival may "breed an insurrection amongst us" (43), and accuses Silvio of being in love, clamining to know the object of his desire. We later discover that this brief hint at an admirer of Silvio's is a reference to the magical and disguised presence of the vanished female protagonist Belvidere. Here, in a parody of the unspoken *droit de seigneur* of postfeudal society, Soto offers to "speak a good word for" him. "Thou shalt have my Lordships countenance to her," Soto promises him, slyly adding, "May be I have had a snap my self, may be ay, may be no, / We Lords are allow'd a little more" (49–52). This parody of sovereign authority acts in a manner akin to the coronation sequence of *Beggar's Bush,* to deflate and criticize easy equations of court and country festivity.

The people are about to begin the morris dance when a captain comes in, demanding that they arm and come to the state's defence against an invasion by the duke of neighboring Siena. He cries:

> Arme, honest friends, arme suddenly and bravely,
> And with your antient resolutions follow me;
> Look how the Beacons show like comets, your poor neighbours
> Run maddingly affrighted through the Villages;
> *Syennas* Duke is up, burnes all before him,
> And with his sword, makes thousand mothers childlesse. (95–96)

Soto, however, is unimpressed, retorting with a simple question: "What's this to our Morrisdancers?" and adding, "There's ne're a Duke in Christendome but loves a May-game" (97, 98), and ask-

ing, "Cannot they let us dance in our owne defence here?" (90).
The captain tries again, urging the farmer to "put your Son on [a
horse], / And arme him well i'th States name, I command ye" (99–
100), yet Soto, completely oblivious to the authority the captain
claims, replies in apparent shock at the soldier's rudeness:

> [T]his is strange, Master Captaine,
> You cannot be content to spoile our sport here,
> Which I do not think your Worship's able to answer,
> But you must set us together by the ears, with I know not who to?
> We are for the bodily part o'th dance. (102–6)

Thus, in the "bodily part o'th dance," the "lower bodily principle"
of carnival contradicts the claims of state on the loyalties of the
countrymen.[59]

The captain, seeing his authority inexplicably flouted, announces that "[t]his is no time to foole," and says "I shall return ye
else, / A rebell to the Generall, State, and Duchesse" (107–8).
Soto still refuses to go, and his father tries offering a bribe which
the Captain refuses. The crux of the matter—which authority is
paramount, the state's or the carnival's—is revealed in Soto's question: "Are ye a man? will ye cast away a May-Lord? / Shall all the
wenches in the Country curse ye?" (114–15). Moreover, this question goes unanswered, since it is deflected by Silvio's sudden offering of himself as substitute. Like a good patriotic hero in a Red
Bull play, he says, "Let me have Horse, and good Armes, ile serve
willingly, / And if I shrinke a foot of ground, Hell take me" (118–
19). The Captain is happy to accept this offer of service; for his
part, Soto hints that Silvio could well be a "May-Lord" himself in
the future. But Silvio simply replies: "Dance you, Ile fight, Sir"
(128). Here in the country, then, there would appear to be room for
two parallel yet hardly compatible realms; at the same time we can
detect a certain ironic acknowledgment of congruence between a
country obsessed with sports and a court with dancing.

If the heroism Silvio shows is not already undercut by the
conflicting claims of Soto's carnival, the fact that the dance simply
continues as soon as the captain and Silvio are out of sight seems to
confirm all the problems of festive irresponsibility. As soon as the
villagers turn back to their dancing, one of their number, a shoe-
maker called Bomby, who is to dance as the Hobby-Horse, decides

he cannot carry on. Bomby, it would seem, has become a Puritan of some sort through his "wives instructions," and he tells himself to "defie these sports" (135, 137). "This Beast of *Babylon*," he announces, "I will never back againe, / His pace is sure prophane, and his lewd wihies / The Songs of *Hymyn,* and *Gymyn,* in the wildernesse" (138–40). The farmer has obviously heard it all before. "Fie neighbour *Bomby,* in your fits againe," he sighs, saying that his "zeale swets" (141–42). But Bomby is not to be stopped now, and he describes the Hobby-Horse as "unseemely" and "lew'd," "[a]nd got at *Rome* by the Popes Coach-Horses," adding that "[h]is mother was the Mare of ignorance" (145–47).

Soto intervenes in a rage, declaring the honesty of the Hobby-Horse's lineage, and provoking a long diatribe from Bomby, expressed in heavy-handed Puritanese, in the course of which he throws off his Hobby-Horse costume:

> I do defie thee, and thy foot-cloth too,
> And thell thee to thy face, this prophaine riding
> I feele it in my conscience, and I dare speake it,
> This unedified ambling, hath brought a scourge upon us,
> This Hobby-horse sincerity we liv'd in
> War, and the sword of slaughter: I renounce it,
> And put the Beast off; thus, the Beast poluted,
> And now no more shall Hope-on-high *Bomby*
> Follow the painted Pipes of worldly pleasures,
> And with the wicked daunce the Devills measures;
> Away thou pamper'd jade of vanity,
> Stand at the Livery of lewd delights now,
> And eat the provender of prickear'd folly,
> My daunce shall be to the pipe of persecution. (154–67)[60]

Soto is enraged by this outburst, and he expresses his anger in a threat which mocks the "mechanick" preacher's brand of personal Protestantism:

> If thou do'st this there shall be no more Shooe-mending,
> Every man shall have a speciall care of his owne soule:
> And in his pocket carry his two Confessors,
> His Lingell, and his Nawle. (177–80)

Bomby retaliates by attacking Sunday sports—" 'Twas the fore-running sin brought in those Tilt-staves, / They brandish 'gainst the Church, the Devill calls May-poles" (182–83)—thereby amplifying his earlier claim that it is pastimes and sports which have brought down vengeance, in the form of the duke of Siena's invasion, on the villagers. The farmer orders him to put his costume back on, but he spits on it and describes it as the "Beast: that signifi'd destruction, / Fore-shew'd ith' falls of Monarchies" (189–90). This is too much for Soto, who orders him to put the Hobby-Horse costume back on, unless he wants to find himself stocked for refusing. Bomby reluctantly succumbs, a martyr to his brethren's cause.

As a critique of Puritan opposition to festivity, this part of the scene is remarkable, and not least for its ambivalences. Puritan objections to pastimes are obviously given very short shrift. Bomby is an early Prynne-figure, who sees dancing as "the Devills measures" (163), and through him the language and idiosyncrasies of Puritan subculture are mocked. Yet there is a certain equation of the theological awkwardnesses of Roman Catholicism and low Protestantism, not least in Soto's mind when he merges Anglican objections to the sectarian tendencies in antinomianism ("Every man shall have a speciall care of his owne soule") with humor at what might seem to be Catholic idolatry ("in his pocket carry his two Confessors, / His Lingell, and his Nawle"). Moreover, Bomby is no Jonsonian Puritan, an unchanging hypocrite from birth, despite his reference to his pious renomination as "Hope-on-high Bomby." After all, he learned his piety from his "wives learned lectures," and the others can recall his fondness for sports before his conversion to sectarianism. Even Soto, in an uncharacteristic moment of gentleness, points out that dancing as the Hobby-Horse is "a thing thou has lov'd with all thy heart *Bomby* / And would'st do still but for the round-breecht Brothers" (197–98). And some of his remarks might well engender a degree of sympathy: it would be difficult for the audience, brought up almost as much on Foxe's *Acts and Monuments*—to which, of course, Fletcher's grandfather had contributed—as on the Bible, not to feel just a little sorry for his plight when he observes that his "daunce shall be to the pipe of persecution" (167).

But Bomby's characteristic tendency to quote from Revelation as often as possible leads him to a moment of potential political danger. His conviction that there is a direct relationship between the invasion and the dance leads him to suggest that the Beast (by denotation the Hobby-Horse, but by connotation the Beast of Revelation) "signifi'd destruction, / Fore-shew'd ith' falls of Monarchies" (189–90). For all the satiric potential in the language and zeal of Puritanism, we are not allowed to forget the darker side of their rejection of worldly matters. And, despite the obvious mockery of Puritanism and Puritanism's objections to country pastimes in the scene, this connection between sports and judgment is uncomfortably close to the bone in view of Soto's earlier rejection of the state's authority in favor of the dance. In this scene, Fletcher manages subtly to interweave satire against the more outspoken Puritan objections to the legitimation of Sunday pastimes in *The Book of Sports* with an implicit warning that there was a certain truth in the Puritans' recognition of the potential for treason in the world-upside-down of festive activity. Fletcher seems on the one hand to agree with James's rejection of the motives and the language of those opposed outright to sports and pastimes, yet on the other to question the possibility, implicit in James's theory of carnival, of an alignment of festival and state. As the relationship of the morris dance to the call-to-arms in this play suggests, the inverted hierarchy intrinsic to festivity may well assert itself against the demands of state and of monarchy, leaving as the only option a mediated settlement. Absolutes are again qualified in favor of a certain complexity and a degree of unease.

FOUR

Collaboration

I

The ocular proof of the censor's intervention in the writing of *Sir John Van Olden Barnavelt* serves to remind us of the broadly (and not always voluntarily or intentionally) collaborative way in which drama was produced in the Jacobean period. It also suggests, as does Fuller's anecdote about collaborative plotting, an intimate connection between collaboration and troublesome politics. The method and the politics of Fletcher's plays demonstrate just such an intimacy. In his analyses of political life, especially the political life of the country, Fletcher appears aware of the essentially collaborative nature of rule, the inadequacy of absolutism, and the correspondent need for a politics of involvement. As we have seen, many of his plays demonstrate the potential energy of popular unrest in the face of failed responsibility, and they dramatize the dangers inherent in political instability. The politics represented in and by these plays are at once collaborative, consensual, and conservative, seeking wider involvement in political processes and rejecting absolutist claims, yet resting on an established hierarchical framework: exactly the kind of politics in favor at the Huntingdons' seat at Ashby-de-la-Zouche. But it is not only his patronage environment but also his professional practice as a playwright that orients Fletcher toward a politics of involvement, a politics of collaboration.

It has become something of a critical commonplace that Renaissance plays were collaboratively written in the most basic sense that the individual actors, the particular theater, the financial exigencies of the moment, and the political, moral, or economic demands upon playwright and company were all as much responsible for the received text as the playwright himself. As G. E. Bentley has phrased it,

[e]very performance in the commercial theatres from 1590 to 1642 was itself essentially a collaboration: it was the joint accomplishment of dramatists, actors, musicians, costumers, prompters (who made alterations in the original manuscript), and—at least in the later theatres—managers.[1]

Despite this acknowledgment, most Renaissance drama studies nonetheless continue to assume the single author in a way that would have made Ben Jonson happy. The norm to which Jonson attempted to give flesh in his *Workes* was that of a single dominant author entirely determining a fully unified and coherent dramatic text. Yet a decade earlier he had acknowledged that alterations were needed to erase the traces of collaboration. In his introduction to *Sejanus,* he admitted that

this Booke, in all nu[m]bers, is not the same with that which was acted on the publike Stage, wherein a second Pen had good share: in place of which I haue rather chosen, to put weaker (and no doubt lesse pleasing) of mine own, then to defraud so happy a *Genius* of his right, by my lothed vsurpation.[2]

It is apparent that Jonson suppressed mention altogether of early collaborative plays such as *Hot Anger Soon Cold* and *Robert II, or the Scot's Tragedy.*[3] Collaboration appears to have been something of an inevitability even for one as classically-minded as Jonson. And if this is true of Jonson's texts, it is much more obviously so of Fletcher's.

Where Jonson fought for authorial privilege and prerogative, and worked to deny the possibility of collaboration by omitting certain texts and any mention of collaboration in his grand, monolithic gesture, the *Workes* of 1616, and in his obvious practical discomfort with his own collaboration on masques with Inigo Jones, Fletcher remained doggedly a collaborator first and foremost. He quite clearly *preferred* to collaborate. As the dramatic quality of, say, the solo plays written for the Christmas season of 1621 shows, there was no need for Fletcher, at least in the later part of his career, to work with others: he must have chosen to do so. He seems to have been financially secure; when Field, Daborne, and Massinger write from jail to beg money of Henslowe, they refer to Fletcher as a collaborator of theirs, but he is not with them in prison.[4] He wrote his solo plays in the gaps between established partnerships, not as a final grand achievement once he became successful. He was even partially involved in a dramatic collaboration with his friend Ben Jonson, of all people.[5]

Yet Jonson avoided such joint activity as soon as he could afford to, attempting to apply the same strictures to the authorship of a play as to the texture of a poem, which, for him, should be "like a Table, upon which you may runne your finger without rubs, and your nayle cannot find a joynt; not horrid, rough, wrinckled, gaping, or chapt."[6] Collaboration, by its nature supplementary, belongs to the stubbornly unclassical, multiple, and generative aspect of drama which Jonson, despite the ongoing evidence of his own work, seems always to have resisted. But it must be remembered both that Jonson was unique in his concern with the texts of his plays and that his efforts to disguise joint authorship were thoroughly atypical.[7] He is, as Bentley points out, "the only active dramatist among Shakespeare's contemporaries who expended anything remotely approaching this effort on his play texts."[8] Fletcher, on the other hand, seems not to have concerned himself with final authorial or authoritative versions of the texts of his plays. Perhaps he recognized the incongruousness of asserting authority over intrinsically collaborative material. He seems to have been known for a certain modesty and restraint: a very different reputation from that of Jonson. Lowin and Taylor, in their dedication printed in the 1652 text of *The Wild-Goose Chase,* explain that "[t]he play was of so Generall a receiv'd Acceptance, that (he *Himself* a *Spectator*) we have known him un-concern'd, and to have wisht it had been none of His; He, as well as the *throng'd Theatre* (in despight of his innate Modesty) Applauding this rare issue of his Brain."[9]

Of the fifty-two extant plays in which Cyrus Hoy's investigations would suggest Fletcher had a hand, only fifteen can be attributed to Fletcher working alone.[10] He wrote something like ten plays in the company of Beaumont, three with Shakespeare, six with Field, one with Rowley, and maybe nineteen with Massinger. Several of these peripherally involved others. Hoy's work, as well as the work of Oliphant, Hensman, Bentley, Hope, and others, in parallel with that of Lake in Middleton studies, has gone a long way toward the appropriate allocation of writing shaares in partic-

134

ular plays.[11] But the linguistic methods they espouse have their limitations, and it remains exceptionally difficult to make clear assumptions about intention and authorial dominance in all of these plays. The collaborative process—meeting in taverns to agree on plots, writing separate scenes apart and then coming together to edit, handing material to one playwright to finish and copy out—is a hermeneutical nightmare. It is in fact difficult to achieve an appropriate working definition of collaboration. Fletcher has always been seen to break the Aristotelian rules for unified drama and to defy the requirement to paste over the cracks. This is exemplified simply enough by the number of modifications and wholesale rewritings that were produced in the late seventeenth and early eighteenth centuries. Rochester, for example, set about revising *Valentinian* because he considered it poorly structured. Robert Wolseley's preface to Rochester's version of the play observes that

[a]s Imperfect as *Valentinian* is left . . . my Lord has made it a Play, which he did not find it, the chief business of it (as *Fletcher* had contriv'd it) ending with the *Fourth Act,* and a new Design, which has no kind of relation to the other, is introduc'd in the *Fifth,* contrary to a Fundamental Rule of the Stage.[12]

Yet Rochester's rewriting is akin in its way to much of Fletcher's work as a collaborator, since, according to Hoy's findings alone, Fletcher himself very often returned to material shelved years earlier, often well after the death of his then co-author, in order to produce a new play from the fragments. Thus plays which for various reasons can date only from late in Fletcher's career, such as *The Noble Gentleman* and *Love's Cure,* appear nonetheless to contain the hand of Beaumont, dead for nearly a decade.[13] This kind of collaboration with the dead is characteristic of Fletcher in other ways, most notably in his insistence upon reworking Shakespearean material and returning to generic and thematic questions first broached in actual collaborative work years earlier. In light of such complications, I would contend that there has as yet been no approach to the reading of Renaissance drama which deals adequately with the collaborative processes which characterize the writing in which Fletcher and every other Jacobean playwright was involved.

2

Astonishingly little work has been done until very recently on the process and nature of collaborative writing in any period of literary history. Most critics share a very negative attitude toward collaboration. Although the *Oxford English Dictionary* makes it clear that the word collaboration acquired the truly negative connotation it has for us only in 1940 and 1941, when it was first used specifically to describe voluntary, treasonable assistance given to an occupying enemy, the word appears nonetheless to have been used pejoratively in a literary context for centuries, thus presumably paving the way for its wartime usage. We have already seen the way in which collaborative plotting led to accusations of treason in Fuller's anecdote. Since the reopening of the theaters, critics have never been comfortable with the collaborative writing technique employed widely in the first quarter of the seventeenth century, exemplified in the collaboration of Beaumont and Fletcher. This has had a lasting negative impact upon criticism of the work of these playwrights. Even at the time of the 1647 Folio, the process of collaboration seems to have puzzled the commenders. Jasper Maine's commendatory verse, for example, in trying simultaneously to explain and dismiss the problem of joint writing, relies upon the unifying perception of the reader:

> Whether one did contrive, the other write,
> Or one fram'd the plot, the other did indite;
> Whether one found the matter, th'other dresse,
> Or the one disposed what th'other did expresse;
> Where e're your parts betweene your selves lay, we
> In all things which you did but one thred see. [14]

By 1691, Gerard Langbaine's anecdote about Fletcher's writing habits suggests a certain distaste rather than just puzzlement:

I have either read, or been inform'd, (I know not well whether) that 'twas generally Mr. *Fletcher*'s practice, after he had finish'd Three Acts of a Play to shew them to the Actors, and after they had agreed on Terms, he huddled up the two last without that care that behoov'd him. [15]

R. C. Rowland comments that in view of the relatively late date of this anecdote and Langbaine's own admitted vagueness about the provenance of the tale it would be unwise to take it as gospel, yet he adds that, "in the curious structure of these plays there is something strongly suggestive of such a practice" (Rowland 331).

It may be possible, though, to read Langbaine's anecdote in a different light. If we accept that the Jacobean playwrights were accustomed to the process of collaboration and, moreover, also accept recent arguments which view the process in a more positive light—suggesting that collaboration was a careful negotiation of scenes and characters in which there was an ongoing and amiable revision process—it is possible to see Langbaine's comment as a criticism of *careless* collaboration rather than of collaboration per se.[16] At the same time, it is equally possible that Langbaine's attitude is the more familiar one which assumes that disunity, which can only be bad, must automatically follow from collaborative writing. This is obviously the presumption of later criticism. For Coleridge, the collaborations of Beaumont and Fletcher were merely "mechanic" while Shakespeare's plays were "organic." He held that "the plays of Beaumont and Fletcher are mere aggregations without unity," constructed "just as a man might fit together a quarter of an orange, a quarter of an Apple, and the like of a Lemon and a Pomegranate, and make it look like one round diverse-coloured fruit."[17]

One curious historical exception to the general rule of silence or distaste on the subject of collaboration, however, is an essay by Brander Matthews called "The Art and Mystery of Collaboration," which prefaced his collection of collaborative stories entitled *With My Friends: Tales Told in Partnership*, published in 1891.[18] Matthews's "principle of collaboration" denies the role of the "disintegrator" (to use E. K. Chambers's tellingly disparaging term for those who seek to determine the identities of the hands involved in collaborative work) from the outset.[19] "In a genuine collaboration," Matthews tells us, "when the joint work is a true chemical union and not a mere mechanical mixture, it matters little who holds the pen" (7). After all, he claims, the question "what was the part of each partner in the writing of the book?" can hardly ever be answered: "even the collaborators themselves are at a loss to specify their own contributions" (1–2). He points out that collaboration "has been most frequent and most fertile among dramatists" (11) rather than poets or novelists, and explains this by means of the level of artifice required to construct a play. The controlling metaphor of Matthews's argument, as will already have been apparent, is sexual, matrimonial. "Collaboration is a sort of marriage" (5), Matthews tells us, and describes the production of the collaborative text from pregnancy to parenthood. Thus, "[t]he putting down on paper of the situation and the character is but the clothing of the babe already alive and kicking" (7). Then the question of legitimacy arises: "Who shall declare whether the father or the mother is the real parent of a child?" (9). And if there are problems, if "the partnership is unprofitable and unnatural," then the disgruntled partner "had best get a divorce as soon as may be" (14–15). Finally, Matthews announces that he "cannot forego the malign pleasure of quoting . . . Mr. Andrew Lang's insidious suggestion to 'young men entering on the life of letters.' He advises them 'to find an ingenious, and industrious, and successful partner; stick to him, never quarrel with him, and do not survive him' " (29).

Matthews's language makes some of the recent claims made by critic Wayne Koestenbaum about the nature of collaborative writing seem self-evident. Koestenbaum has mapped the misogynistic, homoerotic fin de siècle world to which Andrew Lang belonged (perhaps at its most striking in his barely known collaboration with H. Rider Haggard, *The World's Desire*) as part of his recent analysis of what he calls the "erotics of male literary collaboration."[20] He celebrates collaboration, rejecting the attitude that presumes collaborative works to be "promiscuous and unnatural" (1), and he outlines the essential differences that mark collaborative writing:

Collaborative works are intrinsically *different* than books written by one author alone; even if both names do not appear, or one writer eventually produces more material, the decision to collaborate determines the work's contours, and the way it can be read. Books with two authors are specimens of a relation, and show writing to be a quality of motion and exchange, not a fixed thing. (2)

Koestenbaum frequently echoes Matthews's concerns, not least in his personal rejection of the intricacies of attribution: "I am uninterested in apportioning credit or blame, and will not attempt to decide which writer, in a twosome, was responsible for specific passages or for the final product" (2). Koestenbaum's interests lie with literature between 1885 and 1922, since the effects of the Labouchère Amendment (under which Oscar Wilde was impris-

oned for "gross indecency") were, he claims, to shape male behavior in that period and to have a marked effect on the literary
representation of homosexuality from then on. It follows from this
focus that Koestenbaum's "theory of male collaboration" is one
which concentrates on the psychopathology of homoeroticism.
"Collaborators," he claims, "express homoeroticism and they strive
to conceal it," and he employs the term "double talk" as an expression which "embodies collaboration's evasions" (3). His paradigm,
developed primarily from a synthesis of psychoanalytic and feminist methodologies, but principally from the ground-breaking
work of Eve Kosofsky Sedgwick, is "that men who collaborate
engage in a metaphorical sexual intercourse, and that the text they
balance between them is alternately the child of their sexual union,
and a shared woman" (3).[21] Thus for Koestenbaum the collaborative text is "half pathological case history, half egalitarian intellec-
tual dialogue" (4). He does, however, admit the problems of wider
application of his theory:

By beginning with Freud, and relying, throughout, on his vocabulary, I
am discussing not only acts of literary collaboration in general, but a particular sort of writing relationship that existed between men who were
Freud's contemporaries, who were keenly aware of the ascendancy of
female authority, and who shared his conviction that creativity was most
powerfully released in heated male colloquy. The kind of quasierotic
male collaboration that I describe was a cohesive wave in literary and
cultural history. (4)

Direct application of Koestenbaum's theories to another period
would thus seem seriously circumscribed.

Nonetheless, the partnership of Beaumont and Fletcher in many
ways appears perfect material for this kind of reading. Their sexuality has long been a matter for interpretive unease. Sir John
Berkenhead, in his dedicatory verse for the first Beaumont and
Fletcher folio, trying to cope with the collaborative nature of the
text ("Each Piece is wholly Two, yet never splits") reaches an
awkwardly sexual conclusion:

> What strange Production is at last displaid,
> (Got by Two Fathers, without Female aide)
> Behold, two *Masculines* espous'd each other,
> Wit and the World were born without a *Mother*.[22]

The bluntest commentary on the playwrights' sexuality is Aubrey's brief life of Beaumont, which appears to insinuate bisexuality.[23] Aubrey reports that "[t]here is a wonderfull consimility of phansey between [Mr. Francis Beaumont] and Mr. John Fletcher, which caused that dearnesse of friendship between them" (95). He goes on to outline their domestic situation:

They lived together on the Banke side, not far from the Play-house, both batchelors; lay together—from Sir James Hales, etc.; had one wench in the house between them, which they did so admire; the same cloathes and cloake, &c., betweene them.[24]

Aubrey is thus mischievous enough to reify and domesticate the collaborative relationship, and to imply a certain degree of sexual ambiguity, though he appears uneasy about their "lying together" since he feels obliged to cite both an authority (one difficult to pursue) and an et cetera. But if we simply acknowledge Koestenbaum's assertion that collaborators "engage in a metaphorical sexual intercourse" and "balance between them" a text which may be read as "a shared woman," then Aubrey's sketch would appear prime material for such a reading.

Nonetheless, the caveat about applications of the theory to texts prior to the period examined in Koestenbaum's book must be heeded. It remains the case that a coherent, generally applicable theory of collaboration has yet to be written. Part of the problem must be the remit of such a project. How does one define collaboration? With both Matthews and Koestenbaum, as a text with two authors? Or must we acknowledge a broader definition, which acknowledges a certain fluidity of boundary, and allows for inclusion of nonauthorial yet nonetheless shaping voices in the hermeneutic of collaboration, including various aspects of influence and environment? I would suggest that any exclusive focus on intimate partnerships of two is in many ways inappropriate for analysis of Jacobean collaborative writing. For Matthews,

[n]othing of real value is likely to be manufactured by a joint-stock company of unlimited authorship. The literary partner-ships whose paper sells on 'change at par have but two members. It is this association of two, and of two only, to which we refer generally when we speak of collaboration. In fact, literary collaboration might be defined, fairly enough, as "the union of two writers for the production of one book."

This is, of a truth, the only collaboration worthy of serious criticism, the only one really pregnant and vital. (5)

The metaphor of pregnancy again suggests the latent sexuality of Matthews's argument, but it is a reading which, if invoked in the interpretation of Jacobean drama, would deny the material details of collaborative dramatic writing at that time by overprivileging the intimacy required for collaborative production.

There is no need to romanticize the role of collaboration in Jacobean drama. As Kathleen McLuskie has phrased it,

Jacobean dramatists collaborated for the same reason as Hollywood scriptwriters: they were the employees of a booming entertainment industry which demanded a steady output of actable material from which a repertory could be built. [25]

She quotes various examples of the way in which collaborations were constructed. In the lawsuit which followed in the wake of the collaborative play *The Late Murder of the Son upon the Mother, or Keep the Widow Waking* (1624), for example, Thomas Dekker outlined his writing role as "two sheetes of paper conteyning the first Act . . . and a speech in the Last Scene of the Last Act"; and McLuskie adds that she assumes that the other collaborators— Ford, Rowley, and Webster—had similar remits. [26]

Bertha Hensman quotes a number of similar pieces of evidence about the practicalities of collaboration. Henslowe's diaries and papers alone demonstrate how habitual a practice this was; Henslowe "acted as a middleman between playwrights and the various dramatic companies in London" between 1595 and 1614. Robert Daborne, for example, explains in June 1613 why he has not produced a particular play for Henslowe, and in doing so reveals the multiplicity of projects in hand at a given moment:

I have not only labord my own play which shall be ready before they [the actors] come over [to Oxford] but given Cyrill Tourneur an act of ye Arreignment of london to write y^t we may have y^t likewise ready for them. [27]

A year later, Nathan Field wrote to the entrepreneur:

Mr Dawborne and J, have spent a greate deale of time on conference about this plotte, wch will make as beneficiall a play as hath come these seauen yeares. Jt is out of his loue he detaines it for vs, onely x^l is desired in hand, for w^{ch}, we will be bound to bring you in the play finish'd vpon the first day of August.[28]

It is useful to remember that one variable but inevitably important factor in the collaborative process was economic: the evidence of the *Diary* would seem to suggest that the playwrights had Henslowe breathing down their necks as often as not. Such financial pressure is likely to have been a considerable feature in the playwrights' lives, even the more successful and established. Hensman, it should be added, uses such evidence to suggest that when a play has clear-cut evidence of collaborative effort divided between scenes, this indicates the customary well-defined division of labor characteristic of professional collaboration (she includes, of plays in which John Fletcher was involved, *The False One, The Knight of Malta, The Double Marriage, The Custom of the Country,* and *The Little French Lawyer* in this category); and that when there are "no clear-cut lines of demarcation of responsibility" (9), the evidence suggests that these plays (including, of Fletcher's, *The Queen of Corinth, The Lovers' Progress, A Very Woman,* and *The Bloody Brother*) are revisions by another dramatist.[29] This, it is worth observing, is a rather clearer distinction than most commentators are prepared to draw.

It is thus essential to emphasize that active collaboration was the *norm* of Jacobean theater and that the individual artistic autonomy claimed by Jonson is an evasion. Bentley attests that "as many as half of the plays by professional dramatists in the period incorporated the writing at some date of more than one man," adding that "[i]n the case of the 282 plays mentioned in Henslowe's diary (far and away the most detailed record of authorship that has come down to us) nearly two-thirds are the work of more than one man." He also points out that "[t]his troublesome fact has inclined a number of critics to assert that collaboration was a peculiar feature of Henslowe's policy and imposed by him upon the companies he financed," but refutes this, observing that, even in the absence of such clear records as Henslowe's, it is obvious that "joint composition was common in the repertories of the other London troupes of actors."[30] And it is likely that Bentley's rough figure of "as many as half" is conservative, no doubt treating as solo such texts as *Macbeth* or *Timon,* which have recently been recognized to involve more than one hand.

Beyond the purely professional, workmanlike, and effectively random assignment of scenes that generally appears to characterize Jacobean collaborative writing, it must be acknowledged that the case of John Fletcher offers evidence for a certain consistency and intimacy in professional partnerships. Although they remain at an uneasily speculative and homophobic level, the repeated intimations of homosexual relations between Beaumont and Fletcher underline the need for a reading of the plays which can cope with persistent and intimate literary partnership. It is quite plain, from Hoy's investigations alone, that there is a shift in Fletcher's role in the space between his work firstly with Beaumont and then with Massinger. The main Beaumont and Fletcher collaborations—*The Woman Hater* (chiefly Beaumont's), *Cupid's Revenge* (dominated by, and final version by, Beaumont), *Philaster* (chiefly Beaumont's), *The Maid's Tragedy* (chiefly Beaumont's), and *A King and No King* (also chiefly Beaumont's)—provide clear evidence of Fletcher's regular subordination to his younger partner in the writing process. He remained the junior partner in his 1612–13 work with Shakespeare (though the shares begin to appear more evenly balanced). Nonetheless, by 1611, Fletcher had produced a successful solo play, *The Woman's Prize,* and the last Beaumont-and-Fletcher play, *The Captain,* appears to have been mainly Fletcher's work. It was around 1614 or so, in his work with Nathan Field, that Fletcher seems to have adjusted to a dominant collaborative role, and, commencing with the controversial *Barnavelt,* his long partnership with Philip Massinger reveals a clear pattern in which Fletcher is the master and Massinger the apprentice, despite the minimal age disparity between the two playwrights.

The partnership of Fletcher and Massinger is of considerably more importance overall than that of Beaumont and Fletcher. It was only after Beaumont's retirement and death that Fletcher's work became established as the staple of the King's company, and it was once he had come out from under the influence of Beaumont that Fletcher began to develop his own interests. As Bentley points out, "[t]he title of the 1647 folio *Comedies and Tragedies Written by Francis Beaumont and John Fletcher, Gentlemen* has long been recognized as grossly misleading, since at least thirty of the plays were written after Beaumont's death."[31] The earliest criticism of the 1647 folio is that of Sir Aston Cokayne writing to his cousin Charles Cotton shortly after the publication of the volume. "Had

Beaumont liv'd when this Edition came / Forth, and beheld his ever living name / Before Plays that he never writ," asserts Cokayne, "how he / Had frown'd and blush'd at such Impiety," adding that "my good friend Old *Philip Massinger* / With *Fletcher* writ in some that we see there. / But you may blame the Printers."[32] Even at this relatively early stage, however, the sheer size of Massinger's involvement in the folio plays (Fletcher wrote nearly twice as many plays with Massinger as he did with Beaumont) seems to have been forgotten.

Cyrus Hoy has sugggested that the collaboration of Massinger and Fletcher had a lasting negative effect on Massinger's ability to write solo plays. This would appear to be due largely to the specific allocation of duties within that particular partnership. For Hoy, "[t]he most immediately striking fact about Massinger's work as a collaborator is the frequency with which he writes both the opening and closing scenes of a play."[33] Hoy lists the various plays in which Massinger was responsible for the opening and the conclusion—*The Fatal Dowry* (with Nathan Field), *The Virgin Martyr* (with Thomas Dekker), *The Double Marriage, The Little French Lawyer, The Spanish Curate,* and *A Very Woman* (all with John Fletcher)—and expands this list by suggesting that in many more plays, including *The False One, The Elder Brother, The Queen of Corinth, The Fair Maid of the Inn, The Bloody Brother,* and *Beggars' Bush,* Massinger "seems to have been called on, in effect, to put a frame around a play's various actions" (53). Hoy thus believes that in the writing of these plays Massinger was "employed for the express purpose of setting a play in motion, and providing it with a finale" (53).

He goes on to outline the way in which this process works, for better or worse, in several of the collaborations, suggesting that those plays in which Massinger's contribution was almost entirely limited to the opening and closing scenes and maybe "one plot strand in between" generally appear to work better than those in which both dramatists contribute to the same plot. He believes that Massinger ended up composing "scenes that probably held no great interest for him, and that were not really appropriate to his peculiar stylistic timbre" (78). And the outcome of this is that "[i]n the course of the decade" in which he collaborated with Fletcher, "something withered in his dramatic talents, so far at least as his work in collaboration with others is concerned" (79). In the end, he believes, "Fletcher's style was too powerful and too well established in the favour of theatrical audiences to permit a collaborator any role beyond that of a subordinate assistant." As a result, Massinger's "verbal powers never really developed, and most of his dramatic efforts went into the work of reducing to some kind of order the tangled yards of romantic story material that were the inevitable sources for the plots of Jacobean plays" (79). Hoy's arguments about individual plays are in many ways convincing, yet there remains a strong sense that his observations about Massinger's damaged technique depend upon the presumed inferiority of collaborative work. His language, when he addresses the nature of the damage sustained by Massinger at the hands of Fletcher's style, is vague and unspecific, and his attitude both to the collaborative plays themselves and to the processes by which they were written is unnecessarily negative. His inevitable conclusion is that collaboration was thrust upon an unwilling Massinger: "Aspiring as he evidently was during these years to establish himself as an independent playwright, his work as a collaborator must have been understandably onerous; presumably he was driven to it by financial need" (79).

Frustratingly, this negative attitude to collaboration remains prevalent even in the best of contemporary criticism. Kathleen McLuskie, whose chapter on Fletcher's women in her *Renaissance Drama: Feminist Readings* is one of the more sensitive interpretations of Fletcherian drama written in recent years, is nonetheless vague on the subject of authorship attribution (she states simply that "[i]n order to avoid the minefield of the authorship of the Beaumont and Fletcher canon, I am using "Fletcher" to refer to plays by Fletcher and his collaborators"), and her emphasis above all on the "wittiness" of the protagonists tends to minimize the dramatic, as well as the political, potential of the plays.[34] The conclusion to her chapter on collaboration in the *Revels History* is similarly unhelpful:

Dependence on convention . . . was not in itself artistically disabling. It sometimes resulted in dull and repetitive writing but it also provided the dramatic expectations which a writer could either fulfil or deny to create the maximum variety or suspense. It could only emerge in a sophisticated theatre with a regular audience which both knew the forms and enjoyed new variations on them. Collaborations may not have produced works of lasting serious significance, but when the collaborators were congenial and their responses to convention inventive, they provided the staple fare for a successful theatre industry which in its turn sustained creations of individual genius.[35]

"The smoothest and most successful collaborations achieved by the great King's Men team," she admits, "centred on Fletcher" (175); but even here the term "smoothest" jars, and "centred" is arguably not the most appropriate verb to use of these bifurcated texts. When she suggests that most of Fletcher's collaborations "display a stylish dovetailing of the different plots to create suspense and variety as well as a mechanically even division of labour" (175), it is clear that she sees Fletcher and his collaborators as dramatic entertainers rather than as playwrights proper.[36] The echo of Coleridge's pejorative term "mechanic" is not without significance. The corollary of this attitude is the quite reasonable inference that collaborative writing for the Jacobean theater depended heavily on shared knowledge of dramatic conventions, a "series of formulae" (181) which allows for speedy production of joint work with a minimum of consultation. But the implication that Jacobean theater only excelled in single author plays (a notion at least partially undercut by Jonson's admission in his preface to *Sejanus*) and the suggestion that dependence upon convention produces mediocre work are both questionable. It has, after all, been a commonplace of Shakespeare criticism for decades that a substantial proportion of his genius lay in his ability to utilize and develop dramatic convention.

McLuskie acknowledges Sir John Berkenhead's suggestion in his commendatory verse to the 1647 folio that in Fletcher's collaborations, at least with Beaumont, there was "a degree of cooperation which went beyond simply dividing the scenes for comedy" (175):

> Both brought Your Ingots, Both toil'd at the Mint,
> Beat, melted, sifted, till no drosse stuck in't,
> Then in each Others scales weigh'd every graine,
> Then smooth'd and burnish'd, then weigh'd all againe,
> Stamp't Both your Names upon't by one bold Hit,
> Then, then 'twas Coyne, as well as Bullion-Wit.[37]

There is a series of tensions in such commentaries upon Fletcher's collaborations. On the one hand he is seen to have worked very closely indeed with his partners to produce superior collaborative work; on the other he is seen merely as one of a number of journeymen in collaboration who pumped out predictable formulaic dramatic entertainments. Similarly, there is an effort to reduce the various collaborative partners involved in the canon to only two—Beaumont and Fletcher—and, then, like Berkenhead, to attempt to merge even these into one, in order to promote the authority of the plays. At the same time, there is a tremendous emphasis on the limiting effect upon Fletcher's artistry that collaboration imposed. These are contradictions to which no critic has yet faced up.

Such negative attitudes toward collaboration are at their most unhelpful in the work of textual editors dealing with collaborative texts. The editorial process itself is, almost by definition, collaborative; yet the most distinguished editors may fall foul of their presuppositions. A notable example of presumptions obscuring the possibilities of joint authorship is R. A. Foakes's otherwise useful Arden edition of *Henry VIII*, first published in 1957. Foakes, unlike some commentators, has a high regard for the play, and despite his recognition of the inevitability of prejudice—he observes that "[i]t is significant that support for Fletcher has nearly always been associated with condemnation of *Henry VIII* as bad or lacking unity, and belief in Shakespeare's authorship with approval of the play"—he nonetheless promotes single authorship for a series of apparently prior interpretive reasons.[38] "The play shows a unified, if special, conception and spirit" (xxiv), he tells us, adding that "[t]he accusations of Spedding and others that *Henry VIII* is incoherent in design have been opposed by strong claims that it is an organic whole" (xxiv). Despite the linguistic evidence already available to him, Foakes prefers to depend upon arguments of scholarly intuition:

Perhaps after all what points most strongly to Shakespeare in the similarity in compassionate tone and outlook between *Henry VIII* and the other late plays. The spirit of Fletcher's known work is completely alien to this, so that there seem very good grounds for leaving the play where Heminge and Condell put it, amongst Shakespeare's works. (xxv)

The last sentence here is a non sequitur, yet Foakes insists that both the verse and sentiment of *Henry VIII* are generally above the quality that Fletcher was capable of producing. Unfortunately for

Foakes, however, it was not possible to leave the matter there, since Hoy's linguistic evidence for Fletcherian part-authorship appeared shortly after the edition was published. So in 1962, Foakes added a brief postscript to the authorship section of his introduction, in which he both acknowledged Hoy's work and admitted his own attitude:

In my discussion of the authorship of the play, I hoped to do three things: to present fairly the case for Fletcher as part-author; to emphasize the strength of the case for Shakespeare as sole author, or author of most of the text; and to dismiss the whole matter, so that in the remainder of the Introduction and in the commentary the play might be viewed as a whole, and appreciated for what it is. It seemed to me important to ask what the structure of *Henry VIII* is, to appreciate rather than to judge it, because so often in the past critics had attacked it as a "collaboration of such a kind that no unity of conception and design ought to be expected of it." My approach to the play was a sympathetic one, and this no doubt influenced my attitude to the authorship question. The supporters of Fletcher have not let the matter rest, but it should be noted that they tend to begin from the assumption that the play is a poor piece of work, lacking a unified design. (xxvi)

Foakes's exasperation with the supporters of Fletcher is alleviated a little by Hoy's findings, and he closes his postscript by saying that "it would be pleasant if the whole debate could be brought to a halt with [Hoy's] sane conclusion that

the truth about Fletcher's share in *Henry VIII* is to be found where truth generally is: midway between the extreme views that have traditionally been held regarding it. Those who would deny his presence in the play altogether are wrong to do so, for he is assuredly there. Those who award him ten and one-half of the play's sixteen scenes (the usual ascription) claim too much.[39]

Yet Hoy's "sane" conclusion is dependent upon a liberal golden mean premise that hardly seems appropriate in the technical analysis of Jacobean drama.

Even the most recent of Beaumont-and-Fletcher projects—one in which Hoy is involved—falls foul of inappropriate theoretical presumptions. In his foreword to the ongoing New Cambridge edition of *The Dramatic Works in the Beaumont and Fletcher Canon,* Fredson Bowers, the general editor of the series, outlines the editorial method to be employed in all the volumes:

The texts of the several plays have been edited by a group of scholars according to editorial procedures set by the general editor, who closely supervised in matters of substance as well as of detail the initially contrived form of the texts. Thereafter the individual editors have been left free to develop their concepts of the plays according to their own views. We hope that the intimate connexion of one individual, in this manner, with all the different editorial processes will lend to the results some uniformity not ordinarily found when diverse editors approach texts of such complexity. At the same time, the peculiar abilities of the several editors have had sufficient free play to ensure individuality its proper role; and thus, we hope, the deadness of compromise that may fasten on collaborative effort has been avoided, even at the risk of occasional internal disagreement.[40]

This, I would suggest, is an astonishingly inauspicious and inappropriate manifesto for a contemporary editor of Fletcherian drama. Nobody approaching Fletcher's plays should be able to write baldly of "the deadness of compromise that may fasten on collaborative effort," and no editor should attempt to exert a personal hegemony over a corpus of plays which by their very nature defy such attempts. Fletcher made no such attempt in the writing of the plays: "uniformity" does not seem to have been high on his agenda. His practice was developed in the space between "intimate connexion" and "internal disagreement," and at no stage resembled Jonson's project for authorial hegemony. There is a narrowness of vision in Bowers's editorial manifesto which means that his edition can serve only to reinforce the divide between critical and textual approaches to drama and cannot from the start do justice to the work of Fletcher and his collaborators, since his premises with regard both to texts and to collaborative effort seem to take little account of Fletcher's own theory and practice.

3

For the political interpretation of plays in a collaborative canon, understanding of the processes and division of collaborative work is essential, since inappropriate readings may result from inadequate textual knowledge. In deference to Koestenbaum, I shall take as an example of such an inappropriate reading a recent essay by Jonathan Dollimore which addresses the issue of homosexuality in *Love's Cure,* arguably the most difficult to attribute of all the plays in which Fletcher had a hand. The play, as Dollimore points out in a highly perceptive analysis of the gender politics of the play, addresses the possibility that "gender division and inequality are a consequence not of divine or natural law but of social custom."[41] The chief concern of *Love's Cure* is the consequence of patriarchal behavior. One Don Alvarez fled Seville, the play's location, twenty years earlier with his daughter Clara, who as a consequence of life in army camps and elsewhere has grown up rather more masculine than feminine in her lifestyle. Alvarez's wife Eugenia and their son Lucio were unable to leave Seville, and in order to deny their enemies the chance to take revenge by wiping out the possibility of inheritance, Eugenia has brought Lucio up as if he were a little girl.

We learn of this inversion abruptly in the second scene of the play when Lucio, full of domestic concerns, bustles onto the stage. Alvarez's steward Bobadilla provides an exasperated commentary. "Was there ever such an Hermaphrodite heard of?" he asks, "[W]ould any wench living, that should hear and see what I do, be wrought to believe, that the best of a man lies under this Petti-coate, and that a Cod-peece were far fitter here, then a pind-Placket?"[42] He tries to talk Lucio out of his customary femininity:

[T]hough my Lady your mother, for fear of *Vitelli* and his faction, hath brought you up like her daughter, and h'as kept you this twentie year, which is ever since you were born, a close prisoner within dores, yet since you are a man, and are as wel provided as other men are, methinks you should have the same motions of the flesh, as other Cavaliers of us are inclin'd unto. (I. ii. 21–26)

And as Eugenia enters, Bobadilla voices the central preoccupation of the play: "O custom, what ha'st thou made of him?" (I. ii. 47). Eugenia announces Alvarez's imminent return, and instructs Lucio to "change those qualities thou didst learn from me, / For masculine virtues" (I. ii. 81–82). Lucio does not reply.

Clara, for her part, has been ordered by her father to resume her "natural" sexuality, "custome having chang'd," he explains somewhat nervously, "[t]hough not thy sex, the softnesse of thy nature" (I. iii. 21–22). Clara's reply is dutiful but reluctant:

> Sir, I know only that
> It stands not with my duty to gaine-say you,
> In any thing: I must, and will put on
> What fashion you think best: though I could wish
> I were what I appeare. (I. iii. 34–38)

Alvarez's response to this is again a little uneasy, a little uncomfortably sexual: "Endeavour rather / To be what you are, *Clara,* entring here / As you were borne, a woman" (I. iii. 38–40). At home, meanwhile, Lucio appears "in man's attire," and chafes at the change:

> What would you have me doe? this scurvy sword
> So gals my thigh: I would 'twer burnt: pish, looke
> This cloak will ne'r keep on: these boots too hidebound,
> Make me walk stiffe, as if my leggs were frozen,
> And my Spurs gingle, like a Morris-dancer:
> Lord, how my head akes, with this roguish hat;
> This masculine attire, is most uneasie,
> I am bound up in it: I had rather walke
> In folio, againe, loose, like a woman. (II. ii. 12–20)

Lucio is even less ready to acknowledge normal dress codes than his sister; and his sense of the equivalence of "masculine attire" and a bound volume of the printed word appears to relate to the code of violence he is obliged to obey as soon as he enters the masculine world, a code which, as Dollimore usefully demonstrates, is decidedly "uneasie."

For Dollimore, moments such as this make *Love's Cure* "[p]erhaps the most interesting theatrical containment" of what he calls "the transvestite challenge" in the period, yet I would like to question one of the premises upon which he bases his conclusion that the challenge is ultimately contained. Toward the end of the play, both Lucio and Clara fall in love with a member of the correct (i.e., opposite) sex, and rapidly assume attitudes appropriate to their "natural" genders. Thus for Dollimore, "[n]ature succeeds where authority has failed; attraction to the opposite sex awakens the siblings' own 'true' natural instincts, and gender incongruities are resolved" (72). "We might say," he continues, "that *Love's Cure* produces transgression precisely in order to contain it, and in the most insidiously ideological way: desire which initially appeared to contradict nature is reconstituted by nature in accord with her (?) [sic] order" (73). Thus, for this reading, the apparently radical aspect of the play—its critique of natural gender—is thoroughly defused by the way in which the play ends. Yet despite his reliance upon a Foucaultian equilibrium model in which the method of containment is inevitably dependent upon and equivalent to the transgression it contains, Dollimore quite clearly wishes he could claim more for *Love's Cure*. As he observes, in the process of the play, "the very masculine code of honor which is affronted by Lucio's perverse failure of masculinity is shown to border on a perversity even more excessive than his," an assertion which he supports with an analysis of the blood feud of Vitellia and Alvarez, and he recognizes that "[i]t is as if containment, in reinstating nature over culture . . . protests too much" (73).

This aspect of Dollimore's reading could be considerably strengthened by more detailed textual information. He refers to the play simply as "Fletcher's *Love's Cure*," ignoring the problems of attribution and thus making inappropriate assumptions about authorship. The attribution details of *Love's Cure* are especially complex. We have seen already the way in which Fletcher habitually worked in collaboration, apparently preferring to write the central rather than the opening and closing sections of a play, and delegating the work of finishing to his partner. This appears to have been roughly the case with *Love's Cure*. However the extant text came about—whether as a collaboration by Beaumont and Fletcher revised much later by Massinger or as a late Fletcher/ Massinger collaboration—it is clear that Fletcher was much more interested in the setting-up of the problem than in its resolution.[43] Even taking the most complex of the disintegrative attributions— Hoy's—the evidence suggests that Fletcher's hand is present in the majority of the scenes we have referred to so far, the scenes in which the gender inversion is presented, including I. ii ("O custom, what ha'st thou made of him?") and II. ii ("This masculine attire, is most uneasie"). On the other hand, Fletcher's characteristic linguistic habits are conspicuous by their absence in the scenes in which nature reasserts control over Lucio and Clara: it is Massinger, not Fletcher, who provides the words both for Clara's rejection of her erstwhile masculinity—

> I here abjure all actions of a man,
> And wil esteem it happinesse from you
> To suffer like a woman: love, true love
> Hath made a search within me, and expel'd
> All but my naturall softnesse, and made perfect
> That which my parents care could not begin
>
> (IV. ii. 185–90)

—and for Lucio's discovery of his "natural" sexual preferences: "My womanish soul, which hitherto hath governd / This coward flesh, I feele departing from me; / And in me by her beauty is inspir'd / A new, and masculine one" (IV. iv. 54–57).

Recognition of this division of writing can only amplify Dollimore's sense that there is genuine subversion in the writing of the play: Fletcher at least, if not the play as a whole (if whole is an appropriate word), can be seen to have an interest only in the transgression and not the inevitable containment. This distinction between author and work is of course a theoretical labyrinth, yet I would maintain that it is important to be aware of the difference between attributing a certain politics to a particular text and to a particular author: the complexities of collaboration make such a distinction all the more difficult, but all the more important. It is apparent from *Love's Cure,* perhaps the most complex of examples, as well as from the more clear-cut and consistent collaborations with Massinger alone, that Fletcher was fascinated by the setting-up of unlikely and transgressive political situations and effectively uninterested in the necessary process of resolving them, an obligation of writing for the Jacobean stage.[44] *Love's Cure* may, as Dollimore suggests, ultimately offer a conservative resolution to the question of natural gender; John Fletcher, however, as coauthor cannot be held responsible for the resolution provided.

4

Chambers' word "disintegration," which Bentley also uses with a certain amount of distaste, underlines the destructive role many editors and critics assign to those who try to ascertain the respective shares of the dual or multiple authors involved in collaborative texts. All such endeavors are, by definition, inadequate: little more than belated attempts to recreate an indeterminate original state of affairs. Hoy's own recognition of the unfinished condition of many Beaumont-and-Fletcher plays in a sense undermines his project, which assumes a definitive, original collaborative arrangement. None of the linguistic criteria Hoy wields is adequate by itself: even taken together, as Hoy would be the first to admit, they fail in certain cases (*Love's Cure* is a good example) to provide workable answers to the connected questions of source, authorship, and dating. And no matter how many refinements of Hoy's methods, or alternative sets of criteria, are applied, the disintegration of dramatic texts will remain at best mechanical and partial.

Yet, unlike Jeffrey Masten, whose article on collaborative drama appeared as the present study was under revision, I do not see Hoy's project as hopelessly compromised.[45] As Masten observes, "the collaborative project in the theater was predicated on *erasing* the perception of any differences that might have existed, for whatever reason, between collaborated parts" (342). Yet a decision therefore to refuse to analyze the nature of the collaboration is to acquiesce in this particular original intention and to defer to the intentional project as a source of interpretive guidance. This is redolent of the very romanticisms Masten wishes to question. If disintegration is viewed entirely separately from influence, source, performance, and other social and discursive aspects of dramatic production, then it is an inadequate process. But an attempt to distinguish responsibility for the various acts and scenes of a collaborative play seems to me to be a necessary prerequisite of analysis, as I trust I have already made clear in my critique of Dollimore's reading of *Love's Cure*. It is essential to stay alert to the multiple agencies operating in such texts.

In his discussion of Beaumont and Fletcher, Masten asserts a strong version of Foucault's rejection of the author. "Within Hoy's paradigm of collaboration," he points out, "language is fundamentally reflective of, because it is produced by, the individual author; the language one uses is (and identifies one as) one's own. But if we accept that language is a socially produced (and producing) system, then collaboration is more the condition of discourse than its exception" (345). I am very much in agreement with the latter assertion, but I am not clear about its relation to the former. As Jack Stillinger observes, writing of "the joint, or composite, or collaborative production of literary works that we usually think of as written by a single author," "a work may be the collaborative product of the nominal author and a friend, a spouse, a ghost, an agent, an editor, a translator, a publisher, a censor, a transcriber, a printer, or—what is more often the case—several of these acting together or in succession."[46] The logic of collaboration puts paid to the myth of the author as sole controller of the text. The logic of collaboration is the logic of the supplement: if Shakespeare had a collaborator in several of his plays, he cannot have been entirely self-contained.[47] Infection, contamination, compromise, and all the other words used of the collaborative process describe not an atypical situation but the inevitable condition of writing. Yet I do not see that this claim is denied by the suggestion that individuals have distinctive ways with words.

I prefer to argue, with Bakhtin, for the distinctiveness of the individual as an *orchestrator* of voices. In other words, while there is no such thing as original speech—all words have always already been previously voiced in some context or other, which does not contaminate or sully them but rather fills them with the energy, the productive tension, of discourse—there is nonetheless a role for the voice in organizing the innumerable discursive options available at a particular moment.[48] This organization or orchestration can be distinctive without requiring belief in romantic notions of originality. And promoting collaboration is one way of demonstrating the profoundly social, dialogic nature of discourse, which does not deny (though it makes impossible, finally) the attempt to locate a working distinctiveness for the orchestrator of voices, influences, sources, and contexts known to literary history as Fletcher.

FIVE

"Strange carded cunningnesse"

I

By the conclusion of the Coleorton masque, the Beaumonts and their noble guests had witnessed a negotiation of sexual inequality resolved by a kind of linguistic collaboration or mutuality.[1] To begin with, the women masquers think wistfully (and dangerously) of an "Amazonian" world in which "weomen could live & lie with one another," principally because they recognize the inequality of power relations: "Menns overawing tames / And Pedantlike our active Spirits smother." At the end of the masque, sexual difference has been asserted, along with a claim that the metaphoric plenitude of "well-figur'd" men is a prerequisite for female signification. "Themselves unsignificant," women can only have meaning when "[j]oynd" with men in a kind of sexual and linguistic collaboration. Yet the reference to an Amazonian realm has already offered the possibility of projection outside that particular cultural framework. The Coleorton masque highlights a location for this issue in his patronage milieu, but Fletcher's own dramatic assessment of the issues of collaborative meaning-creation between the genders and the politics of sexual inequality is considerably more complex and far-reaching than this might suggest. As is already clear from the unease evoked in the debate about natural and nurtured gender embodied in *Love's Cure,* Fletcher rehearses the problem of the culturally appointed roles of men and women throughout his plays.

In the third Act of *Women Pleased,* the protagonist Belvidere is introduced by her mother to the duke of Siena, whom she is obliged against her will to marry. Her poker-faced comment in response—"Your Grace is a great Master, / And speake too powerfully to be resisted" (III. i. 55–56)—is suggestive both of the man's verbally embedded power as a male aristocrat and of the woman's need to find an appropriately female strategy to reorient power and sovereignty. One distinctively female strategy for dealing with masculine excess is that dramatized many centuries earlier by the Athenian comic playwright Aristophanes. His *Lysistrata,* or *The Flight of the Swallows,* was produced early in 411 B.C., and proposed a radical and comic solution to the war with Sparta by way of a sex strike imposed by the wives of prominent men in various parts of Greece, a rejection of the usual mechanics of difference underpinning social structures. And this is the strategy adopted by the women in their war with the men in *The Woman's Prize,* or *The Tamer Tam'd,* Fletcher's exuberant mock sequel to *The Taming of the Shrew,* written around 1611.

Kate has died. Petruchio has just remarried. His new wife is, again, the elder of the two daughters, Maria and Livia, of a rich man. We learn from the opening debate among his friends that Petruchio's troubles were in fact only just starting at the close of *The Taming of the Shrew.* Fletcher has absorbed the ambiguity of Lucentio's closing line (" 'Tis a wonder, by your leave, she will be tamed so") and made of it only a beginning. "[T]he bare remembrance of his first wife," we discover, "Will make him start in's sleep, and very often / Cry out for Cudgels, Colstaves, any thing; / Hiding his Breeches, out of feare her Ghost / Should walk, and weare 'em yet."[2] "Since his first marriage," says one of his friends, "He is no more the still *Petruchio,* / Then I am *Babylon*" (I. i. 32–38). But worse, it turns out, is in store for the war-weary Petruchio of *The Woman's Prize,* since the second wife intends to outshine the first. She dismisses Kate in a few words: "She was a foole, / And tooke a scurvy course; let her be nam'd / 'Mongst those that wish for things, but dare not do 'em: / I have a new daunce for him, and a mad one" (I. ii. 140–43).

She tells him her intention bluntly a little later on, echoing the language of his younger days:

> You have been famous for a woman tamer,
> and beare the fear'd name of a brave wife-breaker:
> A woman now shall take those honours off,
> And tame you;
> Nay, never look so bigge, she shall, beleeve me,
> And I am she. (I. iii. 268–73)

The play proceeds to map Maria's strategies for accomplishing this aim, which include orchestrating a sex war similar to Lysistrata's, and takes its structure from the pattern of female and male tricks and countertricks, negotiating a careful conclusion most neatly expressed in the Epilogue:

> The Tamer's tam'd, but so, as nor the men
>   Can finde one just cause to complaine of, when
> They fitly do consider in their lives,
>   They should not raigne as Tyrants o'r their wives.
> Nor can the women from this president
>   Insult, or triumph: it being aptly meant,
> To teach both Sexes due equality;
>   And as they stand bound, to love mutually.
> (Epilogue 1–8)

Maria's actions thus invert the resolution of *The Taming of the Shrew.* Yet the focus of comparative interest does not reside solely in the relationship of Petruchio and Maria.

The dual displacement of Shakespeare's Bianca into Fletcher's Livia and Byancha, Maria's sister and cousin respectively, offers a polarity for considering the alternatives presented to Maria in her attempts to find strategy and expression for her rights as a woman and as a wife. In *The Shrew,* we have watched the subtle progress of Bianca from the silence that flouts Kate to her assertiveness with her teachers ["I'll not be tied to hours nor 'pointed times, / But learn my lessons as I please myself" (III. i. 19–20)]; through her description by a disgruntled Hortensio as "this proud disdainful haggard" (IV. ii. 39), a technical term previously exclusive to Kate; and finally to her bluntness about the "foolish duty" expected of women at a time when Kate has come to acknowledge only the futility of resistance. In a sense, the double recharacterization of *this* Bianca as Livia and Byancha in *The Woman's Prize* offers alternative extrapolations from her development in the course of *The Shrew.*

Despite the apparent feminism of her early assertion that "no man shall make use of me; / My beauty was born free, and free Ile give it / To him that loves, not buys me" (I. ii. 36–38), Livia is decidedly wary at first of the revolt planned by Maria and Byancha, and her reason for joining in when she does is chiefly her desire to find a means to secure the affections of her nervy and easily disaffected lover, Rowland. The other two imply their recognition of this by forcing her to swear "by thy Sweet-heart *Rowland*" (II. ii. 46) that she will not betray them. Under Byancha's influence, Maria outlines a fearful revenge if Livia were in fact to let them down:

> Thinke what women shall
> An hundred yeare hence speak thee, when examples
> Are look'd for. . . .
>   . . . [A]ll that ever
> Shall live, and heare of thee, I meane all women;
> Will (like so many furies) shake their Keyes,
> And tosse their flaming distaffes o're their heads,
> Crying Revenge. (II. ii. 80–82; 103–7)

Quite clearly, it is Byancha, and not Maria, who motivates this and accompanying images of sisterhood betrayed. This Byancha is, according to the dramatis personae, "Their Cosin, and Commander in chief," and, although it is Maria who fronts the women's insurrection, Byancha can be seen as the motivator throughout.

The hierarchy of rebellion in this play is rather more complex than in *Lysistrata,* where the protagonist is the sole originator and executor of the action. Again and again, Byancha acts to escalate the subversiveness of Maria's pronouncements by moving away from a focus upon the individual to a general assertion of women's rights. When Maria calls down sterility upon herself until such time as she has successfully tamed Petruchio, Byancha generalizes the effect of her actions, crying, "All the severall wrongs / Done by Emperious husbands to their wives / These thousand yeeres and upwards, strengthen thee: / Thou hast a brave cause" (I. ii. 122–25), revealing that she is the most fully alienated woman of the play, a bitter backstage activist for the Regiment of Women. And later in the play it is to Byancha that Petronius, Maria's father, turns particular venom for her incitement of his daughters. Her most radical expression of the generalizing principle comes in the debate over Livia's trustworthiness. Evoking the conditions of Troy besieged, Byancha gives a warning to Livia which demonstrates the essential difference between the grounds upon which she, Byancha, premises revolt and those upon which Maria (and most of Fletcher's other assertive, witty, successful women) base their stands. "Goe home," she says,

> and tell the merry Greekes that sent you,
> *Ilium* shall burn, and I, as did *Æneas,*
> will on my back, spite of the Myrmidons,
> Carry this warlike Lady, and through Seas
> Unknown, and unbeleev'd, seek out a Land,
> Where like a race of noble *Amazons,*
> We'le root our selves and to our endlesse glory
> Live, and despise base men. (II. ii. 32–39)

In this apocalyptic image she not only successfully appropriates male myth to her own purpose, but reworks the outward urge of the dramatic genre of romance toward a specifically female utopian vision.

Byancha is by no means the only one of Fletcher's female protagonists to desire a woman's utopia of this nature. Her wish receives a curiously optimistic precursor in *The Coxcomb,* a Beaumont and Fletcher play written a year or two before *The Woman's Prize,* in which a distinct learning curve can be plotted from the initial voicing of a utopian alternative. The female protagonist Viola has arranged a tryst with her lover Richardo. Unknown to Viola, however, Richardo has, since they last met, been enticed into a tavern by his companions. Drunk, he and his friends argue over her and, in a scene which amounts to multiple attempted rape, end up brawling in the street. In despair and horror, she wanders away, only to be attacked and tied up by a tinker and his "trull." She is rescued by a country gentleman who, it turns out, has ulterior motives, too. When he announces that he married his wife only for money and then propositions Viola, she cries, "Are you men / All such? wood you wood wall us in a place / Where all we women, that are innocent, / Might live together," a similar desire to that of the women masquers in the later Coleorton masque.[3] And she goes on to voice her disgust in a refiguration of the creation of Eve:

> Woman they say, was onely made of man,
> Methinks tis strange they should be so unlike,
> It may be all the best was cut away
> To make the woman and the nought was left
> Behind with him. (III. iii. 109–13)

This inversion of the Eden myth, despite being undercut by the amusement with which we are apparently expected to view it, suggests that the possibility of utopia lies firmly and only with women.

In the immediate wake of this scene, Viola encounters two milkmaids, who, it turns out, offer something of the separatist utopia she has outlined. They suggest that she join them in their various tasks at the dairy, but one of them warns her: "[B]e sure to keepe the men out, they will mar all that you make else." And they say:

[C]ome you shall een home with us and be our fellow, our house is so honest, and we serve a very good woman, and a Gentlewoman, and we live as merrily, and dance a good dayes after evensong. . . . [Y]ou must be our sister, and love us best, and tell us every thing, and when cold weather comes wee'l ly together . . . (III. iii. 171–77; 184–86)

This low-key separatist environment is, however, quickly dissolved by the announcement of the imminent arrival of the mistress's son, who has been away traveling. The introduction of men sets the women to thinking about sex, and the brief utopia fades away. Richardo, meanwhile, has realized what he has done, and searches for Viola to ask forgiveness. She does indeed forgive him, and their closing dialogue is significant. He acknowledges that "the defective race of envious man / Strives to conceale" women's virtues (V. ii. 148–54), and goes on in the last lines of the play to provide a remarkable analysis of patriarchal relations. "[S]uch an overswayed sex is yours," he says,

> That all the vertuous actions you can do,
> Are but as men will call them, and I sweare,
> 'Tis my beliefe that women want but wayes
> To praise their deeds, but men want deeds to praise.
> (V. iii. 255–61)

Thus, in the wake of Viola's utopian vision, Richardo has recognized that the pressures on women entail that everything a woman does is in fact reinscribed by men, and that this reinscription enforces women's silence.[4] Few of Fletcher's male protagonists, however, are prepared to make such an acknowledgment.

For every heuristic female utopia projected, there is a male dystopia of sorts. Gondarino, the eponym of *The Woman Hater,* suggests a motivation for separatism quite different from that of Byancha or Viola. "The much praysed *Amazones,*" he says,

Knowing their owne infirmities so well,
Made of themselves a people, and what men
They take amongst them, they condemn to die,
Perceiving that their follie made them fit
To live no longer, that would willingly
Come in the worthlesse presence of a woman.

(II. i. 310–16)

Belleur, one of Mirabel's friends in *The Wild-Goose Chase*, a solo
play of 1621, similarly asks:

Is there ne'er a Land
That ye have read, or heard of, (for I care not how far it be,
Nor under what Pestiferous Star it lies)
A happy Kingdom, where there are no Women? . . .
For thether would I Travel; where 'tis Fellony
To confess he had a Mother: a Mistris, Treason.[5]

It is against men such as these rather than the likes of Richardo that
Maria in *The Woman's Prize* and Fletcher's other assertive women are
pitted.

Maria's options, then, as represented by Livia and Byancha, are
clear. Either she adopts the *Lysistrata* principle in a diluted and
self-centered form as Livia does, simply as a means to secure her
limited sexual aims within the framework provided for her (and
thereby creating at best a brief carnival, a temporary, heuristic
world-upside-down) or she bases her revolt, as Lysistrata did, upon
a broader premise. Her choice is perhaps best expressed in her
reappropriation of the most pervasive "figure" with which Petruchio "disfigured" Kate in *The Taming of the Shrew* (I. ii. 112–
13), namely the falconry metaphor of his speech in Act IV scene i.
In attempting to persuade Livia of the significance of her revolt,
Maria gives her opinion of the relative status of man and wife
within marriage:

By the faith I have
In mine own Noble will, that childish woman
That lives a prisoner to her husband's pleasure
Has lost her making, and becomes a beast,
Created for his use, not fellowship (I. ii. 136–40),

and she carries on to outline her metaphoric definition of "the
nature of a woman." "Hang these tame-hearted Eyasses," she cries,

that no sooner
See the Lure out, and heare their husbands halla,
But cry like Kites upon 'em: The free Haggard
(Which is that woman, that hath wing, and knowes it,
Spirit, and plume) will make an hundred checks,
To shew her freedom, saile in ev'ry ayre,
And look out ev'ry pleasure; not regarding
Lure, nor quarry, till her pitch command
What she desires, making her foundred keeper
Be glad to fling out traines, and golden ones,
To take her down again. (I. ii. 147–58)

Maria paints a gloriously breathless picture of the demanding processes of female sexual pleasure, rejecting the blunt strictures of the male orgasm for something more appropriate to woman. Unable to contain the slippage between tenor and vehicle, she pursues the falconry metaphor in direct subversion of Petruchio's "taming" of Kate, seeking linguistic means to express the profound limitations upon her of any sexual model dictated by man.

Yet this astonishing celebration of female sexuality denying phallocentric expectations and reappropriation of the technical language of falconry that so comprehensively contained Kate's threat in *The Shrew* nonetheless fails to achieve the same interpretive status as Byancha's wish for a different realm, a women's commonwealth. Maria's concern is to maximize her freedom within the framework available, that of marriage, but at no stage does she acknowledge the possibility of stepping outside that framework. The speech serves not only as a metaphor of the wealth of female sexuality but also to delimit the extent to which women can express that sexuality. The haggard, no matter how long she takes to "look out ev'ry pleasure," will inevitably eventually return to the glove and acknowledge the keeper. The "foundred" husband is clearly stretched to the limit by the deferral of the climactic moment, but is nonetheless able to keep the danger in check simply because at no stage does the bird reject his rights as keeper. And haggard or no, there is no danger that the keeper will "whistle her off, and let her down the wind / To prey at fortune" in the words of Othello's impotent threat.[6]

Maria thus heralds with this speech both the possibility of a spirited assertion of the "nature of a woman" and at the same time the treading of a negotiated path between the circumscribed vision of a Livia and the genuinely radical stance of a Byancha, remaining ultimately within the commonwealth of men. In the closing scenes of the play, Livia acquires Rowland, and Maria finally acknowledges that she has outwitted Petruchio sufficiently that she can "begin [her] new love" and dedicate her life "in service to [his] pleasure" (V. iv. 48; 57), a retraction, at least partially of her earlier vision. Such a response must be at best unsatisfactory for the radical Byancha, and where in *The Shrew* the third partnership of Hortensio and the Widow appears to have been cobbled together by Shakespeare for purposes of symmetry, in *The Woman's Prize* Byancha remains on stage alone, conspicuously asymmetric to the marital closure. The play thus offers the possibility that in the Fletcherian world there can be two kinds of feminist: the witty woman, like Maria, who, as Kathleen McLuskie has shown in her recent essay on Fletcher's women, succeeds by matching the men at their own game, and the outsider, like Byancha, who remains external to closing symmetries and looks to women's utopia as the only alternative.[7] The debate in these plays thus occupies a space between the manipulation of patriarchal structures to the negotiated advantage of the women and the often trauma-induced desire to move outside those structures into a different form of society, a utopia.

2

We have seen that the "figure" with which Petruchio "disfigures" Katherina in *The Taming of the Shrew* is that of falconry, and we know that despite Maria's appropriation of the metaphor to her own ends in *The Woman's Prize,* she nonetheless fails to escape its strategic bounds, preferring rather to seek the maximum freedom of movement within the confines of the metaphor. On other occasions, however, Fletcher's women can and do employ metaphors from female experience which have the potential to escape the bounds provided by men. Lylia-Biancha in *The Wild-Goose Chase,* for example, who is in part a later reworking of Bianca/Byancha, provides an example, manipulating perhaps the best-known metaphor of patriarchy to her own ends. Her actions, along with those of Oriana, the protagonist, and Rosalura, the other "Aërie Daughter of *Nantolet,*" are oriented towards marriage, yet marriage defined by way of relative equality. Addressing Pinac, one of the travelers, she tells him of the value of a wife:

> I know you are young and giddy,
> And till you have a Wife can govern with ye,
> You saile upon this world-Sea, light and empty;
> Your Bark in danger daily; 'tis not the name neither
> Of Wife can steer ye; but the noble nature,
> The diligence, the Care, the Love, the Patience:
> She makes the Pilat, and preserves the Husband,
> That knowes, and reckons every Ribb, he is built on.
>
> (IV. i. 95–102)

She manipulates both Pinac's favourite image of freedom—sea travel—and the familiar "spare rib" myth of woman's creation from Genesis in such a way that the female partner in marriage becomes the controlling voice.[8] She makes herself attractive to Pinac by presenting herself as a doting wife who will do as she is told while at the same time describing a relationship in which she has the upper hand.

In *The Woman's Prize,* Maria finds a similarly appropriate metaphor in an echo of Lysistrata, who, in trying to explain to the magistrate her methods for promoting peace, employed images from woman's daily experiences: "[T]ake a tangled skein of wool for example," she suggested, explaining that "[w]e take it so, put it to the spindle, unwind it this way, now that way. That's how we'll unravel this war." Lysistrata begins in fact to realize the general applicability of her metaphor to a new attitude to government:

As a matter of fact, it might not be so idiotic as you think to run the whole City entirely on the model of the way we deal with wool. . . . The first thing you do with wool is wash the grease out of it; you can do the same with the City. Then you stretch out the citizen body on a bench and pick out the burrs—that is, the parasites. After that you prise apart the club-members who form themselves into knots and clots to get into power, and when you've separated them, pick them out one by one. Then you're ready for the carding: they can all go into the basket of Civic Goodwill.[9]

Maria follows Lysistrata's example in seeking the same metaphor from experience shared by women in ancient Greece and early

modern England alike, though Maria's classical exemplar is not Lysistrata herself but Penelope. The effect of her argument, though,
is similar to that of both Lysistrata and Lylia-Biancha: when Petruchio has learned better ways, he can at last have what he wants
from her. She has tricked him into saying he will leave her in order
to travel. She picks up the theme willingly:

> For if the Merchant through unknown Seas plough
> To get his wealth, then deer sir, what must you
> To gather wisdom? go, and go alone,
> Only your noble mind for your companion,
> And if a woman may win credit with you,
> Go far. . . .
>   . . . Then when time,
> And fulnesse of occasion have new made you,
> And squard you from a sot into a Signour,
> Or neere from a lade into a courser;
> Come home an aged man, as did Ulysses,
> And I your glad Penelope. (IV. v. 155–60, 168–73)

In this, she is responding to his previously voiced fears by reworking the very weaving metaphor with which he has recently expressed his fears of and failure to comprehend woman. Talking
with Jaques a short while before, Petruchio described Maria as

>   a drench of Balderdash,
> Such a strange carded cunningnesse, the Rayne-bow
> When she hangs bent in heaven, sheds not her colours
> Quicker and more then this deceitfull woman
> Weaves in her dyes of wickednesse. (IV. v. 32–36)

Weaving thus becomes a metaphor by which women express their
intentions and men their fears and frustrations. Petruchio clearly
knows the story well enough, since he responds bitterly to her
description of him as Ulysses and herself as Penelope by describing
her as one "[t]hat must have / As many lovers as I languages, / And
what she do's with one i'th day, i'th night / Undoe it with an other"
(IV. v. 173–76). The metaphor of weaving thus provides an image
with which the women can defend themselves against the linguistic superiority of men, as we have seen it at least partially contain
the threat of Belvidere's assertiveness in *Women Pleased,* and it also

appears as a "figure" with which Maria can in her turn "disfigure" Petruchio.

This tendency to seek classical exemplars to authorize their activities in characteristic of most of Fletcher's assertive women protagonists. We have heard both Byancha's obsession with posterity ("Thinke what women shall / An hundred yeare hence speak thee, when examples / Are look'd for") and Maria's fascination with exemplary behaviour [Byancha: "Thou wilt be chronicl'd." / Maria: "That's all I aime at" (I. ii. 176)]. And it is to Roman history that Maria looks to provide the perfect image of exemplary behavior. The story she invokes is that of a huge chasm opening in the Roman forum which could, according to the soothsayers, be closed again only if Rome's greatest treasure were thrown in. Lacus Curtius rode into it, crying that Rome had no greater treasure than arms and valor, at which the chasm closed above him. Maria sees herself as a modern day Curtius, developing the obviously female sexual imagery of the chasm into a challenge to the norms of sexual politics. [10] "I am perfect," she claims, "Like *Curtius* to redeeme my Countrey, have I / Leap'd into this gulph of marriage, and Ile do it" (I. ii. 66–68).

Most of the examples of this nature invoked by Fletcher's assertive women are drawn from Rome's republican history. Perhaps the most notable instance occurs early in *The Wild-Goose Chase,* when De Gard, brother to the female protagonist Oriana, tells her to be a little more discreet about her love for Mirabel, the wild goose of the play's title, pointing out that people have talked. Oriana is furious, and her reply amounts to a deconstruction of the basis of the patriarchal relations within which she must nonetheless operate:

> Now I say hang the people: He that dares
> Believe what they say, dares be mad, and give
> His Mother, nay his own Wife up to Rumor;
> All grounds of truth they build on, is a Tavern,
> And their best censure's Sack, Sack in abundance:
> For as they drink, they think: they ne'r speak modestly
> Unless the wine be poor, or they want money.
> Beleeve them? beleeve *Amadis de Gaul,*
> The *Knight* o' th' *Sun,* or *Palmerin* of *England;*
> For these, to them, are modest, and true stories.

Pray understand me; if their tongues be truth,
And if in *Vino veritas* be an Oracle,
What woman is, or has been ever honest?
Give 'em but ten round cups, they'll swear *Lucretia*
Dy'd not for want of power to resist *Tarquine,*
But want of Pleasure, that he stayd no longer:
And *Portia,* that was famous for her Pietie
To her lov'd Lord, they'll face ye out, dy'd o'th' pox.

(I. i. 103–20)

Oriana's enraged outburst serves in part to deflect Jacobean patriarchal expectations of woman, in spite of the admission she makes that her "thing is Mariage" (I. i. 123), to foreground the implicit violence of popular male attitudes to women, and to relate patriarchal repressed fears of woman and misogynistic myths to wider issues of political structure.

Oriana's role in the play, beginning with her spirited defence of motive in this first scene, is an ironic reversal of the customary romance plot. She takes on the questing obsession with the object of desire which is usually the domain of the male, yet she disposes of the narrative trappings of such an obsession, laying bare the hypocrisy of motivation and the fear behind male expectations of honor and chastity from women. She will retain her honor, but on her own terms, not on those of men. De Gard suggests that her mistake has not been to fall for Mirabel but rather "[t]o Love undiscreetly," and adds that "[a] Virgin should be tender of her honour, / Close, and secure" (I. i. 97–99). "Secure," of course, in this context implies not so much her physical safety as effective sexual surveillance. She replies by switching the grounds of criticism. "I am as close as can be," she says, "And stand upon as strong and honest guards too, / Unless this Warlike Age need a Portcullis" (I. i. 99–101). Each term of this opening defense can be read doubly: she presents herself in his terms, as "close" and "secure," yet "close" in her sense seems to imply that she is entitled to the silence of her own opinion, and that her security (punning upon her brother's name) is her own business, of which she is quite capable. Furthermore, the question of a "warlike age" and the need for a "portcullis" serves a multiple referential purpose.[11] Firstly, as an implicit reference to the contemporary military struggles in the Palatinate, Bohemia, France, and the Low Countries, it acts to remind the 1621 audience of their own political situation within Europe as a whole, and thus relates Oriana's position as chastized and, in the traditional sense, "besieged" woman to a wider political arena. Secondly, the metaphor of the portcullis in particular invokes patriarchal images—on the one hand, the horror of a chastity belt or such equivalent precautions against female desire as Jacobean comedy had by this time habitually mocked as self-defeating and inhuman, and on the other, in the sense of a portcullis as metal teeth preventing access to an entrance, the *vagina dentata* of misogynist myth.

Oriana premises belief in popular gossip—and therefore in this instance of popular patriarchal attitudes toward women (centered on their supposed lustfulness)—upon nothing better than drunkenness. Such popular views are inadequate grounds for censure: here Fletcher produces a curiously aristocratic feminism. Face value acceptance of ideas gleaned from reading romances is portrayed as both a representative error and the very cause of belief in such nonsense worlds. As Rota Lister observes in her edition of *The Wild-Goose Chase,* the three popular romances which Oriana cites—*Amadis de Gaul, The Knight of the Sun,* and *Palmerin of England*—evoke the opening discussion between Quixote and the Barber in Cervantes's *Don Quixote:* it is these very tales, and the genre they represent, which promote madness. Burton's *Anatomy of Melancholy,* also published in 1621, came to the same conclusion, regarding such tales as "amorous toys" which are the cause of love-melancholy in certain readers.

Moreover, the political effect of the exemplary narratives to which Oriana refers is an uneasy one. She invokes a classical age, and the brief but significant exemplary history she repeats is a specifically republican history, which thereby relates woman's position within patriarchal society to the subject's position within a sovereign state. It is a king, Tarquin, who rapes Lucretia: the tale itself demonstrates the hideous inversion that the combination of drink and misogyny can create in asserting that Lucretia "[d]y'd not for want of power to resist *Tarquine,* / But want of Pleasure, that he stayd no longer."[12] The result, of course, of Lucretia's rape and suicide was the end of kingship in Rome and the establishment of the republican system of government. It is also a strand of republican history that is invoked in the mention of the tale of

Portia and Brutus. Thus, like Maria in her assertion of freedom, Oriana holds up exemplary women from republican history to underline her rejection of the ideological apparatus of masculine sovereignty, thereby relating her own struggle as a woman to a broader political plane. In the language of her outburst, there is a questioning of expected roles for women which is also a questioning of political norms. Implicit in the notion that it is man's point of view which is warped and that men have "squint-eyes" (I. i. 124) is the traditional misogynistic belief in women's enjoyment of rape. All of this is spoken in a manner which is indignant but which also involves a powerful sense of political and social irony: we are aware that Oriana is not naïve about the wild goose's behavior, and that she is not prepared to let him continue in that way.

Oriana's admiration for Portia's choice of suicide in the wake of rape had already received its dramatic correlative in Fletcher's *Valentinian* some years earlier.[13] Despite Lucina's pleas, the emperor Valentinian forces her. After the violence has subsided, she speaks her mind:

> Thou bitter bane o'th Empire, look upon me,
> And if thy guilty eyes dare see these ruines,
> Thy wild lust hath layd levell with dishonour,
> The sacrilegious razing of this Temple,
> The mother of thy black sins would have blushed at,
> Behold and curse thy selfe; the Gods will find thee,
> (That's all my refuge now) for they are righteous,
> Vengeance and horror circle thee; the Empire,
> In which thou liv'st a strong continued surfeit,
> Like poyson will disgorge thee, good men raze thee
> For ever being read again but vicious,
> Women and fearefull Maids, make vows against thee:
> Thy own Slaves, if they heare of this, shall hate thee;
> And those thou hast corrupted, first fall from thee;
> And if thou let'st me live, the Souldier,
> Tyrde with thy Tyrannies, break through obedience,
> And shake his strong Steele at thee. (III. i. 36–52)

Royal corruption can, according to Lucina, lead to legitimate rebellion in the cause of honor. She continues by comparing Valentinian to Romulus and, again, Tarquin:

The curses that I owe to Enemies,
Even those the *Sabines* sent; when *Romulus,*
(As thou hast me) ravished their noble Maydes,
Made more, and heavier, light on thee. . . .
The sins of *Tarquin* be rememberd in thee,
And where there has a chast wife been abusde,
Let it be thine, the shame thine, thine the slaughter,
And last, for ever tine, the feard example.
(III. i. 87–90, 91–94)

Thus again—this time mythologically—she relates the wrongs
done to women to political wrongs, and equates patriarchy and
empire.

Valentinian's answer is an arrant claim for prerogative:

Ye are so excellent, and made to ravish,
(There were no pleasure in ye else) . . .
So bred for mans amazement, that my reason
And every help to hold me right has lost me;
The God of love himselfe had been before me,
Had he but power to see ye; tell me justly,
How can I choose but erre then? . . .
Know I am far above the faults I doe,
And those I doe I am able to forgive too;
And where your credit in the knowledge of it,
May be with glosse enough suspected, mine
Is as mine owne command shall make it: princes
Though they be sometime subject to loose whispers,
Yet weare they two edged swords for open censures:
Your husband cannot help ye, nor the Souldier,
Your husband is my creature, they my weapons,
And only where I bid 'em, strike; I feed 'em:
Nor can the Gods be angry at this action,
For as they make me most, they meane me happiest,
Which I had never bin without this pleasure.
(III. i. 103–4, 105–9, 119–31)

Lucina determines to commit suicide in true Roman fashion, an
intention which is debated almost coolly with her husband Maximus and his fellow soldier Aecius. What makes Maximus decide
she has no choice is his acknowledgment of the truth of Oriana's
observation about the misogynistic assumptions of the people:

I would desire her live, nay more, compell her:
But since it was not youth, but malice did it,
And not her own, nor mine, but both our losses,
Nor staies it there, but that our names must find it,
Even those to come; and when they read, she livd,
Must they not aske how often she was ravishd,
And make a doubt she lov'd that more then Wedlock?
Therefore she must not live. (III. i. 238–45)

No argument from Aecius can save her from destruction at the hands of a tyrant and a misogynistic ethos.

Again and again in Fletcher's plays, the plight of a woman oppressed by a domineering man parallels that of a state in the hands of a corrupt sovereign. In *The Humorous Lieutenant,* for example, the last solo play Fletcher wrote prior to *Sir John Van Olden Barnavelt* and his subsequent steady collaboration with Massinger, the political situation of the female protagonist Celia is represented specifically in terms of sexual politics. The play opens with preparations at court for the arrival of certain ambassadors in Asia Minor. Ushers prepare the scene, and one of them condescendingly explains to another the need for elaborate preparations for the audience. "Make all things perfect," he says, but not with diplomacy in mind. "[W]ould you have these Ladies," he asks,

They that come here to see the Show, these Beuties
That have been labouring to set-off their Sweetnes,
And washd and curld; perfum'd, and taken Glisters
For fear a flaw of wind might over-take 'em,
Lose these and all their expectations?[14]

"Would you have al these slighted?" he asks of his inferior, and expands on the logic of courtly show and the hyperbole of courtly expression:

[W]ho should report then
The Embassadors were hansome men? his beard a neat one?
The fire of his eyes quicker then lightning,
And where it breaks, as blasting? his legs, though little ones,
Yet movers of a masse of understanding?
Who shall commend their cloaths: who shall take notice
Of the most wise behaviour of their feathers? (I. i. 18–24)

Some citizens enter to see the ceremony, but the usher insults them and throws them out.

At this point, Celia enters to see her lover Demetrius and suffers an abusive conversation with the head usher, who immediately assumes that because she is not dressed in finery she must be a whore. "The King is comming," he says, "And shall we have an agent from the suburbs / Come to crave audience too?" (I. i. 64–66). With the protection of the second usher, however, she manages to be in the room when the king and ambassadors enter, followed in due course by Demetrius. He sees her and kisses her, and the attitude of the ushers changes dramatically. "Lord, how they flocke me!" she says, "Before I was affraid they would have beat me; / How these flies play i'th sunshine" (I. i. 230–32). This sets the scene succinctly enough for the court of King Antigonus, who is characterized in the dramatis personae as "an old Man with young desires," and who in due course attempts to seduce Celia with a *Midsummer Night's Dream*-like magic potion which is intended to make "whosoever drinkes [it] violently doat upon [his] person" (IV. iii. 44–45). She, however, Marina-like, is not only unaffected but succeeds in converting him away from his lusts. The terms in which she broaches this conversion represent the bounds of proper kingship:

> What glory
> Now after all your Conquests got, your Titles,
> The ever-living memories rais'd to ye,
> Can my defeat be? my poore wracke, what triumph?
> And when you crowne your swelling cups to fortune,
> What honourable tongue can sing my story?
> Be as your Embleme is, a glorious Lamp
> Set on the top of all, to light all perfectly:
> Be as your office is, a god-like Justice,
> Into all shedding equally your vertues. (IV. v. 46–55)

Her attitude when he intimates that he may choose to rape her states unequivocally that one is a king only as long as one behaves as a king:

> *Antigonus:*   Say I should force ye?
> I have it in my will.
> *Celia:*   Your will's a poore one;
> And though it be a Kings will, a despised one,
> Weaker then Infants leggs, your will's in swadling clouts:
> A thousand waies my will has found to checke ye;
> A thousand doores to scape ye: I dare die sir;

As suddenly I dare die, as you can offer:
Nay, say you had your will, say you had ravish'd me,
Perform'd your lust, what had you purchas'd by it?

(IV. v. 59–67)

The quest for women's sovereignty in this play thus broaches fundamental questions about the nature of rule.

Five years later, Fletcher reworked some of this material in *A Wife for a Month,* a late solo play, licensed for production on 27 May 1624, approximately a year before his death. It begins with what can by now be recognized as a Fletcherian norm, a scene which introduces a corrupt court and a lustful monarch catered to by amoral advisers, beginning a sexual plot against a good noble couple. The king, Frederick, desires a sexual encounter with his adviser Sorano's sister Evanthe, and Sorano is only too happy to oblige on the premise that Evanthe is "a compleat Courtier" and will therefore be responsive to "[l]arge golden promises, and sweet language."[15] Frederick is chary, however, of offending his queen, since Evanthe is one of her ladies-in-waiting. Sorano's insolent response relies upon an attitude to absolutism that Fletcher attacked again and again from *The Maid's Tragedy* onward:

> say she were a fury,
> I had thought you had been absolute, the great King,
> The fountaine of all honours, place and pleasures,
> Your will and your commands unbounded also;
> Go get a paire of beads and learne to pray, Sir. (I. i. 46–50)

Evanthe's reaction to the king's eventual advances turns out to be a model response of upright subject to unjust ruler and depends upon a crucial *parliamentary* context. A king's absolute actions, she implies, are correctly and morally tempered by Parliament:

> *Evanthe:* Shall I be rich do you say, and glorious,
> And shine above the rest, and scorne all beauties,
> And mighty in command?
> *Frederick:*　　　　　Thou shalt be any thing.
> *Evanthe:* Let me be honest too, and then ile thank ye.
> Have you not such a title to bestow too?
> If I prove otherwise, I would know but tis Sir,
> Can all the power you have or all the riches,
> But tye mens tongues up from discoursing of me,

Their eyes from gazing at my glorious folly,
Time that shall come from wondering at my impudence,
And they that read my wanton life, from curses?
Can you do this? have ye this magick in ye?
This is not in your powre, though you be a Prince Sir
(No more then evill is in holy Angels)
Nor I, I hope; get wantonnesse confirm'd
By Act of Parliament an honesty,
And so receiv'd by all, ile harken to ye.
Heaven guide your Grace. (I. i. 106–23)

This is the practical political resolution to Oriana's complaint against popular attitudes to women. Rejection of absolute or divine power in kings and acknowledgment of parliamentary procedure as the arbitrator of moral power provides a defense for Evanthe against Frederick's lusts. Her argument depends entirely upon a political situation in which the absolute tendencies of the monarch, expressed in sexual metaphor as is Fletcher's habit, are tempered by the reasonable response that a parliament might guarantee.

3

The parliamentary model is, in a sense, an incomplete one in the context of *A Wife for a Month,* since it curbs rather than cures a king's tendency toward tyranny. Recalling the ways in which *The Woman's Prize* echoes Aristophanes' *Lysistrata,* however, perhaps suggests a further aspect of Fletcher's political representation of women, one which arguably moves beyond the confines of both the wit game described by Kathleen McLuskie and the tempering model provided by Evanthe's invocation of parliamentary structures in *A Wife for a Month. Lysistrata* comes to a close with a dance in which the husbands and wives are reunited, concluding with a song in praise of Athena, goddess-protectress of all Greece. The context is politics, the politics both of state and of gender, since the aim of the sex strike is to force the men to agree terms for peace. Lysistrata commands the women throughout their sexual rebellion, and as the play draws to a conclusion she succeeds in her plan to reconcile the Spartans and the Athenians. She calls to Reconciliation, "an extremely beautiful and totally unclothed girl," to guide the Athenian negotiators and the Spartan ambassadors to her ("Don't be rough or brusque," she instructs her, "handle them very gently, not in the brutal way men lay hold on us, but the way a lady should—very civilized"), and they rapidly agree terms for a treaty. The play concludes with a song of thanksgiving to Pallas Athena, the presiding goddess:

> Athena, hail, thou Zeus-born Maid!
> Who war and death in Greece hast stayed:
> Hail, fount from whom all blessings fall;
> All hail, all hail, Protectress of us all. (235)

The two sides are thus brought together by the strategies of a woman and the symbolic guidance of Reconciliation, embodied as a woman, and the new-found political unity of Greece is celebrated in a hymn of praise to a female divinity.

This, I would argue, serves not only as a source for the action of *The Woman's Prize,* but as a model for political solutions in a number of Fletcher's plays. In several plays of the early 1620s, political strife is negotiated and resolved by women who are either magical or create artificial magic for the purpose. To demonstrate this, we must return to the politics of the country, since the locus for political resolution in these plays is invariably far from city or court. In *The Pilgrim,* for example, a solo play dating from Christmas 1621, a series of problems of the kind we have already considered in the context of the politics of the countryside are resolved by the intervention of two assertive women, who create a magical context for political and social resolution.

In Act V of *The Pilgrim,* the Governor of Segovia encourages festivities in honor of a dual royal occasion, the king's "birth day, and his marriage."[16] "Use all your sports, / All your solemnities," he encourages the people, to make it "a glad day." A citizen promises to make "*Segovia* ring with our rejoycings," and the Governor outlines a code for appropriate festive behavior:

> Be sumptuous, but not riotous; be bounteous,
> But not in drunken Bacchanals: free to all strangers,
> Easie, and sweet in all your entertainments,
> For tis a Royall day admits no rudenesse. (V. iii. 6–9)

A certain degree of reciprocation is called for, however, by the Governor's people if they are to be dutiful subjects, and they are keen to remind him of the problems they face with outlaws. One citizen says

> I hope your honour has taken into your consideration
> The miseries we have suffered by these Out-laws,
> The losses, howrly feares; the rude abuses
> Strangers that travell to us are daily loaden with.
>
> (V. iii. 12–15)

The Governor tells them of a "Commission from the King" to deal with the outlaws, but the people press on with their complaints:

> *1 Citizen:*   Had we not wals, sir,
> And those continually man'd too with our watches,
> We should not have a bit of meat to feed us.
> And yet they are our friends, and we must think so,
> And entertaine 'em sometimes, and feast 'em,
> And send 'em loden home too, we are lost else.
> *2 Citizen:* They'l come to Church amongst us, as we hope Christians,
> When all their zeale is but to steale the Chalices;
> At this good time now, if your Lordship were not here,
> To awe their violence with your authority,
> They would play such gambals! . . .
> They would drink up all our Wine, pisse out our Bonfires;
> Then, like the drunken Centaures, have at the fairest,
> Nay, have at all: fourscore and ten's a Goddesse,
> Whilst we, like fooles, stand shaking in our cellars. (V. iii. 18–32)

The Governor's observations make it clear, however, that he is aware that Roderigo, the leader of these outlaws and once a courtier, has been the subject of courtly intrigue and jealousy, and that his exile is due to others' desires to take his estate. "Tis pity of their Captaine *Roderigo* . . . / That long neglect bred this, I am sorry for him," he says, describing him as "A wel-bred Gentleman, and a good souldier, / And one, his Majesty has some little reason / To thank, for sundry services, and faire ones." Verdugo adds that "[t]he hope of his estate keeps backe his pardon; / There's divers waspes, that buz about that honey-box, / And long to lick themselves full" (V. iii. 42–49). He goes on nonetheless to point out the difficulty of solving the problem:

> To fetch him in sir,
> By violence, he being now no infant,

Will aske some bloody crowns. I know his people
Are of his owne choice men, that will not totter,
Nor blench much at a Bullet; I know his order,
And though he have no multitude, h'as manhood;
The elder-twin to that too, staid experience.
But if he must be forced, sir, ———. (V. iii. 51–58)

Promising resolution to the problem of the outlaws, they turn to the festivities. As with Silvio's "Dance you, Ile fight, Sir" injunction to Soto in *Women Pleased,* the governor is careful to see action premised on conjunction with festivity. "Come," he says, "to this preparation"; and adds that "when that's done, / The Outlaws expedition is begun." The citizens are satisfied: "We'l contribute all to that," says one, "and help our selves too" (V. iii. 69–71). Once they know that their grievances will shortly be addressed, the citizens are happy to participate in the king's festivities. Rule in the country of *The Pilgrim* is thus by negotiation and collaboration, not prerogative.

The issues of rightful command and prerogative rule had already surfaced earlier in the play. Roderigo, the outlawed aristocrat, sentences Pedro, Alinda's lover and his long-standing enemy, to summary execution. One of his men asks, "What's his fault, Captaine?" to which Roderigo answers only, "Tis my will he perish, / And thats his fault." And Pedro is quick to capitalize on the problems of prerogative. "A Captaine of good government," he cries mockingly, and addresses Roderigo's outlaws:

Come Souldiers, come, ye are roughly bred, and bloody,
Shew your obedience, and the joy ye take
In executing impious commands;
Ye have a Captaine seales your liberall pardons,
Be no more Christians, put religion by,
Twill make ye cowards: feele no tendernesse,
Nor let a thing call'd conscience trouble ye;
Alasse, twill breed delay! (II. ii. 154–63)

He works on their consciences and drives a wedge between their awareness of the difference between prerogative orders and rightful orders. The outlaws consequently refuse to hang him on a political principle: "We will obey things handsome, / And bad enough, and over doe obedience," they say, "But to be made such instruments of mischiefe———" (II. ii. 195–97) Roderigo is beside himself at

178

their disobedience, and concludes that they must have planned it: "Have ye conspir'd, ye slaves?" he rages, while Pedro gives a smug commentary on his short temper: "How vildly this showes / In one that would command anothers temper, / And beare no bound in's own" (II. ii. 202–4). The language that Pedro uses to the outlaws is persistently constitutional. "[K]eepe your obedience," he tells them, as the tables begin to turn against him, "For though your government admit no president, / Keep yourselves carefull in't" (II. ii. 241–42).

It is finally the intervention of the saintly Alinda which saves Pedro, caught as he is between the implacable absolutism of Roderigo and the unwillingness of Roderigo's men to do the deed. Alinda has been portrayed as a woman of some strength from the opening of the play. She is unstinting in her generosity to the poor pilgrims who come to her door, much to the fury of her short-tempered father whose attitude quickly forces her to flee to the woods disguised as a boy. She joins Roderigo's band, and when his men fail to obey his order to execute Pedro, she persuades Roderigo not to kill him by pointing out the advantage of reputation Pedro would have over him afterward: "This man ye rocke asleep, and all your rages / Are Requiems to his parting soule, meere Anthems" (II. ii. 332–33). Her servant Juletta joins her in the woods, and together they plot a way to overcome the violence of the men.

The key scene comes late in the last act. Roderigo and Pedro, now reconciled, find themselves in a particularly idyllic part of the countryside. "How sweet these solitary places are," says Roderigo in a moment of uncharacteristic lyricism, "how wantonly / The wind blowes through the leafes, and courts, and playes with 'em" (V. iv. 1–2). They hear "strange Musicke," and, Ferdinand-like, they follow the sound until they see "inchanted Cels" inhabited by singing birds. For Pedro, the sights and sounds serve to remind him of his lost love, Alinda: "O love," he moans, "In such a harmony art thou begotten, / In such soft Ayre, so gentle, lul'd and nourish'd. O my best Mistris!" (V. iv. 23–26). Roderigo is touched by this: "deere Heaven / Give him his hearts content, and me forgive too," he whispers in an aside (V. iv. 26–27). At this point, Alinda and Juletta appear, dressed as old women and described by Roderigo as "grandame things" and "strange antiquities" (V. iv. 36). Juletta has taken over her mistress's dominant role and become the orchestrator of events, and she assures the amazed Alinda that they cannot be recognized. "They wonder at us," she says, and adds "let's maintaine that wonder" (IV. v. 41). We know that the magic is contrived by way of disguise and other means, but the women aim to "maintaine that wonder" which is the psychological effect of the magic they have orchestrated. "Let them admire," Juletta says, "it makes / For our advantage" (V. iv. 99–100). Pedro and Roderigo are afraid of the women, but they listen as they are told to make their way to Segovia to "repent, and live" (V. iv. 93). The women call the unnerved Roderigo forward. "I shall be hang'd, or whipt now," he says to himself, acknowledging that "[t]hese know, and these have power" (V. iv. 70). Juletta and Alinda take it in turns to admonish him:

> *Juletta:*   See how he shakes.
> A secure conscience never quakes,
> Thou hast been ill; be so no more,
> A good retreat is a great store.
> Thou hast commanded men of might,
> Command thy selfe, and then thou art right.
> *Alinda:* Command thy will: thy foule desires.
> Put out and quench thy unhallowed fires:
> Command thy mind, and make that pure;
> Thou art wise then, valiant, and secure.
> A blessing then thou maist beget.
> *Juletta:* A curse else that shall never set
> Will light upon thee: Say thy Prayers,
> Thou hast as many sins, as haires.
> Thou art a Captain, let thy men
> Be honest, have good thoughts, and then
> Thou maist command, and lead in chiefe,
> Yet thou art bloody, and a thiefe.
> *Roderigo:* What shall I doe? I doe confesse.
> *Alinda:*   Retire,
> And purge thee perfect in his fire:
> His life observe; live in his Schoole,
> And then thou shalt put off the foole.
> *Juletta:* Pray at *Segovia* too, and give
> Thy Offrings up, repent, and live. (V. iv. 70–93)

Once Alinda and Juletta have gone, Roderigo is left to say, "Now I am Catechiz'd, I would ever dwell here, / For here is a kinde of Court of Reformation" (V. iv. 110–11).

When Alinda and Juletta reappear in the closing scene, they are disguised as shepherdesses, and arrive in the midst of solemn prayers at the altar at Segovia. Again, wonder is the chief emotion at their arrival. Alphonso, amazed, can only say, "I had a daughter, / With such a face once: such eyes and nose too, / Ha, let me see, 'tis wondrous like *Alinda*" (V. vi. 45–47). They kneel at the altar and produce offerings for the king, the queen, and for themselves (in that order):

> *Alinda:* Thus we kneele, and thus we pray
> A happy honour, to this day,
> Thus our Sacrifice we bring
> Ever happy to the King.
> *Juletta:* These of Purple, Damask, greene,
> Sacred to the vertuous Queene
> Here we hang.
> *Alinda:*   As these are now
> Her glories ever spring, and show.
> These for our selves: our hopes, and loves,
> Full of pincks, and Ladies gloves,
> Of hartes-ease too, which we would faine
> As we labour for, attaine;
> Heare me heaven, and as I bend,
> Full of hope: some comfort send. (V. vi. 51–64)

It is only at this point, now that the recognition scene has occurred and opposed individuals are reconciled, that Juletta can admit the constructed nature of the magic she has used. She admits she has disguised herself as "a little Foot-Boy," "a Drum," and "a Page" in order to manipulate events, and amazes Roderigo by announcing mischievously that she and Alinda were the old, prophesying women in the woods. She places the motivation for all this action squarely upon her love for her mistress Alinda: "I am strange ayers, and excellent sweet voyces. / I am any thing, to doe her good beleeve me" (V. vi. 113–14). Alphonso tries to recompense her for her arrangement of the general reconciliation by offering her a husband, but she demonstrates perhaps how far toward the role of Byancha from *The Woman's Prize* she has moved by replying, "No I beseech you Sir; / My Mistresse is my husband, with her I'le dwell still" (V. vi. 119–20). As *agente provocateuse,* Juletta must remain, like Byancha, outside the symmetry of marriage relations at the close of the play.

4

Fletcher's early analysis of sexual politics thus draws upon and reacts to Shakespeare's *The Taming of the Shrew*. Later in his career, another play of Shakespeare's seems to be of particular interest to Fletcher and is involved more than once in his later representation of the political roles available to women. In the run up to the publication of the Shakespeare First Folio, Fletcher produced a spate of rereadings of *The Tempest*, the last play Shakespeare wrote alone. One can only assume that the research of fellow King's men Heminges and Condell into Shakespeare's texts at that time had rekindled Fletcher's long-standing fascination with his erstwhile colleague's work. *The Tempest* seems to have meant something special to the Folio compilers, since they gave it pride of place as the first play in the volume, against all interests of chronology and dramatic development. However it came about, the years 1621 and 1622 saw at least four plays from Fletcher's pen which were consciously rooted in one way or another in *The Tempest*.

It is above all the awkward and uneasy moments of *The Tempest* that Fletcher insistently reworks, the moments at which Prospero's power and project are most in question or when the play's utopian impetus is most apparent.[17] *The Double Marriage,* for example, written with Massinger in spring 1621, re-presents a series of key moments from Shakespeare's play. After fourteen years' delay, an exiled duke narrates the tale of his disgrace to his daughter. The narration, however, motivates piracy and revenge, and the re-demptive possibilities customarily inherent in romantic tragicomedy are driven into a tragic process which culminates in the death of a tyrant king of Naples to cries of "Liberty and freedom!": a revolution curiously reminiscent in underlying motive, if not in execution, of the attempted coup of Stephano, Trinculo, and Caliban. Again, *The Wild-Goose Chase,* written in 1621 by Fletcher alone, focuses on a mock Prospero figure in the wild-goose Mirable, a misogynistic Don Juan who keeps a narrative of his conquests which he volunteers to burn at the end of the play, thereby abjuring his unlimited sexual license. *The Sea Voyage,* written, again with Massinger, in the first half of 1622, reworks the colonial aspects of *The Tempest,* beginning with a leveling storm and analyzing the uneasy possibilities of a women's utopia.[18] A month or two earlier in 1622, Fletcher and Massinger had produced in the

The Prophetess perhaps their most puzzling reworking of Prospero the mage in the figure of the prophetess Delphia.

The Prophetess is a strange and difficult play which examines the rise of the emperor Dioclesian to the supreme position in Rome and charts the dangers inherent in the acquisition of power, concluding with a strong affirmation of the virtue of the country life over that of the court. The closing action of the play to some extent mirrors that of *The Pilgrim* and further amplifies the connections of state politics and the politics of gender in Fletcher's plays. Yet the preceding action is, to a certain extent, morally and politically ambivalent. The opening scenes seem remarkably unsophisticated for a Fletcher play of the early 1620s, lacking the subtlety of plot and language of, say, *The Wild-Goose Chase,* and in that sense they echo the conscious formality and archaism of *The Faithful Shepherdess,* written some ten years earlier. Moreover, there are puzzling disjunctions of characterization in the course of the play that make coherent analysis difficult.

The Prophetess is unique within the Fletcher canon for several reasons, but it is the characterization of Delphia which stands out as the most ambivalent and atypical element of the play. Normally in Fletcherian drama (as we have seen in *The Pilgrim*), apparently magical events turn out to have been orchestrated and fabricated by ordinary mortals. Despite their reputation as a canon of "wonder," Fletcher's plays by and large eschew the magical qualities associated with Shakespeare's late plays, preferring to undercut audience expectations of miraculous happenings with a certain wry realism. In one sense, *The Prophetess* is no different. We see that Delphia orchestrates the "music from the spheres" which seems to signal that "the gods approve" of Diocles (as he is named until his accession) as emperor, yet her ability to conjure such music is indeed truly magical. In her role as an alternative controller of political events whose power stems from heaven, she is more than reminiscent of Clorin, the eponymous protagonist of *The Faithful Shepherdess.* On the other hand, when we hear the clown Geta's undercutting remarks at the moment of Diocles's accession—"My Master is an Emperour, and I feel / A Senators Itch upon me: would I could hire / These fine invisible Fidlers to play to me / At my instalment"—we are made aware of the artificiality of his rise to power. [19]

Delphia's role—as a kind of curiously feminized Prospero—is

fraught with moral and theological complications, yet at the same time is clearly politically charged. By 1621, the dramatic representation of women as stalwarts of religious faith in the face of Roman (Catholic) persecution was well established (in, for example, Dekker and Massinger's *The Virgin Martyr,* which was licensed for production on 6 October 1620), and such female religious figures carried with them certain political resonances with the resurgence in the early 1620s of militant Protestant nostalgia for the reign of the Virgin Queen. Dorothea, the heroine of *The Virgin Martyr,* is a thoroughly idealized figure: there are no suggestions of any flaws in her character. By contrast, until the final act of *The Prophetess,* Delphia is at best a figure of moral ambivalence. We have been aware from the beginning, for example, that Ceres is Delphia's particular goddess, and Ceres is present at the resolution of the play, but their relationship has appeared at times a little uneasy. When in act 2 Delphia's niece Drusilla expresses her fear that Dioclesian will be lured from her by courtly ladies, Delphia promises magical surveillance. "No, my Drusilla," she says:

> From *Ceres* will I force her winged Dragons,
> And in the air hang over the Tribunal;
> (The Musick of the Spheres attending on us.)
> There, as his good Star, thou shalt shine upon him,
> If he prove true, and as his Angel guard him.
> But if he dare be false, I, in a moment,
> Will put that glorious light out, with such horrour
> As if the eternal Night has seiz'd the Sun,
> Or all things were return'd to the first Chaos,
> And then appear like Furies. (II. i, p. 336)

Moreover, this "forcing" of the goddess turns into a momentary defection. At the end of the act, Delphia changes allegiance, briefly allying herself with darker forces. "Some Rites I am to perform to *Hecate,*" she says, "To perfect my designs" (II. iii, pp. 345–46). These dark connections resurface when, Faustus-like, she teaches Geta a lesson by conjuring a she-devil to frighten him out of the arrogant attitude he has assumed since his master became emperor. The anxieties and uncertainties that at times characterize Delphia's attitudes are in many ways reminiscent of Prospero's unease about his powers. "Rest then assur'd," she says to Drusilla, "I am the Mistris of my Art, and fear not" (II. i, p. 336).

Yet once Diocles becomes emperor as Delphia has foretold, he immediately forgets his obligations to her and to Drusilla, leaving Delphia to rage, "If he dares prove false, / These glories shall be to him as a dream, / Or an inchanted banquet" (II. iii, p. 344), a further quiet echo of *The Tempest*. When she realizes that Diocles prefers Aurelia to Drusilla, she orchestrates a Persian victory to spoil things:

> *The skilful* Delphia *finding by sure proof*
> *The presence of* Aurelia *dim'd the Beauty*
> *Of her* Drusilla . . .
> *Deals with the* Persian *Legats, that were bound*
> *For the Ransom of* Cassana, *to remove*
> Aurelia, Maximinian, *and* Charinus,
> *Out of the sight of* Rome. (IV. i, pp. 363–64)

Delphia's betrayal of her fellow Romans here is hardly alleviated by the added condition that the Persians "shall not, / On any terms, when they were in their power, / Presume to touch their lives" (IV. i, p. 364). Her behavior is more akin to that of Dionyza in Shakespeare and Wilkins's *Pericles*—who betrays the innocent Marina because the girl constantly outshines her own daughter Philoten—than to the selflessness of a Clorin. Her angry strategizing at such moments involves moral compromises that cannot have sustained the sympathy of the audience.

On the other hand, she acts in an environment of betrayal and broken vows, and her strategies are oriented not only to the advantage of her own niece but to an appropriate political response to state problems. Throughout, we are aware that the threat posed by the ambitiousness of both Maximinian and Aurelia requires radical action. The closing scenes of the play sustain a moral and theological clarity notably absent from the first four acts, moving toward the kind of resolution provided by *The Pilgrim,* a feminocentric political conclusion premised on the moral superiority of country reflection over courtly intrigue. It is as if the negotiated settlements represented in plays such as *Women Pleased* can find a proper resolution only away from kings and their courts, in an idealized countryside governed by a powerful woman. In collaboration now with Massinger, it appears that Fletcher has come full circle from *The Faithful Shepherdess:* the political symbolism of *The Prophetess* turns our minds and memories back toward the days of the Virgin Queen.

The play's political outlook, its rejection of absolutism, is perhaps most bluntly voiced in the leveling comment Geta makes on the smell of putrefaction that assails him when Diocles opens the litter to discover the murdered emperor Numerianus. "An Emperours Cabinet?" he exclaims, "Fough, I have known a Charnelhouse smell sweeter. / If Emperours flesh have this savour, what will mine do / When I am rotten?" (II. ii, p. 340). It is fear of the contradictions of mortality and absolutism that unsettles Dioclesian, even at the height of his power—an appropriate political unease in a play which opens with an emperor dead in his sedan chair. And once he has secured victory in the Persian wars, Dioclesian loses all interest in his role as emperor, becoming painfully aware of the inevitability of his own death:

> I am a man,
> And all these glories, Empires heap'd upon me,
> Confirm'd by constant friends, and faithful Guards,
> Cannot defend me from a shaking Feaver,
> Or bribe the uncorrupted Dart of Death
> To spare me one short minute. Thus adorn'd
> In these triumphant Robes, my body yields not
> A greater shadow, than it did when I
> Liv'd both poor and obscure; a Swords sharp point
> Enters my flesh as far; dreams break my sleep
> As when I was a private man; my passions
> Are stronger tyrants on me; nor is Greatness
> A saving Antidote to keep me from
> A Traytors poyson. Shall I praise my fortune,
> Or raise the building of my happiness
> On her uncertain favour? or presume
> She is mine own, and sure, that yet was never
> Constant to any? Should my reason fail me
> (As flattery oft corrupts it) here's an example,
> To speak how far her smiles are to be trusted;
> The rising Sun, this morning, saw this man
> The *Persian* Monarch, and those Subjects proud
> That had the honour but to kiss his feet;
> And yet e're his diurnal progress ends,
> He is the scorn of Fortune. (IV. vi, pp. 374–75)

At the zenith, then, he decides to retire, and he elaborates on his decision to abdicate his political responsibilities:

> Let it suffice
> I have toucht the height of humane happiness,
> And here I fix *nil ultra.* Hitherto
> I have liv'd a servant to ambitious thoughts,
> And fading glories; what remains of life,
> I dedicate to Vertue; and to keep
> My faith untainted, farewel Pride and Pomp,
> And circumstance of glorious Majestie,
> Farewel for ever. (IV. vi, pp. 375–76)

It is only away from court that Dioclesian can "dedicate" himself "to Vertue." Going into the country, he can obey divine command in marrying Drusilla rather than succumbing to the courtly charms of the sinister and ambitious Aurelia, whom only the audible signs of heavenly displeasure have prevented him from marrying, contrary to his earlier vow. The negative aspects of courtly life are comprehensively embodied in Aurelia's allure and mutability, the positive aspects of the country in the steadfastness of Drusilla, backed by the determining support of heaven. In this context, the emperor seems to have remarkably little divine right. He has been installed by the will of heaven, but can keep the gods' favor eventually only by retiring from the court. His actions seem absolutely predetermined from the start.

In retiring from political life, he gives all he has to his ambitious nephew Maximinian, retaining only "the poor Grange, / The Patrimony which my father left me," and telling Maximinian to stay at court while he will "labour to find content elsewhere" (IV. vi, p. 376). There is thus a stark contrast between honour at court and content in the country, voiced most clearly by Drusilla: "I still lov'd / Your Person, not your fortunes," she says, "in a cottage, / Being yours, I am an Empress" (IV. vi, p. 376). The Chorus who narrates the first scene of the last act is quite explicit about the new role Dioclesian has chosen:

> good Dioclesian,
> *Weary of Pomp and State, retires himself*
> *With a small Train, to a most private Grange*
> *In* Lombardie; *where the glad Countrey strives*

> With Rural Sports to give him entertainment:
> With which delighted, he with ease forgets
> All specious trifles, and securely tastes
> The certain pleasures of a private life. (V. i, p. 377)

Country sports are thus once again drawn in direct opposition to the "specious trifles" of court: there is little acknowledgment here of James's attempt in *The Book of Sports* to put such activities on a par with courtly entertainments. The country harmony Dioclesian finds at his "most private grange" stands in direct contrast to the effects of vicious ambition on Maximinian back at court. "Nearness of blood," he announces, "Respect of pietie, and thankfulness, / And all the holy dreams of vertuous fools / Must vanish into nothing, when Ambition / (The maker of great minds, and nurse of honour) / Puts in for Empire" (V. ii, p. 379). Thus one of the distinctive features of Dioclesian's residence in the country is that he allows and enjoys folk games and sports.

At one point, a group of shepherds discusses his attitude toward the country and their pastimes. The first asks: "Do you think this great man will continue here?" and the second replies:

> Continue here? what else? he has bought the great Farm;
> A great man, with a great Inheritance,
> And all the ground about it, all the woods too;
> And stock'd it like an Emperour. Now, all our sports again
> And all our merry Gambols, our may-Ladies,
> Our evening-daunces on the Green, our Songs,
> Our Holiday good cheer, our Bag-pipes now Boyes,
> Shall make the wanton Lasses skip again,
> Our Sheep-sheerings, and all our knacks. (V. iii, pp. 381–82)

A third shepherd contrasts such games with the sophisticated but artificial entertainments given at court: "He cannot expect now / His Courtly entertainments, and his rare Musicks, / And Ladies to delight him with their voyces," he claims. Instead he can expect "[h]onest and cheerful toyes from honest meanings, / And the best hearts they have" (V. iii, p. 382). Even Geta, whom we have seen swollen with courtly pride in previous scenes, succumbs to the leveling effects of country air. To begin with, he retains his courtly airs, telling the country people to "stand farther off." "[M]ingle not with my authoritie," he instructs them, "I am too mighty for your companie." The third shepherd acknowledges his grandeur but asks him to pay attention to their country sports. In response Geta starts to set himself up as a courtly censor of such activities in what appears to be continuing criticism of *The Book of Sports*—"For your Sports, Sirs," he says, "They may be seen, when I shall think convenient, / When out of my discretion, I shall view 'em, / And hold 'em fit for licence" (V. iii, p. 383)—but before long he relaxes and says: "Come nearer now, / And be not fearfull; I take off my austeritie. . . . / Come, go along with me, / And I will hear your Songs, and perhaps like 'em" (V. iii, p. 383). At this point, Delphia arrives, and gives clerical (and therefore, presumably, divine) approval to the games: "[H]onest friends," she cries, "I know ye are hatching / Some pleasurable sports for your great Landlord: / Fill him with joy, and win him a friend to ye, / And make this little Grange seem a large Empire, / Let out with home-contents" (V. iii, p. 384).

Dioclesian and Drusilla, meanwhile, are discussing the pleasures of country living in direct contrast to life at court:

> *Dioclesian:*   I find now by experience,
> Content was never Courtier.
> *Drusilla:*   I pray ye walk on, Sir;
> The cool shades of the Grove invite ye.
> *Dioclesian:*   O my Dearest!
> When man has cast off his ambitious greatness,
> And sunk into the sweetness of himself;
> Built his foundation upon honest thoughts,
> Not great, but good desires his daily servants;
> How quie[t]ly he sleeps! how joyfully
> He wakes again, and looks on his possessions,
> And from his willing labours feeds with pleasure?
> Here hang no Comets in the shape of Crowns,
> To shake our sweet contents: nor here, *Drusilla,*
> Cares, like Eclipses, darken our endeavours:
> We love here without rivals, kiss with innocence;
> Our thoughts as gentle as our lips; our children
> The double heirs both of our forms and faiths.
> *Drusilla:* I am glad ye make this right use of this sweetness,
> This sweet retiredness.
> *Dioclesian:*   'Tis sweet indeed, love,
> And every circumstance about it, shews it.

How liberal in the spring in every place here?
The artificial Court shews but a shadow,
A painted imitation of this glory.
Smell to this flower, here nature has her excellence:
Let all the perfumes of the Empire pass this,
The carefull'st Ladies cheek shew such a colour,
They are gilded and adulterate vanities. (V. iii, pp. 384–85)

As Dioclesian speaks these words, he hears music which "stirs and joys" him. Confirmation of divine approval for his recent actions is revealed in the form of a spirit rising from a "Crystal Well," with flowers for his "entertainment," a clear echo of *The Faithful Shepherdess* (and perhaps also of the miraculous responses to the prayers of Palamon, Arcite, and Emilia in *The Two Noble Kinsmen*). Delphia brings in the may-game, saying, "here are Country-shepherds; here is some sport too," and telling Dioclesian, "[Y]ou must grace it, Sir; 'twas meant to welcom ye," adding, "A King shall never feel your joy" (V. iii, p. 386). She ushers in a "dance of Shepherds and Shepherdesses; *Pan* leading the men, *Ceres* the maids." But as soon as she has introduced this dance, Delphia sees her messenger appear and shouts "Hold, hold . . . leave off, friends, / Leave off a while, and breathe" (V. iii, p. 386). Dioclesian is puzzled by this interruption and asks her what the matter is: "you are pale, mother", he points out. Delphia simply says, "Be not affrighted, but sit still," and adds, in a curious echo of Christ, "I am with thee," ordering the dancers to continue the dance.

Courtly ambition now intervenes in the form of a murderous Maximinian, and the echo of the moment at which Prospero's masque is broken in *The Tempest* becomes unmistakable. The presiding goddess is once again Ceres, and all traces of the darker potential of Delphia's magic have now faded. There is the same overall structure of a mage "writing" the action with a heavy guiding hand, and it is that mage's pastoral that is abruptly halted by the incursion of violent ambition. But where in *The Tempest* Prospero's pastoral masque remains broken, the masque Delphia directs continues after the interruption, and unlike Prospero, who loses control at his sudden recollection of the plot of Caliban, Stephano, and Trinculo, Delphia remains apparently unmoved by Maximinian's arrival and encourages the country people to "dance out [their] dance" (V. iii, p. 386).

Maximinian, hell-bent on empire, however, makes his intentions plain, rejecting country festivity out of hand:

> I come not to eat with ye, and to surfeit
> In these poor Clownish pleasures; but to tell ye
> I look upon ye like my Winding-sheet,
> The Coffin of my Greatness, nay, my Grave:
> For whilst you are alive . . . I am no Emperour.
>   (V. iii, p. 386)

Until Dioclesian is dead, Maximinian tells them, he is "nothing but [his] own disquiet." Dioclesian responds by warning him of the dangers of ambition and "ungratefulness," but Maximinian orders his soldiers to kill him. The moment, however, brings to the rescue a deus ex machina almost unique in Fletcher's plays. Thunder and lightning, this time in tune with and not fabricated by Delphia, are followed by a "hand with a Bolt" beneath which Maximinian and Aurelia cower. Their soldiers are rendered immobile, and over the sounds of the storm, the prophetess orders the rebels to "read those hot characters, / And spell the will of heaven" (V. iii, p. 388), forcing them to confess and repent. Forgiveness is granted them, and Dioclesian (now, it would seem, no longer portrayed as an emperor but instead as a country gentleman instructing royalty in the right path) tells them to "love your Good more than your Greatness." As the play ends, we hear the sound of drums as Carinus and his soldiers arrive belatedly to help Dioclesian against the rebellion. Delphia's action has thus prevented civil strife. She turns in conclusion to the country people, and says: "Sound your pipes now merrily, / And all your handsom sports." And Diocletian tells them in the last line of the play to "let 'em know, our true love breeds more stories / And perfect joys, than Kings do, and their glories" (V. iii, p. 389).

5

The Prophetess clearly inherits much from *The Tempest:* its similarities to *The Pilgrim,* however, point to the further source we have noted in Fletcher's own pastoral romance *The Faithful Shepherdess.* It would appear, from the careful union of Ceres and Pan as joint presiding deities of Delphia's dance, that we are intended to notice this juxtaposition of images from both *The Tempest* and *The Faithful Shepherdess*. In *The Pilgrim,* the play is brought to an acceptable conclusion only by the transforming activity of the women, who provide the "magical" events needed to wrest the men away from their strife. Alinda, like Clorin, is characterized as a saintlike figure from the play's opening, and is at least partly responsible for putting things right at the close. The king and queen, often referred to in the course of the play, never appear, and political activity is initiated by a governor and, towards the end, the agency of the women protagonists. The conclusion is in part a pastoral scene, in which "shepherdesses" control the action and orchestrate the resolution of problems of masterlessness and un-controlled lust. Clorin's role is in a way split between Alinda and Juletta. At the close, the chief orchestrator denies the ultimate resolution of marriage, preferring to remain outside societal norms and symmetries. In *The Prophetess,* the orchestrator and presiding figure is also a woman, who, like Clorin, rejects the worship offered her. "I am a poor weak woman," Delphia says in the imme-diate wake of a practical demonstration of her power in foiling Maximinian's first attempt to kill her, "to me no worship" (I. iii, p. 332). Her special goddess is Ceres, and accordingly she arranges a conclusion in the country. The pastoral scene she organizes features shepherds with names such as Amaryllis and Alexis. *The Pilgrim* and *The Prophetess* thus clearly glance backward, by way of *The Tempest* and *The Faithful Shepherdess,* to 1610 or thereabouts: in doing so, they tend to adopt a stance critical of the political status quo in the early 1620s.

We have seen already that Oriana's outburst to her brother in act 1 of *The Wild-Goose Chase* (another play from this time which echoes aspects of *The Tempest*) located itself in "this Warlike age" in an apparent reference to political events in Britain and the Conti-nent in 1621. This political location is amplified by the symbolic resonances of her name. The original Oriana was the true love of the hero of the romance *Amadis de Gaul,* one of the tales mentioned by Oriana in her outburst, thus providing something of an ambig-uous context. On the one hand, Oriana develops a very negative and contemptuous view of such romances in her speech. On the other, though, Oriana (like Gloriana) had been one of the many semimythical names applied to Queen Elizabeth, most notably in

Thomas Morley's 1601 song cycle *The Triumphs of Oriana,* the chorus of which repeats the refrain "Long liue faire *Oriana.*"[20] At James's accession, Queen Anne had been initially addressed (in the context of her reappropriation of Elizabeth's womanly symbols) as Ori-Anna: but this echo of Elizabeth seems to have lapsed rapidly. The name was, however, revived in rather different circumstances in 1619 or thereabouts. A set of songs by Thomas Vautor, entitled *The First Set: beeing Songs of diuers Ayres and Natures,* invoked once more the name of Oriana, not in the context of glorifying James's family or reign but rather of the late Jacobean revival of Elizabeth's Accession Day feast on 17 November as overt criticism of James and his pacific policies.

Discontent with Stuart methods of government and a yearning for the days of Elizabeth found an outlet in the bonfires and bell-ringing of that day, as one of Vautor's songs suggests:

> Orian now a saint in heaven is crowned.
>> Both bonfires and bell-ringers
>> She left us, and good singers.
> Sing then, ye nymphs and shepherds of Diana;
>> Farewall, fair Oriana.[21]

It is thus difficult to avoid hearing a double resonance in Fletcher's employment of the name Oriana in 1621, since James's daughter Elizabeth had been viewed poetically at the 1613 celebrations for her marriage to the elector palatine as a reincarnation of the older Elizabeth. Reference to her, however subtle, in the "warlike" context of 1621, can suggest only criticism of James. Echoes of 1610 in *The Pilgrim* and *The Prophetess* amplify this implied criticism of political affairs in the early 1620s, criticism which is the product of a carefully modulated reinterpretation of the role of the chaste and dominant woman away from the destructive tendencies of male-dominated courts. It is in the country, transmuted into a "Court of Reformation" by the power of women, that the dreamed-of female utopias of Fletcher's assertive women in the earlier plays find a practical location.

It is perhaps too fanciful already to hear a half-echo of Oriana / Gloriana in Clorin's name, but it is quite clear that despite the marked change of direction in Fletcher's drama after the failure of *The Faithful Shepherdess* in 1609, certain political strategies begun in that play recur later in his career. Furthermore, Fletcher's political plays arguably reflect the kind of feminocentric country environment that Fletcher seems to have been part of when he visited the Huntingdon seat at Ashby. It was not only Princess Elizabeth whose name encouraged wistful equations with the memory of the dead Queen Elizabeth; another Jacobean aristocrat whose admirers equated her to a certain extent with the memory of Queen Elizabeth was Elizabeth, countess of Huntingdon, Fletcher's friend and patron. Thomas Pestell, for example, is keen in his "Verses of ye Countess of Huntington" to present implicit parallels with the memory of Elizabeth, emphasizing her perfection and near divinity. When he refers to her as "faire, & sweete *Elizabeth. / Stanley & Huntingdon,*" and suggests that someone should "her twoe greate names / Ripp vp, and rake in, to finde Anagrams," he is, however ironically, acknowledging the associations that were drawn between the countess and the dead queen.[22] Moreover, it is possible to see Ashby, with its self-conscious role as an exemplary country estate, as a locus for Delphia's injunction to the countrymen in Act V of *The Prophetess* to "make this little grange seem a large empire," as well as for Roderigo's vision of the country in *The Pilgrim* once he has been influenced by Alinda and Juletta as "a kinde of Court of Reformation," and for Philaster's injunction to the errant courtiers to "go and make your country a vertuous court."[23] It is significant too that Arthur Wilson, secretary to the earl of Essex and a contender for authorship of the Coleorton masque, writing during the interregnum and looking back, used these words of Philaster to praise the first Lord Spencer. According to Wilson, he "made the Countrie a vertuous Court, where his Fields and Flocks brought him more calme and happie contentment, then the various and mutable dispensations of a Court can contribute."[24]

In the context of the Huntingdons, moreover, there is a further curious family connection which ties the plays I have discussed here to the best-known of early modern pastoral entertainments, Milton's "A Masque presented at Ludlow Castle," generally known as *Comus*. Elizabeth Hastings, fifth countess of Huntingdon, was the third daughter of Ferdinando, earl of Derby, and his wife Alice, whose visit to Ashby as dowager countess of Derby in 1607 was, as we have seen, the occasion for which Marston's *Entertainment at Ashby* was written. Elizabeth Stanley/Hastings's sisters were

Anne, whose second husband was Mervyn, earl of Castlehaven, and Frances, who married John, earl of Bridgewater. *Comus* was written for the installation of this same earl of Bridgewater as lord president of Wales in 1634. Milton's *Arcades,* produced a year earlier than *Comus* and clearly its forerunner in a number of ways, was "[p]art of an entertainment presented to the countess dowager of Derby at Harefield," probably sponsored, like *Comus,* by the earl of Bridgewater. The two entertainments thus share connections and concerns and may well have been acted by the same people (including the earl of Bridgewater's daughter Alice, named after her grandmother). In particular, both appear to respond, at least in part, to the revival of *The Faithful Shepherdess* at court around this time, echoing as they do that play's ambivalent emphasis upon chastity. As we have seen, the presence of a character named Amaryllis in *The Faithful Shepherdess* may well have been a quiet compliment to the dowager countess, who had in her youth been the "sweete Amaryllis" of Edmund Spenser's *Colin Clout's Come Home Again.* For Milton to invoke Fletcher's pastoral in his entertainment for the countess would presumably be both to repeat that compliment and to situate himself within an appropriately radical Protestant poetic heritage.[25]

Part of Milton's heritage, obviously enough, is the work both of Shakespeare and of Fletcher. *Comus*'s obvious parallels with *The Tempest* (particularly in several of Ferdinand's speeches) and *The Faithful Shepherdess* have been noted many times: it is nonetheless perhaps worth repeating the most obvious connections that can be drawn between *Comus* and Fletcher's abortive pastoral play. Clorin and Amoret are seen to prefigure the Lady, and the Sullen Shepherd to prefigure Comus himself. Pan is the presiding deity of both play and masque, and the Attendant Spirit of *Comus* takes elements from Pan's Satyr in *The Faithful Shepherdess.* Similarly, the God of the River who rises to save the wounded Amoret serves as something of a prototype for Sabrina. This latter parallel, moreover, suggests the particular but unacknowledged route by which *The Faithful Shepherdess* became part of *Comus,* since the Spirit in the Crystal Well of *The Prophetess* would appear to serve as a bridge between Fletcher's earlier God of the River and Milton's Sabrina; this suggests that *The Prophetess* may well provide an important link between Jacobean uncourtly drama and Milton's work in the 1630s.

Recognizing the relevance of *The Prophetess* as a source for *Comus* means that the route to the Lady's role can thus be mapped directly from Clorin to Delphia. Delphia's presence is apparent too: when, for example, the Attendant Spirit in *Comus* talks of creatures "[d]oing abhorred rites to Hecate," one recalls the prophetess's moment of defection from Ceres: "Some rites I am to perform to Hecatè."[26] As David Norbrook has noted, the prominence of the role that Milton gave to the Lady in *Comus* was a decided innovation in the context of masques in the period.[27] It is, after all, at this time that the court's feminocentricity had begun to provoke cultural crisis over the role of women in society, a process heralded by the involvement of women actors in courtly pastoral performances. The revived *Faithful Shepherdess* was among a group of pastorals put on for Henrietta Maria.[28] But Milton is careful, despite giving the Lady a prominent role and a prophetic voice, to keep her almost entirely clear of the kind of moral ambivalence we have mapped in Delphia's character.

Yet the words of prophetesses were beginning to be seen as potentially subversive in the 1630s, and one prophetess in particular would inescapably have been in the minds of those connected with the earl of Bridgewater.[29] Three years before the first performance of *Comus,* the earl of Bridgewater's brother-in-law, Mervyn, earl of Castlehaven, husband of the countess of Huntingdon's sister Anne, had been executed for vicious and flamboyant sexual activities, including overseeing Anne's rape; and his sister, Lady Eleanor Davies, already notorious as an anti-Laudian prophetess, had defended his cause with vigor, thereby underlining for uneasy observers the dangers of women's prophecy. Milton is very careful to situate his Lady at a distance from this kind of subversive prophecy. There is nonetheless a degree to which the Lady's prophetic speech makes it difficult to avoid such issues, and our knowledge of Delphia's moral lapses prior to her triumph at the close of *The Prophetess* can only serve to emphasize both the reconciliatory powers and the darker possibilities present in the woman's voice, powers and possibilities that Fletcher had insistently explored as part of what I have called his politics of unease.

SIX

Discovery

Did not Columbus himself set sail because
he had read Marco Polo's narrative?[1]

I

When Caliban emerges from his den to face Prospero and Miranda, the words they exchange rehearse the process of colonization. Caliban describes the experience of the naïve and initially responsive native:

> When thou cam'st first,
> Thou strok'st me, and made much of me, wouldst give me
> Water with berries in't, and teach me how
> To name the bigger light, and how the less,
> That burn by day and night; and then I loved thee,
> And showed thee all the qualities o'th'isle,
> The fresh springs, brine pits, barren place and fertile—
> Cursed be I that did so! . . .
> For I am all the subjects that you have;
> Which first was mine own king, and here you sty me
> In this hard rock, whiles you do keep from me
> The rest o'th'island.[2]

Miranda responds to his outburst with the voice of the hurt colonist, whose aims in introducing the native to her own culture were purely philanthropic, yet who has been severely disappointed in her charge. Caliban has tried to rape her, to "people / [t]his isle with Calibans" (I. ii, 353–54), and she is appalled at this near reversal of the colonial project. She simply cannot comprehend his ungrateful behavior. "I pitied thee," she says, "Took pains to make thee speak, taught thee each hour / One thing or other. When thou didst not, savage, / Know thine own meaning, but wouldst gabble like / A thing most brutish, I endowed thy purposes / With words that made them known" (I. ii. 356–61). Caliban fails to see the kindness in this. "You taught me language," he responds bitterly, "and my profit on't / Is I know how to curse" (I. ii. 366–67). For him, the linguistic generosity of the Europeans is simply a means to enslave him. Prospero, after all, recognizes his economic value: "We cannot miss him," he observes. "He does make our fire, / Fetch in our wood, and serves in offices / That profit us" (I. ii. 314–16). Their relationship is that of colonist and enslaved native, and the nervousness of Prospero's art, for all its technological dominance over the native, is correlative to the anxieties of Jacobean colonial venturers as they made their way into the New World.

This reading of the relationships of Prospero, Miranda, and Caliban is by now very familiar. The discourse of colonialism in the writing of *The Tempest* has been the subject of many critical essays over the last ten years or so, and there is no need to repeat the substance of those essays here.[3] Instead, I hope in this chapter to point out that *The Tempest* was not the only Jacobean play and that Shakespeare was not the only Jacobean playwright to dramatize the various promises and problems of colonization. Fletcher, too, shows a sustained curiosity about the question of discovery. Shortly after his collaborations with Shakespeare in 1612–13, he responded in his *Four Plays, or Moral Representations, in One* to what he saw as a naïve reading of the Virginian venture. Reworking Shakespeare's reading of colonial relations in *The Tempest* by way of certain contemporary texts of colonialism (including the accounts of William Strachey and John Nicoll), he produced two plays— *The Island Princess* and *The Sea Voyage*—in the early 1620s which both analyze and mock the processes and dangers of colonial venture. It is quite remarkable that no mention has been made of these plays in recent colonial criticism of Jacobean drama. This omission has assisted in the creation of a monolithic vision of Jacobean colonialist discourse which is only gradually being superseded.[4] Recognition of the similarities and the differences in the representation of the colonial between *The Tempest* and these later plays of discovery plots the development of the discourse across a ten-year period, thereby providing a sense of chronology and process generally lacking in the criticism. Responding in the plays to his patron's interest in colonial venture and involvement in the Virginia Company as well as to popular cynicism about New World voyaging, Fletcher examines the utopian dreams, the material justifications, and the theological premises for colonization, and in both plays provides a memorably uneasy account of the Jacobean urge for discovery.

2

It is apparent from the opening sequence of *The Tempest* that the environment of discovery may not be conducive to good order in general and to monarchical government in particular.[5] There is no doubt that colonists were regarded with a certain degree of suspicion by King James.[6] This, according to Noel Malcolm, explains Thomas Hobbes's silence later in his life about his youthful involvement with the Virginia Company. "In retrospect," he suggests, "the Virginia Company must have seemed, to Hobbes, tainted with anti-royalism."[7] This, obviously, is an assessment made from a later vantage point, and members of the Virginia Company at the time of the composition of *The Tempest* would doubtless have reacted strongly to such charges. Yet a substantial number of the Virginia Company adventurers were at odds in various ways with King James. Samuel Purchas's lengthy commentary on the travels of the colonists, his *Pilgrimes* of 1625, concludes even then, at the very end of the reign, with a dedication in the name not of James but of Elizabeth:

> We have now compassed the World . . . And as in Geometricall compasses one foote is fixed in the Centre, whiles the other mooveth in the Circumference . . . in this English Centre also I have chosen the Centre of that Centre, the Renowmed Name of Queen Elizabeth, to which, because Mortalitie hath deprived us of Her Person, wee have added that of King James, the All that is left us of Queene Elizabeth.[8]

Purchas clearly had little belief in James's centrality to the developing empire.

The interests of the colonists seemed in many ways to stand as a threat to James's sovereignty, and the correlation between radical preference in politics and interest in colonial venture is striking. In January 1624, for example, Sir Nathaniel Rich accused Sir Edwin Sandys, treasurer (that is, principal officer) of the Virginia Company, of "trying to create a Brownist republic in Virginia," an accusation which, voiced by puritan Rich at the very beginning of his association with the duke of Buckingham, must have had much more bite than if it had come from a more obvious courtier.[9] Both Sandys and the earl of Southampton, his successor as treasurer, were at different times accused of republicanism, and their activities promoting other aspects of the militant Protestant cause consistently irritated James. Southampton attempted in 1620 to raise a volunteer force to help the king and queen of Bohemia in their troubles, and according to Simon Adams, "he and his friends were noticeably outspoken during the first session of [the] 1621 [Parliament. A]s a result he and Sandys were imprisoned and [Sir Thomas] Roe sent into virtual exile as ambassador to Constantinople."[10] Roe, who was devoted to Princess Elizabeth, was also a member of the Virginia Company and part, as we have seen, of the Ashby circle. Bearing in mind the political attitudes prevalent at Ashby, it is hardly surprising that the fifth earl of Huntingdon should also have become involved in Virginian ventures. His financial problems, inherited from the third earl in particular and exacerbated by James, are well documented: his need for new sources of funding, combined with his uncourtly politics, would make him prime material for the Virginia Company.[11] A key feature of Fletcher's patronage environment, then, was an active interest in Virginia.

It was the personality of Sir Edwin Sandys, treasurer of the Company from 1619 to 1620 and an outspoken Parliamentarian, which seems to have been the focus of royal unease about Virginia. As Malcolm phrases it, under Sandys's direction, the Company as a whole "was tarred with the brush of his own record of criticism and opposition in parliament" (301). The Company was dominated in the last years before its demise by several members of the Sandys family, and though Sir Edwin has, unlike his younger brother George, never been the subject of a full-length study, he has been consistently at the center of historiographical debate about the politics of the Company.[12] Sandys had already established his credentials as a forthright Parliamentary politician before he became involved with the Virginia Company. He introduced a bill in February 1605 "for the better establishment of true religion," and in February 1607 argued against the Crown's desire to see equal rights and privileges for the Scottish and the English.[13] It was in

1614, however, that he made his most notable speech during a debate on impositions, a speech which appears from the fragmented notes in the *Journal of the House of Commons* to comprise the basic elements of a theory of justified resistance to government on a basis of Natural Law. [14] His arguments in this debate were backed by both by Sir Thomas Roe and by Sir Dudley Digges, another leading light in the Virginia Company (though one who was to oppose Sandys fiercely later on). His expression of reciprocal conditions between monarch and subject and his assertion that an unelected king could be deposed if appropriate force were available led to his examination and temporary confinement by the Privy Council once Parliament had been dissolved.

Curiously, this principle of election and liberty appears to be at odds with one of the basic presumptions of colonial occupation. After all, the simplest and clearest claim to be voiced consistently by colonists was the "right of conquest." Yet Sandys's own political theory would appear to deny the Virginia Company its legitimacy on that basis alone, and some of the documents of the plantation suggest a degree of unease over this issue of legitimacy. The writer of the Council of Virginia's *True Declaration of the estate of the Colonie in Virginia* begins his discourse by marshalling "all those reasons, which may resolue the religious, encourage the personall, confirme the noble, and satisfie the timorous aduenturer" under three headings: "lawfulnesse, possibility, and commoditie." [15] He begins by ensuring that the reader realizes the value of the project, claiming that "our primarie end is to plant religion, our secondarie and subalternate ends are for the honour and profit of the nation," and asking the "plaine question: whether it bee not a determinated truth, that the Gospell should bee preached, to all the world, before the end of the world?" (B1ᵛ). He then dismisses various possible ways to preach the gospel, rejecting Roman Catholic claims to America, and particularly rejecting the kind of "imperiall" preaching which results "when a Prince, hath conquered their bodies, that the Preachers may feede their soules" (B2ʳ). This approach, "to preach the Gospell to a nation conquered, and to set their soules at liberty, when we haue brought their bodies to slauerie" may be, according to the writer, "a matter sacred in the Preachers, but I know not how iustifiable in the rulers" (B2ᵛ). The preferable way to preach is the way chosen by the Virginia adventurers, "who by way of marchandizing and trade, doe buy of them the pearles of earth, and sell to them the pearles of heaven" (B3^r). As Malcolm suggests,

no extensive attempt at a solution to the problem of legitimation was ever offered by the Virginia Company; there was a tendency to regard the actual colonization as a *fait accompli* and to justify its continuation on the grounds of converting infidels. The problem seemed less important after the Great Massacre of 1622, when it became possible to regard any subsequent action against the Indians as self-defence or justifiable retaliation.[16]

By then, however, the pressure to justify the continued cost of the plantation had grown, and the Company had only two years left before its dissolution.

Sandys appears to have been undaunted in the case of the plantation by the issues of legitimation that concerned him in domestic politics. In the six years before the second Parliament of James's reign, he turned his attention fully to Virginia. He had become a member of the Council of the newly formed Company in March 1607, and by April 1619 he had unseated Smith and become treasurer, supported by "a group which included his brother, Sir Samuel Sandys, John and Nicholas Ferrar, the earl of Southampton, Sir Edward Sackville, Sir John Danvers, Sir Dudley Digges, and [William, Lord] Cavendish."[17] As the titles—*The Genesis of the United States* and *The First Republic in America*—of books by one representative historian imply, nineteenth century colonial historiography was keen to find the roots of American political independence in the history of the Virginia Company: histories of the plantation tended to characterize the Sandys faction as the founders of American liberty and to blame the demise of the Company on a combination of James's conspiracy to defeat Sandys's political aims and of the machinations of Count Gondomar, the Spanish ambassador to London.[18] W. F. Craven began the task of revising attitudes toward Sandys and toward the Company under his administration, suggesting that, though the previous administration under Sir Thomas Smith had clearly been inefficient, Sandys was in many ways an equally factional replacement who frequently enacted changes in policy which had already been decided upon prior to his election. Craven nonetheless acknowledges that Sandys had probably been "responsible for much that had been accomplished in the months preceding his election,"[19] and he remained in effective control of the Company when his ally the earl of Southampton took over the treasurership.

His project for restoring the colony involved encouraging both private plantation and the improvement of public land, as well as seeking the fullest available cooperation of the colonists for both facets of the venture. To this latter end, Sandys was involved in instigating the first representative assembly in America, a general assembly of the colony comprising burgesses elected from each "town, hundred, or other particular plantation" in Virginia.[20] This was the lower house of a structure modeled upon Parliament, the upper house comprising the governor and council elected by the Company in England. Sandys's parliamentary mentality thus left its stamp upon Virginia. His treasurership, however, was short-lived, since the king intervened in the process that was intended to lead to his reelection. When the Company remonstrated, the king is said to have replied "that the Company was the seminary for a seditious Parliament, that Sandys was his greatest enemy, and concluded with the remark, 'Choose the devil, if you like, but not Sir Edwin Sandys.'"[21] The election of the earl of Southampton in his place, however, ensured the continued dominance of the Sandys faction, a dominance most readily apparent in Southampton's recommendation of Sir Edwin Sandys's youngest brother, George, to the new post of resident treasurer in 1621.

George Sandys provides early evidence of connections between the Sandys family and the earls of Huntingdon, since Catherine, countess of Huntingdon, wife to the Puritan third earl, was his godmother.[22] The Hastings family seems in fact to have had something of a penchant for colonial ventures. Captain Edward Hastings, brother to the fifth earl of Huntingdon, accompanied Sir Walter Raleigh on his failed expedition to Guyana in 1617 and died there.[23] One of those who capitalized on Sir Edwin Sandys's enthusiasm for private plantation in Virginia was his acquaintance the fifth earl himself. Ashby milieu connections with the Virginia Company, in fact, predate Sandys's privatizing drive by nearly ten years. In March 1611, Sir Thomas Beaumont and the earl of Huntingdon were both recipients of a circular letter sent presumably to those among the nobility and gentry thought most likely to have an interest in matters colonial. The letter was a formal affair, exalting the colony—"The eyes of all Europe," it claims, are "looking upon o^r endeavours to spread the gospell among the heathen peoples of Virginia to plant a^n Englishe nation there and to settle a trade in those parts wch may be peculiar to o^r nation"—and asking the recipient to "procure us such numbers of men, and of such condition, as you are willing and able" for a planned expedition. There is no record of a reply from Sir Thomas, but clearly the Virginia Company was already establishing connections with at least one branch of the Ashby milieu, and by 1620 he was a member of the Company.

The earl of Huntingdon, also a recipient of the circular letter, began his Virginian interest not long after the circulation of this letter, so that under the charter of 1612 he was admitted as a member of the Company. Among the Hastings papers, there are three Bills of Adventure, each for forty pounds, dated 4 April 1610, 16 January 1611, and 2 December 1613, which represent payments for the earl's contribution. There is also a note outlining "what quantity of ground shall be set forth for an Adventurer to Virginia that adventures 120*l*. given my Lord by the merchants." The setting-up of private plantations was a practice "undoubtedly due to the plans which Sir Edwin Sandys set on foot for the building up of the colony,"[24] and is noted as one of the more promising possibilities in face of some of the colony's troubles by 1620:

The Collony beinge . . . weake and the Treasury vtterly exhaust, Itt pleased divers Lords Knights, gentlemen and Citizens (greived to see this great Action fall to nothinge) to take the matter a new in hand and at their pryvate charges (ioyninge themselves into Societies) to sett vpp divers p[ar]ticular Plantac~ons wherof the first of any moment now called Southampton Hundred hath had 310 Persons sent vnto itt, the next called Martines Hundred aboue 200 p[er]sons and some others in like sorte so that att the Cominge away of Captaine Argoll att Easter i6i9 ther were Persons in the Colony neere—1000:.[25]

The earliest of these "Societies" was Smith's Hundred, created in 1617, which in due course became Southampton Hundred. The note goes on to suggest this as the most prestigious available project in which the earl might care to join, carefully ensuring him of the quality of his fellow venturers:

DISCOVERY

If my Lord please to join with any others, that that is called Smith's Hundred is the most honourable and most hopeful, whereof Sir George Yeardly the Governor is Captain in Virginia, and Sir Edwin Sandys is Treasurer here in England. The chief Adventurers are the Earls of Southampton, of Pembroke, of Warwick, the Lord Paget, the Lord Cavendish, the Master of the Wards, Sir Thomas Smith, Sir John Davers, Sir Nicholas Tufton, to the number of 30 knights, gentlemen and merchants of the best account in London, whereof the least Adventurer must have 500 acres. . . .[26]

This note is amplified by a letter written to the earl by Sandys on 11 January 1620. Sandys has learned from John Ferrar, deputy treasurer of the Company, that the earl "hath been pleased . . . to reflect some upon o^r Plantation," and he writes to persuade Huntingdon both to join the council of the Company and to take a share in Smith's Hundred:

Yo^r Lp: is one of o^r principall and most forward Adventurers: and if it please yo^u to enter into the Societie of the Counseil, wherein are many honorable personages of yor Lps rancke and degree, upon notice of yor Lps; honorable favor and help exported will willinglie by their choise of yor Lp testefie their serviceable thankfulnes. . . . [I]f yor Lp wilbe pleased for the planting of yor owne private Land to ioyne in a particular Society of some thirtie persons, whereof my Lo of Southampton is the chief, and my self amonst many of better worth am one: I will therein also be ready to perform to yor Lp; my best service.[27]

The earl took up this offer of a share in Smith's Hundred, taking his allowance of one thousand acres at a place called Nansimahum.

By 1620, then, his interest in the Virginia project had grown substantially. He was admitted to the council on 28 June, and the minutes record that he received special thanks from the Company for his enthusiastic involvement.[28] He had begun employing agents to look after his share of the plantation. There are extant copies of the earl's letters of attorney, dated 5 April 1620, appointing two agents, Nicholas Martiau (or Martian) and Benjamin Blewitt. Martiau was a Huguenot (reminding us again of the fifth earl's religious temperament) whose main claim to fame for the modern reader is as the earliest known American ancestor of George Washington.[29] Blewitt seems to have had connections with the iron works at Falling Creek, and appears to have encouraged Martiau to emigrate to Virginia. The Hastings papers include correspondence between the earl and Martiau, which perhaps suggest something of the real state of the colony after 1620 in a way that the official records inevitably do not.

Disaster, after all, struck unexpectedly in 1622, with the massacre of hundreds of colonists by the Algonquians. A letter written by the fifth earl to Sandys refers to the death of Blewitt, who was probably one of those killed when the iron works were attacked. Martiau also seems to have been living at the iron works at this time, and the earl writes to Sandys to ask if he can be allowed to move elsewhere:

After my very harty Comendacons whereas about two yeares since a servant of mine one Nicholas Martian beinge desirous to goe into Virginia and beinge perswaded by one Beniamin Bluet who went ther as Captain (and had skill in Iron worke) that it would be a ve[ry] good voyage but since wch time by reason of the death of Bluet and divers others of the Choise workmen the worke faylinge this servant of mine as I understand is by comaund of the Companie put to much paines & in some distresse and hath sent to intreat me to be a meanes for his release from them and to live in Southampton hundred.[30]

The earl continues by pointing out Martiau's lack of ironworking skill and repeats his request that his agent be allowed to move to the relative comfort and safety of Southampton Hundred (and presumably to the earl's own plantation in the Hundred) or an equivalent location. Two years later, the situation seems only marginally improved. Writing on 8 July 1624, the earl thanks Martiau for sending him "a Prick of Tobacco and a great quantitie of sassafras," though, noting that in his last letter Martiau had offered a rather gloomy "Epitome of the p^{r}sent state of Virginia," he feels obliged to provide some brief words of encouragement. "[A]s all new plantacons are troublesome and dangerous soe it seemes this is," he writes, adding, "I doubt not but this plantacon will [come] to p[er]fection and all the troubles and difficulties outecome."[31]

3

The earl seems to have been more optimistic than many about the potential for the Virginian plantation. By the 1620s, there was

widespread cynicism about the project, not least in the drama, and
Fletcher's work is no exception. Several of his plays, and not only
those with an obviously colonial location, voice a sense of unease
about the outcome of the various tribulations of colonization.
Leon, asserting his domestic dominance over Margarita in *Rule a
Wife and Have a Wife,* voices a very different view of the relationship between Europe and its colonies from that embodied in the
earl's letter to Martiau. "[Y]ou have Land ith Indies as I take it," he
announces, "Thither weele goe, and view a while those clymats, /
Visit your Factors there, that may betray ye."[32] A little earlier in
the play, Michael Perez has described his emotional state by way of
an extended colonial metaphor:

> I am like the people that live in the sweet Ilands:
> I dye I dye if I stay but one day more here,
> My lungs are rotten with the damps that rise,
> And I cough nothing now but stinks of all sorts,
> The inhabitants we have are two starv'd rats,
> For they are not able to maintain a cat here,
> And those appeare as fearfull as two divells,
> They have eat a map of the whole world up already,
> And if we stay a night we are gone for company;
> . . . [I]s there any thing here to eat
> But one another, like a race of Canniballs?
>   (III. ii. 14–22, 41–42)

In view of the persistence of such images in the drama, it seems
likely that the actors and audiences of the early 1620s had developed a quite different attitude to Virginia from those involved in
the Company.[33] And in Fletcher's dramatic response to New World
issues, we can begin to see a degree of tension between the different
contexts in and for which he wrote.

Several apologists for colonization cite "plaiers" as specific enemies of Virginia. Ralph Hamor's *True Discourse of the Present Estate
of Virginia* (1615) rails at "Papists *and* Plaires, Ammonites *and*
Horonites, *the Scumme and dregges of the people,* [who] *mocke at this
holy Businesse.*"[34] The preacher William Crashaw is equally furious
with the players for sniping at the Virginian venture. In his epistle dedicatory to Alexander Whitaker's *Good newes from Virginia*
(1613), he writes of the "many discouragements that haue attended this glorious businesse of the Virginian plantation," which,

"deuised by the Diuell, and set abroach by idle and base companions, are blowen abroad by Papists, Players and such like, till they haue filled the vulgar eares."[35] Crashaw is most specific about theatrical mockery of Virginia in the sermon he preached before "the Lord Lawarre, Lord Governour and Captaine Generall of Virginea" and the other adventurers as they set sail in February 1609. "[W]ho but the *Diuell,* and *Papists,* and *Players* doe mocke at religion?" he asks, adding, "[T]hat *Players* doe, too many eyes and eares can witnesse."[36] Mockery of religion and mockery of colonization are one and the same thing for Crashaw, but he also attacks the actors for specific satire of Virginia. "[N]othing that is good, excellent or holy can escape them," he asserts, "[H]ow then can this *action?* But this may suffice, that they are *Players:* they abuse *Virginea,* but they are but *Players*" (H4^r). "But why," he asks, "are the *Players* enemies to this Plantation and doe abuse it? I will tell you the causes: First, for that they are so multiplied here, that one cannot liue by another, and they see that wee send of all trades to *Virginea,* but will send no *Players.* . . . Secondly, as the diuell hates vs, because wee purpose not to suffer *Heathens,* . . so doe the *Players,* because wee resolue to suffer no Idle persons in Virginea" (H4^r).

The theaters were thus established as particular enemies in the minds at least of religious apologists for New World ventures, even by 1610. But it seems likely that the actors were responding to as well as creating an increasingly negative public attitude. As Meredith Skura points out, after the initial enthusiasm of the beginning of James's reign, cynicism crept swiftly in:

The official propaganda, optimistic about future profits, was soon countered by a backlash from less optimistic scoffers challenging the value of the entire project, one which sent money, men, and ships to frequent destruction and brought back almost no profit. (55)

She adds in a footnote that "[t]he quantity and quality of the objections, which have not on the whole survived, has been judged by the nature of the many defenses thought necessary to answer them" (55n). Fletcher's colonial plays, though, provide a hint of the way in which criticism of Virginia had developed by the early 1620s, in the theaters at least.

Many of the printed justifications of the Virginian ventures themselves reveal awkward fractures in the construction of the discourse of colonialism even as they strive to hide them. The writer of the 1610 *True Declaration,* for example, explains the *Sea-Venture* affair of a year earlier and then turns to a glowing description of the present state of affairs in Virginia.[37] It is the sheer plenitude and abundance of life that astounds him: "the naturall Pease of the Countrie returne an increase innumerable," he writes, "our garden fruits, both roots, hearbes, and flowers, doe spring vp speedily, all things committed to the earth, do multiply with an incredible usurie" (D4^v-E1^r). Yet recognition of the problems is built into the praise:

If any man shall accuse these reports of partiall falshood, supposing them to be but Vtopian, and legendarie fables, because he cannot conceiue, that plentie and famine, a temperate climate, and distempered bodies, felicities, and miseries can be reconciled together, let him now reade with judgement, but let him not judge before he hath read. (E3^r-E3^v)

So the writer is obliged to recognize the darker side, the reasons for the poor state of the colony on the arrival of Sir Thomas Gates the previous year. This he blames chiefly on "the tempest of dissention: euery man ouervaluing his own worth, would be a Commander: euery man vnderprising an others value, denied to be commanded" (E3^v). "When therfore," he goes on, "licence, sedition, and furie, are the fruits of a headie, daring, and vnruly multitude, it is no wonder that so many in our colony perished" (E4^r). Moreover, "[u]nto Treasons, you may ioyne couetousnesse in the Mariners, who for their priuate lucre partly imbezeled the prouisions" (F2^v). This, along with those mutineers who "stole away the Ship [and] made a league amongst themselues to be professed pirates, with dreams of mountains of gold, and happy robberies" (F1^r), is the worst imaginable behavior in a colony, and led not only to rumors of cannibalism among the English, but also to the near collapse of the colony.

The very justifications for colonization thus inevitably invoke the dangers and problems of the plantation. Purchas's *Virginia's Verger,* a justification of the colony from the end of James's reign, focuses on a series of natural rights as the basic defense, with the theological basis for the right to colonize as the most fundamental consideration:

God is the beginning and end, the Alpha and Omega, that first and last, of whom and for whom are all things. The first and last thing therefore in this Virginian argument considerable, is God; that is, whether we have Commission from him to plant, and whether the Plantation may bring glory to him. (218)

Man was made to reflect God, but fell. Yet

neither did the Fall of Man so cracke this earthen vessell, that all his created excellence ran out: for neither were the substance or faculties of the soul extinct, nor his prerogative over the visible creatures (the spiritual creature naturally excelling the bodily. . .). Hence it is that Christians . . . have and hold the world and the things thereof in another tenure, whereof Hypocrites and Heathens are not capable. (219)

Thus the non-European is neatly gulled out of his land. But "[n]either yet is it lawful for Christians, to usurpe the goods and lands of Heathens; for they are villains not to us; but to our and their Lord" (220). Thus according to the world tenancy European Christians have from God, they

have a naturall right to replenish the whole earth: so that if any countrey be not possessed by other men, (which is the case of Summer Ilands, and hath beene of all Countries in their first habitations) every man by Law of Nature and Humanitie hath right of Plantation, and may not by other after-commers be dispossessed, without wrong to human nature. . . . [T]hus Virginia hath roome enough for her own (were their numbers an hundred times as many) and for others also which wanting at home, seeke habitations there in vacant places, with perhaps better right then the first, which (being like Cain, both Murtherers and Vagabonds in their whatsoever and howsoever owne) I can scarsly call inhabitants. (222–23)

The apparent contrast between the evil of the inhabitants and the goodness of the land itself presents an imbalance (particularly to anyone of Calvinist persuasion) that the colonists must put right:

[C]onsidering so good a Countrey, so bad people, having little of Humanitie but shape, ignorant of Civilitie, of Arts, of Religion; more brutish then the beasts they hunt, more wild and unmanly then that unmanned wild Countrey, which they range rather than inhabite; captivated also to Satans tyranny in foolish pieties, mad impieties, wicked idlenesse, busie and bloudy wickedness: hence have wee fit objects of zeale and pitie, to deliver from the power of darknesse. (231)

Thus there are both past and future theological justifications for colonization, justifications prescriptive and projective: Biblical basis and evangelical intent.

It is, of course, morally essential to prove the natives incapable of the stewardship of God's earth. Caliban is a savage because of his desire to violate a virgin; the process of colonization (especially bearing in mind the "good husbandman" trope by which America is a beautiful woman awaiting the Christian colonists to free her from the clutches of the heathen) must not be seen as such a violation. But clearly the inhabitants have no right to their own land:

[T]hey bee not worthy of the name of a Nation, being wilde and Savage: yet as Slaves, bordering rebells, excommunicates and out-lawes are ly-able to the punishments of Law, and not to the priviledges; So is it with these Barbarians, Borderers and Out-lawes of Humanity. (224)

Emphasis of the liminal qualities of the New World's inhabitants thus supports the motivation for colonization, yet it also produces myths of blind murderousness, incest, and cannibalism. John Nicoll's narrative of his Guyana voyage, for example, suddenly mentions the threat of cannibalism, without accompanying evidence to justify the fear (thus failing to fulfill the promise of a tale of "Men-eaters" contained in the title of the published narrative).[38] Peter Hulme mentions the "complex interplay between expectation and experience" in Gabriel Archer's bemused observation that the natives "are naturally given to trechery, howbeit we could not finde it in our travell up the river, but rather a most kind and loving people."[39] Such myths of fear validate their discursive antitheses—civilisation and manners—yet there is still more than enough room for a degree of slippage. Nicoll almost casually reports the transfer of the fear of cannibalism from the natives to the Europeans:

[W]e continued fifteen days [in a desolate island], having no kind of meat but Perriwinkles or Whelks, Tobacco, & Salt-water, which did nothing at all to nourish us: yet it took away the desire of hunger, and saved us from eating one another. (61)

Even Purchas, in view of moments such as this, feels obliged to underline the point of the colonial exercise:

This should be, and in the most Adventurers I hope is the scope of the Virginian Plantation, not to make Savages and wild degenerate men of Christians, but Christians of those Savage, wild, degenerate men. (*Pilgrimes*, 222)

As Paul Brown observes, "[t]he same discourse which allows for the transformation of the savage into the civil also raises the possibility of a reverse transformation."[40]

It is these reversals which the dramatists seem keen to explore. For Caliban to threaten Miranda with rape is to invert the expected pattern by which the isles will be peopled with white Europeans. The threatened reversal of the preconceived order which such an act would embody, combined with the disruption of Prospero's self-congratulatory masque by his sudden, fearful recollection of Caliban's revolt, offers, as the critics have observed, an image of colonial nightmare far from the dreams of effortless plenitude which motivated discovery. The centrality of material and sexual gain to the psychological motivations for colonization—*pace* the preachers—offers the most powerful focus for dramatization.

So far in this study, I have emphasized the importance of the relationship Fletcher had with the earl and countess of Huntingdon in orienting his political drama. I consider this patronage relationship to be a necessary reference point in examining Fletcher's work. Yet a writer and his or her patron are not one and the same, and patronage is by no means the only cultural input for a writer, least of all a public theater writer. It can often be unhelpful to assume baldly that a writer's political and social attitudes are in all circumstances and throughout a career to be identified fully with those of his or her patrons. We have seen a range of congruences between the politics embodied at Ashby and the politics of Fletcher's plays, and it is certainly reasonable to suppose that the Ashby milieu's fascination with foreign travel and colonial voyaging would have prompted Fletcher's interest in matters colonial, just as Shakespeare's friendship with Southampton and Pembroke may well have prompted him to dramatize certain issues of colonialism in *The Tempest*. Yet it is by no means essential also to presume that Fletcher's own response or the response of the broader culture within and for which he wrote was always in total harmony with that of the earl and countess. In the case of the New World, there is a clear, shared interest, yet there is arguably also a divergence of perspective. It is as if Fletcher stages not just the attitudes in evidence in the earl's reply to Martiau, but the agent's concerns, too, dramatizing the dialogue voiced here between Old World and New.

4

We have seen already that 1613 was a watershed in both the politics and the poetics of the reign of James I. One of the masques performed for the wedding of Princess Elizabeth and Frederick the elector palatine in February 1613 was in part a glorification of a project which the king had consistently viewed with a certain unease. George Chapman's *Memorable Maske of . . . the Middle Temple, and Lyncolns Inne* was published (apparently in some haste) shortly after its performance, and was entered in the *Stationers' Register* in the company of its sister entertainment, Beaumont's *Masque of the Inner Temple and Gray's Inn,* on 27 February. It is a grand affair of Jonsonian structure which glorifies without apparent reserve both James and his court. This is in itself remarkable: Chapman's political outlook was not normally in full sympathy with the king, and the attitudes celebrated by his masque can only be explained in the specific political context of 1612–13. Nonetheless, there is a certain idiosyncratic orientation on Chapman's part, since he sets the piece enthusiastically in the New World, and specifically in Virginia. This location can be explained in part by the relatively close relationship Chapman had with Prince Henry, the heir to the throne, whose premature death a few months before the palatine marriage bereft English militant Protestants of their chief hopes from the Stuart line.[41] The Virginian project was something Prince Henry had keenly supported. Chapman's celebration of a project with which James was notoriously uncomfortable can thus be seen as implicit criticism of the king's reluctance to embrace what to militant Protestants was by far the clearest way by which God's kingdom and England's empire could be simultaneously expanded.

The primary impetus of Chapman's masque, however, is not to glorify the Virginian project per se, but to celebrate the conspicuous consumption of James's court in a way which correlates expenditure with honor and Christian piety. In order "to amplefie yet more the diuine graces of [the] Goddesse [Honour]," we are told in the "Description" of the masque,

Plutus, (or Riches) being by *Aristophanes, Lucian. &c.* presented naturally blind, deformd, and dull witted; is here by his loue of *Honor,* made see, made sightly, made ingenious, made liberall: And all this conuerted and consecrate to the most worthy celebration of these sacred Nuptialls.[42]

The scene is "a rich Iland," in which "(beeing yet in command of the Virginian continent) a troupe of the noblest Virginians inhabiting; attended hether the God of Riches" (52, 56–58). There is an antimasque dance of baboons, which forms a link with Beaumont's masque for the same occasion. Eunomia, the goddess of law, invites the Virginian masquers to leave their pagan ways:

> [R]enounce
> Your superstitious worship of these Sunnes,
> Subiect to cloudy darknings and descents,
> And of your fit deuotions, turne the euents
> To this our Britan *Phoebus,* whose bright skie
> (Enlightned with a Christian Piety)
> Is neuer subiect to black Errors night,
> And hath already offer'd heauens true light,
> To your darke Region. (326–34)

The Virginians oblige by descending and paying homage to James, personified as the sun king; and Plutus's final speech combines the present occasion of the masque, the nature and tastes of the court, with Chapman's own penchant for New World venture:

> Come Virgine Knights, the homage ye haue done,
> To *Loue* and *Bewty,* and our Britan Sun,
> Kinde *Honor,* will requite with holy feasts
> In her faire Temple; and her loued Guests,
> Giues mee the grace t'inuite; when she and I
> (*Honor* and *Riches*) will eternally
> A league in fauour of this night combine,
> In which *Loues* second hallowed Tapers shine;
> Whose Ioies, may Heauen and Earth as highly please
> As those two nights that got great *Hercules.* (405–14)

The great Protestant wedding thus provides a context for the legitimation of conspicuous consumption and for the easy equation of riches and honor, in which wealth and spending become both "ingenious" and "liberall."

This out-of-character glorification of the excesses of James's court prompted rapid criticism from Chapman's friend Fletcher. Probably late in 1613, he collaborated with the actor-playwright Nathan Field to produce a quirky tour de force. *Four Plays, or Moral Representations in One,* is perhaps the strangest item in the Fletcher canon, and one which has been almost entirely neglected in the criticism. Yet recent work would suggest that it is essential to an understanding of the theatrical response to the political events of early 1613 as that year wore on and celebration faded into disillusion. Fletcher reacted swiftly and cynically to the enthusiasms of 1613 in *The Two Noble Kinsmen* and elsewhere, and *Four Plays* provides a very specific negative reaction to one of the wedding masques. In the process, it also registers a degree of unease about the Virginian project, and thus offers a preliminary politics of discovery for Fletcher's plays.

Four Plays is, as Andrew Hickman has recently pointed out, "a showcase, a specimen catalogue of the dramatists' artistic abilities."[43] It eschews five-act structure, and comprises instead four brief playlets or "Triumphs" which represent the generic range available to the stage: comedy, tragicomedy, tragedy, and masque. The influence of the latter is particularly marked throughout the whole, giving the piece an oddly artificial and rather unsettling tone.[44] The collaborative work appears, unusually for plays in which Fletcher had a hand, to have been neatly divided down the middle, Field writing the Induction and the first two pieces— "The Triumph of Honour" and "The Triumph of Love"—and Fletcher the second two—"The Triumph of Death" and "The Triumph of Time."[45] The movement and visual apparatus of all four pieces depend quite heavily upon the masque as a form, but, taken together, the set is overtly critical of the ideology of the Jacobean (that is, the Jonsonian) masque. It has been suggested that *Four Plays* may well actually have been performed for the marriage of Elizabeth and Frederick, but, as Nicoll observes, the stage directions would appear to indicate public theater performance, and Hickman and Gossett rightly point out that the tone of the pieces makes them quite inappropriate for court performance, in 1613 or any other year.[46] Nonetheless, performance quite clearly required much spectacle, spectacle (it would seem) with an edge.

Field's Induction is astonishingly open both about the critical claims of the piece—"wee will censure, not onely the King in the Play here, that reigns his two hours; but the King himself, that is to rule his life time"—and about its politics, which appears to be a politics of incorporation: *"{Y}e are welcome all / To Lisbon, and the Court of Portugall; Where your fair eyes shall feed on no worse sights / Then preparations made for Kings delights."*[47] The scene is the marriage of the king of Portugal, Emanuel, to his queen, Isabella, and the tone of their nuptials clearly reflects that of Frederick and Elizabeth. Field's first piece, "The Triumph of Honour," glances at one of the devices from the February celebrations, but it is Fletcher's closing contribution which appears not only as a response to the wedding entertainments in general but as a specific criticism of Chapman's involvement in the celebrations as author of one of the central wedding masques.

Fletcher's "Triumph of Time," the brief concluding section of the *Four Plays,* is a mock morality which is also a mock masque. It opens with an everyman figure, Anthropos, who is ambivalently characterized as either a courtier or a king. He berates his servant, Desire, for failing to provide him with wealth (thereby equating himself with the grasping courtier of Field's Induction), and Desire's response provides an immediate implied critique of court life, *"Vain delight"* he says,

> has ruin'd ye, with clapping all
> That comes in for support, on clothes, and Coaches
> Perfumes, and powder'd pates; and that your Mistris,
> The Ladie *Pleasure,* like a sea devours
> At length both you and him too. If you have houses,
> Or land, or jewels, for good pawn, he'll hear you,
> And will be readie to supplie occasions:
> If not, he locks his ears up, and grows stupid.
> From him, I went to *Vanity,* whom I found
> Attended by an endlesse troop of Tailors,
> Mercers, Embroiderers, Feather-makers, Fumers,
> All Occupations opening like a Mart,
> That serve to rig the bodie out with braverie;
> And th'row the roome new fashions flew like flyes,
> In thousand gaudie shapes. (i. 19–33)

Desire describes Vanity's servant, Pride, who, he says,

> shew'd me gowns and head-tires,
> Imbroider'd wastcoats, smocks sem'd thorow with cutworks,
> Scarfs, mantles, petticoats, muffs, powders, paintings,
> Dogs, monkeys, parrots, which all seemed to shew me
> The way her money went. (i. 37–41)

He then moves on to Pleasure, who announces, resonantly, that "revels and Masques had drawn her drie alreadie." The uncourtly politics of the piece is already apparent.

Anthropos blusters about his dominance over lesser forms of life and his expectations of service. His servants should be as pliable to his will as are the animals he owns or which simply inhabit the world over which he, representative man, considers himself to rule. His dreams specifically deny mutual responsibility:

> Miserable creatures,
> Born to support and beautifie your master,
> The godlike man, set here to do me service,
> The children of my will; why, or how dare ye,
> Created to my use alone, disgrace me?
> Beasts have more courtesie; they live about me,
> Offering their warm wooll to the shearers hand,
> To clothe me with their bodies to my labours;
> Nay, even their lives they daily sacrifice,
> And proudly press with garlands to the altars,
> To fill the gods oblations. Birds bow to me,
> Striking their downie sails to do me service,
> Their sweet airs ever ecchoing to mine honor,
> And to my rest their plumie softs they send me.
> Fishes, and plants, and all where life inhabits,
> But mine own cursed kind, obey their ruler;
> Mine have forgot me, miserable mine,
> Into whose stonie hearts, neglect of dutie,
> Squint-ey'd deceit, and self-love, are crept closely:
> None feel my wants, not one mend with me. (i. 48–67)

This is the self-pitying politics of material absolutism, a kind of totalitarian utopics which Fletcher has satirized thoroughly by the close of the masque. The passage echoes the material expectations of some of the New World venturers and may well thus involve a double-edged criticism of Chapman's masque. Furthermore, Anthropos immediately recalls one of his servants, Flattery, whom he has not thought of till now, but Desire acknowledges that this one, too, is a lost cause. "[I] made him my first venture," he says,

> But found him in a young Lords ear so busie,
> So like a smiling showr pouring his soul
> In at his portals, his face in a thousand figures
> Catching the vain minde of the man: I pull'd him,
> But still he hung like birdlime; spoke unto him,
> His answer still was, By the Lord, sweet Lord,
> And By my soul, thou master-piece of honour:
> Nothing could stave him off: he has heard your flood's gone;
> And on decaying things he seldom smiles, Sir. (i. 71–80)

The mockery of the flatterer's terminology—"thou master-piece of *honour*" (my italics)—in the context of obsession with the material is again a negative comment on Chapman's masque.

Anthropos, furious, decides to reject his erstwhile followers, in sudden recognition of their worthlessness, and in the process catches a brief glimpse of rural redemption. He addresses Bounty, his "most worthie servant," and advises him to depart. "[G]o plant thyself," he tells him, "In honourable hearts that truely know thee, / And there live ever like thy self, a vertue: / But leave this place, and seek the Countrey, / For Law and lust like fire lick all up here" (i. 91–95). Here again, the negative reference to Law satirizes the role of Eunomia as the go-between for Honor and Riches in Chapman's *Memorable Maske*. Anthropos decides to seek out "[d]espis'd patch'd *Poverty*," with whom he aims to "seek *Simplicity, Content* and *Peace* out" (i. 97–98) in a rural environment. Yet despite his hasty decision to become impoverished (and even though he has accepted Poverty's gifts of Content, Rest and Peace), when Anthropos prays to Jupiter, he asks that the "father of all honour" will "raise again . . . [t]he poor despis'd" out of poverty (i. 126–27). The term by which he describes his state appears an overt sign of regret on Fletcher's part for his own ideological involvement not a year earlier in the writing of *Henry VIII*. "Raise from his ruines once more this sunk Cedar," he asks of Jupiter, "That all may fear thy power, and I proclaim it" (i. 128–29).[48] To quote a central metaphor of James's self-mythologization in such an overt way is surely to play dangerously close to the edge of censorship.

The result of his prayers is a descent of Jupiter and Mercury, who decide that Anthropos, "beguil'd by *Vanity* and *Pleasure,* / *Desire, Craft, Flattery,* and smooth *Hypocrisie*" and "left to *Poverty*" (ii. 7–9) cannot be ruined in that way, and, in an overt parody of the *Memorable Maske,* they summon "golden *Plutus, god of riches,* / Who idly is ador'd," they say, "among the Sun-burnt *Indians*" (ii. 15–17). Plutus then enters, with an antimasque-like dance of worshipping Indians, and is instructed by Time to assist Anthropos. Plutus is decidedly reluctant, and only grudgingly obeys, saying however that he will "change [his] figure:" foe, he says, "when I willingly befriend a creature, / Goodly, and full of glory I shew to him; / But when I am compell'd, old, and decrepid, / I halt, and hang upon my staff" (iii. 14–18). When Plutus departs, Anthropos reappears with the Christian virtues of Honesty, Simplicity, Humility, and Poverty, and it becomes apparent that, in the morality scheme of this "Moral Representation," the gods have inverted their expected role by introducing vices to the stage. The virtues, good angels, speak to Anthropos of the advantages of his "divorce / From *Mundus*" (iv. 1–2), a parting which has clearly saddened him. Simplicity tells him of an alternative form of self-government to his earlier totalitarian utopics. "Crown thy minde," she tells him,

> With that above the worlds wealth, joyful suff'ring,
> And truely be the master of thy self.
> Which is the noblest Empire; and there stand
> The thing thou wert ordain'd, and set to govern. (iv. 16–20)

Fletcher thus writes a Protestant-political critique of courtly motivations for empire, which combines implicit criticism of ill-founded colonization projects with a suggestion of the nature of true, Christian sovereignty.

Time and Plutus enter suddenly and the virtues are forced to break off their song of "the worlds shame" and to flee "betray'd" (iv. 21–22). Time personally ejects Poverty, and announces that he has brought Riches to Anthropos. "Have I found pitie then?" asks Anthropos. Time's reply is ambivalent. "Thou hast," he says, "and *Justice* / Against those false seducers of thine honour" (iv. 32–33), thereby leaving us uncertain if the "seducers" are the vices or the Christian virtues we have just seen conclusively thrown off the stage. Time's provision for Anthropos acknowledges neither moral polarity—careless wealth nor abject poverty—as an undoubted good. We see the vices in discomfort at the close, certainly. The virtues, though, never reappear, banished for the duration. We cannot (with King Emanuel) forget that, in the process of Time's solution for the ills that have befallen Anthropos, essential Christian virtues have been denied.

Time now dis-covers Industry, the Arts, and Labour to an amazed Anthropos. There is a certain uneasy fragmentation of the text at this point, since the Arts are both revealed and superseded in the same moment by the appearance of Labour. The Arts are thus marginalized, but we are presented with the need to recognize wealth as the product of a mutual relationship between Anthropos, Industry, and Labour. In this company, Anthropos is shown a "glorious mine of metal" (iv. 38), and he gives ambivalent joint praise to both Jupiter and Plutus. The latter, reluctant from the start, leaves for America, bequeathing Anthropos a "book and mattock," the necessary props to the appropriate acquisition of wealth; and Plutus, Industry, Labour, and (presumably) the Arts, leave the stage.[49] We are left aware, nonetheless, that in some uneasy way we have been witness to a mythologized uncovering of the means of production. Anthropos is now affluent once more ["his riches envi'd / As far as Sun or Time is; his power fear'd too" (iv. 49–50)], yet he has learned the hard way the necessity of work and of the acquisition of wealth. Jupiter descends once more "in glory" at the close, and Time triumphs over the courtly vices, Vain Delight, Pleasure, Craft, Lucre, and Vanity. King Emanuel's reaction to the piece he has seen performed necessitates interpretation of Anthropos as representative king as well as representative man, and recalls the opening premise of "censure [of] the King himself." "By this we note," he says sententiously,

> in Kings and Princes
> A weaknesse, even in spite of all their wisedoms.
> And often to be master'd by abuses:
> Our natures here describ'd too, and what humors
> Prevail above our Reasons to undo us.
> But this the last and best: when no friend stands,
> The gods are merciful, and lend their hands.
> (4 Interlude 1–7)

Yet we are by no means convinced that the price paid for the match of honor and new wealth is acceptable.

The price of masquing was of course rarely acceptable. "Summing up the expense" was not pleasant for either the Inner Temple or Gray's Inn after the performance of Beaumont's masque in 1613, which, as Philip Edwards points out, "put both Inns deeply into debt." In the same vein, Chapman was kept waiting for payment for his work for the Middle Temple.[50] As late as June, the Gray's Inn authorities were still trying to persuade the masquers to return their wildly expensive costumes; they were even reduced to the threat of fines and expulsion for noncompliance with the request for return of properties. The relations of production of court entertainment, the interchange of labor and art, are thus perhaps most apparent in the aftermath of a masque. And a year later, Fletcher had glossed a curious correlation between Labour and the Arts— oddly interchangeable anyway in "The Triumph of Time"—in the epilogue to the *Four Plays,* a correlation which successfully invokes a certain participation for the theater in the politics of collaboration:

> Now as the Husbandman, whose Costs and Pain,
> Whose Hopes and Helps lie buried in his Grain,
> Waiting a happie Spring, to ripen full
> His long'd-for Harvest, to the Reapers pull;
> Stand we expecting, having sown our Ground
> With so much charge (the fruitfulnesse not found)
> The Harvest of our Labours: For we know
> You are our Spring; and when you smile, we grow:
> Nor Charge nor Pain shall binde us from your Pleasures,
> So you but lend your hands to fill our Measures.
>
> (Epilogue 1–10)

This recalls both the fate of *The Faithful Shepherdess* in performance and the colonizing Prospero's uneasy plea to the audience at the close of *The Tempest.* The husbandman trope thus underlines a kind of kinship between theatrical production and the labor of plantation, which is far from the natural opposition cited by the preachers.

A reading of *Four Plays* thus requires analysis of the motivations and ramifications of the fledgling colonial enterprise of the 1610s and claims theatrical interest in the venture. It foregrounds above all the material principle to which the colonists adhered. After all, acknowledging the adventurers' genuine enthusiasm to convert the natives to true religion, the Virginia Company was essentially a practical business, a mercantile venture rather than a spiritual or philanthropic gesture to a heathen nation. In his later discovery plays, Fletcher maintains this focus on the material principle of colonization, but he turns also, as did Shakespeare, to the further metaphoric resonance of the husbandman trope in the realms of the sexual.

5

The most obvious field of simultaneous desire and danger in the New World context is the sexual. The colony, after all, is repeatedly metaphored as a woman. Samuel Purchas cries, "[L]ooke upon Virginia," begging those who doubt the practicality of the venture to

view her lovely looks (howsoever like a modest Virgin she is now vailed with wild Coverts and shadie Woods, expecting rather ravishment then Mariage from her Native Savages) survay her Heavens, Elements, Situation; her divisions by armes of Bayes and Rivers into so goodly and well proportioned limmes and members; her Virgin portion nothing empaired, nay not yet improoved, in Natures best Legacies; the neighbouring Regions and Seas so commodious and obsequious; . . . in all these you shall see, that she is worth the wooing and loves of the best Husband.[51]

This equation of the colonial realm with patriarchal notions of plenitude and boundless, untapped sexual possibility is a commonplace in New World texts: the sexual and the colonial seem interchangeable in their strategies for empire. The best-documented case of this discursive crossover between the sexual and the colonial in the Jacobean period is one which recent critics have considered in some depth and is ironically rehearsed in Fletcher's play *The Island Princess*.[52]

In 1614, John Rolfe, a survivor of the much-publicized wreck of the *Sea Venture* five years earlier, wrote to the governor of Virginia asking his permission to marry the Virginian princess Pocahontas and providing a series of justifications of his desire for such a marriage. Rolfe's letter exemplifies the colonists' struggle to come to terms with the colonial other and the way in which this is conducted in relation to the female body. The arguments by which John Rolfe justifies his marriage to Pocahontas are the arguments by which Purchas justifies colonization. He claims to have striven with all his

power of boddy and mynde in the vndertakinge of soe waighty a matter (noe waye leade soe farr foorth as mans weaknes may p[er]mytt, wth the vnbridled desire of Carnall affection) for the good of the Plantacon, the hono^r of o^r Countrye, for the glorye of God, for myne owne salvacon, and for the Convertinge to the true knowledge of God and Iesus Christ an vnbeleivinge Creature, namely Pohahuntas: To whome my hart and beste thoughte are and haue byn a longe tyme soe intangled.[53]

The controlling metaphor of colonization is inverted. Rolfe's relationship to the woman becomes that of a husbandman to the land. He was created, he says,

to labour in the Lordes vyneyard there to sowe and plant, to nourishe and encrease the Fruytes thereof, daylie addinge wth the good husband of the Gospell somewhat to the Tallent: that in the ende the Fruytes may be reaped to the Comfort of [the] Labo[ur]er in this lyfe, and in the worlde to come. (118^v)

His reasons echo those of the Council of the Virginia Company for the plantation: that it is right for the colonists to "possesse part of their land, and dwell with them . . . because there is no other, moderate, and mixt course, to bring them to conversion, but by dailie conversation, where they may see the life, and learne the language each of other."[54] Thus, says Paul Brown, Rolfe's letter may be said

to produce Pocahontas as an other in such a way that she will always affirm Rolfe's sense of godly duty and thus confirm him as a truly civil subject. . . . The letter, then, rehearses the power of the civil subject to maintain self-control and to bring the other into his service, even as it refers to a desire which might undermine that mastery. (49–50)

From this perspective, colonialism can be seen both to consist of and to create the very elements that subvert it.

For Foucaultian critics, the subversive quality of the discourse of colonialism is largely unconscious. Despite authority's attempts to eradicate the subversive, subversion is inescapable: the corollary of this is that all attempts to subvert are involved in and compromised by the very authority they wish to overturn. This involuntary involvement is seen as the inevitable effect of discourse. Yet Fletcher's case in part questions these assumptions. In *The Island Princess,* Fletcher's analysis of the colonial and the sexual is highly conscious of the contradictions of colonialism and broaches the very questions usually considered submerged into the unconscious operations of discourse. He dramatizes wryly the colonists' obsessive focus upon the deceit of the native, the material abundance of the New World, and the metaphoric sexuality of the colony.

The widely publicized and discussed material relating to the princess Pocahontas is thoroughly rehearsed, though geographically transposed, in *The Island Princess,* by way of its title character, Quisara. Rolfe's letter is not an obvious, direct verbal source; yet the play, like the letter, demonstrates through the metaphor of the native woman as object of desire the anxieties which seem characteristic of the colonial. The play is not ostensibly Virginian. As with *The Tempest,* the stated location of *The Island Princess* is in fact far from America. The islands of Tidore and Ternata, upon which the dramatic action takes place, belong to the Moluccan archipelago situated to the south of the Philippines, spice islands key to colonial trade. Thus the play's location as it is given in the dramatis personae of the Second Folio—"India"—probably connotes as vague an area as "the Indies," a term applied to new-found lands both to the west and to the east of Europe. Yet the play bears clear traces of the American experience from the very first scene, and these traces are supported by source-study.

The principal differences between *The Island Princess* and its chief source, Le Sieur de Bellan's *Histoire Memorable de Dias Espagnol,* serve to demonstrate the way in which American narratives become interweaved into Fletcher's Moluccan tale.[55] By focusing upon and amplifying a tale of colonial intermarriage within a romantic framework, Fletcher investigates the sexual construction of the colonial. The choice of Quisara's story, with its clear echoes of the problems and questions surrounding Rolfe's desired marriage with Pocahontas, enables both an ironic dramatization of the sexual component of colonialist discourse and a considerably greater degree of female agency than that allowed to Miranda by Shakespeare.

The play's first scene provides discussion of the colonial situation and the relations of colonist and islander that becomes an analysis of the female colonial other. To begin with, we hear the wary Europeans warning each other of the treachery and viciousness of the natives. Pyniero describes the islanders as "false and desperate people, when they find / The least occasion open to encouragement, / Cruell, and crafty soules."[56] Christophero takes up the refrain—"[T]hat Governour's a feirce knave, / Unfaithful as he is feirce too, there's no trusting," he claims (I. i. 14–15)—and introduces one of the play's central concerns, the peculiarly complex question of the psychological playoff that the colonists had to make between their contempt for natives who seemed to them to be less than human and their reverence for royalty of any nationality and creed. The Governor's opening gambit has been to take captive the King of Tidore, who is confederate with the colonists, while the latter was enjoying a little recreational rowing "between the islands." This prompts a question from Christophero and an uncompromising response from Pyniero:

> *Christophero:* I wonder much how such poore and base pleasures,
> As tugging at an oare, or skill in steerage,
> Should become Princes.
> *Pyniero:* Base breedings love base pleasures;
> They take as much delight in a Baratto,
> A little scurvy boate, to row her tithly,
> And have the art to turne and wind her nimbly,
> Thinke it as noble too, though it be slavish
> . . . As we Portugalls, or the Spaniards do in riding,
> In managing a great horse which is princely,
> The French in Courtship, or the dancing English,
> In carrying a faire presence. (I. i. 16–27)

The natives are defined by Western standards alone: in this light, they become "false," "cruel," "crafty," and "base." Yet the comedy of the last lines of Pyniero's speech—the mock contrasts of European princely pleasures—undercuts presumptions of cultural absolutes and of European superiority at the same time as it maintains them, a technique which is subtly pursued throughout the play, especially in the mouth of Pyniero, who acts as a kind of mock narrator for the play.

The natives may be irredeemably "base" and "fierce," but the native princess is worthy of admiration both for her beauty and for her almost western sense of honor. She is much sought after by suitors—including a Portuguese Captain (being only a native princess, it seems, she need not be matched with European roy-alty)[57]—and has proved her nobility by her anguish at the capture of her brother, since she stands to gain by his demise:

> . . . the nobler
> Still it appears, and seasons of more tendernes,
> Because his ruin stiles her absolute
> And his imprisonment adds to her profit. (I. i. 31–34)

Despite all this, the worldly-wise Pyniero refuses to be "fool'd," showing on the one hand a profound racism, while on the other ef-fecting a highly cynical deconstruction of the mystique of royalty:

> *Pyniero:* Peace, peace, you are fool'd, sir;
> Things of these natures have strange outsides *Pedro,*
> And cunning shadowes set 'em far from us,
> Draw 'em but neare, they are grosse, and they abuse us;
> They that observe her close, shall find her nature,
> Which I doubt mainly will not prove so excellent;
> She is a Princesse, and she must be faire,
> That's the prerogative of being royall:
> Let her want eyes and nose, she must be beautious,
> And she must know it too, and the use of it,
> And people must beleeve it, they are dam'd else:
> Why, all the neighbour Princes are mad for her.
> *Christophero:* Is she not faire then?
> *Pyniero:*　　　　But her hopes are fairer. . . . (I. i. 39–51)

The refutation of the possibility of native royalty has gone too far here and has become a critique of social hierarchy. Royalty, in Pyniero's eyes, is a matter of social convention alone; he stares insolently at the nakedness which is the emperor's new clothes. The debate is hierarchical: which runs deeper, royalty or race? Can baseness of race be overcome by natural nobility? Or can both be overcome by the revelation of artifice? Pyniero satirizes the social convention of reading the signifier as the signified, though later in the play he does admit that Quisara is physically attractive. Nonetheless, he retains his cynical belief that her primary attractiveness resides in her royal blood and hopes.

Pyniero's admission of Quisara's beauty (echoing de Bellan) has to be qualified. De Bellan apologizes for digressing, but announces that he feels obliged to explain that Quisara was truly attractive despite being non-European:

> Maybe you are surprised that the Princess's eyes could perform such wonders, and above all that they had such power over men born and brought up in Europe who had therefore not been used to recognizing the shafts of a beauty obscured by a tawny colour or even a Moorish colour. . . . [But in fact w]hile the men are indeed black because [of] the strength of the sun, . . . the women there, who protect themselves from the sun in all sorts of ways, are quite white.[58]

Fletcher closely echoes this digression of de Bellan's in a brief speech by Christophero:

> For by my life I hold her a compleate one,
> The very Sun I thinke, affects her sweetnesse,
> And dares not as he does to all else, dye it
> Into his tawny Livery. (I. i. 59–62)

Quisara, then, is only "compleate" in Christophero's eyes by virtue of being, unlike her fellow Moluccans, white; moreover, she is naturally pale in the play, though de Bellan's natives manage the feat only by artificial means.

In the source-text, the further problems of royalty and religion (particularly the latter) are simply stumbling blocks en route to marriage between Quisara and Ruy Dias. But if de Bellan, at least, seems content that Portuguese "of good family" are an adequate match for Moluccan royalty, Fletcher on the other hand (maybe recalling James's immediate concern about Rolfe's request to marry a princess) complicates matters. Early on, Ruy Dias comments:

> I wou'd I were of worth, of something neare you,
> Of such a royall peece, a King I wou'd be,
> A mighty King that might command affection,
> And bring a youth upon me might bewitch ye,
> And you a sweet sould Christian. (I. ii. 42–46)

There is perhaps a degree of mockery of John Rolfe's overqualified expression of his desire to marry Pocahontas both in the way in which Quisara entices the half-reluctant Dias to admit his love—

> *Quisara:* And could you wish me Christian brave Ruy Dias?
> *Ruy Dias:* At all the danger of my life great Lady,
> At all hopes, at all—
> *Quisara:*   Pray ye stay a little,
> To what end runs your wish?
> *Ruy Dias:*   O glorious Lady,
> That I might—but I dare not speake.
> *Quisara:*   I dare then,
> That you might hope to marry me—(I. ii. 49–54)

and in Pyniero's later ironic undercutting of the play's emphasis on the need to convert. Wooing Panura near the close of the play, he says, "If thou wilt give me leave, Ile get thee with Christian, / The best way to convert thee" (V. iv. 14–15), a clear exposure of the way in which the female colonial other is produced to justify both sexual desire and the sense of godly duty that in itself justifies the entire colonial exercise.

Fletcher dis-covers the colonial mentality through an orchestration of voices from American narratives. In the first act, Pyniero voices the fundamental ethos of adventure as a kind of prologue to the arrival of Armusia:

> The nature of our country . . . brings forth
> Stirring, unwearied soules to seeke adventures;
> Minds never satisfied with search of honour:
> Where time is, and the sunne gives light, brave countrimen,
> Our names are known, new worlds disclose their riches,
> Their beauties, and their prides to our embraces;
> And we the first of nations find these wonders. (I. iii. 6–12)

Armusia replies in terms which remain the mainstay of colonial desire for decades, waxing lyrical about the natural abundance of the isles, a cornucopic abundance which seems specifically there for the colonists' benefit.[59] The point at which Pyniero interrupts his speech, however, provides a significant moment in the play's conscious critique:

> These noble thoughts sir, have intic'd us forward,
> And minds unapt for ease to see these miracles,

In which we find report a poore relater;
We are arriv'd among the blessed Islands,
Where every wind that rises blowes perfumes,
And every breath of aire is like an Incence:
The treasure of the Sun dwels here, each tree
As if it envied the old Paradice,
Strives to bring forth immortall fruit; the spices
Renewing nature, though not deifying,
And when that fals by time, scorning the earth,
The sullen earth, should taint or sucke their beauties,
But as we dreamt, for ever so preserve us:
Nothing we see, but breeds an admiration;
The very rivers as we floate along,
Throw up their pearles, and curle their heads to court us;
The bowels of the earth swell with the births
Of thousand unknowne gems, and thousand riches;
Nothing that beares a life, but brings a treasure;
The people they shew brave too, civill manner'd,
Proportion'd like the Mastres of great minds,
The women which I wonder at—
Pyniero: Ye speake well.
Armusia: Of delicate aspects, faire, clearly beauteous,
And to that admiration, sweet and courteous. (I. iii. 13–36)

The climax of the speech is the slippage once again from abundance of land to abundance of women. Presumably the women ought to "court" the colonists with as much enthusiasm as the other natural products there to be appropriated at will by Europeans.[60] Yet the romantic nature of the play compromises this.

The key motifs of romance (as well as its general emphases on wandering and voyages) seem to underline the genre's particular aptness for analyzing questions of discovery. The romantic obsession with nomination and with questions of identity is clearly appropriate to a colonial context, where the process of reappropriation was always heralded by renomination. The Algonquian names for the plantations are forgotten, replaced by appropriately Eurocentric ones such as Jamestown or Virginia. Pyniero is proud that "Where time is, and the sun gives light, brave countrimen, / *Our names are known,* new worlds disclose their riches, / Their beauties, and their prides to our embraces," and Dias bemoans his loss by admitting that Armusia "[h]as trod [him] like a name in sand to nothing."[61] But the romantic quest that Quisara initiates allows her to hold a certain sway over the Europeans. Whereas in de Bellan's tale, Quisara's proclamation that she will marry whoever liberates her brother is presented primarily as a trick to secure Dias, in *The Island Princess* the task is presented as a love-quest through which Dias must prove to her his true nobility:

> Do some brave thing that may entice me that way,
> Some thing of such a meritorious goodnesse,
> Of such an unmatcht noblenesse, that I may know
> You have a power beyond ours that preserves you;
> 'Tis not the person, nor the royall title,
> Nor wealth, nor glory that I look upon,
> That inward man I love that's lin'd with vertue.
>
> (I. ii. 57–63)

Dias gives a romantically hyperbolic response: "Command deare Lady, / And let the danger be as deep as hell, as direfull to attempt—" (I. ii. 71–73), but fails utterly not only to complete his sentence but also to achieve the required standard. The quest Quisara demands from him mocks the expectations of romance. But in order to avoid the suggestion that the Europeans might fail such a quest, Fletcher rearranges de Bellan's conclusion by the substitution of the Portuguese Armusia for the Moluccan Salama. The play thus closes with a thoroughgoing sexual and familial infiltration of Moluccan culture by the Portuguese which enables colonial appropriation through "legitimate" inheritance. There has nonetheless been the real danger that the island princess might be seen to demand a certain level of behavior which a European is not able to fulfill.

The fulfillment of the quest by Armusia is, after all, enabled by artificial, technological means. Fletcher, again ventriloquizing many of the narrative voices, the majority of whom speak of the devastating effects of Western technology on the psychology of the natives, once more significantly supplements de Bellan's tale. In the play, Armusia uses gunpowder to start a fire as a decoy while freeing the King of Tidore. Fletcher thus focuses what in de Bellan is praise for Armusia's share in the universal virtue of courage into the specific strategies of colonialism. Armusia is well aware of the potential effects of his use of Western resources, which are akin to the psychological effects of the New World tempest on the Europeans:[62]

> My thoughts have not been idle, nor my practice:
> The fire I brought here with me shall doe something,
> Shall burst into materiall flames, and bright ones,
> That all the Island shall stand wondring at it,
> As if they had been stricken with a Comet:
> Powder is ready, and enough to worke it,
> The match is left a-fire. (II. ii. 37–43)

Where de Bellan describes a local operation by one of the King's subjects and relatives in which fire, spread naturally by the wind, serves to draw away from the inhabitants of the island, Fletcher specifically relates the rescue attempt to the colonial context, not only by substituting Pyniero for Salama (thereby denying Quisara a Tidorean suitor from the beginning and enforcing the difficult question of mixed marriage and inheritance) but also by emphasizing that the rescue is achieved by dint of the superiority of the colonists' technical knowledge over the naïve natives. Even the otherwise sophisticated Governor and his Captain seem stupid, not recognizing the sound of exploding gunpowder.[63]

Armusia refers to this rescue mission tellingly as "our discovery" (II. iii. 55), and the scene of highly inflammable native houses succumbing to fire ignited by Europeans rehearses familiar colonists' narratives.[64] Later in the play, artillery is used to frighten the natives, and at no stage is the colonists' militarism far below the surface:

> *Ruy Dias:* We are Masters of the Fort yet, we shall see
> What that can doe.
> *Pyniero:*　　　Let it but spit fire finely,
> And play their turrets and their painted Palaces
> A frisking round or two, that they may trip it,
> And caper in the aire. (V. i. 68–72)

The ploy is obviously effective. Fletcher echoes travel narrative descriptions of native fear and ignorance in the face of European technological superiority in an uneasily carnivalesque destruction scene:

1 Townes-man: Heaven blesse us, what a thundring's here? What fire-spitting? We cannot drinke, but our Cans are mald amongst us. . . . Are these the Portugall Bulls—How loud they bellow?
2 Townes-man: Their horns are plaguie strong, they push down Pallaces. . . . (V. iii. 1–3, 13–16)

The audience's amusement at the expense of the colonized, both here and in the earlier scene of burning, effectively incorporates them into the processes of colonization.

The contradictions of the colonial project are most thoroughly glossed in *The Island Princess* at the moment when the Governor of Ternata, disguised as a priest, attempts to persuade the King of Tidore of the dangers posed by the Portuguese colonists. We are aware that the Governor is up to no good: his frequent asides— "My maine end is to advise / The destruction of you all" (IV. i. 79–80)—reinforce his role as a negative trickster. We know that the prophecy he produces must be false: yet he voices a simple analysis of the process of colonization from the viewpoint of the colonized, and like so many of the trickster figures of Jacobean drama, drawing upon the emotional resources of the Morality play, he is at least as sympathetic as he is evil. If Caliban's response to Prospero, cursing him for the occupation of the island and his own subjugation, is a representation of the situation of the native under colonial rule, the Governor's reaction to the Portuguese in *The Island Princess* is an expansion and a sophistication of that response.

The analysis of colonial enterprise in the play hinges on this reaction, a prophetic speech denouncing the Europeans. On the one hand, the Governor is an enemy king from a neighboring island seeking both the destruction of Tidore and the removal of the Europeans from the area. Yet on the other, he describes without exaggeration the process of colonization, from the colonists' arrival from Europe, weak, vulnerable and apparently harmless, to their consolidation on the island and the emergence of oppressive policy:

> These men came hether as my vision tells me,
> Poore, weatherbeaten, almost lost, starv'd, feebled,
> Their vessels like themselves, most miserable;
> Made a long sute for traffique, and for comfort,
> To vent their childrens toyes, cure their diseases.
> They had their sute, they landed, and too th'rate
> Grew rich and powerful, suckt the fat, and freedome

Of this most blessed isle, taught her to tremble;
Witnesse the Castle here, the Cittadell,
They have clapt upon the necke of your Tidore,
This happy town, till that she knew these strangers,
To check her when she's jolly. (IV. i. 44–55)

He shows himself aware also of the frequently reported tendency for the inhabitants of newly discovered lands to think of the colonists as gods:

[T]houghe you be pleas'd to glorifie that fortune,
And thinke these strangers Gods, take heed I say,
I finde it but a hansom preparation,
A faire fac'd Prologue to a further mischiefe. (IV. i. 57–60)

All this echoes Caliban's bitter description of his own colonization and enslavement at the hands of Prospero. But later in *The Island Princess,* the Governor moves beyond such echoes of *The Tempest,* speaking subversive words to Quisara which demonstrate his sophisticated recognition of the religious and civil domination the colonists require and the psychological means by which they will gain ideological superiority, and foreshadowing Armusia's later hysterical stand upon Christianity in face of Quisara's pagan faith:

The Portugals like sharpe thornes (marke me Lady)
Sticke in our sides; like razors, wound religion,
Draw deep, they wound, till the life bloud followes,
Our gods they spurne at, and their worships scorne,
A mighty hand they beare upon our government.
                              (IV. ii. 155–59)

This is an astonishing deconstruction of colonial motivation: the Governor's perceptions here echo Pyniero's earlier wry dis-covery of the arbitrary definition of royal beauty.

The key problem of intermarriage and "legitimate" inheritance by sexual tie is the potential for the Europeans to be sucked into the native culture; there is, in other words, an abiding danger that the colonist may "go native." At one end of the spectrum is the omnipresent threat of cannibalism; at the other the kind of fears that one can read between the lines of Rolfe's letter. But one area of crucial danger, to the Jacobean mind, is religion, the primary justification stated for the colonial enterprise. In *The Island Princess,* the religious motivation of colonization is subjected to its share of dramatic scrutiny. Quisara entices Ruy Dias to declare his desire to marry her by suggesting that he might "make her Christian." Yet she appears to have no intention of converting to Christianity, and the religious crux of the play comes at the moment when she attempts to reverse Armusia's presumptuous expectation that marriage would mean conversion: *hers*, to *his* faith. Her demand—"[C]hange your religion, / And be of one beleefe with me" (IV. v. 34–35)—instantly obliterates his professed love for her. He reacts in a manner which is hysterical and hyperbolic even in the context of the times. He cries:

> Love alone then, I'le love diseases first,
> Doate on a villaine that would cut my throat,
> Wooe all afflictions of all sorts, kisse crueltie;
> Have mercy heaven, how have I beene wandring?
> Wandring the way of lust, and left my maker?
> How have I slept like Corke upon a water,
> And had no feeling of the storme that lost me?
> Trod the blinde paths of death? forsooke assurance,
> Eternitie of blessednesse for a woman?
> For a young hansome face hazard my being? (IV. v. 53–62)

His frenzy grows:

> Your eyes resemble pale dispaire, they fright me,
> And in their rounds a thousand horrid ruines,
> Methinkes I see; and in your tongue heare fearefully
> The hideous murmurs of weake soules have suffer'd;
> Get from me, I despise ye, and know woman,
> That for all this trap you have laid to catch my life in,
> To catch my immortall life, I hate and curse ye,
> Contemne your deities, spurne at their powers,
> And where I meet your maumet Gods, I'le swing 'em
> Thus o're my head, and kick 'em into puddles,
> Nay I will out of vengeance search your Temples,
> And with those hearts that serve my God, demolish
> Your shambles of wild worships. (IV. v. 106–18)

The depth of his rage is matched only by his ignorance of her presumed religion, Islam.

The primary theme of the play—that of religion—thus occupies a compromised space. Armusia's hysterical response to Quisara's desire for his conversion to her religion is clearly awkward.

No matter how embarrassing the hyperbole of his outburst might seem to us, it is obviously impossible to suggest that a stand for the "glorious crosse" could, in 1621, be subject to overt satire; yet here, suddenly, Armusia seems to be reduced to the status of a Bomby, the sectarian fanatic in *Women Pleased*. As we have seen, de Bellan's tale ends with both Portuguese suitors dead and Quisara married to one of her distant relatives, while Fletcher's play closes with distinct advantage to the colonists: Armusia married to Quisara, and Pyniero given Ternata's main town and fortress. The Portuguese colonial hold, in Fletcher's play, is secure. Moreover, any suggestion that the play may offer a comprehensive subversion of colonialism, despite the thoroughness with which the discourse is dissected and analyzed, is defused not only by the closure effected in the last act but also by Quisara's ultimate willingness to convert to Christianity in respect for Armusia's absolute stubbornness and honor. She describes herself to him as a "virgin won by your faire constancy" (V. ii. 109). Armusia becomes for her "the perfect schoole of worth" and the "temple of true honour" (V. ii. 115–16), and she sees him as a "mirrour" of his creed. Even the King, her brother, is "halfe perswaded . . . to be a Christian" (V. v. 66).[65] Yet only "halfe." And this, surely, is the point of the play. At best, militant evangelism and its brother-in-arms, colonial enterprise, as dramatized in *The Island Princess,* only "halfe perswade."

6

"I revolt from, I am like, these savage foresters."[66]

We have seen that the women protagonists of Fletcher's plays at times long for a separatist utopia, a woman's realm where they can be free from the oppressions of men. In response, the misogynists in the plays dream of the opposite kind of utopia, "a Land," to quote Belleur in *The Wild-Goose Chase,* "where there are no women." The possibility exemplified here that one person's utopia may be another's dystopia emerges strongly from much of Fletcher's writing, but it is not until 1622, with his collaborative play *The Sea Voyage,* that he fully explores the dramatic possibilities of a commonwealth of this reversible nature. *The Sea Voyage* extends the analysis begun in *The Island Princess* of the relationship between the sexual and the colonial, pitching us onto an American island inhabited by a "commonwealth of women," the youngest member of which, like Miranda in *The Tempest*—the play upon which *The Sea Voyage* is overtly based—has never seen a man. The decay of the women's utopia into a dystopia of frustration and rebellion upon the introduction of shipwrecked men closely parallels the transformation of the New World paradise into a place of greed and betrayal upon the intrusion of the colonists.

As it happens, the first English dystopia came out of the Ashby milieu. The future bishop Joseph Hall's unlovely Latin allegory *Mundus Alter et Idem* was dedicated in 1605 to the fifth earl of Huntingdon, to whom Hall was in various ways indebted. Translated into English four years later by John Healey as *The Discovery of a New World,* it was then dedicated to the earl of Pembroke, a combination of dedicatees which underlines the broad political allegiances of the piece.[67] *Mundus Alter et Idem* is a burlesque of contemporary travel narratives which, though it draws upon the general model of Thomas More's *Utopia,* does so with the apparent intention of debunking the serious political ideals that motivate that work. John Milton, whose Puritan preferences were much affronted by it, considered *Mundus Alter et Idem* the "idlest and paltriest Mime that ever mounted upon banke," contrasting it with Plato's *Critias,* Bacon's *New Atlantis,* and More's *Utopia,* works which, for Milton, taught "this our world better and exacter things, then were yet known."[68] Hall's work, he claims, fails the essentially moral task of satire, offering "neither reproofe nor better teaching" (295). Yet the dedication to Healey's translation asks that the author be left "alone to beate all their disgraces about their owne eares, and the whole worlds, in a true Satyrick furie" (3).

The Discovery of a New World comprises four books, each devoted to a mythical land stemming from popular comic tradition: Tenterbelly, a land of Cockaigne dedicated to eating and drinking; Shee-landt, a commonwealth of Amazons; Fooliana, a country of fools and clowns; and Theevingen, a republic of robbers. Healey's marginal notes suggest satiric parallels with European courts, but Milton's rejection of the piece perhaps suggests that the criticism did not go very far. As a satire, its relevance to this study lies first in the manner in which it merges popular expectations of the New World and certain traditions of the (Old) world-upside-down within the framework of a burlesque both of contemporary travel narratives and of Renaissance political utopias, and second in its position as a source for *The Sea Voyage*. Its mockery of the clichés of travelers' tales is at best unsubtle: Healey's long-winded and pseudomystical claim that the text is "A discoverie and no discoverie, of a world and no world, both knowne and unknowne, by a traveller that never travelled" somehow falls short of the subtlety of More's brief coinage, "Utopia."

Nevertheless, *Mundus Alter et Idem* serves to underline the double-edged popular response to America, credulity and mockery mixed. Fooliana, the location of the third book, is inhabited by a race of half-wits who resemble the natives of the New World in contemporary descriptions: "The inhabitants goe all in painted fethers, as the *Indians* doe" (84).[69] They are fickle, as seen again in colonists' reports of the "treachery" of the Indians: "They vse a stranger for the very first daie as if hee were their owne brother, (though they never saw him before): marry the next daie they will passe you by, and forget that ever they knew yee" (84). The marginal notes suggest that this is satire of courtly behavior, but the immediate context of criticism is obviously the many accounts of colonists' relations with the Indians.[70] Elsewhere in Fooliana, in the region of Cholerikoye, the natives are cannibals: "They neuer make any iourney forth, but they eyther bring blowes home, or leave some behinde them. If one chance to kill his enemy, hee feedes vpon him immediatly, for they eate raw flesh altogether, and drinke warme bloud, and this is the best esteemed fare" (95). These elements pick up on some of the most familiar formulae for describing the savagery of the American natives, but are otherwise unremarkable. The second book, however, offers a source for *The Sea Voyage* and a new topography for the dramatisation of gender-relations.

This second book, "The Description of *Shee-landt*, or *Woman-decoia*," is (mercifully) brief. While traveling in Tenterbelly, the narrator is seized by a band of marauding Sheelandresses and taken "to the Chiefe cittie of the land, called Gossipingoa" (63). The land is a dystopian adaptation of classical accounts of Amazons, divided into two regions, each of which draws from one of two main Amazonian traditions. Gossipingoa and Cockatrixia are occupied and run entirely by women: any men found in their bounds are imprisoned. In the latter, men are brought out only temporarily for sexual purposes:

Others, they lay their ambushes for, and fetch them in first by loose allurements, then by praiers, and then by pence, and if none of these meanes will worke, they compell them to serve their wanton desires by force. And when they have done so, iust as you see stallion horses kept for breede, so are they stowed into custody, dieted with Eringo's, Potatoes, Cullises, and other dishes of lust devising, vntill *Venus* send her second summons. [71]

Shrewes-bourg, on the other hand, is more truly a world-upside-down, where the women are in control, and the men exist in a state of domestic slavery. "Ah what a beastly sight was it to see a distaffe and a Spindle in a mans hand, and a sword and buckler in a womans," we are told (73). The narrator arrives first in Gossipingoa, and escapes the clutches of the women by the power of his rhetoric, though not without a false start. He is captured on the borders of Letcheritania, and his plea for sympathy clearly affects the younger women in a way that fails to affect the older:

Well these good words I can tel yee wrought so prettily well, that the poore yong wenshes began many of them to weepe: yet the old countesses were not so much ouer-swaied by mine oration, but that I must go to prison to a great house in the market place called *Cold and comfortlesse,* vntill my country and cause of trauell were truely manifested vnto the *Shee-counsell.* (65–6)

His narrow escape from the law of the land provokes the narrator into a description of the Amazonian forms of government:

Their state (for ought that I could observe) is popular; each one seeking superiority, and auoyding obedience. They have no lawes at all, but do every thing by the numbers of voices. But the giuing vp of their voices struck me into a wonder, being vnacquainted therewith for they set vp a crie all together, none giues eere, but each one yells as if shee were horne mad. Is not this able to abash a good mans spirit? (67)

The land as a whole is described, like Virginia, as "ill-husbanded" (64). Hall's Latin coinage translated by Healey as "Shee-landt" is "Gynia Nova," and his marginal note reads: "New Guinea is generally represented as the easternmost part of the unknown Southern Continent, very near to the kingdom of Maletur and Beach. I have represented Gynia as situated there likewise" (223). Hall divides

Gynia Nova (with rather more etymological coherence than his translator) into "Gynaecopolis" and "Gynandria or Amazonia," but he notes that the latter "was formerly an American power, but by reason of the doughty spirit of the settlers, it is now ours" (223), thus suggesting a verbal slippage from Guinea to Guiana, from East Indies to West. Furthermore, in the process of translation, Healey amplifies this American connection. He calls the land "*Sheelandt* . . . or *Womandecoia,* & makes it a part of Virginia" (64). In the same vein, he calls it "Viraginia," land of viragoes. More-over, "Wingandacoa," a semi-homonym of "Womandecoia," was the Algonquian name for the region that the English named Vir-ginia.[72] Healey's version of Hall's satire thus locates the meta-phoric geography of his Amazonian dystopia in the New World.

It is impossible to know if Fletcher and Hall were acquainted by way of Ashby, but it is clear that Fletcher, in collaboration with Massinger, draws on Hall's Amazonia for the commonwealth of women, which is the central interest of *The Sea Voyage* of 1622.[73] The play begins on board a French ship during a tempest, in the course of which Old World hierarchies are put under severe strain. Two Portuguese gentlemen, Sebastian and Nicusa, who have been stranded on a barren island by French pirates, watch the sailors come ashore from the ship, which is in fact still intact. Once on the island, the French argue among themselves. When the Portuguese arrive, the French treat them as monstrous natives until they realize that they are in fact Europeans. Sebastian and Nicusa tell them how barren the island is and mention that the next island is much more promising but frustratingly out of reach. They also show the new arrivals piles of gold, washed up on the shore, over which, they explain, their companions had quarreled until all were dead except themselves. The newcomers instantly begin to argue over the gold, and Sebastian and Nicusa capitalize on the moment by sailing off in the French ship, apparently stranding the new-comers in their place. Act Two opens with the female protagonist, Aminta, binding the wounds the hero, Albert, has received in the struggle over the gold. They hear hunting sounds on the far island, and Albert decides to cross the gulf to the far side. The scene switches abruptly to the other island, where we discover a com-monwealth of women. When Albert crawls ashore, it is his turn to be treated as a monstrous creature, since the youngest of the island's Amazons, Clarinda, has never before seen a man. His experiences at the hands of the women echo those of the narrator of Hall's satire, but the narrative is modified and complicated as it is informed by a network of further influences and sources.

Four major sources apart from Hall's dystopia can be isolated for *The Sea Voyage:* one poetic, one dramatic, and two narrative, the influence of each of which is at its clearest in the opening scenes. The poetic source is *The Faerie Queene.* In the fourth canto of book 5, Spenser's Artegall deals justice between two brothers who are fighting over an inheritance which consists of two juxtaposed islands, one waste, the other fertile, and a coffer of dowry treasure which has been washed up on one of the islands after a "cruell ship-wracke."[74] Shortly afterward, Artegall encounters the "Queene of the Amazons" (IV. xxxiii. 5), Radigund, to whom he succumbs in battle. She imprisons him among

> Many brave knights, whose names right well he knew,
> There bound t'obay that Amazons proud law,
> Spinning and carding all in comely rew. . . .
> Amongst them all she placed him most low,
> And in his hand a distaffe to him gave,
> That he thereon should spin both flax and tow.
> (V. xxii. 2–4, xxiii. 1–3)

Artegall is held in prison by the youngest Amazon, Clarinda, who falls for him and is jealous of her mistress's power over him; the knight is finally freed by his lady, Britomart. These events and situations are clearly echoed in one way or another in *The Sea Voyage.* Juxtaposed yet opposed islands—one barren, the other abundant—act as the setting; dowry treasure motivates action; men are imprisoned by Amazons; and an Amazon named Clarinda falls for the hero. The triumph of patriarchy asserted in Spenser's text, however, comes under ironic and complex scrutiny in the course of the play.

The Tempest is the obvious dramatic source for *The Sea Voyage.* Samuel Pepys was the first to comment on the similarities between the two plays, and in none too complementary terms either. In his diary for 25 March, 1668, he writes that he went with his wife "to the King's Playhouse to see 'the Storme' [an alternative Restoration title for *The Sea Voyage*], which we did, but without much pleasure, it being but a mean play compared with *The Tempest*."[75] Dryden also notes the connection of the plays—again putting Fletcher's in an inferior light—in the prologue to his and Davenant's adaptation of *The Tempest:*

> The Storm which vanish'd on the Neighb'ring shore,
> Was taught by *Shakespear's* Tempest first to roar.
> That innocence and beauty which did smile
> In *Fletcher,* grew on this Enchanted Isle.
> But *Shakespear's* Magick could not copy'd be.[76]

Since that time, Fletcher's play has been generally considered to be inferior. Yet Fletcher did not attempt to copy "*Shakespear's* Magick": the magical elements of *The Tempest* are conspicuous by their absence from *The Sea Voyage*.[77] The opening scenes of storm and shipwreck are so obviously dependent upon *The Tempest* that any basic difference such as the absence of magic must be deliberate, and a series of key moments in *The Sea Voyage* depend for their effect upon the audience's knowledge of *The Tempest*. Albert's decision to cross to the other island because he hears the sound of hunting echoes Ariel's musical enticement of Ferdinand to a different part of Prospero's island. The safe arrival on the island of all the Europeans, including the unscrupulous and potentially mutinous ones, is common to both plays, as is the combined sexual and political naïveté of the daughter of the island's ruler. The possibility of starvation in paradise is underlined in both plays, and in both a table is set with a feast as a ploy to discover the viciousness of certain of the Europeans. Yet rejecting the magical aspects of Prospero's "art," Fletcher and Massinger choose to concentrate on the problems of practical government by human resources, following two colonial narratives, one which Shakespeare had already partially dramatized in *The Tempest,* William Strachey's "A true reportory of the wrack," and the other apparently unknown to Shakespeare, John Nicoll's *An Houre Glass of Indian News*.[78]

These narrative sources are rather more difficult to locate and analyze than the poetic sources. Fletcher and Massinger, in extending the storm scene, draw more closely than Shakespeare upon the Bermuda narratives and most obviously upon that of Strachey, which even by 1622, after the author's death, was still not in print.[79] According to Stephen Greenblatt, Strachey's "letter on the events of 1609–10 was unpublished until 1625, not for want of interest but because the Virginia Company was engaged in a vigorous propaganda and financial campaign on behalf of the colony, and the company's leaders found Strachey's report too disturbing to allow it into print."[80] To echo Shakespeare's use of Strachey's tale and to quote overtly a series of passages from the narratives of Strachey and Nicoll was to invoke the very features of colonial life that the Virginia Company most wanted hidden—the possibility of unease and unrest in paradise. Moreover, for Fletcher and Massinger to quote passages from Strachey and Nicoll in June 1622 appears even more calculated, since the events of only three months earlier had showed exactly how vulnerable the colony was.

There had already been hints prior to George Sandys's arrival as resident treasurer that the local tribes, disturbed by the increasing numbers of men and ships arriving at Jamestown, might be considering an attack. Company instructions of 24 July 1621 had encouraged fraternization with the natives in the interests of their conversion to Christianity: this, however, seems to have made the attack easy. The Algonquians overran the colony on the morning of 22 March, killing between three and four hundred settlers, including six members of the Council, among whom was almost certainly John Rolfe, the widower of Pocahontas.[81] The ironworks at Falling Creek was destroyed, as were several outlying plantations, and the surviving colonists withdrew to the fortifications at Jamestown to begin again. It is a pity that the anonymous Curtain play entitled *A Tragedy of the Plantation of Virginia,* dating from August 1623, is not extant, since it may well have provided a useful counterpart to Fletcher's colonial plays.[82] But it is clear that speedy work in the immediate wake of the massacre (which perhaps explains the atypical nature of the collaboration) would produce a play which, while avoiding reference to the massacre, would nonetheless retain a good deal of topical resonance.

The two American narratives are deployed in succession: Fletcher and Massinger seem to have drawn upon Strachey's narrative for their description of the storm itself and upon Nicoll's for the immediate events on shore. Strachey notes early on that "in the beginning of the storm we had received likewise a mighty leake" (8). In the opening scene of *The Sea Voyage,* Albert cries, "I never saw, since I have known the Sea, / . . . so rude a tempest," and asks, "In what state are we?" to which the Master replies, "Dangerous enough Captain, / We have sprung five leaks, and no little ones" (3). Strachey also reports that "Sir George Summers, when no man dreamed of such happinesse, had discovered, and cried Land" (13). In *The Sea Voyage*, a sailor cries midstorm: "We have discover'd Land, Sir, / Pray let's make in, she's so drunk else, / She may chance to cast up all her lading" (2). Strachey goes on to describe the psychological effects of the tempest, which Fletcher dramatizes through the female protagonist Aminta. Strachey reports:

[The sky] turned blacke upon us, so much the more fuller of horror, as in such cases horror and feare use to overrunne the troubled, and overmastered sences of all, which (taken up with amazement) the eares lay so sensible to the terrible cries, and murmurs of the windes, and distraction of our Company, as who was most armed, and best prepared, was not a little shaken. . . . For it is most true, there ariseth commonly no such unmercifull tempest, compound of so many contrary and divers Nations, but that it worketh upon the whole frame of the body and most loathsomely affecteth all the powers thereof. (6)

Aminta cries out in a blind terror for which she later apologizes to Albert: "Oh miserable fortune, / Nothing but horror sounding in mine ears, / No minute to promise to my frighted soul." The cynical Tibalt, counterpart to Pyniero in *The Island Princess,* shouts her down: "Peace woman," he cries mockingly, "We ha storms enough already; no more howling." But Aminta is beside herself, and asks "Must I die here in all the frights, terrors, / The thousand several shapes death triumphs in?" (3–4).

Strachey notes too the various measures taken to save the ship: "[We] threw over-boord much luggage, many a Trunke and Chest (in which I suffered no meane loss)" (12). In the play, the ship's master gives the command: "It must all overboard." The gentlemen voyagers are distraught at the loss of their fortunes. "Must my Goods over too?" cries Lamure, begging, "Oh save one Chest of Plate," but Tibalt enjoys their suffering, crying, "Away with it lustily, Sailors; / . . . Over with the Trunks, too" (5–6). Strachey notes the breaking down of class divisions at this moment of stress: "[S]uch as in all their life times had never done houres worke before," he observes sarcastically, "were able twice fortie eight houres together to toile with the best" (192). As Stephen Greenblatt points out, the word "best" in this leveling context finds a new and inverted meaning.[83] The boatswain calls "In with her of all hands," and the Master echoes this: "Come Gentlemen, come Captain, ye must help all" (6). Fletcher and Massinger thus in various ways draw much more closely both on Strachey's structure and on his turn of phrase than does Shakespeare in the opening scene of *The Tempest*.

Once the Europeans are ashore, the narrative base changes to that of Nicoll. Fletcher places his island near Guyana, adhering both to Hall's geography and to that of Hakluyt in his *Principal Navigations,* who describes a certain tribe of Amazons who live "not far from Guiana."[84] John Nicoll's *An Houre Glass of Indian News* tells the tale of colonists "sent for a supply to the planting in Guiana in the yeare 1605," who become lost and then are stranded en route upon the island of St. Lucia.[85] Immediately before they land on St. Lucia, Nicoll reports: "We went ashore upon the . . . Isle of Mayo to take in fresh water and salt, where we found five Portugals, which had been robbed by the French, and there set ashore" (49). Nicoll goes on to describe events on the journey to Guyana:

[W]ith a merry gale we sailed towards our desired place to the country of Guiana: but missing of our expectation, here began the first scene of our ensuing miseries. . . . [W]andering as it were in a wilderness of woe, betwixt hope and despair, the time passed away and with the time our victuals, the only hope of our health exceedingly wasted. . . . [I]t was so exceeding hot, that with the vehemency thereof many of our men fell marvellous weak, and some of them died. . . . This extremity caused us (though against our stomachs) to entreat the master to bring us to the nearest shore he could. (49)

The English go ashore to tend their sick, and decide to stay there for a while, bringing muskets and a cannon onto the land. They also keep the ship's boat "for we did not know what needs we might have of such a commodity afterward" (50). This irritates the sailors who remained on board, and they fire the ship's cannon at those on shore—"as it should seem in revenge of their Boat" (50)—before sailing away, leaving them to fend for themselves. Those left ashore later find Spanish goods on the island, left over from ships which had foundered nearby:

A little before our arrival, three Spanish ships were cast away, and much of the goods these Indians had saved with their Boats, and hid it in the Woods . . . insomuch that if we had a Barque of forty tons burthen, we could have laden her home with such commodities as would have made a saving voyage. (52)

The English encounter the ship and its crew again a while later at a different point on the island:

The next morning Captain Sen-Johns went in the Boat, with fifteen more in his company, to trade . . . for Roan cloth, which he had saved at sea great store: but when we came there, contrary to our expectation, we found our ship there trading with them, who had incensed the Indians sore against us, telling them that we were bad people, and would take all they had from them, and would cut their throats. (51)

In *The Sea Voyage*, Fletcher and Massinger adhere to this sequence of events, but remove all traces of aboriginal inhabitants.

In the play, Sebastian and Nicusa, two Portuguese gentlemen, have been stranded as a result of French piracy upon an island near Guiana. The French protagonists of the play, coming ashore, find the stranded Portuguese, who show them heaps of gold and jewels on the beach left from an earlier shipwreck. This inspires a realization of potential profit among the French, and while they argue over the gold, Aminta runs back to point out that the Portuguese have joined forces with some of the sailors and are making off with the ship:

> *1 Sailor:* They have cut the Cables,
> And got her out; the Tide too has befriended 'em.
> *Master:* Where are the sailors that kept her?
> *Boatswain:* Here, here [in] the mutiny, to take up money,
> And left no creature, left the boat ashore too. (14)

A while later, those who have apparently fled for good with the ship reappear. Nicoll's narrative is thus even more firmly embedded in the texture of *The Sea Voyage* than Strachey's. These clear echoes of New World narrative thus situate the fears and motivations dramatized in *The Sea Voyage,* providing a base in the equivocal literature of colonization for the uneasy attitude rehearsed by the play.

The Europeans' initial utopian motivations are clear enough. Sebastian provides a bitter commentary on the way in which he and his fellow voyagers encountered Old World robbers in the very process of traveling "[i]n hope to find some place free from such robbers" (7). For others, the utopia they desire is perhaps not so different from the Old World: Lamure bewails the loss of "the Money I ha wrackt by usury, / To buy new Lands and Lordships in new Countreys" (5). Yet descriptions of the dreams of plenitude that inspired the sea voyage are couched primarily in terms of bitterness and loss. Wrecked on the barren island, the voyagers are well aware of the dichotomy between their dreams and their predicament:

> Here's nothing but rocks and barrenness,
> Hunger, and cold to eat; here's no vineyards
> To cheer the heart of man, no Christal rivers,
> After his labour, to refresh his body. . . .
> Nature that made those remedies,
> Dares not come here, nor look on our distresses,
> For fear she turn wild, like the place, and barren. (7)

Even nature herself, the willing nature of abundance that the colonists dreamed of, is in danger of "going native." Sebastian expands on such lost dreams. There is, he says,

> No summer here, to promise anything;
> Nor autumn, to make full the reaper's hands;
> The earth obdurate to the tears of heaven,
> Lets nothing shoot but poison'd weeds.
> No rivers, nor no pleasant groves, no beasts;
> All that were made for man's use, flie this desart;
> No airy fowl dares make his flight over it,
> It is so ominous. (12)

It was in such moments that colonial experience and utopian expectation divided, creating fractures which colonialism had to assimilate.

The question of production was crucial. Much voyaging was premised on the grounds of easy wealth—gold there for the taking—and the early colonists were, as Tzvetan Todorov has underlined, obsessed by the thought of gold.[86] Fletcher and Massinger are obviously aware of this. When the women ask for "assurances of ample Joynters" (37) over the reproductive arrangement set up towards the end of the play, the men take them to see the piles of gold they have found on the beach. Tibalt voices the colonists' belief in the superiority of money to other forms of persuasion: " 'twill speak for us," he says, "More than a thousand complements or cringes, / Ditties stolen from Petrarch, or Discourses from Ovid" (37). In a representative eulogy of venture capitalism, each European male voices his own particular interest, whether it be luxury, commerce, nobility, sex, or adventure:

> *Albert:* See the Idol of the Lapidary.
> *Tibalt:* These Pearls, for which the slavish Negro
> Dives to the bottom of the Sea.
> *Lamure:* To get which the industrious Merchant
> Touches at either pole.
> *Franville:* The never-fayling purchase
> Of Lordships, and of honors.
> *Morillat:* The Worlds Mistriss,
> That can give everything to the possessors.
> *Master:* For which the Saylors scorn tempestuous Winds,
> And spit defiance in the Sea. (38)

But the drama counters this enthusiasm, recognizing the disjunction between utopian hopes and capitalist dreams and the bare facts of colonization. We recall that Prospero does not wish to lose Caliban (even at the expense of acknowledging a certain identity with him) since Caliban is useful, more than useful, as worker and slave. Twice in *The Sea Voyage,* the Europeans are betrayed by their obsession with wealth. This time, they show the gold to women, associating possession of wealth with the procurement of sexual opportunity. It turns out that that which is found apparently awaiting the Europeans in fact belongs to those already on the island, to the very women they wish to manipulate with it. The treasure, originally belonging to the Old World, both mocks their Old World haste in believing in the myth of New World plenitude and undermines the colonial justification based on the premise of the apparent absence of prior ownership.

The barren island on which the French are initially stranded is contrasted with the isle of plenitude upon which the women live.[87] The women's isle presents (at least to begin with) the other side of the coin: a utopia untainted by Old World problems and an answer to dreams of plenitude. This is made clear from the moment Albert and Aminta catch sight of it for the first time:

> The air clears too;
> And now, we may discern another Island,
> And questionless, the seat of fortunate men:
> Oh that we could arrive there. (18)

Sebastian and Nicusa have already described the impossibility of crossing to this "shadow of a place inhabited" (12). But Albert decides to brave the channel, reassuring Aminta in oddly prescient terms:

> 'Tis nor hope, nor fear, of my self that invites me.
> To this extream; 'tis to supply thy wants; and believe me
> Though pleasure met me in most ravishing forms,
> And happiness courted me to entertain her,
> I would nor eat nor sleep, till I return'd
> And crown'd thee with my fortunes. (18)

Already, then, a suggestion of utopian possibilities, blended with romantic echoes of enchanted lands, governs Albert's actions. He tells Aminta to sleep and to dream: dream, he says, that "you have sent me for discovery / Of some most fortunate Continent, yet unknown, / Which you are to be Queen of" (18).

We first encounter the Amazons as they are hunting. According to Crocale, the stag they have chased has led them to the very margin of their land:

> When we believ'd the Stag was spent, and would take soil,
> The sight of the black lake which we suppos'd
> He chose for his last refuge, frighted him more
> Than we that did pursue him.
> *Julietta:* That's usual; for, death itself is not so terrible,
> To any beast of chase.
> *Hippolita:* Since we liv'd here, we ne'er could force one to it.
> *Crocale:* 'Tis so dreadful
> Birds that with their pinions cleave the air
> Dare not fly over it. (19)

The geographical difference between island and island underlines gender difference. The male, desert island seems a hell and the channel a hellish river across which Albert's romantic love propels him:

> Sure something more than human keeps residence here,
> For I have past the *Stygian* gulph,
> And touch upon the blessed shore? 'tis so;

This is the *Elizian* shade; these happy spirits,
That here enjoy all pleasures. (21)

A little later the sexual inference is made even clearer. Aminta asks
him what he has "discover'd"; he replies: "a paradise, / A paradise
inhabited with Angels" (32). But, even in paradise, there are
problems. We soon hear of discontent among the women, a rest-
lessness which coincides with the arrival of the Europeans. Clarinda, daughter to the island's ruler Rosellia, has become separated
from the others, but Crocale points out irritably that they need not
"fear her safety, this place yields not / Fawns nor Satyrs, or more
lustful men." This observation moves her to a wistful description
of their realm, which turns into unrest. "Here we live secure," she
says, "And have among our selves a Common-wealth, / Which in
our selves begun, with us must end," to which Juletta bursts out,
"I, there's the misery" (20).

Crocale defines the tyranny of the island by way of a generational
scale:

> The strictness of our Governess, that forbids us,
> On pain of death, the sight and use of men,
> Is more than tyranny: for her self, she's past
> Those youthful heats, and feels not the want
> Of that which young maids long for: and her daughter
> The fair Clarinda, though in few years
> Improv'd in height and large proportion,
> Came here so young,
> That scarce remembering that she had a father,
> She never dreams of man; and should she see one,
> In my opinion, a would appear a strange beast to her. (20)

Juletta observes bitterly, " 'Tis not so with us," and Hippolita
adds, "For my part, I confess it, I was not made / For this single
life; nor do I love hunting so, / But that I had rather be the chace
myself" (20). Crocale describes "strange visions" which came to her
in her sleep: "As I lay in my Cabin, betwixt sleeping and waking"
(20), an erotic dream thwarted at the climax, and Albert appears
on the shore at this precise moment, fittingly exhausted by his
exertions. He begs them for help, thinking them divine:

> my last breath
> Is for a Virgin. . . . O pitty her,
> And let your charity free her from that desart,

If Heavenly charity can reach to Hell,
For sure that place comes near it: and where ere
My ghost shall find abode,
Eternally I shall powre blessings on ye. (21)

Clarinda arrives, and, Miranda-like, falls instantly for this example of the brave New World.[88] She seemed initially other than
human, a prelapsarian state defined by her never having seen a
man. It is "as if / She were made of Air and Fire, / And had not part
of earth in her." But along with her new-found infatuation comes
jealousy: "What fury / For which my ignorance does not know a
name, / Is crept into my bosome?" (23). The fall of man is thus
reenacted in a woman's Eden.

A fall of this nature has clearly already taken place in the European males well before their discovery. The gallants are Jonsonian
in their greed: their arrival on the desert island and the disappointment of their hopes drive them rapidly to savagery, the state so
dreaded by the narrators of colonial venture. Lamure and Franville
made their motives for travel abundantly clear during the storm.
Already rogues at the beginning of the play, the gallants descend
not unwillingly to the level of savages. The possibility that Europeans in the New World could move from civility to savagery has,
after all, already been evoked by Albert's arrival on the women's
beach. He thinks he is in heaven, yet he appears to the women as
subhuman or inhuman, as the Portuguese appear to the newly
stranded French, shorn of all identity, like Pericles ashore from
shipwreck. These repeated encounters with "unaccommodated"
Europeans question and undermine the absolutism of discoverers'
expectations of otherness, turning the tables in an unsettling way.

Moreover, this recognition of cultural relativity finds its fearful
correlative when hunger drives the gallants towards cannibalism.
Heralded by the grotesque suggestion that they are so hungry they
could eat the "great Wen" that the Surgeon had earlier cut "from
Hugh the saylers shoulder" (28) had he kept it handy, the notion of
cannibalism is in fact suggested not by the island context but by
memories of the written—not spontaneous savagery, but action
drawn from "civilised" memory. "I have read in stories . . ." begins Morillat, and Lamure picks up the theme: "Of such restoring
meates, / We have examples," he claims (29). The gallants thus

make to kill Aminta. She wakes up, and in terror asks them their intentions in a scene that hints at a kind of grotesque communion. She asks, "Shall I be with ye Gentlemen?" and the gallants answer mockingly:

> *Lamure:* Yes marry shall ye: in our bellies Lady.
> We love you well—
> *Aminta:* What said you Sir?
> *Lamure:* Mary wee'll eat your Ladiship.
> *Franville:* You that have buried us in this base Island,
> Wee'll bury ye in a more noble monument.
> *Surgeon:* Will ye say your prayers, that I may perform Lady?
> *Aminta:* Are ye not *Christians?*
> *Lamure:* Why, do not *Christians* eat Women? (30–31)

As they are about to pounce, she is saved by the timely arrival of Tibalt, the Master, and the sailors. Tibalt forces the gallants to realize the savagery of what they have done by plainly calling them "damn'd canibals" (32), and noting with disgust their bestial behavior when Albert brings them food. "See," he cries, "they snarle like dogs" (32). Later, in prison, Morillat freely admits the transformation: "We were handsome men, and Gentlemen, and sweet men," he says, "And were once gracious in the eyes of beauties, / But now we look like Rogues; / Like poor starv'd rogues" (52). This is a far cry from the material-utopian hopes with which they began their voyage.

The viciousness that results from such disappointment with colonial expectations begins to affect the Amazons, too. Yet this Old World tainting stands in direct contrast to the possibility of utopia the women had created for themselves on the abundant isle. The Commonwealth of Women was founded to avoid such tainting. Rosellia describes the beginnings:

> We took a solemn Oath, never to admit
> The curs'd society of men: necessity
> Taught us those Arts, not usual to our Sex,
> And the fertile Earth yielding abundance to us,
> We did resolve, thus shap'd like Amazons
> To end our lives. (63)

They created a convent-republic, in which they placed their "happiness / In cold and chaste embraces of each other" (34). Such a society clearly requires mutual discipline, a rigor which equally clearly fails. Crocale admits: "Every hour something tels me I am forsworn" (20). Yet Rosellia demands the maintenance of this rigor, as she demands an end to patriarchy:

> the Soveraignty
> Proud and imperious men usurp upon us,
> We confer on our selves, and love those fetters
> We fasten to our freedomes. Have we, Clarinda,
> Since thy fathers wrack, sought liberty,
> To lose it un-compel'd?[89] Did fortune guide,
> Or rather destiny, our Barke, to which
> We could appoint no Port, to this blest place,
> Inhabited heretofore by warlike women,
> That kept men in subjection? (24–25)

Her motivation, however, is impure. As in *The Tempest,* where Prospero, displanted, builds an island kingdom to protect the prospects of a daughter, here Rosellia creates the woman's realm to protect her daughter not out of pure opposition to patriarchy but in remembrance of lost inheritance. And it is the instinct for inheritance, for reproduction, that Clarinda evokes in her arguments against the strict maintenance of separatism. "Should all women use this obstinate abstinence / You would force upon us," she says, "in a few years / The whole World would be peopled / Only with Beasts" (25), a chilling echo of Caliban's stated motivation for his attempted rape of Miranda.[90]

Thus a reproductive arrangement is initiated:

> Each one shall choose a husband, and injoy
> His Company a month, but that expir'd,
> You shall no more come near 'em; if you prove fruitful,
> The Males ye shall return to them, the Females
> We will reserve our selves: this is the utmost
> Ye shall e'er obtain. (26)

For Rosellia, the change from one form of Amazonian government, heralded by the arrival of Albert and the rebellion he causes among the women, is a move toward weakness, at best a rash compromise. She admired the aboriginal Amazons, whose system she emulated in constructing the commonwealth, the "warlike women, / That kept men in subjection" (25), a system the imprisoned gallants comically beg for later in the play:

Lamure: Put us to any service.
Franville: Any bondage,
Let's but live.
Morillat: We'll get a world of children,
For we know ye are hainously unprovided that way;
And ye shall beat us when we offend ye;
Beat us abundantly, and take our meat from us. (52)

But she realizes that a change is inescapable. When first she sees
Albert, she points out, like the older women in Hall's Amazonia,
the patriarchal authority latent in rhetorical fluency, knowing that
"every word he speaks [is] a Syrens note, / To drown the careless
hearer."[91] "Have I not taught thee," she asks, "The falshood and
the perjuries of Men? / On whom, but for a woman to shew pity, /
Is to be cruel to her self" (24). She maintains that it was ordained
that they, the women, should be wrecked upon an island where
matriarchy was aboriginal. It is man—European man—who becomes the very monster of otherness that the colonists feared inhabited such islands.

But events drag even Rosellia into the dilution of her ideals. She
begins reluctantly to enjoy the sexual frisson of the situation when
Tibalt flatteringly and strategically chooses her as his partner in
the reproductive negotiations, so that when apparent betrayal (in
the form of the treasure) is discovered, her fury is redoubled by
recollection of her own weakness, and she determines upon a fierce
revenge. She orders the men to be killed in bitter sacrifice, but her
motivation focuses on the memory of men:

                    She that moves me
        For pity or compassion to these Pirats,
        Digs up her Fathers, or her Brothers Tomb,
        And spurns about their ashes.
        Couldst thou remember what a Father thou hadst once,
        'Twould steel thy heart against all foolish pity.
        [T]hey shall fall the sacrifices to appease
        His wandring Ghost. (55–56)

Thus, paradoxically, both the sacrifice of the men and the continued sexual self-denial of the women are premised on ultimately
patriarchal grounds.[92] And the women find that they have a stark
choice: either they must settle for a single-generation utopia—
"have among our selves a Common-wealth, / Which in our selves
begun, with us must end" (19)—or else succumb to a patriarchy

which would, in the words of the Spenserian source, "changing all that forme of common weale, / The liberty of women . . . repeale."[93]

There is thus a distinct sense of unease at the close of *The Sea Voyage*. Moreover, not only is the closing marriage allocation quite as arbitrary as the earlier mechanical reproductive arrangement—reducing Clarinda, for example, to an Isabella-like silence in face of an arranged marriage—but the very tone of the final recognition-scene shares with *The Winter's Tale* and *Pericles* the realization that the deferral of reunion has in fact been far too prolonged. Sebastian sees Rosellia again after years apart, and, though their daughter Clarinda is now, for Sebastian, identical with his wife in her prime—"a perfect model of thy self, / As thou wert when thy choice first made thee mine" (64)—there is no escape from the loss to time. Rosellia's features are "wrinkled now with time / Which Art cannot restore" (64). Just as the religious resolution of *The Island Princess* only "halfe perswaded," the colonial resolution of *The Sea Voyage* can only half-restore. The economics of discovery appears unsound.

7

At one point in *The Island Princess*, Pyniero and Quisara are in conversation. She thinks he has come to plead on behalf of his cowardly uncle Ruy Dias, but he denies the charge. "I am no Uncles agent, I am mine owne, Lady," he says, "I scorne my able youth should plough for others, / Or my ambition serve for pay; I ayme, / Although I never hit, as high as any man, / And the reward I reach at shall be equall" (III. i. 218–22). At this moment, his curious blend of idealism and cynicism smacks more of the malcontent of revenge drama than the satiric voice of tragicomedy. The sarcastic asides he makes at the expense both of Quisara and of his mission all through the play (but most volubly at this point) still fail to undermine the desire for autonomy apparent in this outburst. This essential doubleness—a dream of agency matched by a cynical recognition of circumstances—seems to me characteristic of Fletcher's work.

Writers, like the characters they create, seek a certain autonomy of action, yet the conditions in which they write inevitably resist this desire. As a working playwright in Jacobean London, Fletcher was at the mercy of financial considerations, of his audiences, of the censor, of the city authorities, and of many other determining factors. His connections with the earl and countess of Huntingdon and with the Ashby milieu appear to have allowed him a degree of independence from London and the court as well as from his company's royal patron, yet these connections may be said simply to have freed him into another kind of determinism: to echo the concerns of those whose hearts lay with the memory of an earlier monarch and a more conscious and militant Protestantism than that favored by the king. This particular politics was in his blood, and there is nothing to suggest strain in his dramatizations of the dangers of absolutism and the need to resist in certain conditions.

Yet his response to Jacobean colonial endeavor suggests a typical degree of tension among the various discourses that determined the shape of his work. I have shown a variety of ways in which his connections with the Ashby circle influenced the orientation of his work, and fascination with the ramifications of the discovery of America is one obvious arena of shared interest. At the same time, he was writing for a theater audience with very different points of view from those of his country patrons, and he was experimenting with forms, genres, and inheritances, seeking a distinctive dramatic voice. As a Jacobean playwright with patronage roots outside London, Fletcher was neither an autonomous creator of autotelic literary texts nor a circumscribed subject wholly determined in his output by arbitrary discursive forces. The politics of his plays is rather the product of putting into play aspects of agency, influence, and interest in the context of a popular theater repertoire.

His attitude to the New World thus appears a wry one, both producing and produced by certain central cultural definitions of the colonial project, and providing, as Thomas More's *Utopia* did, with its obvious location in the New World, a locus for reinforcement and satire of English practices and institutions. He mocks the desires and demands of the adventurers and shows the dangers inherent in such expectations, yet he also demonstrates the utopian possibilities of escape from the Old World; by invoking certain well-known New World travel narratives in the writing of his two plays of discovery, he provides a comprehensive dramatization of the discursive contexts of colonization. Fletcher's discovery plays are thus the product of negotiation among a range of intentions—his own attitudes, the attitudes of his patrons, and the attitudes of the audiences in the theatre—which are finally impossible to disentangle. It is the tensions produced by this negotiation which give the plays their characteristic quality of unease.

CODA

"Strange bifronted posture"

A little speculation by way of conclusion. In 1622, the same year as *The Sea Voyage,* the Oxford hispanist James Mabbe published *The Rogue,* his translation of Matheo Alemán's *Guzmán de Alfarache,* with dedicatory verses by his fellow translator Leonard Digges, by Ben Jonson, and by one "I. F." The latter provided two poems, a brief one in Latin and a longer one in English. The longer poem welcomes Guzmán to these shores and praises his Protean nature:

> his life alone,
> Is Precept with Example; So that none
> Can better teach by worse meanes; who by strange
> Bifronted posture, Ill, to good, doth change.
> So Vipers flesh, the Vipers cure hath bin:
> And sinfull surfets, Antidotes for sin.
> So an old Bawdes face, Chastnesse doth suggest:
> Vices true Picture, makes us Vice detest,
> More then Grave *Platoes* wish. (A4ʳ)

"I. F." is almost certainly John Fletcher, who would presumably have known Mabbe through Jonson, and whose dependence upon Spanish literary sources has long been acknowledged. Here he rehearses the early modern moral theory of satire, proposing an antiplatonic aesthetic with irony as the vehicle of instruction. He praises Guzmán for a kind of doubleness or duplicity, a "strange bifronted posture," which also has tremendous resonance for his own work and which lies at the heart of what I have called his politics of unease.

Bearing in mind the politics I have mapped for Fletcher, including the overt wish for war with Spain he voiced in his verse letter of around this time to the countess of Huntingdon, this penchant for Spanish literature, particularly in a context of duplicity, might seem problematic. But the dedicatory poem is careful to separate literary appreciation from political implication. Through the voice of the picaresque hero, Fletcher detaches enjoyment of Spanish literature from complicity in Spanish politics:

> I come no Spy, nor take
> A Factious part; No sound of Warre I make,
> But against sinne; I land no forraine mates;
> For Vertues Schooles should Free be in all states. [1]

This separation of literature and politics is a standard attitude among literary-minded English Protestants at this time. Despite his lifelong commitment to the language and literature of Spain, the translator Mabbe's own politics were by no means pro-Catholic or pro-Spanish: it is possible, for example, that he did a little spying for England while he lived in Madrid. [2] More to the point, an earlier translation from the Spanish offers a militant Protestant context for the attitude Fletcher expresses. Thomas Wilson's translation of Montemayor's *Diana* was never published, but its full title suggests paradoxical tastes: *Diana de Monte Mayor Done out of Spanish by Thomas Wilsõ Esquire, in the Yeare 1596 & Dedicated to the Erle of Southamptõ Who Was Then uppon y*ᵉ *Spanish Voiage w*ᵗʰ *My Lord of Essex. Wherein under the Names and Vailes of Sheppards and Theire Lovers Are Covertly Discoursed Manie Noble Actions & Affections of the Spanish Nation, as Is of y*ᵉ *English of y*ᵉ *Admirable and Never Enough Praised Booke of Sr Phil: Sidneyes Arcadia.* Wilson is careful to cite Sidney as a precursor of the kind of writing he is promoting, and Southampton and Essex, taking translations from the Spanish with them even as they sail to raid Cadiz, demonstrate that such works could be acceptable reading for the most militant of Protestants.

Fletcher was immensely influenced by Spanish literature. I have shown already that 1613 was, for various reasons, a key year in his career, and one event of that year which has not been mentioned so far but which would turn out to be of crucial importance to him was the publication of Cervantes's *Novelas Exemplares*. It is not clear that Fletcher knew Spanish, but he certainly knew French, and the *Exemplary Tales* were translated into French in 1615. Certainly, he made use of various of the *Tales* as the sources of his plays well prior to 1624, the year they were translated into English by Thomas Shelton. He clearly favored Spanish sources when writing his plays, and he treated material from Lope de Vega, Calderon, de Argensola, and others as well as Cervantes. But ever since Beaumont's obviously *Quixote*-inspired *Knight of the Burning Pestle* and their subsequent collaborative use of the 1608 French translation of *The Curious Impertinent* from *Don Quixote* as a source for *The Coxcomb*, Fletcher had maintained a particular interest in the writings of Cervantes, and he went on to make use of his work in thirteen further plays.[3]

He treated material from *Don Quixote* in the lost Shakespeare collaboration *Cardenio* (to judge from its title and its relation to the later play, *The Double Falsehood,* which is supposedly based on it), and in *The Double Marriage, The Pilgrim, The Wild-Goose Chase, The Prophetess,* and *The Noble Gentleman;* and material from *Persiles y Sigismunda* appeared in *The Custom of the Country,* shortly after the English translation was published.[4] Treatments of various of the *Novelas Exemplares* are apparent in *Love's Pilgrimage* ("La Dos Doncellas"), *The Queen of Corinth* ("La Fuerza de la Sangre"), *Beggars' Bush* ("La Gitanilla"), *Rule a Wife and Have a Wife* ("El Casamiento Engañoso"), *The Chances* ("La Señora Cornelia"), and *The Fair Maid of the Inn* ("La Ilustre Fregona").[5] Even where the origin of a play is neither Spanish literature in general nor Cervantes in particular, a connection can sometimes be found, such as with *The Island Princess,* where the principal source is a tale appended to the French translation of the *Novelas Exemplares.* A thorough examination of Fletcher's dependence upon Spanish sources would obviously be a study in its own right, and I do not propose in concluding the present volume to attempt such an analysis. But I would like to suggest that Fletcher's praise for Guzmán's "strange bifronted posture" echoes some of the primary concerns and problems of his plays and to speculate on a possible future direction for Fletcher studies.

This "Bifronted posture" or doubleness is a key feature of Fletcher's work, from his habitual practice of collaboration to the characteristic mixed genre of his plays, tragicomedy. I have argued that Fletcher's plays negotiate a variety of intentional and cultural inputs, from the religious preferences of his family to the political orientation of his patrons, and from his culture's obsessions with the problems of gender and discovery to the particular political issues of his day, such as rural unrest. It is from these negotiations that the plays take their characteristic productive tension, the politics of unease that rejects monolithic or absolute solutions and seeks instead a recognition of the inevitability of collaboration and dependence. The political resistance to absolutism has its literary correlative in the doubleness of the plays, the resistance to resolution and to a single author or viewpoint. At the same time, this collaborative Fletcherian politics has its vehicle in tales of individuals, whether seeking resolution to riddles, such as Silvio in *Women Pleased,* or creating transformed power structures by way of spirited defence, such as Maria in *The Woman's Prize,* or rejecting received cultural norms and inheritances, such as Valentine in *Wit Without Money.* With Valentine's rejection of "title troubles" in mind, it is perhaps not surprising that Fletcher should voice his appreciation of the Protean picaresque hero of *The Rogue* in the way that he does; the picaresque is clearly an important genre for Fletcher, both in its forthright humor and in its self-conscious, generic opposition to romance. In this generic issue Fletcherian doubleness is at its most marked.

I would speculate, then, that in the self-consciousness and anti-romance of certain Spanish texts—perhaps especially *Guzmán de Alfarache* and the writings of Cervantes—Fletcher found a prose correlative to his own generic experiments on the stage. Beaumont and Fletcher are generally described in the criticism as writers of overblown and uncritical "romantic tragicomedy"; yet from Rafe's conquests in *The Knight of the Burning Pestle* and the resonantly named Lazarillo's quest for the fish's head in *The Woman Hater* to Oriana's outburst against the readers of romance in *The Wild-Goose Chase* and the reversible utopia of *The Sea Voyage,* romance elements are simultaneously utilized and ironized, first in the work of Beaumont and Fletcher, and then in Fletcher's later solo and collaborative work, creating the tension and unease that characterize Fletcherian drama. Failure to recognize and accept this simultaneity of antitheses has always weakened criticism of Fletcher's plays, leading not only to a continued inability to acknowledge the generic and political ramifications of collaboration but also to an almost total failure to recognize the essential ironies of Fletcherian writing.

The modern critic or director is in good company, though, since the original audiences also initially missed the point, and not long after Fletcher's death began once more to misread the plays. Walter

Burre, in his dedicatory epistle to Beaumont's *The Knight of the Burning Pestle,* seethes at its failure on stage, which he attributes firmly to the inability of the audience to understand "the privie marke of irony about it." Annabel Patterson has suggested that this inability to recognize irony is key to the failure on stage as well as the continued inadequate comprehension of Fletcher's *The Faithful Shepherdess.* As Patterson shows, already by 1634, only nine years after his death, Fletcher's play had been performed in a wholly inappropriate Platonic context, that of the court of Henrietta Maria, who "reinvented *The Faithful Shepherdess,* or caused it to be reinvented on her behalf, translating it from Jacobean camp into the queen's pastoral, making it 'new.' "[6] In this irony or "camp" and in his persistently ambivalent response to romance, at once depending upon and mocking the genre, Fletcher echoes the experiments and achievements of his Spanish sources.

Even if one rejects as overstated Foucault's view of *Don Quixote* as forming an absolute break with previous writing, it is difficult not to see in the self-awareness of Cervantes' work a central articulation of the early modern condition, and it is apparent that at the end of the sixteenth and the beginning of the seventeenth century, Spanish writers were producing a mass of self-conscious, generically aware, picaresque antiromances which nonetheless depended upon romance for their structure and impetus.[7] The works of these writers had a profound influence on Fletcherian drama, and the paradox of the "strange bifronted posture" he praises in *The Rogue* lies, as I have suggested, at the heart of his own politics of unease.

In the illogic of "none can better teach by worse meanes," it is possible to hear echoes of the paradoxical, controlling mood of achievement, bewilderment, and loss voiced by Palamon at the conclusion of *The Two Noble Kinsmen,* as he bewails the arbitrary and ironic behavior of the gods and the apparently inevitable duplicity of life:

> That we should things desire, which doe cost us
> The losse of our desire; That nought could buy
> Deare love, but losse of deare love. (V. iv. 110–12)

Palamon here voices the essential structural contradiction of the new genre, recognizing the paradox that the vehicle of its regenerative teleology is dispersal, dissemination, and loss. He thus provides an alternative way of reading the "middle mood" that Eugene Waith ascribed to Fletcher's plays, defining that mood not as a bland, middle way between the absolute genres of tragedy and comedy, but rather as a radically liminal response to the particular cultural and political conditions of the Jacobean theater.[8]

Innovation at the Globe did not cease with the retirement of Shakespeare: Fletcher's achievement is a putting into practice of the generic implications both of a resistance to the politics of absolutism and of a writing practice which rejects the single author and the self-possessed text. It is perhaps only now, centuries later, that readers of his plays (and, with luck, audiences) will be able to respond as positively as did the audiences of the 1610s and 1620s to the doubleness, the duplicity, and the productive unease of Fletcher's plays.

Family Trees of Beaumont, Fletcher, Huntingdon

Family Tree of Beaumont

Sir Thomas Beaumont — Philippine (dau. of
(Seigneur de Basqueville)   Thomas Maureward
(d. 1547)   of Cole Orton)

Thomas — Anne Moton

Sir John — Joan D'Arcy

Thomas — Anne Harcourt
Thomas (d. 1531–2)

Edward — Anne Milgate

Mary   Dorothy   John — Elizabeth Hastings

Beaumonts of Barrow-upon-Trent

Francis — Ursula Isley

Elizabeth   Frances

Sir John (b. 1446)

George — Joan Pauncefote

William (d. 1529)   Henry   William   Richard   Robert
m. Mary Basset

Edmund m. Katherine Laxham

Anne m. 1) ? Francis
2) William Turner

Mary — Sir Matthew Charnock

John (rector of Cole Orton)   Anthony m. Anne Armstrong   William   Cicely m. Henry Fenton

Katherine m. Leonard Bardsey

Francis   Thomas   Mary

Maurice

Mary — 1) Sir George Villiers
2) Sir William Rayner
3) Sir Thomas Compton
(brother of 1st Earl of Northampton)

George Villiers (1st Duke of Buckingham)

Catherine

Nicholas (1529–1585) — Anne Saunders

Richard — Colette Clerke
of Cole Orton (d. 1538)

George m. Elizabeth Leigh   Edward   Simon

Mary m. 1) ? Sharpe 2) ? Hatcliffe

Avery (d. 1601) — Thomas Findern   Anne   Dorothy

Thomas

Sir Henry — Elizabeth Lewis (d. 1608)
(d. 1607)

Francis (d. 1624)

Sir Thomas (d. 1614) m. Catherine Farnham

Huntingdon m. ? Holland

Dorothy m. William Read

Catherine

Sir Thomas — Elizabeth Sapcote
(later 1st Viscount
Beaumont of Swords)

Sir Henry — Elizabeth Turpin

Sir Thomas (1st Bt. of Sroughton Grange)

Elizabeth m. 1) Sir Thomas Waldron
2) Henry Hastings

Mary — Francis Manby

Sapcote — 1) Bridget Monson
(2nd Viscount
Beaumont of Swords)

Henry   Thomas   Robert   Francis   Henry   Anne   Gervase   Catherine   George   Mary   Charles

Sir John
(2nd Bt. of
Grace-Dieu
1607–1644)

Sir Thomas
(3rd Bt. of
Grace-Dieu
1620–1686)

John — Elizabeth Hastings

Dorothy   Francis (d. 1598) — Anne Pierrepoint   Henry

Elizabeth — William, Lord Vaux of Harrowden   Jane   Francis   Mary   Henry

Thomas Seyliard m. Elizabeth

Sir Henry (1581–1605) — Barbara Faunt

Sir John (1st Bt. of Grace-Dieu) — Elizabeth
(1582–1627)   of Grace-Dieu
(1582–1627)

Barbara

Family Tree of Fletcher

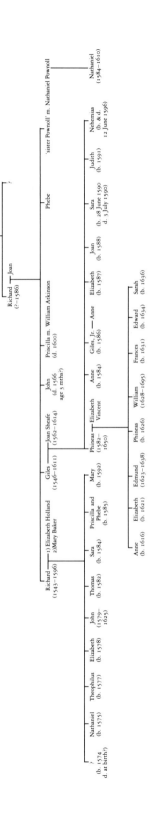

Family Tree of Huntingdon

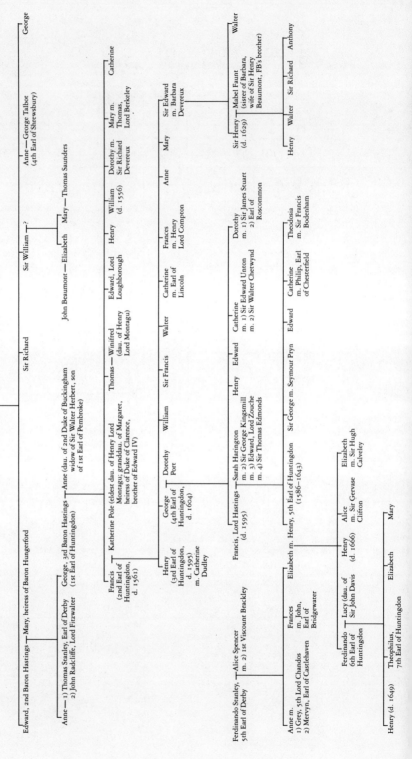

APPENDIX 2

Chronology for the Plays of
John Fletcher and His Collaborators

[*The History of Madon, King of Britain*	1605?	Beaumont (lost)]
The Woman Hater	Probably early 1606; (published 20 May 1607)	Beaumont, with some revision by Fletcher
The Knight of the Burning Pestle	[Autumn?] 1607	Beaumont
Cupid's Revenge	1607–8	Beaumont and Fletcher (final form by Beaumont)
Philaster	1608–9	Beaumont and Fletcher (mainly Beaumont)
The Faithful Shepherdess	1608–9	Fletcher
The Coxcomb	1608–10	Beaumont and Fletcher, revised by ?
The Maid's Tragedy	1610	Beaumont, with a little Fletcher
The Woman's Prize	1611	Fletcher
The Night Walker	1611 (revised 1633)	Fletcher (revised by Shirley)
A King and No King	performed 26 December 1611	Beaumont, with a little Fletcher
The Captain	1609–12 (performed 1612)	Fletcher, with some Beaumont
Bonduca	1609–14	Fletcher
Valentinian	1610< >November 1612	Fletcher
Monsieur Thomas	1610–13	Fletcher
[*Cardenio*	performed Christmas 1612	Fletcher and Shakespeare (lost)]
Masque of Inner Temple and Gray's Inn	performed 20 February 1613	Beaumont
Henry VIII	14 February< >29 June 1613	Fletcher and Shakespeare
The Two Noble Kinsmen	1613	Fletcher and Shakespeare
The Honest Man's Fortune	after March 1613	Field, with a little help from Fletcher and Massinger
The Scornful Lady	probably 1613; (after 27 May)	Fletcher, with a little Beaumont (Beaumont final form)
Thierry and Theodoret	[late?] 1613 [?]	Fletcher, Beaumont, Massinger [?]
[untitled lost play	in or around 1613	Fletcher, Massinger, Field, Daborne]

Four Plays . . .	1613 [?]	Field and Fletcher
Wit Without Money	1614? [after August?]	Fletcher, revised by ?
Love's Pilgrimage	late [?] 1616	[Beaumont and]? Fletcher [with interpolated Jonson]
The Mad Lover	late [?] 1616	Fletcher
[The Jeweller of Amsterdam	late [?] 1616	Fletcher, Field and Massinger (lost)]
A Very Woman	[1616–]1617[?]; revised 1634	Fletcher and Massinger, revised Massinger
The Chances	1617	Fletcher
The Queen of Corinth	[mid-]1617	Fletcher, Field and Massinger [or Fletcher and Field, rev. Massinger]
The Bloody Brother	[Summer] 1617; rev. 1627–30	Fletcher and Massinger, with a little Chapman and Jonson
Women Pleased	[May–December] 1618	Fletcher
The Knight of Malta	November 1618	Fletcher and Field, with a little Massinger
The Loyal Subject	16 November 1618	Fletcher
[The Laws of Candy	1618–19?	Ford?]
The Humorous Lieutenant	mid-late 1619	Fletcher
Sir John Van Olden Barnavelt	perf. 14–27 August 1619	Fletcher and Massinger
The Custom of the Country	probably late 1619	Fletcher and Massinger
The Double Marriage	later [?] 1620	Fletcher and Massinger
The Little French Lawyer	late March [?] 1621	Fletcher and Massinger
The False One	late [? Christmas?] 1621	Fletcher and Massinger
The Island Princess	performed Christmas 1621	Fletcher
The Wild Goose Chase	performed Christmas 1621	Fletcher
The Pilgrim	composed 18 September–31 December 1621; performed 1 January 1622	Fletcher
The Prophetess	licensed 14 May 1622	Fletcher and Massinger
The Sea Voyage	licensed 22 June 1622	Fletcher and Massinger
The Spanish Curate	licensed 24 October 1622	Fletcher and Massinger
Beggars' Bush	performed 27 December 1622	Fletcher and Massinger
The Maid in the Mill	licensed 29 August 1623; revised 1 November	Fletcher and Rowley
[The Devil of Dowgate	performed 17 October 1623	Fletcher? (lost)]
The Lovers' Progress	licensed 6 December 1623 as The Wandering Lovers [7 May 1634 as Cleander or The Lovers' Progress]	Fletcher, [rev. Massinger (1634)]
A Wife for a Month	licensed 27 May 1624	Fletcher
Rule a Wife and Have a Wife	licensed 19 October; performed 2 November and 26 December 1624	Fletcher
The Elder Brother	composed 9 January– 27 March 1625	Fletcher, I and V virtually rewritten by Massinger

[1625: 27 March, James dies, theaters close; 29 August, Fletcher dies; early December, theaters reopen]

Love's Cure	[160? and 1625?]	Massinger revision of conjectured early Beaumont and Fletcher

CHRONOLOGY

The Fair Maid of the Inn	licensed 22 January 1626	Massinger, Webster, and Ford, with a little Fletcher [?]
The Noble Gentleman	licensed 3 February 1626 [written 1611–1615?]	Fletcher revision of early Beaumont [?]

TEXTUAL NOTE

Throughout this study, I have quoted where possible from the ongoing Cambridge edition of the plays in the Beaumont and Fletcher canon, general editor Fredson Bowers. Where plays have not yet appeared in Bowers, I have quoted from the previous Cambridge edition, edited by Glover and Waller. I therefore provide here a list of the plays included in each of these editions. References to Glover and/or Waller refer to page rather than line numbers, since the edition has no lineation. I have cited other editions, such as that of Dyce, on occasion in the notes, but for quotations I have depended upon Bowers, with backup from Glover and Waller. See appendix for authorship attribution and dating of individual plays. In quotations from early modern texts, long 's' has been silently modernized. I have also given speech prefixes in full.

The Works of Francis Beaumont and John Fletcher. Ed. Arnold Glover and A. R. Waller. 10 vols. Cambridge: Cambridge UP, 1905–12.

Vol. 1 (1905), ed. Glover: *The Maid's Tragedy,* 1–74; *Philaster,* 75–148; *A King and No King,* 149–230; *The Scornful Lady,* 231–301; *The Custom of the Country,* 302–88.

Vol. 2 (1906), ed. Glover and Waller: *The Elder Brother,* 1–59; *The Spanish Curate,* 60–145; *Wit Without Money,* 146–207; *Beggars' Bush,* 208–80; *The Humorous Lieutenant,* 281–371; *The Faithful Shepherdess,* 372–445.

Vol. 3 (1906), ed. Waller: *The Mad Lover,* 1–75; *The Loyal Subject,* 76–169; *Rule a Wife and Have a Wife,* 170–235; *The Laws of Candy,* 236–99; *The False One,* 300–72; *The Little French Lawyer,* 373–454.

Vol. 4 (1906), ed. Waller: *Valentinian,* 1–92; *Monsieur Thomas,* 93–173; *The Chances,* 175–245; *The Bloody Brother,* 246–313; *The Wild-Goose Chase,* 314–90.

Vol. 5 (1907), ed. Waller: *A Wife for a Month,* 1–73; *The Lovers' Progress,* 74–152; *The Pilgrim,* 153–229; *The Captain,* 230–319; *The Prophetess,* 320–89.

Vol. 6 (1908), ed. Waller: *The Queen of Corinth,* 1–78; *Bonduca,* 79–159; *The Knight of the Burning Pestle,* 160–231; *Love's Pilgrimage,* 232–320; *The Double Marriage,* 321–407.

Vol. 7 (1909), ed. Waller: *The Maid in the Mill,* 1–77; *The Knight of Malta,* 78–163; *Love's Cure,* 164–236; *Women Pleas'd,* 237–310; *The Night-Walker,* 311–84.

Vol. 8 (1909), ed. Waller: *The Woman's Prize,* 1–90; *The Island Princess,* 91–170; *The Noble Gentleman,* 171–239; *The Coronation,* 240–307; *The Coxcomb,* 308–78.

Vol. 9 (1910), ed. Waller: *The Sea Voyage*, 1–65; *Wit at Several Weapons*, 66–142; *The Fair Maid of the Inn*, 143–219; *Cupid's Revenge*, 220–89; *The Two Noble Kinsmen*, 290–377.

Vol. 10 (1912), ed. Waller: *Thierry and Theodoret*, 1–70; *The Woman Hater*, 71–142; *Nice Valour*, 143–98; *The Honest Man's Fortune*, 202–80; *The Masque of the Inner Temple and Gray's Inn*, 281–86; *Four Plays*, 287–364.

The Dramatic Works in the Beaumont and Fletcher Canon. Gen. Ed. Fredson Bowers. 7 vols. to date. Cambridge: Cambridge UP, 1966–present.

Vol. 1 (1966): *The Knight of the Burning Pestle*, ed. Cyrus Hoy, 1–110; *The Masque of the Inner Temple and Gray's Inn*, ed. Fredson Bowers, 111–44; *The Woman Hater*, ed. George Walton Williams, 145–259; *The Coxcomb*, ed. Irby B. Cauthen, Jr., 261–366; *Philaster*, ed. Robert K. Turner, 367–540; *The Captain*, ed. L. A. Beaurline, 541–670.

Vol. 2 (1970): *The Maid's Tragedy*, ed. Robert K. Turner, 1–166; *A King and No King*, ed. George Walton Williams, 167–314; *Cupid's Revenge*, ed. Fredson Bowers, 315–448; *The Scornful Lady*, ed. Cyrus Hoy, 449–565; *Love's Pilgrimage*, ed. L. A. Beaurline, 567–695.

Vol. 3 (1976): *Love's Cure*, ed. George Walton Williams, 1–111; *The Noble Gentleman*, ed L. A. Beaurline, 113–223; *Beggars' Bush*, ed. Fredson Bowers, 225–362; *The Tragedy of Thierry and Theodoret*, ed. Robert K. Turner, 363–481; *The Faithful Shepherdess*, ed. Cyrus Hoy, 483–612.

Vol. 4 (1979): *The Woman's Prize*, ed. Fredson Bowers, 1–148; *Bonduca*, ed. Cyrus Hoy, 149–259; *The Tragedy of Valentinian*, ed. Robert K. Turner, 261–414; *Monsieur Thomas*, ed. Hans Walter Gabler, 415–540; *The Chances*, ed. George Walton Williams, 541–645.

Vol. 5 (1982): *The Mad Lover*, ed. Robert K. Turner, 1–149; *The Loyal Subject*, ed. Fredson Bowers, 151–288; *The Humorous Lieutenant*, ed. Cyrus Hoy, 289–440; *Women Pleased*, ed. Hans Walter Gabler, 441–538; *The Island Princess*, ed. George Walton Williams, 539–670.

Vol. 6 (1985): *Wit Without Money*, ed. Hans Walter Gabler; *The Pilgrim*, ed. Cyrus Hoy, 111–224; *The Wild-Goose Chase*, ed. Fredson Bowers, 225–354; *A Wife for a Month*, ed. Robert K. Turner, 355–482; *Rule a Wife and Have a Wife*, ed. George Walton Williams, 483–605.

Vol. 7 (1989): *Henry VIII*, ed. Fredson Bowers, 1–144; *The Two Noble Kinsmen*, ed. Fredson Bowers, 145–298; *Wit at Several Weapons*, ed. Robert K. Turner, 299–424; *The Nice Valour*, ed. George Walton Williams, 425–512; *The Night Walker*, ed. Cyrus Hoy; *A Very Woman*, ed. Hans Walter Gabler.

Vol. 8 (1992): *The Queen of Corinth*, ed. Robert K. Turner, 1–111; *The False One*, ed. Robert K. Turner, 113–221; *Four Plays, Or Moral Representations, in One*, ed. Cyrus Hoy, 223–344; *The Knight of Malta*, ed. George Walton Williams, 345–482; *The Tragedy of Sir John Van Olden Barnavelt*, ed. Fredson Bowers, 483–632; *The Custom of the Country*, ed. Cyrus Hoy, 633–758.

Unless otherwise specified, all quotations from the works of Shakespeare are taken from

William Shakespeare: The Complete Works. Gen. Eds. Stanley Wells and Gary Taylor. Oxford: Clarendon P, 1986.

All HA-numbered documents are quoted from microfilm copies of the Hastings Papers manuscripts in the Huntington Library in San Marino, California: *The Aristocracy, the State and the Local Community: The Hastings Collection of Manuscripts from the Huntington Library in California. Part One: The Hastings Correspondence 1477–1701.* Brighton: Harvester Microform, 1986.

NOTES

One. Parentage and Patronage

1. John Foxe, *Actes and Monuments of matters most speciall and memorable, happenyng in the Church. Newly reuised and recognised,* 2 vols. (London, 1583), 2:1679–80. The account of Wade's death appears with a note: "Spectatores praesentes, Richardus Fletcher pater, nunc Minister Ecclesiae Crambroke [*sic*]; Richardus Fletcher filius, Minister Ecclesiae Riensis." For detailed analysis of Richard Fletcher senior's ministry in Cranbrook, see Patrick Collinson, "Cranbrook and the Fletchers: Popular and Unpopular Religion in the Kentish Weald," in P. N. Brooks, ed., *Reformation Principle and Practice: Essays in honour of A. G. Dickens* (London: Scolar P, 1980), 171–202; reprinted in Collinson, *Godly People* (London: Hambledon P, 1983), 399–428, 422n. Subsequent references to Collinson's *Godly People* will be given parenthetically in the text.

2. Abram Barnett Langdale, *Phineas Fletcher: Man of Letters, Science and Divinity* (New York: Columbia UP, 1937), 5. Langdale is a very unreliable biographer, and rarely documents his claims.

3. The inscription, which can be found on the north side of altar of the Parish Church of St. Mary the Virgin, Rye, runs as follows:

RICHARDUS FLETCHER EX EBORACE[N]SI PROVINCIAE HON-
ESTIS PARENTIBUS NATUS; A QUIBUS CANTABRIGIA MISSUS
BONUS ARTIBUS SESE EXERCUIT DONEC ARTIVM MAGISTER
FACTVS EST; HINC REGNUM INEUNTE EDOVARDO VI°, IN
SACRVM MINISTERIVM, ASSVMPTVS EST A SANCTISSIMO
VIRO AC MARTYRE NI; RIDLEIO. LONDINENSI EPISCOPO (EX
EORV[M] NVMERO Q[UI]TVM P[RI]MO PRO MORE AC RITV
ECCL[ES]IAE REFORMATAE, SACRIS ORDINIBVS INITIATI
SV[N]T,) IN CVIVS DIOCOESI VERBI MINISTERIO DILIGENTER
I[N]CVBVIT; POSTEA TEMPORIBVS MARIANIS CVM FERRO ET
FLAM[M]A EVA[N]GELICI PETERE[N]TVR ADVERSA MVLTA
ET VI[N]CVLA PERTVULIT; SED RESTITVTO EVANGELIO ET
IPSE SACRO MUNERI RESTITVTVS EST; ET HVIC ECCL[ESI]AE
PASTOR DESIGNATUS A[?]I SERENISSIMAE PRI[N]CIPIS ELIZ-
ABETHAE HIC PUBLICE VERBO: PRIVATI VITA, PRAEDI-
CA[N]DO PAVPERIBVS EROGA[N]DO: O[M]NIBVS CONSV-
LENDO: (QVA[N]TV[M] IN IPSO FVIT) I[N]TEGER AC BONIS
O[M]NIBVS CHARVS, CVM PER XXVI ANOS ET MENSES VII
HVIC ECCL[ESI]AE PRAEFVISSET TANDEM EX HAC VITA AD
COELOS DEMIGRAVIT A° AETATIS QVARTO, SVPRA, SEXA-
GESIMV[M] FILIOS SVPERSTITES RELIQVIT DVOS QVOS VIDIT

ALTERV[M] THEOLOGIAE ALTERV[M] LEGV[M] DOCTOREM ILLV[M] CAPELLANV[M] REGIV[M] DECANV[M] PETRIBVRG NV[N]C EPISCOPV[M] BRISTOLL, ET REGIAE MA^{tis}, ELEEMO-SYNARIV[M] SVM[M]VM; HVC EIDEM, M^{ti} AD MAGNVM RVS-SIAE, IMPERATOREM, LEGATVM. OBIIT, MVNDO, 12° DIE MENSIS, FEBR, A° 1585 VIVIT DEO AD AETERNITATE CORPVS IN AREA INFERIORI, SVB PROXIMO, SAXO RECONDITVR.

4. See Robert Clutterbuck, *The History and Antiquities of the County of Hertford,* 3 vols. (London, 1815–1827), 3: 254.

5. Robert Masters, *The History of the College of Corpus Christi in the University of Cambridge* (London, 1753), part 2, "Of its Principal Members," 285. Subsequent references to Masters will be given parenthetically in the text.

6. Staller left his fellowship in 1570, and in 1573 became rector of All Hallows in Lombard Street, to which he added the rectory of St. Mary Hill on 24 June 1574, both of which he kept until his death. For the likes of Fletcher and Staller, pluralism and staunch Protestantism do not seem to have appeared incompatible.

7. There appears to be some confusion over dating here. According to Dyce, Norgate succeeded to the Mastership on 22 August 1573 (Alexander Dyce, ed., *The Works of Beaumont and Fletcher,* 11 vols. [London, 1843–46], viiin). Yet Collinson gives May 1573 as the date of Richard Fletcher's marriage to Elizabeth Holland (Collinson 418n). Clearly Fletcher would not have been elected to the post if he were already married at that point; nor is it likely that he would be elected if it were known he was to be married within a couple of weeks.

8. "Some books inaccurately describe Fletcher as vicar of Rye. The true situation was one of some complexity. In Fletcher's time the vicarage was leased and the fruits were a matter of litigation and for a time sequestered. Attempts by the mayor and jurats [the Rye magistrates] and by the bishop of Chichester to resolve this impasse were unsuccessful. Fletcher was in receipt of some benefit from the fruits of the vicarage and of a further 'augmentation' or 'benevolence' from the town of £10, £5 of which was paid by the churchwardens and £5 by the town chamberlain. His normal style was 'preacher [or minister] of the word of God at Rye'" (Collinson 418n). According to Graham Mayhew, "it would appear that Richard Fletcher . . . did obtain the vicarage (the right of presentation to which, after the Reformation, belonged to the Sackville family) after some lobbying by the corporation" (Graham Mayhew, *Tudor Rye* [Falmer: Centre for Continuing Education, U of Sussex, 1987], 78). Subsequent references to Mayhew will be given parenthetically in the text.

9. See Collinson 421–22; Mayhew 42–48.

10. See John Strype, *Annals of the Reformation* (London, 1728), 385–88. Strype prints a lengthy passage from a manuscript entitled *The Order and Manner of the Execution of Mary Queen of Scots, Feb. 8 1586,* which he supposes to have been written by Beal, clerk to the Council, at the Lord Treasurer's orders, and which gives the substance of Richard Fletcher's exhortation to the condemned queen.

11. See Dyce 1:viii–ix; and Francis Godwin, *De Praesulibus Angliae Commentarius* (Cambridge, 1743), 1:193n.

12. See Daniel Neal, *The History of the Puritans or Protestant Non-Conformists, from the Reformation under King Henry VIII. to the Act of Toleration under King William and Queen Mary,* 2nd ed., 2 vols. (London, 1754), 1:388–89.

13. Sir John Harington, *A Briefe View of the State of the Church of England, As it stood in Q. Elizabeths and King James his Reigne, to the Yeere 1608. Being a Character and History of the Bishops of those times* (London, 1653), 26. Subsequent references to Harington will be given parenthetically in the text.

14. See John Dart, *The History and Antiquities of the Cathedral Church of Canterbury* (London, 1726), 74.

15. Thomas Fuller, *The History of the Worthies of England* (London, 1662), Kent, 73. Subsequent references to Fuller's *Worthies* will be given parenthetically in the text.

16. "On the Marriage of Lady Mary Baker to Richard Fletcher, Bishop of London," in Robert Krueger, ed., *The Poems of Sir John Davies* (Oxford: Clarendon P, 1975), 175–79. This is a brief sequence of five satires suggesting that where "John London [i.e., John Aylmer, Fletcher's predecessor, who had been accused of reducing his diocese's income by selling timber from episcopal land] was condemnd for spoiling wood, . . . now Dick London Commons doth enclose," and concluding tastelessly that "[t]he preist must after all the people goe."

17. See Dyce 1:xii.

18. Dyce is not convinced by Harington's account that "in a while [Fletcher] found means to pacifie her so well, as she promised to come, and I think did come, to a house he had at Chelsey. For there was a stayre and a dore made of purpose for her in a bay window" (Harington 27).

19. Dyce quotes this letter from ms., pointing out that the version quoted by Strype in his *Life and Acts of the Most Reverend Father in God, John Whitgift, D.D.,* 4 vols. (London, 1718), Appendix xx, omits a passage by mistake (Dyce xii).

20. Thomas Fuller, *The Church-History of Britain: from the Birth of Jesus Christ Untill the Year M. DC. XLVIII* (London, 1655), 9:233.

21. G[erald] E[ades] Bentley, *The Jacobean and Caroline Stage,* 7 vols. (Oxford: Clarendon P, 1956–1968), 3:306. Subsequent references to this work will be cited as "Bentley," and volume number. Nina Taunton, in a brief article entitled "Did John Fletcher the Playwright Go to University?" in *Notes and Queries* 235, 2 (June 1990): 170–72, attempts (unconvincingly) to show that the evidence for Fletcher's matriculation at Ben'et College is inadequate.

22. Charles Mills Gayley, *Beaumont, the Dramatist* (New York: Russell and Russell, 1914), 62.

23. *The Woman Hater* dates, arguably, from early to mid–1606. Strictly speaking, since it appears (at least according to Cyrus Hoy's analysis—see his 'The Shares of Fletcher and his Collaborators in the Beaumont and Fletcher Canon[III]," *Studies in Bibliography* 11 [1958]: 98–99)—to be a Beaumont composition revised by Fletcher, the latter may only have become involved in the project at a later date. Composition certainly predates the 11 February 1607 publication of Ben Jonson's *Volpone,* for which Beaumont and Fletcher penned separate commendatory verses, since the Paul's boys, for which *The Woman Hater*

was clearly written, are last heard of in July 1606 (see E[dmund] K. Chambers, *The Elizabethan Stage*, 4 vols. [Oxford: Clarendon P, 1923], 3:220). The revised version of *The Woman Hater* was published by 20 May 1607. The commendatory verses would appear to suggest that both Fletcher and Beaumont were part of dramatic circles already by the beginning of 1607. Beaumont had of course published the poem *Salmacis and Hermaphroditus* as early as 1602, and his *Grammer Lecture* was given at Gray's Inn probably in 1605. It seems likely that he wrote the lost *History of Madon, King of Britain* as early as 1605, very possibly before meeting Fletcher. An early version of *Love's Cure, or The Martial Maid,* by either Beaumont alone or conceivably by Beaumont and Fletcher may well date from just before *The Woman Hater,* and may therefore be a trace of the first Beaumont-and-Fletcher collaboration. It is impossible to say. In any event, by 1607, when Fletcher was 28 and Beaumont still only 21, both were established in dramatic circles and acquainted with Jonson (who, for perspective's sake, was 35).

24. Lawrence B. Wallis, *Fletcher, Beaumont & Company: Entertainers to the Jacobean Gentry* (Morningside Heights, NY: King's Crown P, 1947), 179.

25. See Logan Pearsall Smith, *The Life and Letters of Sir Henry Wotton,* 2 vols. (Oxford: Clarendon P, 1907).

26. Lloyd E. Berry, ed., *The English Works of Giles Fletcher, the Elder* (Madison: U of Wisconsin P, 1964), 36.

27. Giles Fletcher's statement to the Privy Council, which from his later acquittal and the corroboration of the evidence of others would appear substantially accurate, serves to amplify what we know of his own religious attitudes: "On Thursday or Fryday beefore the Earle of Essex his cooming into London in that tumultuous and seditious manner I mett with Maister Temple who tould mee that thear wear certein Iesuits and Seminary priests that lodged in divers places of the Citie, who had vowed to kill the Earle of Essex, and that they had divised and cast abroad certein Libels to make him odious to the people. Which beeing reported by him (as it seemed) in good sadnes I did then beelieve, bycause it seemed not improbable, that beeing so followed by the militarie men and making profession of religion more then after an ordinary manner, they might suppose that the sayed Earle stood in their way and might hinder their designes, if they intended any practise against hir Maiestie and the State. The end of his talk was that if I lighted vpon any of those Libels I would gett a copie and send it to him. Which (bycause it seemed to bee spoken in no ill meaning) I promised to doe" (Berry 45).

28. It is, however, probable that Beaumont wrote *Madon, King of Britain* for a children's company, which may very possibly have been Paul's.

29. See Chambers, *Elizabethan Stage,* 2:19.

30. J. H. Lupton, 'Richard Mulcaster,' in Signey Lee, ed., *Dictionary of National Biography,* vol. 13 (London: Smith, Elder & Co., 1909), 1172–73. Subsequent references to *D.N.B.* will be given parenthetically in the text.

31. I can find no evidence to explain this late professional interlude. Richard DeMolen's various essays on Mulcaster are silent on the subject.

32. "The Copie of a Letter," 50–59, 64–65, in Percy Simpson, "Two Poems

of Philip Massinger," *The Athenaeum,* 8 September 1906, 273–74. These lines were first published this century by Percy Simpson, who was unfortunately mistaken about which earl of Huntingdon was Fletcher's patron. "I assume that this patron is . . . George, the fourth Earl," he says, "who succeeded his brother Henry in 1595, and died himself in 1604. Henry is too early; Fletcher was a boy of fourteen when he died. The little that was known of Fletcher's opening career would fit in with the fourth Earl. Fletcher's father, Richard, Bishop of London, died on June 15th, 1596, in debt to the Exchequer. The suggestion has been made that his son's career at Cambridge was interrupted at this point; in any case, we may conjecture that it was a time when a patron would be peculiarly helpful. The Earl's death in 1604 would occur too early in Fletcher's career for any form of literary acknowledgement, such as a dedication in verse, to be possible; he does not emerge as a playwright until about 1608" (274). Simpson seems not to realize that the point of Massinger's letter to Pembroke is to cite precedents of successful *literary* patronage, not philanthropy, and that therefore it must refer to Fletcher during his writing career. He concludes that "[i]t is not likely that the fifth Earl, Henry, grandson of George, was the patron; he was younger than Fletcher, being born in 1586, and he lived till 1643. Help from him could hardly have been ignored by the poet throughout his career" (274). It is certainly odd at first glance that Fletcher never dedicated work to the fifth Earl. Simpson, however, was not to know that, though none of the extant plays is dedicated to Huntingdon, Fletcher did indeed acknowledge his friendship with the earl and countess in correspondence.

33. Philip Edwards and Colin Gibson, ed., *The Plays and Poems of Philip Massinger,* 5 vols. (Oxford: Clarendon P, 1976), 1:xxxiii. See also David M. Bergeron, "Women as Patrons of English Renaissance Drama," in Guy Fitch Lytle and Stephen Orgel, ed., *Patronage in the Renaissance* (Princeton: Princeton UP, 1981), 280.

34. R. C. Rowland, "The Plays of John Fletcher: A Critical Study," D. Phil. thesis (University of Oxford, 1955), 28.

35. Relations between the Hastingses and the Beaumonts had certainly not been cordial to this point. On the suppression of the monasteries, John Beaumont, Francis's grandfather, was given a grant of Grace-Dieu, but was challenged for possession by a claim from the earl of Huntingdon. Beaumont wrote to Lord Cromwell in defense of his right to the property "for Ido feyre the seyd erle and his sonns do seke my lyfe, and all for the truthe sake." The situation was only resolved through marriage. See Alexander B. Grosart, ed., *The Poems of Sir John Beaumont* (privately printed, 1869), xiv.

36. Francis Beaumont and John Fletcher, *Comedies and Tragedies* (London, 1647), XXX3v–XXX4r.

37. The impression of Fletcher as an inhabitant of the counties of Northamptonshire and Leicestershire was lasting. While Fuller places Richard and Giles Fletcher correctly among the "Worthies" of Kent, he associates John Fletcher, despite his birth in Kent, with Northamptonshire (see Fuller, *Worthies* [Northamptonshire], 2:168).

38. Sir John Beaumont to "the Right Honourable, my Singular good Lord,

the Earle of Huntingdon," 26 January 1618, quoted from microfilm copy, *The Aristocracy, the State and the Local Community: The Hastings Collection of Manuscripts from the Huntington Library in California. Part One: The Hastings Correspondence 1477–1701* (Brighton: Harvester Microform, 1986), HA672 (Reel 3, Box 7): "whereas your Lo:ᴾ by your letter desireth liberty to drive a sough thorough my ground. I acknowledge myselfe so many wayes bound to your Lo:ᴾ as that your Lo:ᴾ may iustly commaund me & mine in this & in a farre greater matter, referring the satisfaction to your owne Honourable consyderation. And for Coles in my ground (if any such shall proue) I assure your Lo:ᴾ that you (and none other) shall haue them upon such reasonable termes, as shall be agreed betweene us." Subsequent references to Hastings papers on microfilm will be made by HA number and reel/box location only.

39. See below for further comment on Drayton's connections with the Ashby circle. Philip J. Finkelpearl suggests a connection of Beaumont and Fletcher as early as 1602: "I base this on a reference in John Nichols, *The History and Antiquities of the County of Leicestershire* (London, 1795–1815), vol. 3, part 2, 659: 'Mr. Whalley . . . preserves a copy of verses "on Mr. Frances Beaumont, on his Imitation of Ovid," signed J. F.; which, he says[,] is undoubtedly by John Fletcher.' This may be the poem prefatory to *Salmacis* that is signed 'A.F.' in the 1602 edition but 'J.F.' in the 1640. In any case Whalley's Fletcher poem, referring to Beaumont's Ovidian *Salmacis* published in 1602, suggests an acquaintance three or four years before their first known collaboration"; see Finkelpearl, *Court and Country Politics in the Plays of Beaumont and Fletcher* (Princeton: Princeton UP, 1990), 25n; see also Finkelpearl, "The Role of the Court in the Development of Jacobean Drama," *Criticism* 24.2 (Spring 1982): 138–58.

40. Beaumont and Fletcher, *Comedies and Tragedies* (1647), gʳ.

41. For Skipwith's masque, see the luckless Peter Levi's *A Private Commission: New Verses by Shakespeare* (London: Macmillan, 1988), and the ensuing debate, esp. James Knowles, "WS MS," *Times Literary Supplement*, 29 April 1988, 472, 485. For Marston's piece, see John Marston, "The *hoᵇˡᵉ*: Lorde & Lady of Huntingdons Entertainment of theire right Noble Mother Alice: Countesse Dowager of Darby the firste nighte of her honors arrivall att the house of Ashby," in Arnold Davenport, ed., *The Poems of John Marston* (Liverpool: Liverpool UP, 1961), 189–207.

42. Mulcaster may have been peripherally connected with the Huntingdons, though evidence is decidedly tenuous. His second known piece of work is a 1568 pageant for the Merchant Taylors' Company marking the inauguration as lord mayor of London of Sir Thomas Roe, grandfather to the Sir Thomas Roe who was part of the Ashby circle (see below). See Richard DeMolen, "Richard Mulcaster and Elizabethan Pageantry," *Studies in English Literature* 14 (1974): 209–21.

43. It is perhaps in recognition of the connection of the countess and Fletcher that B.L. Add. MS 25707 juxtaposes some untitled "verses by Jack: Flecher" (which are the verses known as "Upon an Honest Man's Fortune" and appended to the printed version of that play; see also Bodleian MS Rawl. poet. 160, 45ʳ–46ʳ) with Pestell's "verses of yᵉ Countess of Huntingdon."

44. *Historical Manuscripts Commission Report on the Manuscripts of the late Reginald Rawdon Hastings, Esq.*, ed. Francis Bickley [hereafter referred to as HMC *Hastings*], vol. 2 (London: HM Stationery Office, 1930), 58–59. See also Samuel A. Tannenbaum, "A Hitherto Unpublished John Fletcher Autograph," *Journal of English and Germanic Philology* 28 (1929), 35–40.

45. Phineas Fletcher, *A Father's Testament* (London, 1670), sigs. B^v–B2^r.

46. Francis Beaumont and John Fletcher, *The Maid's Tragedy*, ed. Robert K. Turner, Bowers 2:1–166; I. i. 11.

47. The full phrase, translated as "with the sole right to print," is *cum privilegio ad imprimendum solum* (cf. Biondello's inaccurate Latin in William Shakespeare, *The Taming of the Shrew*, Stanley Wells and Gary Taylor, eds., *William Shakespeare: The Complete Works* (Oxford: Clarendon P, 1986), 29–61; IV. iv. 90–91). Fletcher mocks this printing monopoly tag elsewhere, cf. *The Captain:*

> Her looks are nothing like her; would her faults
> Were all in Paris print upon her face,
> *Cum Privilegio*, to use 'em still.

I would write an Epistle before it, on the inside of her masque, and dedicate it to the whore of *Babilon*, with a preface upon her nose to the gentle Reader; and they should be to be sold at the signe of the Whore's head i'th pottage pot, in what street you please. (IV. iv. 3–11)

I am grateful to James Knowles for the suggestion that the reference in Fletcher's letter is a hint of the family's royal background.

48. James Montague, bishop of Bath and Wells, to his cousin Henry, fifth earl of Huntingdon, 28 January 1612, HMC *Hastings* 2:54–55.

49. On the third earl of Huntingdon, see Claire Cross, *The Puritan Earl* (London: Macmillan, 1966).

50. Finkelpearl *Court and Country,* 30.

51. James Knowles, "Pious Patronage: the fifth Earl of Huntingdon," unpublished essay on Ashby patronage.

52. Fifth earl of Huntingdon to earl of Marlborough, 22 January 1627, HMC *Hastings* 2:70.

53. Henry, fifth earl of Huntingdon to his son, "Henry [Hastings], 1627, Jan 23. Dunnington," HA5515 (Reel 4 Box 12); see also HMC *Hastings* 2:70. It is tempting to compare the earl's sentiments here with observations made in several of Fletcher's plays, perhaps especially *The Custom of the Country,* in which Guiomar, wondering why her son Duarte has turned out so badly, says, "I sent him to the Emperours Court, / . . . and there maintain'd him, in such bravery and height, / As did become a Courtier," to which Manuel replies, " 'Twas that spoil'd him. . . . / The Court's a School indeed, in which some few / Learn vertuous principles, but most forget / What ever they brought thither good and honest." See Fletcher and Massinger, *The Custom of the Country,* Glover 1:302–88; 2. i, 317–8.

54. George Abbot, archbishop of Canterbury, to Henry, fifth earl of Huntingdon, 2 February 1613, HA2 (Reel 3 Box 7); see also HMC *Hastings* 2:55.

55. I am grateful to James Knowles for this and other details and suggestions

about the fifth earl, though I should add that he is not to be held responsible for any errors in my reading of the Ashby milieu. See his "WS MS," 485 for further details about Skipwith and Huntingdon.

56. In a letter of 1625, Hildersham expresses a keen interest in the education of the earl's heir, Henry Hastings, as well as his gratitude to the earl: "I should hartilly welcome any opportunity of doing yor Lordship service," he writes, "My desire may perhaps transport me soe farr, that I may meddle in this businesse of my Lord Hastings his education too much . . . out of my duty, and desire of yor heires good." And he adds, "yor former and later favours vouchsafed to me, would in mine own secret thoughts check me, if I should not returne to you upon all occasions a thankefull acknowledgment of the same" (Samuel Hildersam [sic] to fifth earl of Huntingdon, sent from Emmanuel College, Cambridge, 9 November 1625, HA6758 [Reel 4, Box 11]).

57. As David Bergeron and others have shown, women were frequent patrons of dramatic writing, and the fifth countess could count several such patrons among her relatives, including her mother and sister-in-law. See Bergeron, "Women as Patrons of English Renaissance Drama," in Lytle and Orgel, 275–90.

58. From a letter of Sir Thomas Roe to Elizabeth, countess of Huntingdon, at Ashby, written from "Adsmere, the camp of the Great Mogol, Emp[eror] of Indya" on 30 October 1616. See HMC *Hastings* 2:56. Sadly, I am unable to quote directly from the ms. letter because the microfilm copy (HA10561 [Reel 3 Box 7]) is unreadable, presumably because the ink has faded almost completely.

59. Finkelpearl, *Court and Country,* 34.

60. See Stanley Lane-Poole, "Sir Thomas Roe," Lee, ed., *D.N.B.,* 17:89–93.

61. Sir John Holles "to my LORD HUNTINDON [sic] touching my Lord Hastings. February 1603," in *Historical Manuscripts Report on the Manuscripts of His Grace the Duke of Portland* (London: HMSO, 1923), 9: 78–79.

62. Fifth earl of Huntingdon to his son Henry Hastings, 23 January 1627, HA5515 (Reel 4, Box 12).

63. See John Yoklavich, "Donne and the Countess of Huntingdon," *Philological Quarterly* 43 (1964): 283–88.

64. John Donne, "To the Countess of Huntingdon" (January 1615?), in A. J. Smith, ed., *John Donne: The Complete English Poems* (Harmondsworth: Penguin, 1971), 236–38. I give dates suggested by Robin Robbins in recent unpublished research.

65. Donne, "To the Countess of Huntingdon" (c. 1608–9?), in Smith, ed., *John Donne,* 238–41.

66. On the fifth earl and the Virginia Company, see ch. 5 below.

67. Thomas Pestell, "Verses of ye Countess of Huntington," in Hannah Buchan, ed., *The Poems of Thomas Pestell* (Oxford: Blackwell, 1940), 87–90, ll. 9–10, 13–18. Subsequent references to the poem will be given parenthetically in the text.

68. See also Pestell, "Born of a woman," Buchan 65–66.

69. For Fletcher's dramatic representation of this question, see ch. 3 below.

70. From MS Dyce 36 in the Victoria and Albert Museum, London; see Rudolf Brotanek, *Die Englischen Maskenspiele* (Vienna and Leipzig, 1902), 328–37. See also David Lindley's forthcoming edition of this masque in an Oxford World's Classics volume of masques. I am grateful to Lindley for discussion of this masque and for letting me see a draft of his edition.

71. Several attempts have been made to provide an author for the Coleorton masque. David Norbrook has suggested either Arthur Wilson or Thomas Pestell [see Norbrook, "The Reformation of the Masque," in David Lindley, ed., *The Court Masque* (Manchester: Manchester UP, 1984, 109n)]. Philip Finkelpearl has recently suggested that it may have been written by Fletcher "for various reasons too complex to mention" in his book (*Court and Country Politics*, 38n). Certainly, it displays some of Fletcher's stylistic characteristics, but the text is too brief for a comprehensive linguistic comparison with his plays.

72. See Bergeron, "Women as Patrons of English Renaissance Drama," in Lytle and Orgel 277.

73. On the dedicatees of *The Faithful Shepherdess*, see text pp. 55–70.

74. Leah Marcus, *Puzzling Shakespeare: Local Reading and its Discontents* (Berkeley: U of California P, 1988), 36.

75. For a helpful overview of recent historiography, see Glenn Burgess, "On revisionism: an analysis of early Stuart historiography in the 1970s and 1980s," *The Historical Journal*, 33. 3 (1990): 609–27.

Two. "This is a pretty Riot"

1. Michael Drayton, *Poemes Lyrick and Pastorall* (1606), Ode 1, "To himselfe and the Harp," ll. 16–20.

2. HMC *Hastings* 2: 49–51.

3. John E. Martin, *Feudalism to Capitalism: Peasant and Landlord in English Agrarian Development* (London: Macmillan, 1983), 161–63. Subsequent references to Martin will be given parenthetically in the text.

4. Martin 174. See also Roger B. Manning, *Village Revolts: Social Protest and Popular Disturbances in England, 1509–1640* (Oxford: Clarendon P, 1988), 235. Subsequent references to Manning will be given parenthetically in the text. See also Edwin F. Gay, "The Midland Revolt and the Inquisition of Depopulation of 1607," *Transactions of the Royal Historical Society* n.s. 18 (1904): 195–244.

5. British Library Harleian ms. 787, 9ᵛ; see also Frederick J. Furnivall, ed., *Ballads from Manuscripts*, 2 vols. (London, 1868–1872), 1: 37.

6. Sir Edward Montagu reported "several grievances, which were enjoined him . . . by the country to make known to the House," one of which was "the dis-population and daily excessive conversion of tillage into pasture." See *Historical Manuscripts Commission Report on the Manuscripts of Lord Montagu of Beaulieu* (London: HM Stationery Office, 1900), 42.

7. See the 1631 edition of John Stow's *Annales, or A Generall Chronicle of England*, augmented by Edmund Howes (London, 1631), 890.

8. On the Treshams, see Mary E. Finch, *The Wealth of Five Northamptonshire Families 1540–1640*, Northamptonshire Record Society, vol. 9 (Oxford: Ox-

ford UP, 1956). Dislike of the Tresham family may in part have been compounded by their well-known recusancy. Francis Tresham, heir of Sir Thomas Tresham of Rushton (who had been fined £1000 by the Court of Queen's Bench in 1600 for violations of the 1597 Tillage Act [see Manning 249)] and a notorious encloser himself, had been implicated in both the Essex rebellion and the Gunpowder Plot, in the latter case in the company of other Catholic gentlemen from Northamptonshire and Warwickshire. For Manning, it is "something more than a coincidence that of the four Northamptonshire townships where violent disorders broke out in the spring of 1607, in three of them—Rushton, Haselbech, and Newton—the rioting was directed against enclosures made by members of the Tresham family" (Manning 237). One of the other Midlands recusant families caught up in the aftermath of the Gunpowder Plot, incidentally, was that of Vaux of Harrowden, to which Francis Beaumont's family was closely related.

9. See, for example, the Privy Council's injunction to the fifth earl to deal firmly with "those that tooke upon them wth Drummes and Bagpipes to be the encouragers of the rest of the Rebels" (Letter from the Council to the fifth earl of Huntingdon, 12 June 1607, HA4169 [Reel 2, Box 6]).

10. Howes suggests that some levelers only used weapons for their hedge-breaking until they were provided with proper mattocks and spades. See Stow, *Annales* (1631 edition), 890.

11. See "A Proclamation for suppressing of persons riotously assembled for the laying open of Inclosures," 30 May 1607, in *A Booke of Proclamations, published since the beginning of his Maiesties most happy Reigne ouer England, &c.* (London, 1609), 139–140. Reprinted in James F. Larkin and Paul L. Hughes, ed., *Stuart Royal Proclamations,* vol. 1, *Royal Proclamations of King James I 1603–1625* (Oxford: Clarendon P, 1973), 152–54. See also Manning 231.

12. See Martin 170.

13. L. A. Parker, "The Agrarian Revolution at Cotesbach 1501–1612," *Transactions of the Leicestershire Archaeological Society* 24 (1948): 41–77. 57. Subsequent references to Parker will be given parenthetically in the text.

14. See Parker 73. John Quarles is almost certainly related to Francis Quarles, the poet, though this connection is hardly to the latter's credit; John Quarles's business dealings seem to have been sharp at best. Quarles was a London draper who was closely tied to various contractors to the armed forces toward the end of Elizabeth's reign, at least one of whom, James Quarles, seems to have been a close relative. They were connected with Sir Thomas Sherley, who made substantial sums out of speculation with official money before being caught in December 1596. It appears to have been through William Beecher, Sherley's fellow speculator and a relation by marriage, that John Quarles became interested in Cotesbach. There are too many individuals known as "John Quarles, draper" in London at this time to be absolutely certain that John Quarles of Cotesbach is related to the Ufford branch of the family, of which the poet was a part. However, the poet's great uncle was a "John Quarles, draper, of London": his second son by his second wife Dorothy was very probably the John Quarles who bought Cotesbach. See Parker 57; Alexander B. Grosart, ed., *The Complete*

Works in Prose and Verse of Francis Quarles, 3 vols. (London, 1880), 1:ix–xi; Samuel Tymms, ed., *The East Anglian* (London, 1869), 3:155–58, 184–87.

15. Privy Council to the fifth earl of Huntingdon, 12 June 1607, HA4169 (Reel 2, Box 6).

16. There seems to have been a distinct fear that the militia were likely to be sufficiently in sympathy with the rebels that they would not perform their duties adequately. See Manning 232. Sir Anthony Mildmay was the son of Sir Walter Mildmay, whose attitude to the court the fifth earl much later recommended to his own errant son.

17. Sir Roger Wilbraham's account underestimates the slaughter: "[Y]et they continue [in face of the royal proclamation which was read to them] until Sir A. Mildmay with some horsemen using force slay some ten in hot blood; and thus they were put down. Afterwards at the assizes . . . two or 3 were hanged as an example. So that, as the King says, the punishment of a few may impress the majority with fear," Harold Spencer Scott, ed., "The Journal of Sir Roger Wilbraham . . . For the Years 1593–1616" in *The Camden Miscellany,* vol. 10 (London, 1902), 92. The journal entries are translated by Scott from Wilbraham's form of Jacobean personal Franglais. John Nichols quotes a letter of Shrewsbury of 11th June: "You cannot but have heard what courses have been taken in Leicestershire and Warwicksh' by the two lo' lieutenants theare, and by the gentlemen before their lo' coming downe, and also by the deputy lieutenants in Northamptonshire; and, lastlie, how sir Anth. Mildmay and sir Edw. Montacute repaired to Newton, Mr. Tho. Tresham's towne, wheare 1000 of thease fellowes who term themselves levelers weare busily digging, but weare furnished with many halfe pykes, pyked staves, long bills, and bowes and arrowes, and stoanes. Thease gentlemen, fynding great backwardnes in the trained bands, weare constrained to use all the horse they could make, and as many foote of their owne servants and followers as they could trust; and first read the proclamacion twice unto them, using all the best perswasions to them to desist that they could devise; but, when nothing would prevaile, they charged them thoroughlie both with their horse and foote. But the first charge they stoode, and fought desperatelie; but at the second charge they ran away, in which theare weare slaine som 40 or 50 of them, and a verie great number hurt" (John Nichols, *The History and Antiquities of the County of Leicester* [London, 1807], 4.1:83.

18. James I to Henry, fifth earl of Huntingdon, 3 June 1607, HA4166 (Reel 2, Box 6); see also HMC *Hastings* 4:192.

19. HMC *Hastings* 4:192.

20. Privy Council to the fifth earl of Huntingdon, 3 June 1607, HA4166; cf. n. 19.

21. HMC *Hastings* 4:159–82.

22. Henry, fifth earl of Huntingdon to Robert, first earl of Salisbury, 6 June 1607, HA5421 (Reel 2, Box 6); see also HMC *Hastings* 4:193. Howes elaborates: "*Iohn Reynoldes* they surnamed Captaine *Powch,* because of a great leather pouch which he wore by his side, in which purse he affirmed to his company, that there was sufficient matter to defend them against all comers, but afterward

when hee was apprehended, his Pouch was searched, and therein was onely a peece of greene cheese. Hee told them also, that hee had Authority from his Maiestie to throw downe enclosures, and that hee was sent of God to satisfy all degrees whatsoeuer, and that in this present worke hee was directed by the Lord of Heauen, and thereupon they generally inclined to his direction, so as hee kept them in good order, he commaunded them not to sweare, nor to offer violence to any person" (Stow, *Annales* [1631], 890).

23. Henry, fifth earl of Huntingdon, to the lords of the Council, 7 June 1607, HA5422 (Reel 2, Box 6); see also HMC *Hastings* 4:193.

24. Lords of the Council to Henry, fifth earl of Huntingdon, 9 June 1607, HA4168 (Reel 2, Box 6); see also HMC *Hastings* 4:194.

25. Lords of the Council to Henry, fifth earl of Huntingdon, 12 June 1607, HA4169 (Reel 2, Box 6).

26. Henry, fifth earl of Huntingdon, to the lords of the Council, 14 June 1607, HA5423 (Reel 2, Box 6); see also HMC *Hastings* 4:194.

27. The general state of local government during the revolt cannot have comforted the central authorities. The Northampton mayor seems also to have been less than entirely enthusiastic, and he and the county JPs were prosecuted in Star Chamber for their failure to mobilize the militia to deal with riots. The Privy Council was also irritated that the county authorities of Warwickshire had negotiated rather than fought with the levelers, pointing out that they should have "vsed them as rebells and traytors." See Gay 241 and Manning 231. A letter dating from around Christmas 1607 from the countess to the earl provides an interesting corollary to the involvement of Leicester people in the revolts, since she writes to inform him that the "townesmen of Lecester" have given her a gift of a dapple-grey gelding in the hope that she might press her husband "to imbrace the love of those that formerly had erred" (Elizabeth, countess of Huntingdon, to Henry, fifth earl of Huntingdon, c. Christmas 1607, HA4815, Reel 2, Box 6).

28. Lords of the Council to Henry, fifth earl of Huntingdon, 9 June 1607, HA4168 (Reel 2, Box 6).

29. See Manning 221–29 and 233.

30. Moreover, on 28 June, James proclaimed that no one could "in this particular case of depopulation . . . make doubt but it must be farre from our inclination to suffer any tolleration of that which may be any occasion to decay or diminish our people," and he speaks of "our great mislike of Depopulation in generall." See "A Proclamation signifying his Maiesties pleasure aswell for suppressing of riotous Assemblies about Inclosures, as for the reformation of Depopulations," 28 June 1607, in *A Booke of Proclamations:* 141–2. Reprinted in Larkin and Hughes, *Stuart Royal Proclamations,* 1:154–58.

31. Lords of the Council to Henry, fifth earl of Huntingdon, 23 July 1607, HA4173 (Reel 2, Box 6); see also HMC *Hastings* 4:195.

32. "A Proclamation signifying his Maiesties gracious pardon for the Offendours about Inclosures," 24 July 1607, *A Booke of Proclamations,* 146–51. Reprinted in Larkin and Hughes, *Stuart Royal Proclamations,* 1:161–62.

33. Robert Wilkinson was chaplain to the earl of Exeter and later chaplain-in-

ordinary to King James and vicar of St. Olave's, Southwark. He calls himself "One of your Highnesse Soule-Physicians" in his epistle dedicatory to a sermon preached to Prince Charles in 1614 (Robert Wilkinson, *A Paire of Sermons svccessively preacht to a paire of Peereless and succeeding Princes. The Former as an Ante-Fvnerall to the late Prince Henry, Anno Dom. 1612. October 25. The first day of his last and fatall sicknesse. The Latter preacht this present yeere 1614. Ianuar. 16. To the now liuing Prince Charles, as a preseruer of his life, and life to his Soule* [London, 1614]). He also came under the patronage of Exeter's son-in-law, Sir Edward Denny, later earl of Norwich, and preached at the "royally mediated" wedding of Denny's daughter Honoria to Lord Hay in 1606 (Robert Wilkinson, *The Merchant Royall. A Sermon preached at White-Hall before the Kings Maiestie, at the Nuptials of the Right Honourable the Lord Hay and his Lady, vpon the Twelfe day last being Ianuar. 6. 1607* [London, 1607]). On the "royall mediation," see Vicary Gibbs, ed., *The Complete Peerage,* vol. 3 (London: St. Catherine P, 1913), 32]. The title pages of the printed versions of his Northampton sermon and this wedding sermon both bear the Exeter wheat sheaf symbol. Wilkinson's other sermons include *Lots Wife. A Sermon preached at Pavles Crosse* (London, 1607), dedicated to Denny.

34. Robert Wilkinson, *A Sermon preached at North-Hampton the 21. of Iune last past, before the Lord Lieutenant of the County, and the rest of the Commissioners there assembled vpon occasion of the late Rebellion and Riots in those parts committed* (London, 1607), A4r. Subsequent references to this sermon of Wilkinson's will be given parenthetically in the text.

35. Annabel Patterson, *Shakespeare and the Popular Voice* (Oxford: Blackwell, 1989), 138. Subsequent references to Patterson will be given parenthetically in the text. I am grateful to Patterson for letting me see an early version of the relevant chapter of her book before its publication.

36. E. C. Pettet, "*Coriolanus* and the Midlands Insurrection of 1607," *Shakespeare Survey* 3 (1950): 34–42. Subsequent references to Pettet's essay will be given parenthetically in the text.

37. Jonathan Dollimore, *Radical Tragedy: Religion, Ideology and Power in the Drama of Shakespeare and His Contemporaries* (Brighton: Harvester, 1984), 218–30, esp. 225–26. For an alternative (psychoanalytic) reading of the play which does take the Revolt into account, see Janet Adelman, " 'Anger's My Meat': Feeding, Dependency, and Aggression in *Coriolanus,*" in Murray M. Schwartz and Coppélia Kahn, eds., *Representing Shakespeare: New Psychoanalytic Essays* (Baltimore: Johns Hopkins UP, 1980), 129–49; reprinted in revised form in Adelman, *Suffocating Mothers: Fantasies of Maternal Origin in Shakespeare's Plays, Hamlet to* The Tempest (New York: Routledge, 1992), 146–64.

38. Patterson, preliminary draft of *Coriolanus* section from *Shakespeare and the Popular Voice.* See also Wells and Taylor 1199.

39. Shakespeare, *Antony and Cleopatra,* Wells and Taylor 1127–66; I. i. 16.

40. Shakespeare would presumably be aware of multiplicity of motive for revolt from his source in Plutarch, who emphasizes the basis for rebellion in both usury and corn shortage.

41. Shakespeare, *Coriolanus,* Wells and Taylor 1199–1239; III. i. 263–65

(my italics). It is of course known that Shakespeare had at least one practical personal encounter, late in life, with the problem of enclosure—over the question of the common land at Welcombe—but this occurred too late to be conveniently incorporated as biographical corroboration for arguments about *Coriolanus*. It is also worth noting the references to enclosure in *Pericles*, which dates from c. 1607, and (according to Wells and Taylor) immediately precedes *Coriolanus:*

> *3 Fisherman:* Master, I marvel how the fishes live in the sea.
>
> *1 Fisherman:* Why, as men do a-land—the great ones eat up the little ones. I can compare our rich misers to nothing so fitly as to a whale: a plays and tumbles, driving the poor fry before him, and at last devours them all at a mouthful. Such whales have I heard on o'th'land, who never leave gaping till they swallowed the whole parish, church, steeple, bells, and all. . . .
>
> *3 Fisherman:* But, master, if I had been the sexton, I would have been that day in the belfry.
>
> *2 Fisherman:* Why, man?
>
> *3 Fisherman:* Because he should have swallowed me too; and when I had been in his belly, I would have kept such a jangling of the bells, that he should never have left till he cast bells, steeple, church, and parish up again. But if the good King Simonides were of my mind . . . [w]e would purge the land of these drones that rob the bee of her honey. (Shakespeare and Wilkins, *Pericles, Prince of Tyre,* Wells and Taylor 1167–98; scene 5, 67–75, 77–85, 87–88)

There are, however, attribution difficulties with this passage; see William Shakespeare, *Pericles,* ed. F. D. Hoeniger (London: Methuen, 1963), appendix B.

42. See Marston, "Entertainment," in Davenport, ed., *Poems of John Marston,* 189–207; Knowles, "WS MS"; and Knowles's Oxford D. Phil. thesis (in preparation).

43. See HMC *Hastings* 4:197.

44. See Finkelpearl, *Court and Country Politics,* 34–35, 114; also Finkelpearl, "John Fletcher as Spenserian Playwright: *The Faithful Shepherdess* and *The Island Princess,*" *Studies in English Literature* 27 (1987): 285–302. "A decade after the author's death," suggests Finkelpearl, "*The Faithful Shepherdess* would have looked like another work by one of the Spenserian Fletchers, John being the first cousin of Milton's admired Giles Jr. and Phineas" (285), though he does not fully support this claim from the texts of the various Fletchers.

45. See David Norbrook, *Poetry and Politics in the English Renaissance* (London: RKP, 1984), esp. chapter 8, for commentary on the Spenserians. Subsequent references to Norbrook, *Poetry and Politics,* will be given parenthetically in the text. See also Norbrook's doctoral thesis, "Panegyric of the Monarch and its Social Context under Elizabeth I and James I," D. Phil. thesis (University of Oxford, 1978); William B. Hunter, ed., *The English Spenserians: The Poetry of Giles Fletcher, George Wither, Michael Drayton, Phineas Fletcher and Henry More* (Salt Lake City: U of Utah P, 1977); Joan Grundy, *The Spenserian Poets* (London:

Arnold, 1969); Richard F. Hardin, *Michael Drayton and the Passing of Elizabethan England* (Lawrence: UP of Kansas, 1973).

46. George Puttenham, *The Arte of English Poesie,* ed. Gladys Doidge Willcock and Alice Walker (Cambridge: Cambridge UP, 1936), 38. On politics and pastoral, see Annabel Patterson, *Pastoral and Ideology: Virgil to Valéry* (Berkeley: U of California P, 1988).

47. Louis Adrian Montrose, " 'Eliza, Queene of Shephearder,' and the Pastoral of Power," *English Literary Renaissance* 10 (1980): 153–82: 154.

48. Hebel 5:184; 2:517.

49. Finkelpearl, "John Fletcher as Spenserian Playwright," 288–89. For discussion of the dating and authorship of *The Woman Hater,* see ch. 3 below. *Cupid's Revenge,* which, according to James E. Savage ("The Date of Beaumont and Fletcher's *Cupid's Revenge,*" ELH 15 [1948]: 286–294) dates from approximately a year before *The Faithful Shepherdess,* bears the hallmarks of an evenly shared Beaumont and Fletcher collaboration (see Cyrus Hoy, *Studies in Bibliography* 11 [1958]: 90–91).

50. John Fletcher, *The Faithful Shepherdess,* ed. Cyrus Hoy, Bowers 3:483–612; 494, ll. 23–26. Subsequent references to Hoy's edition will be given parenthetically in the text. On *The Faithful Shepherdess* and pastoral, see W[alter] W. Greg, *Pastoral Poetry and Pastoral Drama: a literary inquiry, with special reference to the pre-Restoration stage in England* (London: Bullen, 1906); Lee Bliss, "Defending Fletcher's Shepherds," *Studies in English Literature* 23 (1983): 295–310; V. M. Jeffrey, "Italian Influence in Fletcher's *Faithful Shepherdess,*" *Modern Language Review* 21 (1926): 147–158; Annabel Patterson, *Censorship and Interpretation: The Conditions of Writing and Reading in Early Modern England* (Madison: U of Wisconsin P, 1984), 172–74; Gordon McMullan and Jonathan Hope, "Introduction: the politics of tragicomedy, 1610–1650," in McMullan and Hope, eds., *The Politics of Tragicomedy: Shakespeare and After* (London: Routledge, 1992), 1–20.

51. Bowers 3:497, ll. 10–17. Fletcher's emphasis on herb lore in *The Faithful Shepherdess* recalls the Ninth Eglogue of Drayton's *Pastorals* (1606), where there is an exchange of appropriate flowers and herbs by country lovers which is immediately followed by a politicizing comment: "In Cotes such simples, simply in request, / Wherewith proud Courts in greatnesse scorne to mell, / For Countrey toyes become the Countrey best, / And please poore Shepheards, and become them well" (Hebel 2, 564; ll. 25–28).

52. Cf. Sir Philip Sidney, *The Countess of Pembroke's Arcadia (The Old Arcadia),* ed. Katherine Duncan-Jones (Oxford: Oxford UP, 1985), 50: "[The Arcadian shepherds] were not such base shepherds as we commonly make account of, but the very owners of the sheep themselves, which in that thrifty world the substantiallest men would employ their whole care upon." It is interesting to note that, in the closing scene of *The Faithful Shepherdess,* the Priest tells the shepherds to "[s]ing to the God of sheepe, that happy laye / The honest *Dorus* taught ye, *Dorus* hee, / That was the soule and God of melody" (V. v. 215–17). Dyce (2: 118n) takes this to refer to Spenser, but it seems far more likely, with the *Arcadia* in mind, to be a reference to Sidney. Cf. also the use of the term

"golden world" in Chapman's dedicatory verse, echoing Sidney's formulation of the achievements of poetry in *An Apology for Poetry,* ed. Geoffrey Shepherd (Manchester: Manchester UP, 1973), 100, l. 33.

53. See William Shakespeare, *A Midsummer Night's Dream,* ed. Harold F. Brooks (London: Methuen, 1979), xxxvi; E. K. Chambers, *William Shakespeare: A Study of Facts and Problems* (Oxford: Clarendon P, 1930), 1: 360 and 2: 99–101. See also Manning 224–5.

54. William Shakespeare, *A Midsummer Night's Dream,* Wells and Taylor 351–76; II. i. 93–100, 111–114.

55. On the 1596 rebellion, see Manning, ch. 9, esp. 221–29.

56. It may also be of interest to note certain possible family connections between the plays by way of context. It has been suggested that *A Midsummer Night's Dream* may very well have been performed for a wedding, though this is not an especially current view. One of the contenders has been named as the wedding of William, earl of Derby, and Elizabeth Vere at Greenwich on 26 January 1596. William was brother to Ferdinando, earl of Derby, who had died in 1594, leaving a widow, Alice (the dowager countess) and three daughters: Anne, who firstly married Grey, fifth Lord Chandos, and then Mervyn, earl of Castlehaven; Frances, who married John, earl of Bridgewater; and Elizabeth, who married Henry Hastings to become fifth countess of Huntingdon. A visit to Ashby by the dowager countess was the occasion for the festivities of July 1607 for which Marston's *Entertainment at Ashby* was penned. There might thus be family reasons for a member of the Ashby circle to rework aspects of the *Dream* in 1607, particularly as the long-lived dowager countess had been the dedicatee of Spenser's *Tears of the Muses* and was personified as the "sweet Amaryllis" of *Colin Clout's Come Home Again.* Fletcher's use of the name Amaryllis may be an oblique compliment to his patroness's mother: I am troubled, though, by the change in character of Amaryllis, who hardly seems material for compliment in *The Faithful Shepherdess.* There is, however, a further possible literary link since the earl of Bridgewater was the sponsor of Milton's *Comus.* See below pp. 194–96 for analysis of the relationship of *The Faithful Shepherdess* and of Fletcher and Massinger's later tragicomedy *The Prophetess* to Milton's masque.

57. Hebel 4:iv. Aston (yet not, oddly enough, Drayton, though he later apologized for the omission) was one of the many elegists for Prince Henry's untimely death in 1612.

58. I consulted Bodleian Library MS Eng. Poet. f. 9:194–99; the other copies are Yale, Osborn Collection, b. 148:143–46; and Trinity College Dublin MS 877, fols. 264r–266v. See W. Milgate, ed., *The Satires, Epigrams and Verse Letters of John Donne* (Oxford: Oxford UP, 1967), 293–94; and Dennis Kay, "Poems by Sir Walter Aston, and a Date for the Donne / Goodyer Verse Epistle 'Alternis Vicibus,'" *Review of English Studies* 37 (1986): 198–210. Subsequent references to Kay's article will be given parenthetically in the text.

59. It may be worth noting that Drayton mentions his friendship with the Beaumonts in the same breath as that with William Browne, the author of the Spenserian *Britannia's Pastorals.* In Drayton's "Of Poets and Poesie," written for Henry Reynolds, the poet mentions "the two *Beamounts* and my *Browne*" as his

"deare companions whom [he] freely chose / [his] bosome friends" (*Works*, ed. Hebel, 4:230). *Britannia's Pastorals* even draws from *The Faithful Shepherdess* for the moment at which Marina is saved from drowning by a river god (see Grundy 146).

60. After conviction for recusancy on 2 May 1607, Sir John Beaumont lost two-thirds of his property to James Sempill, an old friend of the king's from the Edinburgh court, and retired to Grace-Dieu, which he was at least allowed to keep. On Sir John, see introduction to Roger Sell, ed., *The Shorter Poems of Sir John Beaumont* (Åbo: Åbo Akademi, 1974).

61. Michael Drayton, "Eglogue the Eighth," *Pastorals. Contayning Eglogues* (1619), Hebel 2:515–73.

62. On Skipwith, see Knowles, "WS MS," and Mary Hobbs, "A WS manuscript," *TLS*, June 10–16, 1988, 647.

63. British Library Add. MS 25707 includes poems by Skipwith, Pestell, Goodyer, and the Beaumont brothers, among others, as well as some verses attributed to Henry Skipwith (Sir William's father) but apparently by Sir Walter Aston. Public Record Office MS SP 14/115/34* juxtaposes poems by Beaumont and Skipwith. Pestell was rector of Coleorton from 1611 under the patronage of Sir Thomas Beaumont. In 1615 he also became chaplain to the third earl of Essex, who was in retirement about twenty miles away at Chartley, Staffs., in the wake of his humiliating divorce. Pestell not only wrote a verse letter to, and two elegies for, the fifth countess of Huntingdon, but also an elegy on the death of Francis Beaumont and an epitaph for Arthur Hildersham, the most prominent of the silenced ministers supported by Huntingdon, Skipwith et al.

64. The dedication read: "The testimony of my Affection, and Observance to my noble Freind Sr Robert Townseehend wch I desire may remayne wth him and last beyond Marble," see Herford and Simpson 1:30–31n. See also Rosalind Miles, *Ben Jonson: His Life and Work* (London: RKP, 1986), 67. This is interesting in terms of the earl of Northampton's apparent perception that there was "treason" in *Sejanus*. Philip Ayres suggests that this "treason" related particularly to the trial of Ralegh in 1603: "it is highly likely that Northampton thought the play in part a comment on the trial of Ralegh and for that reason brought Jonson before the Council"; see Ben Jonson, *Sejanus His Fall*, ed. Philip J. Ayres (Manchester: Manchester UP, 1990), 17. For a context of violence and riot, see Act V, ll. 815–23:

> *Lepidus:* But what hath followed?
> *Terentius:*   Sentence, by the Senate,
> To lose his head—which was no sooner off,
> But that and th'unfortunate trunk were seized
> By the rude multitude; who, not content
> With what the forward justice of the state
> Officiously had done, with violent rage
> Have rent it limb from limb. A thousand heads,
> A thousand hands, ten thousand tongues and voices,
> Employed at once in several acts of malice!

65. See John Nichols, *The Progresses, Processions, and Magnificent Festivities of King James the First*, 4 vols. (London, 1828), 1:114–18; and David Riggs, *Ben Jonson: A Life* (Cambridge, MA: Harvard UP, 1987), 97.

66. See Finkelpearl, *Court and Country Politics*, 109–10; James J. Yoch, "The Renaissance Dramatization of Temperance: the Italian Revival of Tragicomedy and *The Faithful Shepherdess*," in Maguire, ed., *Renaissance Tragicomedy*, 114–38.

67. See Sukanta Chaudhuri, *Renaissance Pastoral and its English Development* (Oxford: Clarendon P, 1989), 371.

68. Richard Helgerson, "The Land Speaks: Cartography, Chorography, and Subversion in Renaissance England," 353, in Stephen Greenblatt, ed., *Representing the English Renaissance* (Berkeley: U of California P, 1988), 326–61; reworked in Helgerson, *Forms of Nationhood: The Elizabethan Writing of England* (Chicago: U of Chicago P, 1992), 105–47.

69. Hebel 4:532–40.

70. *Wit Without Money* is generally dated to 1614 because of one or two specific references to events of that year in the text and because, when the play was published in 1639, it formed part of the repertoire of Queen Henrietta's men and Beeston's boys, a provenance which suggests that the play originally belonged either to the Children of the Queen's Revels or Lady Elizabeth's Men. Since Fletcher's known connection with the Children of the Queen's Revels terminates in 1614, that year is the latest possible date for the play. Gabler (Bowers 4:3–5) conflates the suggestions of Cyrus Hoy (*Studies in Bibliography* XII [1959], 110–12) and Baldwin Maxwell (*Studies in Beaumont, Fletcher, and Massinger* [Chapel Hill: U of North Carolina P, 1939], 194–209) with the ownership evidence to suggest revision in c. 1625 by James Shirley of a Fletcherian original of 1614.

71. See Martin Butler, *Theatre and Crisis 1632–1642* (Cambridge: Cambridge UP, 1984), 159.

72. John Fletcher, *Wit Without Money* (1614), ed. Hans Walter Gabler, Bowers 6:1–109; I. i. 7–10, 11. Subsequent references to *Wit Without Money* will be given parenthetically in the text.

73. In 1600, for example, the Court of Queen's Bench had imposed a fine of £1000 on Sir Thomas Tresham for violations of the Tillage Act of 1597 (see Manning 249).

74. See Melville, "Barrington Isle and the Buccaneers," in *Putnam's Monthly Magazine* 3 (April 1854):346–47. Also see D. Mathis Eddy, "Melville's Response to Beaumont and Fletcher: A New Source for *The Encantadas*," *American Literature* 40 (1968): 374–80. Melville's version is "How bravely now we live, how jocund, how near the first inheritance, without fear, how free from little troubles!"

75. Although *The Night-Walker* seems to have been written in 1611, the extant version dates from 1633 and has been revised by Shirley in all but three scenes (according to Hoy). It is thus effectively impossible to be completely certain of the date of any given passage.

76. John Fletcher (revised James Shirley), *The Night-Walker, or the Little Thief: A Comedy*, Waller 7:311–83; 1:311–12.

77. William Shakespeare, *The Tempest,* Wells and Taylor 1315–1340; II. i. 165–66.

78. *"Andeluria"* is presumably a misreading of secretary-hand Andeluçia. Gabler has kept the 1639 Quarto reading, even though, from the Second Folio on, *"Andeluzia"* is the preferred form (see Bowers 6:104).

79. Cf., much later, *The Elder Brother,* probably the play Fletcher was working on when he died, in which Andrew refers to "[d]eer, those that men fatten for their private pleasures, and let their Tenants starve upon the Commons." See *The Elder Brother: A Comedy,* Glover and Waller 2:1–59; III. iii, p. 24. Also cf. Sir Thomas More, *Utopia,* trans. Turner, 46–47, on sheep eating men.

80. I. i. 222, 225–27; my punctuation modifications.

81. John Fletcher and Francis Beaumont, *The Scornful Lady,* ed. Cyrus Hoy, Bowers 2:449–565. See Cyrus Hoy, *Studies in Bibliography* 11 (1958): 96, for authorship attribution.

82. V. ii. 62–84. I have supplied a few spelling modifications for sense. On courtiers, cf. Leon's apparently mad comment in *Rule a Wife and Have a Wife* (1624): "Courtiers are but tickle things to deale withall, / A kind of march-pane men that will not last Madame, / An egge and pepper goes farther then their potions, / And in a well built body, a poore parsnip / Will play his prize, above their strong potabiles" (Bowers 6:483–605; III. i. 79–83); and cf. Montague's insult to a courtier—"thou silk-worm"—in V. iii. of *The Honest Man's Fortune* (see Waller 10:273).

83. When Falstaff "misuse[s] the King's press damnably," he presses "none but such toasts-and-butter" (William Shakespeare, *The First Part of King Henry the Fourth,* ed. A. R. Humphreys [London: Methuen, 1960], IV. ii. 12, 20–21). Humphreys glosses the term with a passage from Fynes Moryson's *Itinerary* (London, 1617): "Londiners, and all within the sound of Bow-Bell, are in reproch called Cocknies, and eaters of buttered tostes," (Pt. iii, i. 53).

Three. The Reason in Treason

1. Thomas Middleton, *A Game at Chess,* ed. J. W. Harper (London: Ernest Benn, 1966), II. ii. 222–25.

2. Thomas Fuller, *The History of the Worthies of England,* ed. John Nichols, 2 vols. (London, 1811), 2:168.

3. Francis Beaumont and John Fletcher, *The Woman Hater,* ed. George Walton Williams, Bowers 1:145–259; Prologue 6–11. Subsequent references to *The Woman Hater* will be given parenthetically in the text. Finkelpearl assumes that the missing word from "his ——— mallice" is "majesty's" (*Court and Country Politics,* 72).

4. Marginal note in British Library Add. MS. 18653; Fletcher and Massinger, *The Tragedy of Sir John Van Olden Barnavelt,* ed. T. H. Howard-Hill (Oxford: Malone Society, 1980); John Fletcher and Philip Massinger, *The Tragedy of Sir John Van Olden Barnavelt: anonymous Elizabethan play edited from the manuscript,* ed. Wilhelmina Frijlinck (Amsterdam, 1922); T. H. Howard-Hill, "Buc and the Censorship of *Sir John Van Olden Barnavelt* in 1619," *Review of*

English Studies 39 (February 1988): 39–63. See also Jerzy Limon, *Dangerous Matter: English Drama and Politics 1623/4* (Cambridge: Cambridge UP, 1986), 5–6.

5. See Fletcher and Massinger, *Sir John Van Olden Barnavelt,* ed. Howard-Hill, ll. 433–41.

6. I shall spend a little time on *The Woman Hater,* despite the fact that Fletcher's involvement was probably only a minor one, and possibly only as reviser, since it broaches several crucial shared themes and is a play which, as I hope to show in due course, Fletcher echoes more than once in his later work. For helpful readings of this and other plays involving Beaumont, see Lee Bliss, *Francis Beaumont* (Boston: Twayne, 1987).

7. William Shakespeare, *Measure for Measure,* Wells and Taylor 893–924; V. i. 366–67.

8. There are, I would suggest, further echoes of *Measure for Measure* in *The Woman Hater,* one of which perhaps acts as a bridge from Shakespeare's tragicomic problem play to *Pericles,* his first full-fledged (and collaborative) venture into romantic tragicomedy. When the courtiers arrive, disguised, at the brothel to find out what is going on, Arrigo admits he has been there already: "I know the house to be sinfull ynough, yet I have bin here tofore, and durst now, but for discovering of you [i.e., the Duke], appeare here in my owne likenesse" (IV. i. 291–93). And a little later he gives himself away once more when he points out that there is a back door. The Duke observes wryly that "[i]t seemes you are acquainted with the house," to which Arrigo can only reply, "I have bin in it" (IV. ii. 355–56). Cf. the arrival of Lysimachus, disguised, at the brothel in *Pericles,* Wells and Taylor 1167–98; scene 19.

9. Francis Beaumont and John Fletcher, *The Maid's Tragedy,* ed. Robert K. Turner, Bowers 2: 1–166; I. i. 7–11.

10. Beaumont and Fletcher, *The Maid's Tragedy,* I. i. 15.

11. See Janet Clare, *'Art made tongue-tied by authority': Elizabethan and Jacobean Dramatic Censorship* (Manchester: Manchester UP, 1990), 165–68.

12. Francis Beaumont and John Fletcher, *Cupid's Revenge* (1607–8), ed. Fredson Bowers, Bowers 2: 315–448. For authorship ascription by scene, see Cyrus Hoy, *Studies in Bibliography* 11 (1958): 90–91.

13. John Fletcher, *Bonduca,* ed. Cyrus Hoy, Bowers 4:149–259; IV. iv. 15–26.

14. John Fletcher, *Valentinian,* ed. Robert K. Turner, Bowers 4:261–414; I. iii. 41–42, 43, 44–45.

15. See Norbrook 204 and Norbrook thesis 254. The Venetian Ambassador, writing to the Doge and Senate on 16 November 1612, observed that "the four Colleges [i.e., Inns of Court] in which are five hundred of the wealthiest gentlemen of this Kingdom, are, in obedience to the Prince's orders and at great expense, preparing jousts, banquets, liveries and other sumptuous entertainments" ([*Calendar of State Papers*] *Venetian,* 1610–13, 446–47).

16. See Thomas Campion, *The Lords' Masque,* ed. I. A. Shapiro, in *A Book of Masques: in honour of Allardyce Nicoll* (Cambridge: Cambridge UP, 1967), 95–123. For *The Masque of Truth,* see Norbrook thesis, appendix, 294–305.

17. George Chapman, *The Memorable Maske of the two Honorable Houses or Inns of Court; the Middle Temple, and Lyncolns Inne* (1613), ed. G. Blakemore Evans, in Allan Holaday, ed., *The Plays of George Chapman: The Comedies* (Urbana: U of Illinois P, 1970), 557–94. For rocks reference, see "Masque," 1–14.

18. Francis Beaumont, *The Masque of the Inner Temple and Gray's Inn,* ed. Fredson Bowers, Bowers 1:111–44; 124.

19. John Chamberlain, *The Letters of John Chamberlain,* ed. N. E. McClure, 2 vols. (Philadelphia: U of Pennsylvania P, 1939), 1:426 (letter to Alice Carleton, 18 February 1613); quoted in [Spencer and Wells], *A Book of Masques,* 130.

20. It is generally agreed by editors that Fletcher wrote all of the last act except the first scene: see, *inter alia,* Wells and Taylor 1343; Hoy, *Studies in Bibliography* 15 (1962): 76–85); and Jonathan Hope, "Socio-historical linguistic evidence for the authorship of Renaissance plays: test cases in the Shakespeare, Fletcher, and Massinger canons," Ph.D. dissertation (University of Cambridge, 1990), 197; under revision as *The Authorship of Shakespeare's Plays* (Cambridge: Cambridge UP, forthcoming).

21. Fletcher and Shakespeare, *Henry VIII,* V. iv. 17–55.

22. John Fletcher, *Bonduca,* ed. Cyrus Hoy, Bowers 4: 149–259; IV. iv. 15–26.

23. Shakespeare and Fletcher, *The Two Noble Kinsmen,* ed. Bowers, Bowers 7: 145–298; V. iv. 110–12. On the relationship between the play and the events of 1612–13, see John Fletcher and William Shakespeare, *The Two Noble Kinsmen,* ed. Richard Proudfoot (London: Arnold, 1970); Muriel C. Bradbrook, "Shakespeare as Collaborator," *The Living Monument: Shakespeare and the Theatre of His Time* (Cambridge: Cambridge UP, 1976), 227–41, esp. 235–41; and Glynne Wickham, "'The Two Noble Kinsmen' or 'A Midsummer Night's Dream, Part II'?" G. R. Hibbard, ed., *Elizabethan Theatre* 7 (London: Macmillan, 1980), 167–96.

24. Wells and Taylor 1379.

25. Beaumont, *Masque of the Inner Temple and Gray's Inn,* Bowers 1:133. Lois Potter also notes that *"The Lord's Masque,* which Campion wrote for the same occasion, includes a woodland setting with a thicket out of which a wild man comes (like Palamon in Act III)": see Lois Potter, "Topicality or politics? *The Two Noble Kinsmen,* 1613–1634," McMullan and Hope, *Politics of Tragicomedy,* chapter 4.

26. *Henry VIII,* V. iv. 53–4.

27. Dyce 9:29.

28. On *Beggars' Bush* as a source for Caroline "country" plays, see Butler, *Theatre and Crisis,* 331n.

29. Dating and attribution of *Beggars' Bush* are fraught with difficulty. Fredson Bowers, while admitting that there are problems with Hoy's attribution of I and V. ii. 1–65 to Massinger, II and V. i, ii. 65–254 to Beaumont, and III–IV to Fletcher, nonetheless accepts it as "a working hypothesis" (Bowers 3:228). Assuming that all three are there as collaborators, the play must date from the only year in which they could have worked together, *viz.* 1613. Yet the only certain date we have is for the court performance on 27 December 1622. Oliphant ac-

cepts Fleay's suggestion that the play was a Princess Elizabeth's company play transferred to the King's men in 1616 (see Oliphant 257–59), but both Bentley (3:312–18) and Bowers (3:228n) rejects this notion. If Massinger were present as reviser rather than collaborator, the play could of course be an earlier Beaumont and Fletcher collaboration revised for the 1622 performance. The problem with Bowers's dependence on the attributions offered by Hoy is the tenuous nature of the latter's argument. He acknowledges that assigning II and parts of V to Beaumont is based on a "single linguistic feature . . . the use of the contraction *ha'* for *have."* This, he states, is a feature which "might be reasonably associated with the work of Beaumont," and he cheerfully accepts from here on that what he calls "pattern number three" in *Beggars' Bush* is Beaumont's. "And yet," he admits, "to speak of a linguistic pattern for Beaumont is something of an anomaly" (*Studies in Bibliography* 11 [1958]: 88). Thus, when Bowers states that he is happy to accept his friend Hoy's "peculiar expertise" in this matter, it becomes apparent that both are basing their judgments upon intuitive rather than empirical evidence. For my argument I am assuming that the case for assigning II. i. to Beaumont is inadequate: the contraction *'em,* for example, generally assumed to be a characteristic of Fletcher's hand, is present in II. i., e.g. ll. 81, 132.

30. Beggars' Bush was apparently the name of a tree which stood on the left hand side of the London road from Huntingdon to Caxton. See Dyce 9: 18.

31. John Fletcher and Philip Massinger, *Beggars' Bush,* ed. Fredson Bowers, Bowers 3:225–362; II. i. 102–21.

32. I am particularly grateful to Robin Robbins for discussion of this speech.

33. Francis Beaumont and John Fletcher, *Philaster, or Love Lies a-Bleeding,* ed. Robert K. Turner, Bowers 1:367–540; IV. v. 89–90, 91–92, 96–97.

34. Francis Beaumont and John Fletcher, *Phylaster, Or Loue lyes a Bleeding* (London, 1620).

35. The gentleman's sword is apparently highly unusual for the ornate nature of its hilts. I used the 1620 illustration on the publicity for a conference a while ago, and was somewhat surprised to receive a letter from the Tower Armouries asking for further information, not about the conference but about the sword.

36. Finkelpearl, *Court and Country Politics,* 157n; see also Finkelpearl, "Beaumont, Fletcher, and 'Beaumont & Fletcher': Some Distinctions," *English Literary Renaissance* 1 (1971): 144–64.

37. Bowers 1:388, 394.

38. Bowers 1:375, 380.

39. Francis Beaumont and John Fletcher, *Philaster. Or, Loue lies a Bleeding* (London 1622), A2r.

40. See James E. Savage, "The 'gaping wounds' in the text of *Philaster,"* *Philological Quarterly* 28 (1949): 443–57; and Clare, *"Art made tongue-tied by authority,"* 184–87.

41. See Shakespeare, *The Tragedy of King Lear,* Wells and Taylor 1063–1098; IV. v. 225–49. I am grateful to Robin Robbins for suggesting the relevance of this scene to an analysis of *Philaster.*

42. See *Philaster,* IV. v. 90.

43. Clare, *"Art made tongue-tied by authority,"* 184.

44. *Philaster*, I. i. 38–39.

45. It is interesting to note that *The Two Noble Kinsmen* seems to have been revived around this time. According to Lois Potter, "[t]here is some evidence— a fragment of a note—that the play may have been given a court performance in 1619 or 1620. . . . To recall the circumstances of Elizabeth's wedding at this time would have been to invoke the warlike sentiments for which Prince Henry had been so much admired and the popular support for the war," (Potter, "Topicality or politics," McMullan and Hope, *Politics of Tragicomedy,* chapter 4).

46. The polarization of court and country has tended to focus general histo- riographical debate over the early Stuart period. "Whig" and Marxist historians have been keen to see continuity throughout the period and clear development towards constitution or revolution. Perez Zagorin, in *The Court and the Country: The Beginnings of the English Revolution* (London: RKP, 1969), for example, cheerfully talks of the "formation of the Country opposition in the 1620s" (ix), and the subtitle of his book makes his attitude plain enough. He pinpoints Nicholas Breton's *The Court and Country* as a clear indication of developing oppositionism in James's reign [see Breton, *The Court and Country, or A Briefe Discourse betweene the Courtier and Country-man; of the Manner, Nature, and Condi- tion of their liues* (London, 1618)] and he quotes from various speeches given in Parliament in 1625 to defend his claims. Derek Hirst, "Court, Country, and Politics before 1629," in Kevin Sharpe, ed., *Faction and Parliament: Essays on Early Stuart History* (Oxford: Clarendon P, 1978), 105–37, on the other hand, questions the apparently monolithic distinction drawn between court and coun- try in Zagorin's study, and demonstrates the political fickleness of so-called country figures such as Sandys. For a useful overview of this debate, see Richard Cust and Ann Hughes, "Introduction: after revisionism," in Cust and Hughes, eds., *Conflict in Early Stuart England: Studies in Religion and Politics, 1603–1642* (London: Longman, 1989), 1–46. Recent literary studies, and not only the New Historicist, have tended to return to kinds of historicism: see, for example, Finkelpearl, *Court and Country;* Margot Heinemann, *Puritanism and Theatre: Thomas Middleton and Opposition Drama under the Early Stuarts* (Cambridge: Cambridge UP, 1980); and Albert Tricomi, *Anticourt Drama in England, 1603– 1642* (Charlottesville: UP of Virginia, 1989).

47. Fletcher and Rowley, *The Maid in the Mill,* Waller 7: 1–77; III. i, p. 30.

48. C. H. McIlwain, ed., *The Political Works of James I* (Cambridge, MA: Harvard UP, 1918), 343–44.

49. Leah S. Marcus, *The Politics of Mirth: Jonson, Herrick, Milton, Marvell, and the Defense of Old Holiday Pastimes* (Chicago: U of Chicago P, 1986), 2.

50. See analysis of *Women Pleased* below.

51. James I, *The King's Maiesties Declaration to His Subjects, concerning lawfull Sports to be vsed* (London, 1618), 6–7. Quoted in Marcus 3–4.

52. Marcus, *Politics of Mirth,* 37.

53. Lucy Hutchinson, *The Life of Colonel Hutchinson,* ed. James Sutherland (London: Oxford UP, 1973), 42–4. Quoted in Marcus, *Politics of Mirth,* 6.

54. See appendix for datings.

55. It is interesting that the reference to bear-baiting "in the churchyard after

even song" is omitted from the Folio text of the play, presumably as a result of censorship by Sir Henry Herbert in 1633. See John Fletcher, *The Woman's Prize or The Tamer Tamed,* ed. George Ferguson (The Hague: Mouton, 1966), 34. See below for further analysis of this play.

56. The former notion is favored by Oliphant (159), the latter by Bentley (3:432). For a summary, see Hans Walter Gabler's textual introduction in the Bowers edition (Bowers 5: 443–46). See below for closer analysis of the dating possibilities for *Women Pleased.*

57. Bowers 5:445.

58. John Fletcher, *Women Pleased,* ed. Hans Walter Gabler; Bowers 5:441–538; IV. i. 1–6.

59. I take the term "lower bodily principle" from the writings of Mikhail Bakhtin, especially his *Rabelais and His World,* trans. Hélène Iswolsky (Bloomington: Indiana UP, 1984), the introduction to which provides the clearest analysis of the "carnivalesque" in his work. See also Bakhtin, *The Dialogic Imagination: Four Essays,* ed. Michael Holquist, trans. Caryl Emerson and Michael Holquist (Austin: Texas UP, 1981). See also Katerina Clark and Michael Holquist, *Mikhail Bakhtin* (Cambridge, MA: Belknap P, 1984), and Tzvetan Todorov, *Mikhail Bakhtin: The Dialogical Principle,* trans. Wlad Godzich (Minneapolis: U of Minnesota P, 1984). For attempts (with varying degrees of success) to apply Bakhtin's critical principles to the study of Renaissance dramatic texts, see Michael D. Bristol, *Carnival and Theater: Plebeian Culture and the Structure of Authority in Renaissance England* (New York: Methuen, 1985); Peter Stallybrass and Allon White, *The Politics and Poetics of Transgression* (London: Methuen, 1986); and Peter Womack, *Ben Jonson* (Oxford: Blackwell, 1986).

60. "Away thou pamper'd jade of vanity" is a satiric echo of Tamburlaine's "Holla, ye pampered Jades of *Asia*" (Christopher Marlowe, *Tamburlaine,* 71–252, in Fredson Bowers, ed., *The Complete Works of Christopher Marlowe,* vol. 1 [Cambridge: Cambridge UP, 1973], part 2, IV. iii. 1.) I would have corrected Gabler's "wihies" at IV. i. 139 to "winies," except that elsewhere Fletcher quotes the same line and precedes the quotation with a similarly onomatopoeic whinny: "weehee my pampered Jade of *Asia*" (Francis Beaumont and John Fletcher, *The Coxcomb,* ed. Irby B. Cauthen, Jr., Bowers 1: 261–366; II. ii. 74).

Four. Collaboration

1. Gerald Eades Bentley, *The Profession of Dramatist in Shakespeare's Time* (Princeton: Princeton UP, 1971), 198.

2. Ben Jonson, *Sejanus His Fall* (London, 1605), ¶2ᵛ. It has been tentatively suggested that Chapman's is the "second Pen." See R. P. Corballis, "The 'Second Pen' in the Stage Version of *Sejanus,*" *Modern Philology* 76 (1979): 273–77.

3. See Bentley, *The Profession of Dramatist,* 201–2.

4. [Philip Henslowe], *Henslowe Papers: Being Documents Supplementary to Henslowe's Diary,* ed. Walter W. Greg (London: A. H. Bullen, 1907), 65–67.

5. In *The Bloody Brother.* See chronology below.

6. Ben Jonson, *Timber: or, Discoveries,* 626, in Herford and Simpson 8: 555–649.

7. On Jonson's concern with texts, see Joseph Loewenstein, "The Script in the Marketplace," in Greenblatt, *Representing the English Renaissance*, 265–78.

8. Bentley, *Profession of Dramatist*, 207.

9. John Fletcher, *The Wild-Goose Chase* (London, 1652), π2^v.

10. See authorship/chronology list in appendix.

11. See Cyrus Hoy, "The Shares of Fletcher and his Collaborators in the Beaumont and Fletcher Canon, 1–7," *Studies in Bibliography* 7–9, 11–15 (1956–62); E. H. C. Oliphant, *The Plays of Beaumont and Fletcher: An Attempt to Determine their Respective Shares and the Shares of Others* (New Haven: Yale UP, 1927); Bertha Hensman, *The Shares of Fletcher, Field, and Massinger in 12 Plays of the Beaumont and Fletcher Canon*. 2 vols. Jacobean Drama Studies 6 (Salzburg: Institut für Englische Sprache und Literatur, Universität Salzburg, 1974); Bentley, *Jacobean and Caroline Stage;* Jonathan Hope, *Authorship of Shakespeare's Plays* (forthcoming); David J. Lake, *The Canon of Thomas Middleton's Plays: Internal Evidence for the Major Problems of Authorship* (Cambridge: Cambridge UP, 1975).

12. [J. Wilmot,] *Valentinian: A Tragedy As 'tis Alter'd by the late EARL of ROCHESTER* (London, 1685), A2^r–A2^v.

13. On *The Noble Gentleman*, see Bentley 3: 387–91, and Finkelpearl, *Court and Country Politics*, 249–54. On *Love's Cure*, see Bentley 3: 363–66, and Bliss, *Beaumont*, 17–19.

14. Jasper Maine, "On the Workes of *Beaumont* and *Fletcher*, now at length printed," commendatory verse to Beaumont and Fletcher, *Comedies and Tragedies* (London, 1647), d1^r.

15. Gerard Langbaine, *An Account of the English Dramatic Poets* (Oxford, 1691), 144.

16. See Carol A. Chillington, "Playwrights at Work: Henslowe's, Not Shakespeare's, *Book of Sir Thomas More*," *English Literary Renaissance* 10.3 (Autumn 1980): 439–79, for an account of the care with which collaborators might customarily have taken over their textual negotiations.

17. Samuel Taylor Coleridge, *Coleridge's Literary Criticism*, ed. J. W. Mackail (Oxford: Oxford UP, 1908), 250; Coleridge, *Lectures 1808–1819: On Literature*, ed. R. A. Foakes (2 vols.), vol. 5 of *The Collected Works of Samuel Taylor Coleridge*, (London: Routledge, 1987), 2:147.

18. Brander Matthews, *With My Friends: Tales Told in Partnership, with an Introductory Essay on the Art and Mystery of Collaboration* (London: Longmans, 1891). Page references will be given parenthetically in the text.

19. See E. K. Chambers, "The Disintegration of Shakespeare," Annual Shakespeare Lecture, 1924, in *Proceedings of the British Academy 1924–1925* (London: Oxford UP, 1925), 89–108.

20. Wayne Koestenbaum, *Double Talk: The Erotics of Male Literary Collaboration* (London: Routledge, 1989). All references will be given parenthetically in the text.

21. See especially Eve Kosofsky Sedgwick, *Between Men: English Literature and Male Homosocial Desire* (New York: Columbia UP, 1985).

22. Beaumont and Fletcher, *Comedies and Tragedies* (1647), d4^v.

23. *'Brief Lives,' chiefly of Contemporaries, set down by John Aubrey, between the Years 1669 & 1696*, ed. Andrew Clark (Oxford: Clarendon P, 1898), 1:95–96. I

am grateful to Kate Bennett for letting me see the relevant portion of the transcription for her forthcoming edition of Aubrey's *Brief Lives.*

24. Aubrey, *Brief Lives,* ed. Clark, 96.

25. Philip Edwards, Gerald Eades Bentley, Kathleen McLuskie, and Lois Potter, eds., *The Revels History of Drama in English,* vol. 4, 1613–1660 (London: Methuen, 1981), 169.

26. Edwards et al., *Revels History of Drama in English,* 4:170; also Bentley 3:255.

27. *Henslowe Papers,* 72; see also Bertha Hensman, "The Collaboration of Massinger and Fletcher," D. Phil. thesis (University of Oxford, 1960), 6.

28. *Henslowe Papers,* 84; Hensman 7.

29. Hensman also places *The Laws of Candy* in the latter category. I follow Hoy in rejecting that play from the canon and treating it as wholly Ford's.

30. Bentley, *Profession of Dramatist,* 199, 205–6.

31. Bentley, *Profession of Dramatist,* 208.

32. Sir Aston Cokayne, *A Chain of Golden Poems* (London, 1658), 91–92. In the same volume, Cokayne provides evidence of the closeness of Fletcher and Massinger in his "*Epitaph on Mr.* John Fletcher, *and Mr.* Philip Massinger, *who lie buried both in one Grave in* St. Mary Overie's Church *in* Southwark" (186).

33. Cyrus Hoy, "Massinger as Collaborator: The Plays with Fletcher and Others," in Douglas Howard, ed., *Philip Massinger: A Critical Reassessment* (Cambridge: Cambridge UP, 1985), 52.

34. Kathleen McLuskie, "A maidenhead, *Amintor,* at my yeares!" chapter 8 of *Renaissance Dramatists: Feminist Readings* (Hemel Hempstead: Harvester Wheatsheaf, 1989); reprinted as " 'A Maidenhead, Amintor, at my Years?': chastity and tragicomedy in the Fletcher plays," in McMullan and Hope, *Politics of Tragicomedy,* chapter 5.

35. Edwards et al., *Revels History of Drama in English,* 4:182.

36. This attitude is most clearly expressed in Wallis, *Fletcher, Beaumont, and Company.*

37. Sir John Berkenhead, "Oh the happy Collection of Master *Fletcher's* Works, never before Printed," commendatory verse to Beaumont and Fletcher, *Comedies and Tragedies* (1647), e1ᵛ.

38. William Shakespeare, *King Henry VIII,* ed. R. A. Foakes (Arden edition [London: Methuen, 1957; "reprinted with minor corrections 1964"]), xxii. Subsequent references to Foakes's edition will be given parenthetically in the text.

39. Foakes xxvii–xxviii, quoting Cyrus Hoy, "The Shares of Fletcher and his Collaborators in the Beaumont and Fletcher Canon: VII," *Studies in Bibliography* 15 (1962): 79.

40. Bowers 1:vii.

41. Jonathan Dollimore, "Subjectivity, Sexuality, and Transgression: the Jacobean Connection," *Renaissance Drama* 17 (1986): 53–81.

42. *Love's Cure,* ed. George Walton Williams, Bowers 3:1–112; I. ii. 6–10.

43. Hoy divides the play as follows [*Studies in Bibliography* 14 (1961): 48]: Beaumont: III. i, iiib (from entrance of Malroda to Malroda's "Do ye ask?").

Fletcher: II. iia (to first exit of Bobadilla); III. iiia (to entrance of Malroda), v. Massinger: I. i, iii; IV. i, ii, iiia (to entrance of Alvarez, Lucio, Bobadilla), iiic (from entrance of Alguazier to end), iv; V. i, ii, iiic (final speech). Beaumont & Fletcher: II. i, iic (from Clara's "No, he do's not" to end); V. iiib (from Bobadilla's "I am not regarded" to final speech). Fletcher & Massinger: I. ii; II. iib (from first exit of Bobadilla to Clara's "No, he do's not"); III. ii, iiic (from Malroda's "Do ye ask?" to end), iv; IV. iiib (from entrance of Alvarez, Lucio, Bobadilla to entrance of Alguazier). Beaumont & Fletcher & Massinger: V. iiia (to Bobadilla's "I am not regarded").

44. Kathleen McLuskie makes an observation not unakin to this in her discussion of *The Maid's Tragedy,* though she transfers the hermeneutic to the audience: "The pleasure of the play lies less in the happy and conventional conclusion than in the wit with which Fletcher holds . . . potentially offensive material within the bounds of decorum while mocking decorum at every turn." See McLuskie, *Renaissance Dramatists,* 200.

45. Jeffrey Masten, "Beaumont and/or Fletcher: Collaboration and the Interpretation of Renaissance Drama," *ELH* 59 (1992): 337–56. I look forward to publication of Masten's larger project.

46. Jack Stillinger, *Multiple Authorship and the Myth of Solitary Genius* (New York: Oxford UP, 1991), v.

47. I take the idea of the supplement, from the work of Jacques Derrida. See, for example, *Grammatology,* trans. Gayatri Chakravorty Spivak (Baltimore: Johns Hopkins UP, 1976), 141ff.

48. See Mikhail Bakhtin, "Discourse in the Novel," in *The Dialogic Imagination,* 259–422.

Five. "Strange carded cunningnesse"

1. For references and more detailed analysis of this masque, see chapter 1 above.

2. John Fletcher, *The Woman's Prize, or The Tamer Tamed,* ed. Fredson Bowers, Bowers 4:1–148; I. i. 31, 33–36.

3. Fletcher and Beaumont, *The Coxcomb,* ed. Irby B. Cauthen, Jr., Bowers 1:261–366; III. iii. 53–56.

4. Fletcher's fullest analysis of a woman's utopia came in *The Sea Voyage,* written with Philip Massinger in 1622, but I shall return to this in the closing chapter.

5. John Fletcher, *The Wild-Goose Chase,* ed. Fredson Bowers, Bowers 6:225–354; V. ii. 22–25; 28–29.

6. William Shakespeare, *Othello,* Wells and Taylor 925–64; III. iii. 266–67. I am grateful to Helen Cooper for reminding me of the relevance of this line.

7. See McLuskie, *Renaissance Dramatists,* chapter 8.

8. The Genesis myth was of course the chief vehicle and target in the debate over women in the period. See, for example, Æmilia Lanyer, *Salve Deus Rex Iudæorum* (London, 1611), esp. "Eves Apologie in defence of Women," D1ʳ–D3ᵛ; and Simon Shepherd, *The Women's Sharp Revenge: Five Women's Pamphlets*

from the Renaissance (London, Fourth Estate, 1985), esp. Speght and Sowernam. On the debate, see Katherine Usher Henderson and Barbara F. McManus, eds., *Half Humankind: Contexts and Texts of the Controversy about Women, 1540–1640* (Urbana: U of Illinois P, 1985).

9. Aristophanes, *Lysistrata and Other Plays,* trans. Allan H. Sommerstein (Harmondsworth: Penguin, 1973), 203–4. See also Aristophanes, *Lysistrata,* ed. Jeffrey Henderson (Oxford: Clarendon P, 1987).

10. The Curtius story clearly comes to mind at sexually unsettling moments. After he has been put to service in a brothel catering to gentlewomen, Rutilio in *The Custom of the Country* says: "ô the Divell! women? / *Curtius* gulfe was never halfe so dangerous," John Fletcher and Philip Massinger, *The Custom of the Country,* Bowers 8:633–758; IV. v. 11–12.

11. See Rota Herzberg Lister, ed., *A Critical Edition of John Fletcher's Comedy 'The Wild-Goose Chase'* (New York: Garland, 1980), 21n.

12. One Fletcherian would-be rapist even assumes the role of Tarquin willingly. Lavall, the vicious heir to the Duke in "The Triumph of Death," one of the *Four Plays,* attempts to rape Casta, crying, "Then like lustie *Tarquin* / Turn'd into flames with *Lucrece* coy denyals, / His blood and spirit equally ambitious, / I force thee for my own." See John Fletcher and Nathan Field, *Four Plays or Moral Representations in One,* Glover and Waller 10:287–364, 350. Elsewhere, it is a woman, Cassandra the bawd, who voices the patriarchal attitude on behalf of the king in *A Wife for a Month:*

> Had *Lucrece* e're been thought of, but for *Tarquin?*
> She was before a simple unknowne woman,
> When she was ravisht, she was a reverent Saint;
> And do you think she yeelded not a little?
> And had a kinde of will to have been re-ravisht?
> Believe it yes: There are a thousand stories
> Of wondrous loyall women, that have slipt,
> But it has been e're the ice of tender honour,
> That kept 'em coole still to the world; I think
> You are blest, that have such an occasion in your hands
> To beget a Chronicle, a faithfull one.   (IV. iii. 40–50)

See John Fletcher, *A Wife for a Month,* ed. Robert K. Turner, Bowers 6:355–482; IV. iii. 40–50. See also Beliza's comment on the male attitude toward rape in *The Queen of Corinth:* "What joys thou canst expect from such a Husband, / To whom thy first, and what's more, forc'd embraces, / Which men say heighten pleasure, were distasteful," John Fletcher, Nathan Field, and Philip Massinger, *The Queen of Corinth: A Tragicomedy,* Glover and Waller 6:1–78; V. iv. p. 74. On rape in Fletcher's plays, see Suzanne Gossett, " 'Best Men are Molded out of Faults': Marrying the Rapist in Jacobean Drama," Arthur F. Kinney and Dan S. Collins, eds., *Renaissance Historicism: Selections from English Literary Renaissance* (Amherst: U of Massachusetts P, 1987), 168–90.

13. See Gossett, "Marrying the Rapist," 170–72.

14. John Fletcher, *The Humorous Lieutenant,* ed. Cyrus Hoy, Bowers 5:289–440; I. i. 10–15.

15. I. i. 41, 40. *The Humorous Lieutenant*'s Celia, incidentally, turns out by the end of the play to be a king's daughter named Enanthe.

16. John Fletcher, *The Pilgrim*, ed. Cyrus Hoy, Bowers 6:111–224; V. iii. 3. Subsequent references to *The Pilgrim* will be given parenthetically in the text.

17. David Norbrook, "'What cares these roarers for the name of king?': language and utopia in *The Tempest*," in McMullan and Hope, *The Politics of Tragicomedy*, chapter 2.

18. For analysis of *The Sea Voyage*, see chapter 6 below.

19. John Fletcher and Philip Massinger, *The Prophetess*, Waller 5:320–89; II, iii, p. 343.

20. Thomas Morley, *Cantvs Madrigales. The Triumphs of Oriana, to 5 and 6 voices: composed by diuers seuerall aucthors* (London, 1601).

21. Thomas Vautor, *The First Set: beeing Songs of diuers Ayres and Natures* (London, 1619), quoted in Roy Strong, "Queen Elizabeth I as Oriana," *Studies in the Renaissance* 6 (1959): 251–60. See also Strong, "The Popular Celebration of the Accession Day of Queen Elizabeth I," *Journal of the Warburg and Courtauld Institutes* 21 (1958): 86–103, and David Cressy, *Bonfires and Bells: National Memory and the Protestant Calendar in Elizabethan and Stuart England* (London: Weidenfeld and Nicolson, 1989), esp. 130–40.

22. Buchan, ed., *Pestell*, 89.

23. *The Prophetess*, IV. ii, p. 384; *Philaster*, I. i. 301–2; *The Pilgrim*, V. iv. 110–11.

24. Arthur Wilson, *The History of Great Britain* (London, 1653), 162.

25. On *Arcades, Comus*, and their contexts, see Cedric C. Brown, *John Milton's Aristocratic Entertainments* (Cambridge: Cambridge UP, 1985).

26. John Milton, *A Masque presented at Ludlow Castle*, in John Carey, ed., *John Milton: Complete Shorter Poems* (London: Longman, 1968), 168–229, l. 534.

27. See Norbrook, *Poetry and Politics*, 249–50.

28. See Sophie Tomlinson, "'She that plays the King': Henrietta Maria and the threat of the actress in Caroline culture," McMullan and Hope, *Politics of Tragicomedy*, chapter 9.

29. Norbrook, *Poetry and Politics*, 258.

Six. Discovery

1. Tzvetan Todorov, *The Conquest of America: The Question of the Other*, trans. Richard Howard (New York: Harper, 1984), 13.

2. William Shakespeare, *The Tempest*, Wells and Taylor 1315–40; I. ii. 335–42; 344–47. Subsequent references will be given parenthetically in the text.

3. See, among many others, Francis Barker and Peter Hulme, "'Nymphs and reapers heavily vanish': the discursive con-texts of *The Tempest*," in John Drakakis, ed., *Alternative Shakespeares* (London: Methuen, 1985), 191–205; Paul Brown, "'This thing of darkness I acknowledge mine': *The Tempest* and the discourse of colonialism," Jonathan Dollimore and Alan Sinfield, ed., *Political Shakespeare: New Essays in Cultural Materialism* (Manchester: Manchester UP, 1985), 48–71; Charles Frey, "*The Tempest* and the New World," *Shakespeare*

Quarterly 30 (1979): 29–41; Stephen Greenblatt, "Learning to Curse: Aspects of Linguistic Colonialism in the Sixteenth Century," Fredi Chiappelli, ed., *First Images of America: The Impact of the New World on the Old,* 2 vols. (Berkeley: U of California P, 1976), 2:561–80; Peter Hulme, *Colonial Encounters: Europe and the Native Caribbean, 1492–1797* (London: Methuen, 1986), 89–136; Ania Loomba, *Gender, Race, Renaissance Drama* (Manchester: Manchester UP, 1989); Otare Mannoni, *Prospero and Caliban: The Psychology of Colonization,* trans. Pamela Powseland (London: Methuen, 1956), esp. 97–109; Stephen Orgel, "Prospero's Wife," *Representations* 8 (1985): 1–13. For a book-length study which responds to the above essays, see Alden T. and Virginia Mason Vaughan, *Shakespeare's Caliban: A Cultural History* (Cambridge: Cambridge UP, 1991), esp. 118–43.

4. For helpful analyses of the "discourse of colonialism" in recent criticism, see Meredith Anne Skura, "Discourse and the Individual: The Case of Colonialism in *The Tempest,*" *Shakespeare Quarterly* 40 (1989): 42–69; and David Norbrook, " 'What cares these roarers for the name of king?': language and utopia in *The Tempest,*" in McMullan and Hope, *Politics of Tragicomedy,* 21–54, esp. 38–47.

5. See Norbrook, "What cares these roarers for the name of king?" *passim.*

6. On the history and politics of the Virginia Company, see Charles M. Andrews, *The Colonial Period of American History,* vol. 1: *The Settlements* (New Haven: Yale UP, 1934); Wesley Frank Craven, *The Dissolution of the Virginia Company: The Failure of a Colonial Experiment* (New York: Oxford UP, 1932); Susan M. Kingsbury, ed., *Records of the Virginia Company of London* (Washington, 1906); Edward D. Neill, *History of the Virginia Company of London* (Albany, NY, 1869); Neill, *The English Colonization of America During the Seventeenth Century* (London, 1871); Herbert L. Osgood, *The American Colonies in the Seventeenth Century,* vol. 1: *The Proprietary Province in its Earliest Form; The Corporate Colonies of New England* (New York: Columbia UP, 1930; first published 1904).

7. Noel Malcolm, "Hobbes, Sandys, and the Virginia Company," *The Historical Journal* 24.2 (1981): 297–321.

8. Samuel Purchas, *Purchas His Pilgrimes,* 20:130.

9. See Simon L. Adams, "Foreign Policy and the Parliaments of 1621 and 1624," Kevin Sharpe, ed., *Faction and Parliament: Essays on Early Stuart History* (Oxford: Clarendon P, 1978), 139–71: 144n, quoting from HMC *VIIIth Report of the Royal Commission on Historical manuscripts,* Appendix 2: *Manuscripts of his Grace the Duke of Manchester* (Darlington: HM Stationery Office, 1881), 45. And this despite the fact that one of Sandys's own bills in Parliament had been designed to subject Brownists and Barrowists to the same penalties as those inflicted on recusant Catholics. See *D.N.B.* 17: 775, and Sir Symonds D'Ewes, *The Journal of Sir Simonds D'Ewes: from the beginning of the London Parliament to the opening of the trail of the earl of Strafford,* ed. Wallace Notestein (New Haven: Yale UP, 1923), 471, 474, 478, 481, 500, 502.

10. Adams adds that in the examination of Southampton and Sandys after that session of Parliament, "the Privy Council was particularly interested in their contacts with the King and Queen of Bohemia" (145n).

11. See Brown, *Milton's Aristocratic Entertainments,* 19, and Finkelpearl, *Court and Country Politics,* 30.

12. See Richard Beale Davis, *George Sandys: Poet-Adventurer* (London: Bodley Head, 1955).

13. See E[dward] S[eton] Sandys, *History of the Family of Sandys,* vol. 1 (Barrow-in-Furness, 1930), 94.

14. The somewhat enigmatic notes run as follows:

That the King of *Fraunce,* and the rest of the imposing Princes, do also make Laws:—That will, in short time, bring all to a tyrannical Course, where Confusion both to Prince and People—Death of the last great imposing Prince.—No successive King, but First elected.— Election double; of Person, and Care; but both come in by Consent of People, and with reciprocal Conditions between King and People.— That a King, by Conquest, may also (when Power) be expelled.—That no Argument, that the King of *Fraunce* may impose; *ergo,* the King of *England* may.

See Journals of the House of Commons, vol. 1, 1547–1628 (London, 1803), 493; partly quoted in Malcolm 302. It is, incidentally, due to a motion by Sir Edwin Sandys of June 1607 that the *Journals* for the period were kept regularly for the first time.

15. Councell of Virginia, *A True Declaration of the estate of the Colonie in Virginia, With a confutation of such scandalous reports as haue tended to the disgrace of soworthy an enterprise* (London, 1610), B1ᵛ. All subsequent references to the *True Declaration* will be given parenthetically in the text.

16. Malcolm 304.

17. Malcolm 300.

18. Alexander Brown, *The Genesis of the United States,* 2 vols. (London, 1890); Brown, *The First Republic in America* (Boston, 1898). Brown's predecessors include Rev. William Stith, *History of the First Discovery and Settlement of Virginia* (Williamsburg, VA, 1747) and Peter Peckard, *Memoirs of the Life of Mr. Nicholas Ferrar* (Cambridge, MA, 1790). See Craven, *Dissolution of the Virginia Company,* 1–23.

19. Craven 88.

20. Osgood 1:92.

21. Sandys, *Family of Sandys,* 98. As Craven has shown, the source of this anecdote, Arthur Wodenoth's *A Short Collection of the Most Remarkable Passages from the originall to the dissolution of the Virginia Company* (London, 1651) would appear to be untrustworthy. See Craven 16–19. Yet even if the king did not express himself in quite the way Wodenoth claims, it is undeniable that he did intervene directly in the election to prevent Sandys retaining the treasurership.

22. See Davis, *George Sandys,* 25; also Jonathan Haynes, *The Humanist as Traveler: George Sandys's "Relation of a Journey begun An. Dom. 1610"* (London: Associated University Presses, 1986). On George Sandys, see also Michael Drayton, "To Master George Sandys, Treasurer for the English Colony in Virginia," Hebel 3:206–8. Sandy's *Relation of a Journey* is a source for Fletcher, Field, and Massinger's *The Knight of Malta.*

23. See *The Huntingdon Papers: The Archives of the Noble Family of Hastings* (London: Maggs, 1926), x. Edward's loss, incidentally, relieved the earl of one of his many inherited financial obligations.

24. Andrews 1:130.

25. Kingsbury, *Records of the Virginia Company,* 1:350.

26. HMC *Hastings* 2:58.

27. Sir Edwin Sandys to fifth earl of Huntingdon, 11 January 1620, HA10673 (Reel 3, Box 8).

28. Court held on 28 June, 1620: "Then was there further chosen to be of his Maties: Counsell for Virginia the Earle of Dorsett then present The Earle of Huntington, and m^r Doctor Anthony. And vppon the reporte of mr Thr~er of the many and great favours that the Earle of Huntington and Bath had this year done this Company in the procuringe of many fitt and vsefull p[er]sons sent to Virginia Itt was ordered that the Courtes especiall thanks should be signified to them by letters." See Kingsbury, *Records of the Virginia Company,* 1:383.

29. See John Baer Stoudt, *Nicolas Martiau: The Adventurous Huguenot, the military engineer and the earliest American ancestor of George Washington* (Morristown, PA: Morristown P, 1932), an unscholarly account which verges on the fictional in places.

30. Draft of a letter of fifth earl of Huntingdon to Sir Edwin Sandys, 2 September 1622, HA 5466 (Reel 3, Box 9).

31. Fifth earl of Huntingdon "to Captaine Martian," 8 July 1624, HA5486 (Reel 4, Box 10). In a postscript, the earl notes that he is sending Martiau a gift of "a sute of apparell and a cloke of cloth six shirts two paire of black and two paire of russett boots and fower paire of shooes." At the end of 1625, though, Martiau still appears to be awaiting the earl's instructions for the planting of Nansimahum. See Nicolas Martian to the fifth earl of Huntingdon, HA9169 (Reel 4, Box 12): "yor honnor hath written unto me about y^r Land, wich is due unto you, wich is a matter of 1200 ackers; & that I should putt itt to best profitt for you, the wich I am verye willing & rady to doe yor Honnor all the service that possible I can heer in Virginia: but ther is no profitt to be raysed frome the Land, unlese it be planted, & if yor honnor be mynded to have a Plantatione; & to supplye itt with menne & such thinges as are necessarye. I will be allwayes readye for to direct theme & advise theme, the best that my poore Industrie shall." For a comparison with the earl's optimism in face of tribulation, see Christopher Brooke, *A Poem on the Late Massacre in Virginia* (London, 1622). Brooke had helped to arrange finance for Chapman's 1613 masque (see Norbrook, *Poetry and Politics,* 211).

32. Fletcher, *Rule a Wife and Have a Wife,* ed. George Walton Williams, Bowers 6:483–605; IV. iii. 199–201.

33. See Skura, "Discourse and the Individual," esp. 52–57.

34. Ralph Hamor, *A True Discourse of the Present Estate of Virginia, and the success of the affaires there till the 18 of June. 1614* (London, 1615), A4^r.

35. William Crashaw, epistle dedicatory to Alexander Whitaker, *Good newes from Virginia. Sent to the counsell and company of Virginia* (London, 1613), A2^r.

36. William Crashaw, *A Sermon preached in London before the right honorable the*

Lord Lawarre, Lord Governour and Captaine Generall of Virginea, and others of his Maiesties Counsell for that Kingdome, and the rest of the Adventurers in that Plantation, known as "A New-yeeres Gift to Virginea" (London, 1610), H1ᵛ. Subsequent references will be given parenthetically in the text. For this and the previous two references, see Skura 54.

37. In May 1609, a fleet of ships under the command of Sir Thomas Gates and Sir George Summers sailed to relieve the beleagured plantation in Virginia. A storm drove the ships apart, separating Gates's ship, the *Sea-Venture,* from the rest. The ship went aground on the Bermudas, and the crew all came safely ashore. The other ships arrived at Jamestown, and assumed that the *Sea-Venture* had been lost. Eventually, after various mutinies and tribulations, Gates and his men built a new boat, set sail, and finally arrived in Virginia a year or so late.

38. John Nicoll, *An Houre Glass of Indian News or A True and tragicall discourse, shewing the most lamantable miseries, and distressed Calamities indured by 67 English-men, which were sent for a supply to the planting in Guiana in the yeare. 1605. Who not finding the saide place, were for want of victuall, left ashore in Saint Lucia, an Island of Caniballs, or Men-eaters in the West-Indyes* (London, 1607), ed. Rev. C. Jesse, *Caribbean Quarterly* 12.1 (March 1966): 46–67. On Nicoll, see Peter Hulme, "Hurricanes in the Caribees: the Constitution of the Discourse of English Colonialism," in Francis Barker et al., eds., *1642: Literature and Power in the Seventeenth Century* (Chelmsford: U of Essex P, 1981), 55–83, and Hulme, *Colonial Encounters,* 128–31.

39. [Gabriel Archer,] "A Breif discription of the People," memorandum to "A relatyon of the Discovery of our River, from James Forte into the Maine," Public Record Office, State Papers, Colonial, CO 1/1, fols. 55–56ᵛ, quoted from David B. Quinn, ed., *New American World: A Documentary History of North America to 1612,* 5 vols. (New York: Hector Bye, 1979), 5:276.

40. Brown in Dollimore and Sinfield, *Political Shakespeare,* 57.

41. On Chapman, Henry, and Virginia, see Norbrook, *Poetry and Poetics,* 204.

42. Chapman, *The Memorable Maske of the Middle Temple, and Lyncolns Inne* (1613), ed. Evans, in *The Plays of George Chapman: The Comedies,* Holaday ed., 557–89; "Description," 229–34.

43. Andrew J. Hickman, "The Influence and Dramatic Use of the Masque in the Plays and Collaborations of John Fletcher," D. Phil. thesis (University of Oxford, 1986), 166.

44. See Hickman 165–84; also Allardyce Nicoll, *Stuart Masques and the Renaissance Stage* (London: Harrap, 1937), 141–42.

45. See Hoy, *Studies in Bibliography* 12 (1959): 95–97.

46. See Suzanne Gossett, "Masque Influence on the Dramaturgy of Beaumong and Fletcher," *Modern Philology* 69 (1972): 199–208; Gossett, "The Term 'Masque' in Shakespeare and Fletcher, and *The Coxcomb,*" *Studies in English Literature* 14 (1974): 285–95; Hickman 166.

47. Fletcher and Field, *Four Plays, or Moral Representations, in One,* ed. Cyrus Hoy, in Bowers 8:223–344; Induction 64–66, 73–76.

48. Cf. Fletcher and Shakespeare, *Henry VIII,* V. iv. 52–54.

49. Hoy follows Simpson and Dyce in emending "book" to "hook," but I am

not convinced the context warrants this conjecture: the mattock and the book
are presumably the props of Industry and the Arts respectively.

50. See Spencer and Wells, *A Book of Masques,* 128, and Braunmuller, *A
Seventeenth-Century Letter-Book,* 297.

51. Samuel Purchas, *Virginia's Verger; Or a Discourse shewing the benefits which
may grow to this Kingdome from American English Plantations, and specially those of
Virginia and Summer Ilands,* in *Hakluytus Posthumus or Purchas His Pilgrimes*
(Glasgow, 1906), 19:242. Subsequent references to Purchas's *Pilgrimes* will be
given parenthetically in the text.

52. See Brown, "This thing of darkness," and Hulme, *Colonial Encounters.*

53. John Rolfe, to Sir Thomas Dale, Bodleian MS. Ashmole 830, folios
118ʳ–119ᵛ; 118ʳ.

54. Councell of Virginia, *True Declaration,* 10.

55. Le Sieur de Bellan, *Histoire Memorable de Dias Espagnol, et de Quixaire
Princesse des Moluques, Tirée des Memoires des Indes, & composee par le sieur de Bellan,*
in *Les Nouuelles de Miguel de Ceruantes Saauedra ov sont contenves plvsievrs rares
advantures* (Paris, 1640). The verbal echoes of de Bellan in the play are too
numerous to note in their entirety: it is sufficient to observe that the story that
de Bellan made from the materials in the play's Spanish-language source, Bartholomé Juan Leonardo de Argensola's history of the Moluccas, the *Conquista de
las Islas Malucas* (Madrid, 1609), and added as a supplement to his translations
of Cervantes's *Historias Exemplares* is as clear a comprehensive source for the play
as the earlier Spanish history. For discussion of this question, see Edward M.
Wilson, "Did John Fletcher Read Spanish?" *Philological Quarterly* 27 (1948):
187–90. His use of de Bellan's tale implies that Fletcher knew the *Exemplary
Tales* in French rather than Spanish.

56. John Fletcher, *The Island Princess,* ed. George Walton Williams, Bowers
5:539–670; I. i. 4–6. All further references to the play will be to this edition
and will be given parenthetically in the text. There is very little criticism of *The
Island Princess* apart from Philip Finkelpearl's recent essay, "Fletcher as Spenserian Playwright," and an unhelpful piece by Herbert Blau, "The Absolved
Riddle: Sovereign Pleasure and the Baroque Subject in the Tragicomedies of
John Fletcher," *New Literary History* 17.3 (Spring 1986): 539–54.

57. Though this was not everyone's immediate reaction. When Pocahontas
was described to him as an Indian princess, James wanted to know why Rolfe,
being a mere commoner, had not asked for royal permission to marry her. See
Louis Booker Wright, ed., *The Elizabethans' America: A Collection of Early Reports
by Englishmen on the New World* (London: Arnold, 1965), 12–13.

58. My translation. The French text runs as follows: "Peut-estre que
quelqu'vn s'estonnera que les yeux de cette Princesse ayent faict tant de mer-
ueilles. Et sur tout qu'ils ayent eu tant de puissance sur des hommes nais et
nourris en l'Europe, comme s'ils n'eussent point esté accoustumez à ne cog-
noistre les traicts de la beauté, qui est obscurcie par vne couleur bazanee, ou tout
à fait More couleur. . . . Que bien que les hommes foient fort bazanez à cause de
l'ardeur du Soleil . . . si bien que les femmes qui s'en deffendent auec toutes
sortes d'artifices, y font extrémement blanches" (De Bellan 688).

59. Compare Anthropos's speech in *Four Plays* (*The Triumph of Time*, i. 48–67), and Andrew Marvell, who, thirty years later, still promotes a strong myth of spontaneous natural plenitude in his "Bermudas":

> What should we do but sing his Praise
> That led us through the watry Maze,
> Unto an Isle so long unknown,
> And yet far kinder than our own?
> [God] does in the Pomegranates close,
> Jewels more rich than *Ormus* show's.
> He makes the Figs our mouths to melt;
> And throws the Melons at our feet.
> . . . With Cedars, chosen by his hand,
> From *Lebanon,* he stores the Land.
> And makes the hollow Seas, that roar,
> Proclaime the Ambergris on shoar (5–22, 25–28)

in H. M. Margoliouth, ed., *The Poems and Letters of Andrew Marvell,* revised by Pierre Legouis with E. E. Duncan-Jones (Oxford: Clarendon P, 1971), 1:17–18. In Marvell's case, a nonconformist theological (ecclesiastical) motive for descriptions of plenitude in exile is clear, but toned down from myth to metaphor—the exaggeration is in the *ease* of plenitude rather than in legends of the exotic.

60. Note the "court us" (l. 28) / "courteous" (l. 36) echo.

61. I. iii. 9–11; III. i. 52. My emphasis in the first of the two quotations.

62. See below in *Sea Voyage* section for Strachey's description of the effects of the storm on the European mind.

63. See II. iii. 21–29.

64. The scene of burning is most familiar, perhaps, from the account by the merchant John Sarracoll of the wanton destruction of a deserted west African village which is included by Hakluyt in his *Principal Navigations* and which Stephen Greenblatt memorably quotes in his essay on Marlovian "self-fashioning." See Richard Hakluyt, ed., *The Principal Navigations, Voyages, Traffiques & Discoveries of the English Nation,* 12 vols. (Glasgow, 1903–5), 11:206–7; and Stephen Greenblatt, *Renaissance Self-Fashioning: From More to Shakespeare* (Chicago: U of Chicago P, 1980), 192.

65. Cf. Lucinda in Fletcher, Field, and Massinger, *The Knight of Malta,* ed. George Walton Williams, in Bowers 8: 345–482: "I am halfe a Christian, / The other half, I'le pray for" (III. iv. 159–160). The aptly named Colonna has already expressed the logic of sexually motivated conversion:

> [I]n *Constantinople* have I liv'd,
> Where I beheld this Turkish Damosell first.
> A tedious suitor was I for her love,
> And pittying such a beauteous case should hide
> A soul prophan'd with infidelity,
> I laboured her conversion with my love,
> And doubly won her; to fair faith her soul
> She firsr betroth'd, and then her faith to me. (V. ii. 167–74)

Cf. Philip Massinger and Thomas Dekker, *The Virgin Martyr,* ed. Fredson Bowers, *The Dramatic Works of Thomas Dekker,* (Cambridge: Cambridge UP, 1966), 3:365–480; II. iii. 84–90.

66. John Berryman, "Homage to Mistress Bradstreet," stanza 17, line 8, *Homage to Mistress Bradstreet and Other Poems* (London: Faber, 1959), 16.

67. Joseph Hall, *Mundus alter et idem sive terra australis nuperrime lustrata auth: Mercurio Britannico* (London, 1608); Joseph Hall, *The discovery of a new world, or a description of the South Indies, by an English Mercury,* trans. J[ohn] H[ealey] (London, 1609); Joseph Hall, *The Discovery of a New World,* ed. Huntington Brown, trans. John Healey (Cambridge, MA: Harvard UP, 1937).

68. John Milton, *Works,* ed. Frank A. Patterson (New York: Columbia UP, 1931), III, part 1:294.

69. Cf., for example, Jonson's "volatees" in his masque *Newes from the New World Discover'd in the Moon* (1620), Herford and Simpson 7:511–25.

70. In this context, it is relevant to note Franck's critique of courtiers in Fletcher's *The Captain:* "For my single selfe, I'de sooner venture / A new conversion of the *Indies,* / Then to make Courtiers able men or honest" (I. ii. 79–81). The compliment is in effect returned a little later when Angilo, a courtier, tries to persuade his friend Julio not to fall in love with Lelia by saying: "As I have a soule, I had rather venture / Upon a savage Island, then this woman" (III. i. 78–79).

71. Hall, trans. Healey 70. There are possible echoes of this in *The Sea Voyage.* See III. i, p. 33 for bawdy references to "Eringoes" and "Potatoes."

72. "[T]he country [is called] Wingandacoa and now by her Majestie Virginia" from the narrative of the travels of "Captaines M. Philip Amadas and M. Arthur Barlowe, who discovered part of the Countrey now called Virginia, Anno 1584," Hakluyt 6:124, 121.

73. John Fletcher and Philip Massinger, *The Sea Voyage,* Waller 9:1–65. I will repeat Oliphant's sentiment about *The Sea Voyage:* "Why this excellent comedy attracts so little notice or gets so little praise I do not understand" (246). *The Sea Voyage* presents attribution problems which are insurmountable by the means available at present for linguistic analysis. The work of both Fletcher and Massinger is apparent, but it is impossible to determine whether the extant text is a Fletcherian original partially revised by Massinger or a collaboration in which, for once, Fletcher took the task of providing the final form. Hoy thinks the latter is the more likely of the two, yet, as we have seen, it would have been very much against the collaborators' usual practice. If Fletcher did finish the text, it perhaps suggests a stronger than usual level of personal interest in the play. Whatever the original arrangement, Hoy's tentative allocation of I and IV to Fletcher and II, III, and V to Massinger seems questionable. See Hoy, *Studies in Bibliography* 9 (1957): 153.

74. Ray Heffner, ed., *The Faerie Queene Book Five,* in Edwin Greenlaw et al., eds., *The Works of Edmund Spenser: A Variorum Edition* (Baltimore: Johns Hopkins P, 1936), IV, xiii. 8.

75. Bentley 3:412.

76. Preface to John Dryden and William Davenant. *The Tempest: or, The Enchanted Island* (London, 1670). See Bentley 3:414.

77. What magic there is—the apparent response by sound to Albert's plea to Nature for mercy—is of the more usual romantic variety: fleeting or hidden divine assistance.

78. William Strachey, *A true reportory of the wracke, and redemption of Sir Thomas Gates Knight; upon, and from the Ilands of the Bermudas: his comming to Virginia, and the estate of that Colonie then, and after, under the government of the Lord La Warre, July 15. 1610,* Purchas 19: 5–72; John Nicoll. On Strachey, see S. G. Culliford, *William Strachey, 1572–1621* (Charlottesville: UP of Virginia, 1965).

79. It is generally assumed that Shakespeare read the narratives in manuscript, since they were published just after *The Tempest* was first produced.

80. Stephen Greenblatt, *Shakespearean Negotiations: The Circulation of Social Energy in Renaissance England* (Oxford: Clarendon P, 1988), 148.

81. See Davies 126–27.

82. See Bentley 5:1395–56.

83. Greenblatt, *Shakespearean Negotiations,* 149.

84. Hall may also have been guided by Hakluyt in his choice of location for the Amazon nation. Hakluyt, 7:295–96.

85. On the geographical context of Nicoll, see Ripley P. Bullen, "The First English Settlement on St. Lucia," *Caribbean Quarterly* 12. n. 2 (June 1966): 29–35.

86. See Todorov, *Conquest of America.*

87. See Earl Miner, "The Wild Man through the Looking Glass," in Edward Dudley and Maximilian E. Novak, eds., *The Wild Man Within: An Image in Western Thought from the Renaissance to Romanticism* (Pittsburgh: U of Pittsburgh P, 1972), 87–114, esp. 97–99. A two-island structure is of course an obvious feature of *The Island Princess,* too.

88. The name Clarinda, taken presumably from Spenser, is also neatly divided between the two young aristocratic women named in *The Tempest:* Miranda and Claribel.

89. Simon Shepherd, in his *Amazons and Warrior Women: Varieties of Feminism in Seventeenth Century Drama* (Brighton: Harvester, 1981) misreads this sentence. The "fetters" are self-imposed: the discipline of life without men, not the iniquities of patriarchy masochistically enjoyed.

90. As Earl Miner observes (Dudley and Novak 97), there is no Caliban here to people the island with versions of himself. Fletcher appears interested here in the effects of New World experience on Europeans, not in the New World inhabitants themselves (except as a pattern for Amazonian society).

91. It is interesting to note the Amazonian inversion of a classical norm here: the Siren, usually portrayed as a false, beguiling woman, becomes a false, beguiling man. Cf. Massinger and Fletcher (revised Massinger), *A Very Woman,* ed. Gabler, in Bowers 7:639–743; II. iii. 212–15 (a Fletcher scene): "I am no *Hellen,* nor no *Hecuba,* / To be deflowred of my loyaltie / With your fair language." And see above, chapter 5, for other Fletcherian strategies to offset the linguistic advantage men wield over women.

92. Emphasis rests on patriarchal inheritance, not primarily on the worth of individual fathers. Despite Rosellia's glorification of the memory of Sebastian, the play's ending emphasises *generational* inheritance in general, not the particu-

lar father's right of primacy. Raymond and Albert can only forgive each other on recognition of their fathers' errors. Raymond notes that "our Fathers crimes / Are in us punish'd. Oh, Albert, the course / They took to leave us rich, was not honest" (59).

93. Edmund Spenser, *The Faerie Queene*, Book V: 7. xlii. 4–5. Once Britomart (a woman, of course) has freed him from the clutches of the Amazon Queen, Artegall sets about putting society to (man-centered) rights again.

Coda. "Strange bifronted posture"

1. James Mabbe, *The Rogue, or The Life of Guzmán de Alfarache, Written in Spanish by Matheo Alemán* (London, 1622), A4ʳ.

2. See P. E. Russell, "A Stuart Hispanist: James Mabbe," *Bulletin of Hispanic Studies* 30 (1953): 75–84. Mabbe is of course better known to Shakespearean scholars as the author of one of the dedicatory poems to the First Folio. See E. A. J. Honigmann, *The Stability of Shakespeare's Text* (London: Arnold, 1965), 24–25, 34–35.

3. The publisher of *The Knight*, Walter Burre, attempts to deny the influence of Cervantes in his dedicatory epistle: "Perhaps it will be thought to be of the race of *Don Quixote*," he writes, adding that he and Beaumont "both may confidently swear it is his elder above a year." Though Shelton's English translation did not appear until 1612, this sounds suspiciously like too much protesting, particularly since Beaumont and Fletcher made use of Baudouin's French translation, published in 1608, in writing *The Coxcomb*.

4. For a useful summary of the current state of knowledge about *Cardenio*, see Wells and Taylor 1341.

5. For dating and authorship details of each of these plays, see chronology below, as well as the relevant sections of Bentley 3:305–433.

6. Annabel Patterson, *Censorship and Interpretation: The Conditions of Writing and Reading in Early Modern England* (Madison: U of Wisconsin P, 1984), 174.

7. See Michel Foucault, *The Order of Things: An Archaeology of the Human Sciences*, trans. Alan Sheridan-Smith (London: Tavistock, 1966), 46–50; and E. C. Riley, "Cervantes: A Question of Genre," in F. W. Hodcroft, D. G. Pattison, R. D. F. Pring-Mill, and R. W. Truman, eds., *Mediaeval and Renaissance Studies on Spain and Portugal in Honour of P. E. Russell* (Oxford: Society for the Study of Mediaeval Languages and Literature, 1981), 84.

8. Eugene M. Waith, *The Pattern of Tragicomedy in Beaumont and Fletcher* (New Haven: Yale UP, 1952).

BIBLIOGRAPHY

Primary Sources

Manuscripts

Bodleian Library: Ashmole 830; Eng. Poet. f. 9; Rawl. poet. 160. British Library: Additional 18653; Additional 25707; Harleian 787 (art. 11). Public Record Office: SP 14/115/34.* Victoria and Albert Museum: Dyce 36.

Letters

The Aristocracy, the State and the Local Community: The Hastings Collection of Manuscripts from the Huntington Library in California. Part One: The Hastings Correspondence 1477–1701. Brighton: Harvester Microform, 1986. Reel 2, Box 6; Reel 3, Boxes 7, 8, and 9; Reel 4, Boxes 10, 11, and 12. Referred to as HA.

Historical Manuscripts Commission Report on the Manuscripts of the late Reginald Rawdon Hastings, Esq. Ed. Francis Bickley. Volumes 2 and 4. London: His Majesty's Stationery Office, 1930. Referred to as HMC *Hastings.*

Historical Manuscripts Commission Report on the Manuscripts of His Grace the Duke of Portland. Volume 9. London: His Majesty's Stationery Office, 1923.

Printed Sources

Adams, Simon L. "Foreign Policy and the Parliaments of 1621 and 1624." In Sharpe, ed., 139–71.

Adelman, Janet. " 'Anger's My Meat': Feeding, Dependency, and Aggression in *Coriolanus.*" In Schwartz and Kahn, eds., 129–49.

———. *Suffocating Mothers: Fantasies of Maternal Origin in Shakespeare's Plays, Hamlet to The Tempest.* New York: Routledge, 1992.

Andrews, Charles M. *The Colonial Period of American History.* Vol. 1: *The Settlements.* New Haven: Yale UP, 1934.

Appleton, William W. *Beaumont and Fletcher: A Critical Study.* London: Allen & Unwin, 1956.

[Archer, Gabriel.] "A Breif discription of the People." Memorandum to "A relatyon of the Discovery of our River, from James Forte into the Maine" (1607). In Quinn, ed., 5: 276.

Aristophanes. *Lysistrata.* Ed. Jeffrey Henderson. Oxford: Clarendon P, 1987.

———. *Lysistrata and Other Plays.* Trans. Allan H. Sommerstein. Harmondsworth: Penguin, 1973.

Aubrey, John. *'Brief Lives,' chiefly of Contemporaries, set down by John Aubrey, between the Years 1669 & 1696.* Ed. Andrew Clark. Oxford: Clarendon P, 1898.

Bakhtin, Mikhail. *The Dialogic Imagination: Four Essays*. Ed. Michael Holquist. Trans. Caryl Emerson and Michael Holquist. Austin: Texas UP, 1981.

———. *Rabelais and His World*. Trans. Hélène Iswolsky. Bloomington: Indiana UP, 1984.

Bald, Robert C. *Bibliographical Studies in the Beaumont & Fletcher Folio of 1647*. Oxford: Oxford UP, 1938.

Barker, Francis, and Peter Hulme. " 'Nymphs and reapers heavily vanish': the discursive con-texts of *The Tempest*." In Drakakis, ed., 191–205.

Barker, Francis, et al., eds. *1642: Literature and Power in the Seventeenth Century*. Chelmsford: U of Essex P, 1981.

Beaumont, Francis. *Grammer Lecture*. Ed. Mark Eccles. "Francis Beaumont's *Grammar Lecture*." *Review of English Studies* 16 (1940): 402–14.

———. *The Knight of the Burning Pestle*. Ed. John Doebler. London: Arnold, 1967.

———. *The Knight of the Burning Pestle*. Ed. Sheldon P. Zitner. Manchester: Manchester UP, 1984.

———. *The Knight of the Burning Pestle*. London, 1613.

———. *The Masque of the Inner Temple and Gray's Inn*. Ed. Fredson Bowers. Bowers 1: 111–44.

———. *The Masque of the Inner Temple and Gray's Inn*. Ed. Philip Edwards. In Spencer and Wells, eds., 125–48.

———. "Salmacis and Hermaphroditus." *Poems. by Francis Beaumont, gent*. London, 1640.

Beaumont, Francis, and John Fletcher. *Comedies and Tragedies*. London, 1647.

———. *Fifty Comedies and Tragedies*. London, 1679.

———. *The Dramatick Works of Beaumont and Fletcher*. Ed. George Colman. 10 vols. London, 1778.

———. *The Works of Beaumont and Fletcher*. Ed. Henry Weber. 14 vols. Edinburgh, 1812.

———. *The Works of Beaumont and Fletcher*. Ed. George Darley. 2 vols. London, 1840.

———. *The Works of Beaumont and Fletcher*. Ed. Rev. Alexander Dyce. London, 1843–46.

———. *The Works of Francis Beaumont and John Fletcher*. Variorum edition. Gen. Ed. A. H. Bullen. 4 vols. London: Bell & Sons, 1904–12.

———. *The Works of Francis Beaumont and John Fletcher*. Ed. Arnold Glover and A. R. Waller. 10 vols. Cambridge: Cambridge UP, 1905–12.

———. *The Dramatic Works in the Beaumont and Fletcher Canon*. Gen. Ed. Fredson Bowers, 7 vols. to date. Cambridge: Cambridge UP, 1966–present.

———. *The Captain*. Ed. L. A. Beaurline. Bowers 1:541–670.

———. *The Coxcomb*. Ed. Irby B. Cauthen. Bowers 1:261–366.

———. *Cupid's Revenge*. Ed. Fredson Bowers. Bowers 2:315–448.

———. *Cupid's Revenge*. London, 1615.

———. *A King and No King*. Ed. George Walton Williams. Bowers 2: 167–314.

———. *A King and No King*. London, 1618.

————. *The Maid's Tragedy.* Ed. Robert K. Turner. Bowers 2: 1–166.

————. *The Maid's Tragedy.* Ed. T. W. Craik. Manchester: Manchester UP, 1988.

————. *The Maides tragedy.* London, 1619.

————. *Philaster, Or, Loue lies a Bleeding.* London, 1622.

————. *Philaster, or Love Lies a-Bleeding.* Ed. Andrew Gurr. London: Methuen, 1969.

————. *Philaster, or Love Lies a-Bleeding.* Ed. Robert K. Turner. Bowers 1: 367–540.

————. *Phylaster. Or, Loue lyes a Bleeding.* London, 1620.

————. *The Scornful Ladie.* London, 1616.

————. *The Scornful Lady.* Ed. Cyrus Hoy. Bowers 2: 449–565.

————. *The Woman Hater.* Ed. George Walton Williams. Bowers 1: 145–259.

————. *The Woman Hater.* London, 1607.

Beaumont, Francis, and John Fletcher, with Ben Jonson. *Love's Pilgrimage.* Ed. L. A. Beaurline. Bowers 2: 567–695.

Beaumont, Sir John. *The Poems of Sir John Beaumont.* Ed. Alexander B. Grosart. London: Privately printed, 1869.

————. *The Shorter Poems of Sir John Beaumont.* Ed. Roger Sell. Åbo, Sweden: Åbo Akademi, 1974.

Bentley, Gerald Eades. *The Jacobean and Caroline Stage.* 7 vols. Oxford: Clarendon P, 1956–1968.

————. *The Profession of Dramatist in Shakespeare's Time 1590–1642.* Princeton: Princeton UP, 1971.

Bergeron, David. "Women as Patrons of English Renaissance Drama." in Lytle and Orgel, eds., 275–90.

Berry, Lloyd E. "Biographical Notes on Richard Fletcher." *Notes and Queries,* n.s. 7 (1960): 377–78.

————. "Phineas Fletcher's account of his father." *Journal of English and Germanic Philology* 60 (1961): 258–67.

Berryman, John. *Homage to Mistress Bradstreet and Other Poems.* London: Faber, 1959.

Birch, Thomas. *Memoirs of the Reign of Queen Elizabeth, From the Year 1581 till her Death.* 2 vols. London, 1754.

Blau, Herbert. "The Absolved Riddle: Sovereign Pleasure and the Baroque Subject in the Tragicomedies of John Fletcher." *New Literary History* 17.3 (Spring 1986): 539–54.

Bliss, Lee. "Defending Fletcher's Shepherds." *Studies in English Literature* 23 (1983): 295–310.

————. *Francis Beaumont.* Boston: Twayne, 1987.

Bowers, Fredson. *The Dramatic Works in the Beaumont and Fletcher Canon.* See under Beaumont, Francis, and John Fletcher.

Bradbrook, Muriel C. "Shakespeare as Collaborator." In *The Living Monument: Shakespeare and the Theatre of His Time.* Cambridge: Cambridge UP, 1976. 227–41.

Braunmuller, A. R., ed. *A Seventeenth-Century Letter-Book: A Facsimile Edition of Folger MS. V. a. 321.* Newark: U of Delaware P, 1983.

Braunmuller, A. R., and J. C. Bulman, eds. *Comedy from Shakespeare to Sheridan: Change and Continuity in the English and European Dramatic Tradition: Essays in Honor of Eugene M. Waith.* Newark: U of Delaware P, 1986.

Breton, Nicholas. *The Court and Country, or A Briefe Discourse betweene the Courtier and Country-man; of the Manner, Nature, and Condition of their liues.* London, 1618.

Bristol, Michael D. *Carnival and Theater: Plebeian Culture and the Structure of Authority in Renaissance England.* New York: Methuen, 1985.

Brooke, Christopher. *A Poem on the Late Massacre in Virginia. With particular mention of those men of note that suffered in that disaster.* London, 1622.

Brooks, P. N., ed. *Reformation Principle and Practice: Essays in Honour of A. G. Dickens.* London: Scolar Press, 1980.

Brotanek, Rudolf. *Die Englischen Maskenspiele.* Vienna and Leipzig, 1902.

Brown, Alexander. *The First Republic in America.* Boston, 1898.

———. *The Genesis of the United States.* 2 vols. London, 1890.

Brown, Cedric. *John Milton's Aristocratic Entertainments.* Cambridge: Cambridge UP, 1985.

Brown, Paul. " 'This thing of darkness I acknowledge mine': *The Tempest* and the discourse of colonialism." In Dollimore and Sinfield, eds., 48–71.

Browne, William. *Britannia's Pastorals.* London, 1613.

Bullen, Ripley P. "The First English Settlement on St. Lucia." *Caribbean Quarterly* 12.2 (June 1966): 29–35.

Burgess, Glenn. "On Revisionism: An Analysis of Early Stuart Historiography in the 1970s and 1980s," *The Historical Journal* 33.3 (1990): 609–27.

Butler, Martin. "Politics and the Masque: *The Triumph of Peace.*" *The Seventeenth Century* 2. n. 2 (July 1987): 117–41.

———. *Theatre and Crisis 1632–1642.* Cambridge: Cambridge UP, 1984.

Calendar of State Papers. *Venetian.* Ed. Allen B. Hinds. London: HMSO, 1911: vol. 16 (1610–13).

Campion, Thomas. *The Lords' Masque.* Ed. I. A. Shapiro. In Spencer and Wells, eds., 95–123.

Cervantes Saavedra, Miguel de. *Les Nouuelles de Miguel de Ceruantes Saavedra, tr. par F. de Rosset et le sr. d'Audiguier. Auec L'histoire de Ruis Dias, & de Quixaire princesse des Moluques, par le sieur de Bellan.* Paris, 1640.

Chamberlain, John. *The Letters of John Chamberlain.* Ed. N. E. McClure. 2 vols. Philadelphia: U of Pennsylvania P, 1939.

Chambers, E[dmund]. K[erchever]. *The Elizabethan Stage.* 4 vols. Oxford: Clarendon P, 1923.

———. *William Shakespeare: A Study of Facts and Problems.* Oxford: Clarendon P, 1930.

Chapman, George. *The Memorable Maske of the two Honorable Houses or Inns of Court; the Middle Temple, and Lyncolns Inne* (1613). Ed. G. Blakemore Evans. In *The Plays of George Chapman: The Comedies.* Gen. ed. Allan Holaday. Urbana: U of Illinois P, 1970. 557–94.

Chapman, George, Ben Jonson, and John Marston. *Eastward Hoe!* Herford and Simpson IV: 487–619.

Chaucer, Geoffrey. *The Wife of Bath's Tale.* In *The Riverside Chaucer.* 3rd edition. Ed. Larry D. Benson. Oxford: Oxford UP, 1988. 116–22.

Chaudhuri, Sukanta. *Renaissance Pastoral and Its English Development.* Oxford: Clarendon P, 1989.

Chelli, Maurice. *Étude sur la collaboration de Massinger avec Fletcher et son groupe.* Paris: U de Paris, 1926.

Chiappelli, Fredi, ed. *First Images of America: The Impact of the New World on the Old.* 2 vols. Berkeley: U of California P, 1976.

Chillington, Carol A. "Playwrights at Work: Henslowe's, Not Shakespeare's, *Book of Sir Thomas More.*" *English Literary Renaissance* 10.3 (Autumn 1980): 439–79.

Clare, Janet. *'Art made tongue-tied by authority': Elizabethan and Jacobean Dramatic Censorship.* Manchester: Manchester UP, 1990.

Clark, Katerina, and Michael Holquist. *Mikhail Bakhtin.* Cambridge, MA: Belknap P, 1984.

Clutterbuck, Robert. *The History and Antiquities of the County of Hertford.* 3 vols. London, 1815–1827.

Cokayne, Sir Aston. *A Chain of Golden Poems.* London, 1658.

Coleridge, Samuel Taylor. *Coleridge's Literary Criticism.* Ed. J. W. Mackail. Oxford: Oxford UP, 1908.

———. *Lectures 1808–1819: On Literature.* In 2 vols. Ed. R. A. Foakes. Vol. 5 in *The Collected Works of Samuel Taylor Coleridge.* London: Routledge, 1987 2: 147.

Collinson, Patrick. "Cranbrook and the Fletchers: Popular and Unpopular Religion in the Kentish Weald." In Brooks, ed., 171–202.

———. *Godly People.* London: Hambledon P, 1983.

Cooper, Helen. "The shape-shiftings of the Wife of Bath, 1395–1670." In *Chaucer Traditions: Studies in Honour of Derek Brewer.* Ed. Ruth Morse and Barry Windeatt. Cambridge: Cambridge UP, 1990. 168–84.

Corballis, R. P. "The 'Second Pen' in the Stage Version of *Sejanus.*" *Modern Philology* 76 (1979): 273–77.

Cotgrave, Randle. *A Dictionarie of the French and English Tongues.* London, 1611. Reprint. Menston: Scolar P, 1968.

Councell of Virginia. *A True Declaration of the estate of the Colonie in Virginia, With a confutation of such scandalous reports as haue tended to the disgrace of so worthy an enterprise.* London, 1610.

Crashaw, William. "A New-Yeeres Gift to Virginia": *A Sermon preached in London before the lord Lawarre, lord governour of Virginea.* London, 1610.

Craven, Wesley Frank. *The Dissolution of the Virginia Company: The Failure of a Colonial Experiment.* New York: Oxford UP, 1932.

Cressy, David. *Bonfires and Bells: National Memory and the Protestant Calendar in Elizabethan and Early Stuart England.* London: Weidenfeld and Nicolson, 1989.

Cross, Claire. *The Puritan Earl: the life of Henry Hastings, third Earl of Huntingdon, 1536–1595.* London: Macmillan, 1966.

Culliford, S. G. *William Strachey, 1572–1621.* Charlottesville: UP of Virginia, 1965.

Cust, Richard, and Ann Hughes, eds. *Conflict in Early Stuart England: Studies in Religion and Politics, 1603–1642.* London: Longman, 1989.

Danby, John F. *Poets on Fortune's Hill: Studies in Sidney, Shakespeare, and Beaumont and Fletcher.* London: Faber, 1952.

Dart, John. *The History and Antiquities of the Cathedral Church of Canterbury.* London, 1726.

Davies, Sir John. *The Poems of Sir John Davies.* Ed. Robert Krueger. Oxford: Clarendon P, 1975.

Davis, Richard Beale. *George Sandys: Poet-Adventurer.* London: Bodley Head, 1955.

De Bellan, Le Sieur. *Histoire Memorable de Dias Espagnol, et de Quixaire Princesse des Moluques, Tirée des Memoires des Indes, & composee par le sieur de Bellan.* From *Les Nouvelles de Migvel de Cervantes Saavedra ov sont contenves plvsievrs rares advantures.* Paris, 1640.

Dekker, Thomas. *The Dramatic Works of Thomas Dekker.* Ed. Fredson Bowers. 4 vols. Cambridge: Cambridge UP, 1953–1961.

DeMolen, Richard. "Richard Mulcaster and Elizabethan Pageantry." *Studies in English Literature* 14 (1974): 209–21.

Derrida, Jacques. *Of Grammatology.* Trans. Gayatri Chakravorty Spivak. Baltimore: Johns Hopkins UP, 1976.

D'Ewes, Sir Symonds. *The Journal of Sir Simonds D'Ewes: from the beginning of the London Parliament to the opening of the trial of the Earl of Strafford.* Ed. Wallace Notestein. New Haven: Yale UP, 1923.

Dictionary of National Biography. Ed. Sir Leslie Stephen and Sir Sidney Lee. London: Smith, Elder, & Co., 1908–9.

Dollimore, Jonathan. *Radical Tragedy: Religion, Ideology and Power in the Drama of Shakespeare and his Contemporaries.* Brighton: Harvester, 1984.

———. "Subjectivity, Sexuality, and Transgression: The Jacobean Connection." *Renaissance Drama* 17 (1986): 53–81.

Dollimore, Jonathan, and Alan Sinfield, eds. *Political Shakespeare: New Essays in Cultural Materialism.* Manchester: Manchester UP, 1985.

Donne, John. *The Complete English Poems.* Ed. A. J. Smith. Harmondsworth: Penguin, 1971. 236–38.

———. *The Satires, Epigrams and Verse Letters of John Donne.* Ed. W. Milgate. Oxford: Oxford UP, 1967.

Drakakis, John, ed. *Alternative Shakespeares.* London: Methuen, 1985.

Drayton, Michael. *The Works of Michael Drayton.* Ed. J. William Hebel. 5 vols. Oxford: Shakespeare Head P, 1931–41.

———. *Pastorals. Contayning Eglogues* (1619). Hebel 2: 515–73.

———. *Poemes Lyrick and Pastorall.* London, 1606.

———. *Poly-Olbion* (1612). Hebel 4.

————. Dryden, John, and William Davenant. *The Tempest: or, The Enchanted Island.* London, 1670.

Dudley, Edward, and Maximilian E. Novak, eds. *The Wild Man Within: An Image in Western Thought from the Renaissance to Romanticism.* Pittsburgh: U of Pittsburgh P, 1972.

Dyce, Rev. Alexander, ed. *The Works of Beaumont and Fletcher.* See under Beaumont, Francis, and John Fletcher.

Eddy, D. Mathis. "Melville's Response to Beaumont and Fletcher: A New Source for *The Encantadas.*" *American Literature* 40 (1968): 374–80.

Edwards, Philip, Gerald Eades Bentley, Kathleen McLuskie, and Lois Potter, eds. *The Revels History of Drama in English.* Vol. 4 (1613–1660). London: Methuen, 1981.

Field, Nathan, and John Fletcher. *Four Plays or Moral Representations in One.* Bowers 8: 223–344.

Field, Nathan, with John Fletcher and Philip Massinger. *The Honest Man's Fortune.* Glover and Waller 10: 202–80.

Finch, Mary E. *The Wealth of Five Northamptonshire Families 1540–1640.* Northamptonshire Record Society. Vol. 9. Oxford: Oxford UP, 1956.

Finkelpearl, Philip J. "Beaumont, Fletcher, and 'Beaumont and Fletcher': Some Distinctions." *English Literary Renaissance* 1 (1971): 144–64.

————. *Court and Country Politics in the Plays of Beaumont and Fletcher.* Princeton: Princeton UP, 1990.

————. "The Date of Beaumont and Fletcher's *The Noble Gentleman.*" *Notes and Queries* 24 (1977): 137–140.

————. "John Fletcher as Spenserian Playwright: *The Faithful Shepherdess* and *The Island Princess.*" *Studies in English Literature* 27 (1987): 285–302.

————. "The Role of the Court in the Development of Jacobean Drama." *Criticism* 24.2 (1982): 138–58.

Fleay, Frederick Gard. *A Biographical Chronicle of the English Drama, 1559–1642.* 2 vols. London, 1891.

Fletcher, Giles, Sr. *The English Works of Giles Fletcher, the Elder.* Ed. Lloyd E. Berry. Madison: U of Wisconsin P, 1964.

Fletcher, John. *Bonduca.* Ed. Cyrus Hoy. Bowers 4: 149–259.

————. *The Chances.* Ed. George Walton Williams. Bowers 4: 541–645.

————. *The Faithful Shepherdess.* Ed. Cyrus Hoy. Bowers 3: 483–612.

————. *The Faithful Shepherdess.* Ed. Florence Ada Kirk. New York: Garland, 1980.

————. *The faithfull shepheardesse.* London, 1610[?].

————. "A Hitherto Unpublished John Fletcher Autograph." [Ed.] Samuel J. Tannenbaum. *Journal of English and Germanic Philology* 28 (1929): 35–40.

————. *The Humorous Lieutenant.* Ed. Cyrus Hoy. Bowers 5: 289–440.

————. *The Humorous Lieutenant: A Critical Edition.* Ed. Philip Oxley. New York: Garland, 1987.

————. *The Island Princess.* Ed. George Walton Williams. Bowers 5:539–670.

————. *The Loyal Subject.* Ed. Fredson Bowers. Bowers 5: 151–88.

————. *The Mad Lover.* Ed. Robert K. Turner. Bowers 5: 1–149.

————. *Monsieur Thomas.* Ed. Hans Walter Gabler. Bowers 4: 415–540.

————. *The Pilgrim.* Ed. Cyrus Hoy. Bowers 6: 111–224.

————. *Rule a Wife and Have a Wife.* Ed. George Walton Williams. Bowers 6: 483–605.

————. *The Tragedy of Valentinian.* Ed. Robert K. Turner. Bowers 4: 261–414.

————. *A Wife for a Month.* Ed. Robert K. Turner. Bowers 6:355–482.

————. *The Wild-Goose Chase.* Ed. Fredson Bowers. Bowers 6:225–354.

————. *The Wild-Goose Chase.* London, 1652.

————. *A Critical Edition of John Fletcher's Comedy 'The Wild-Goose Chase.'* Ed. Rota Herzberg Lister. New York: Garland, 1980.

————. *Wit Without Money.* Ed. Hans Walter Gabler. Bowers 6: 1–109.

————. *Wit Without Money.* London, 1639.

————. *The Woman's Prize or The Tamer Tamed.* Ed. George Ferguson. The Hague: Mouton, 1966.

————. *The Woman's Prize.* Ed. Fredson Bowers. Bowers 4: 1–148.

————. *Women Pleased.* Ed. Hans Walter Gabler. Bowers 5:443–6.

Fletcher, John. Revised Francis Beaumont (?). *The Noble Gentleman.* Ed. L. A. Beaurline. Bowers 3: 113–223.

Fletcher, John. Revised Philip Massinger. *The Lovers' Progress.* Glover and Waller 5: 74–152.

Fletcher, John. Revised James Shirley. *The Night-Walker, or the Little Thief: A Comedy.* Ed. Cyrus Hoy. Bowers 7: 513–637.

Fletcher, John, and Francis Beaumont. Revised Philip Massinger (?). *Love's Cure.* Ed. George Walton Williams. Bowers 3: 1–112.

Fletcher, John, Francis Beaumont, and Philip Massinger. *The Tragedy of Thierry and Theodoret.* Ed. Robert K. Turner. Bowers 3: 363–481.

Fletcher, John, Nathan Field, and Philip Massinger. *The Knight of Malta.* Glover and Waller 7: 78–163.

————. *The Queen of Corinth.* Bowers 8: 1–111.

Fletcher, John, and Philip Massinger. *Beggars' Bush.* Ed. Fredson Bowers. Bowers 3: 225–362.

————. *The Custom of the Country.* Bowers 8: 633–758.

————. *The Double Marriage.* Waller 6:321–407.

————. *The Elder Brother: A Comedy.* Glover and Waller 2: 1–59.

————. *The False One.* Bowers 8: 113–221.

————. *The Little French Lawyer.* Waller 3: 372–454.

————. *The Prophetess: A Tragical History.* Waller 5: 320–389.

————. *The Sea Voyage.* Waller 9: 1–65.

————. *The Spanish Curate.* Glover and Waller 2: 60–145.

————. *The Tragedy of Sir John Van Olden Barnavelt.* Ed. Fredson Bowers. Bowers 8: 483–632.

————. *The Tragedy of Sir John Van Olden Barnavelt.* Ed. T. H. Howard-Hill. Oxford: Malone Society, 1980.

————. *The Tragedy of Sir John Van Olden Barnavelt: anonymous Elizabethan play edited from the manuscript.* Ed. Wilhelmina Frijlinck. Amsterdam, 1922.

————. *A Very Woman.* Ed. Hans Walter Gabler. Bowers 7: 639–743.

————. *A Very Woman.* Edwards and Gibson 4: 201–289.

Fletcher, John, and Philip Massinger, with George Chapman and Ben Jonson. *The Bloody Brother.* Waller 4: 246–313.

————. *Rollo, Duke of Normandy, or The Bloody Brother.* Ed. John D. Jump. Liverpool: Liverpool UP, 1969.

Fletcher, John, and William Rowley. *The Maid in the Mill.* Waller 7: 1–77.

Fletcher, John, and William Shakespeare. *All is True (Henry VIII).* Wells and Taylor, 1343–78.

————. *Henry VIII.* Ed. Fredson Bowers. Bowers 7: 1–144.

Fletcher, Phineas. *A Father's Testament.* London, 1670.

Foster, Joseph. *Alumni Oxonienses: The Members of the University of Oxford, 1500–1714.* Oxford, 1891.

Foucault, Michel. *The Order of Things: An Archaeology of the Human Sciences.* Trans. Alan Sheridan-Smith. London: Tavistock, 1966.

Foxe, John. *Actes and Monuments of matters most speciall and memorable, happenyng in the Church. Newly reuised and recognised.* 2 vols. London, 1583.

Frey, Charles. "*The Tempest* and the New World." *Shakespeare Quarterly* 30 (1979): 29–41.

Fuller, Thomas. *The Church-History of Britain: from the Birth of Jesus Christ Untill the Year M. DC. XLVIII.* London, 1655.

————. *The History of the Worthies of England.* London, 1662.

————. *The History of the Worthies of England.* Ed. John Nichols, 2 vols. London, 1811.

Furnivall, Frederick J., ed. *Ballads from Manuscripts.* 2 vols. London, 1868–1872.

Gasper, Julia. *The Dragon and the Dove: The Plays of Thomas Dekker.* Oxford: Clarendon P, 1990.

————. "The Protestant Plays of Thomas Dekker." D. Phil. thesis. University of Oxford, 1987.

Gay, Edwin F. "The Midland Revolt and the Inquisition of Depopulation of 1607." *Transactions of the Royal Historical Society,* n.s. 18 (1904): 195–244.

Gayley, Charles Mills. *Beaumont, the Dramatist.* New York: Russell and Russell, 1914.

Gibbs, Vicary, ed. *The Complete Peerage.* Vol. 3. London: St. Catherine P, 1913.

Godwin, Francis. *De Praesulibus Angliae Commentarius.* Cambridge, 1743.

Gossett, Suzanne. " 'Best Men are Molded out of Faults': Marrying the Rapist in Jacobean Drama." In Kinney and Collins, eds., 168–90.

————. "Masque Influence on the Dramaturgy of Beaumont and Fletcher." *Modern Philology* 69 (1972): 199–208.

————. "The Term 'Masque' in Shakespeare and Fletcher, and *The Coxcomb.*" *Studies in English Literature* 14 (1974): 285–95.

Gower, John. *Confessio Amantis.* In *The Complete Works of John Gower: The English Works.* Ed. G. C. Macaulay, 1: 74–86. Oxford: Clarendon P, 1901.

Greenblatt, Stephen J. "Learning to Curse: Aspects of Linguistic Colonialism in the Sixteenth Century." In Chiappelli, ed., 2: 561–80. Reprinted in Greenblatt. *Learning to Curse: Essays in Early Modern Culture.* New York: Routledge, 1990.

———. *Renaissance Self-Fashioning: from More to Shakespeare.* Chicago: U of Chicago P, 1980.

———. *Shakespearean Negotiations: The Circulation of Social Energy in Renaissance England.* Oxford: Clarendon P, 1988.

———., ed. *Representing the English Renaissance.* Berkeley: U of California P, 1988.

Greg, W[alter] W. *Pastoral Poetry and Pastoral Drama: a literary inquiry, with special reference to the pre-Restoration stage in England.* London: Bullen, 1906.

Grundy, Joan. *The Spenserian Poets.* London: Arnold, 1969.

Hakluyt, Richard. *The Principal Navigations Voyages Traffiques & Discoveries of the English Nation.* Ed. John Masefield. London: Dent, 1927.

———, ed. *The Principal Navigations, Voyages, Traffiques & Discoveries of the English Nation.* 12 vols. Glasgow, 1903–1905.

Hall, Joseph. *The discovery of a new world, or a description of the South Indies, by an English Mercury.* Trans. by J[ohn] H[ealey]. London, 1609.

———. *The Discovery of a New World.* Ed. Huntington Brown. Trans. John Healey. Cambridge, MA: Harvard UP, 1937.

[Hall, Joseph.] *Mundus alter et idem sive terra australis nuperrime lustrata auth: Mercurio Britannico.* London, 1608.

Hamor, Ralph. *A true discourse of the present estate of Virginia, till 18 June 1614.* London, 1615.

Hannay, Margaret Patterson, ed. *Silent But for the Word: Tudor Women as Patrons, Translators, and Writers of Religious Works.* Kent, Ohio: Kent State UP, 1985.

Hardin, Richard F. *Michael Drayton and the Passing of Elizabethan England.* Lawrence: UP of Kansas, 1973.

Harington, Sir John. *A Briefe View of the State of the Church of England, As it stood in Q. Elizabeths and King James his Reigne, to the Yeere 1608. Being a Character and History of the Bishops of those times.* London, 1653.

Hawk, Grace E. "England's Literary Debt to Spain." B. Litt. thesis. University of Oxford, 1954.

Hebel, J. William, ed. See Drayton, Michael. *The Works of Michael Drayton.*

Heinemann, Margot. *Puritanism and Theatre: Thomas Middleton and Opposition Drama under the Early Stuarts.* Cambridge: Cambridge UP, 1980.

Helgerson, Richard. *Forms of Nationhood: The Elizabethan Writing of England.* Chicago: U of Chicago P, 1992.

———. "The Land Speaks: Cartography, Chorography, and Subversion in Renaissance England." In Greenblatt, ed., 326–61.

Henderson, Katherine Usher, and Barbara F. McManus, eds. *Half Humankind: Contexts and Texts of the Controversy about Women, 1540–1640.* Urbana: U of Illinois P, 1985.

[Henslowe, Philip.] *Henslowe Papers: Being Documents Supplementary to Henslowe's Diary.* Ed. Walter W. Greg. London: A. H. Bullen, 1907.

Hensman, Bertha. "The Collaboration of Massinger and Fletcher." D. Phil. thesis. University of Oxford, 1960.

————. *The Shares of Fletcher, Field, and Massinger in 12 Plays of the Beaumont and Fletcher Canon.* 2 vols. *Jacobean Drama Studies* 6. Salzburg: Institut für Englische Sprache und Literatur, Universität Salzburg, 1974.

Herford. C. H., and Percy and Evelyn Simpson. *Ben Jonson.* See under Jonson, Ben.

Herrick, Marvin T. *Tragicomedy: Its Origin and Development in Italy, France, and England.* Urbana: U of Illinois P, 1955.

Hickman, Andrew J. "The Influence and Dramatic Use of the Masque in the Plays and Collaborations of John Fletcher." D. Phil. thesis. University of Oxford, 1986.

Hirst, Derek. "Court, Country, and Politics before 1629." In Sharpe, ed., 105–37.

Historical Manuscripts Commission. *Report on the Manuscripts of Lord Montagu of Beaulieu.* London: HM Stationery Office, 1900.

————. *Report on the Manuscripts of the late Reginald Rawdon Hastings, Esq.* Ed. Francis Bickley. 4 vols. London: HM Stationery Office, 1928–47.

————. *VIIIth Report of the Royal Commission on Historical manuscripts.* Appendix II (*Manuscripts of his Grace the Duke of Manchester*). Darlington: HM Stationery Office, 1881.

Hobbs, Mary. "A WS manuscript." *Times Literary Supplement,* June 10–16, 1988, 647.

Holaday, Allan, ed. *The Plays of George Chapman.* See under Chapman, George.

Honigmann, E. A. J. *The Stability of Shakespeare's Text.* London: Arnold, 1965.

Hope, Jonathan. "Applied historical linguistics: socio-historical linguistic evidence for the authorship of Renaissance plays." *Transactions of the Philological Society* (1990): 201–26.

————. "Socio-historical linguistic evidence for the authorship of Renaissance plays: test cases in the Shakespeare, Fletcher, and Massinger canons." Ph.D. dissertation. University of Cambridge, 1990. Under revision as *The Authorship of Shakespeare's Plays.* Cambridge: Cambridge UP, forthcoming.

Howard, Douglas, ed. *Philip Massinger: A Critical Reassessment.* Cambridge: Cambridge UP, 1985.

Howard-Hill, T. H. "Buc and the Censorship of *Sir John Van Olden Barnavelt* in 1619." *Review of English Studies* 39 (February 1988): 39–63.

Hoy, Cyrus. "Massinger as Collaborator: The Plays with Fletcher and Others." In Howard, ed., 51–82.

————. "The Shares of Fletcher and His Collaborators in the Beaumont and Fletcher Canon I–VII." *Studies in Bibliography* 8 (1956): 129–46; 9 (1957): 143–62; 11 (1958): 85–106; 12 (1959): 91–116; 13 (1960): 77–108; 14 (1961): 45–67; 15 (1962): 71–90.

Hulme, Peter. *Colonial Encounters: Europe and the Native Caribbean, 1492–1797.* London: Methuen, 1986.

————. "Hurricanes in the Caribbees: the Constitution of the Discourse of English Colonialism." In Barker et al., eds., 55–83.

Hunter, William B., ed. *The English Spenserians: The Poetry of Giles Fletcher,*

George Wither, Michael Drayton, Phineas Fletcher and Henry More. Salt Lake City: U of Utah P, 1977.

[Huntingdon]. *The Huntingdon Papers: The Archives of the Noble Family of Hastings.* London: Maggs, 1926.

Hutchinson, Lucy. *The Life of Colonel Hutchinson.* Ed. James Sutherland. London: Oxford UP, 1973.

James I, King of England. *The King's Maiesties Declaration to His Subjects, concerning lawfull Sports to be vsed.* London, 1618.

————. *The Political Works of James I.* Ed. Charles Howard McIlwain. Cambridge, MA: Harvard UP, 1918.

————. "A Proclamation for suppressing of persons riotously assembled for the laying open of Inclosures" (30 May 1607). *A Booke of Proclamations, published since the beginning of his Maiesties most happy Reigne ouer England, &c.* London, 1609. 139–40. Reprinted in Larkin and Hughes 1: 152–54.

————. "A Proclamation signifying his Maiesties gracious pardon for the Offendours about Inclosures" (24 July 1607). *A Booke of Proclamations.* 146–51. Reprinted in Larkin and Hughes 1: 161–62.

————. "A Proclamation signifying his Maiesties pleasure aswell for suppressing of riotous Assemblies about Inclosures, as for the reformation of Depopulations" (28 June 1607). *A Booke of Proclamations.* 141–42. Reprinted in Larkin and Hughes 1: 154–58.

Jeffrey, V. M. "Italian Influence in Fletcher's *Faithful Shepherdess.*" *Modern Language Review* 21 (1926): 147–58.

Jonson, Ben. *Ben Jonson.* Ed. C. H. Herford and Percy and Evelyn Simpson. 11 vols. Oxford: Clarendon P, 1925–1952.

————. *News from the New World Discover'd in the Moon.* Herford and Simpson 7: 701–29.

————. *Sejanus His Fall.* Ed. Philip J. Ayres. Manchester: Manchester UP, 1990.

————. *Sejanus His Fall.* London, 1605.

————. *Timber: or, Discoveries.* Herford and Simpson 8: 555–649.

————. *Volpone or the foxe.* London, 1607.

Kay, Dennis. "Poems by Sir Walter Aston, and a Date for the Donne/Goodyer Verse Epistle 'Alternis Vicibus.'" *Review of English Studies* 37 (1986): 198–210.

Kingsbury, Susan Myra, ed. *The Records of the Virginia Company of London.* 4 vols. Washington: Library of Congress, 1906–35.

Kinney, Arthur F., and Dan S. Collins, eds. *Renaissance Historicism: Selections from English Literary Renaissance.* Amherst: U of Massachusetts P, 1987.

Knowles, James. "Pious Patronage: the fifth Earl of Huntington." Unpublished paper, 1990.

————. "WS MS." *Times Literary Supplement,* 29 April 1988, 472, 485.

Koeppel, Emil. *Quellen-Studien zu den Dramen Ben Jonson's . . . und Beaumont's und Fletcher's.* Munich, 1895.

Koestenbaum, Wayne. *Double Talk: The erotics of male literary collaboration.* London: Routledge, 1989.

Lamb, Charles. "Old China." In *The Works of Charles and Mary Lamb*. Vol. 2: *Elia and the Last Essays of Elia*. Ed. E. V. Lucas, 281–86. London: Methuen, 1912.

Langbaine, Gerard. *An Account of the English Dramatic Poets*. Oxford, 1691.

Langdale, Abram Barnett. *Phineas Fletcher: Man of Letters, Science and Divinity*. New York: Columbia UP, 1937.

Lanyer, Æmilia. *Salve Devs Rex Ivdæorvm*. London, 1611.

Larkin, James F., and Paul L. Hughes, eds. *Stuart Royal Proclamations*. Vol. 1: *Royal Proclamations of King James I, 1603–1625*. Oxford: Clarendon P, 1973.

Leech, Clifford. *The John Fletcher Plays*. London: Chatto, 1962.

Leonardo de Argensola, Bartholomé Juan. *Conquista de las Islas Malucas*. Madrid, 1609.

Levi, Peter. *A Private Commission: New Verses by Shakespeare*. London: Macmillan, 1988.

Lindley, David, ed. *The Court Masque*. Manchester: Manchester UP, 1984.

Loomba, Ania. *Gender, Race, Renaissance Drama*. Manchester: Manchester UP, 1989.

Lytle, Guy Fitch, and Stephen Orgel, eds. *Patronage in the Renaissance*. Princeton: Princeton UP, 1981.

Mabbe, James. *The Rogue, or The Life of Guzmán de Alfarache, Written in Spanish by Matheo Alemán*. London, 1622.

McIlwraith, A. K. "The Life and Works of Philip Massinger." D. Phil. thesis. University of Oxford, 1931.

MacKeithan, Daniel M. *The Debt to Shakespeare in the Beaumont-and-Fletcher Plays*. Austin, TX: privately printed, 1938.

McLuskie, Kathleen. *Renaissance Dramatists: Feminist Readings*. Hemel Hempstead: Harvester Wheatsheaf, 1989.

McMullan, Gordon, and Jonathan Hope, eds. *The Politics of Tragicomedy: Shakespeare and After*. London: Routledge, 1992.

Maguire, Nancy Klein, ed. *Renaissance Tragicomedy: Explorations in Genre and Politics*. New York: AMS Press, 1987.

Malcolm, Noel. "Hobbes, Sandys, and the Virginia Company." *The Historical Journal* 24.2 (1981): 297–321.

Manning, Roger B. *Village Revolts: Social Protest and Popular Disturbances in England, 1509–1640*. Oxford: Clarendon P, 1988.

Mannoni, Otare. *Prospero and Caliban: The Psychology of Colonization*. Trans. Pamela Powseland. London: Methuen, 1956.

Marcus, Leah S. *The Politics of Mirth: Jonson, Herrick, Milton, Marvell, and the Defense of Old Holiday Pastimes*. Chicago: U of Chicago P, 1986.

———. *Puzzling Shakespeare: Local Reading and Its Discontents*. Berkeley: U of California P, 1988.

Marlowe, Christopher. *Tamburlaine*. Ed. Fredson Bowers. *The Complete Works of Christopher Marlowe*. Cambridge: Cambridge UP, 1973. 1: 71–252.

Marston, John. "The *ho^ble*: Lorde & Lady of Huntingdons Entertainment of theire right Noble Mother Alice: Countesse Dowager of Darby the firste nighte of her honors arrivall att the house of Ashby." In *Poems of John Marston*. In Davenport, ed., 189–207.

————. *The Poems of John Marston*. Ed. Arnold Davenport. Liverpool: Liverpool UP, 1961.

Martin, John E. *Feudalism to Capitalism: Peasant and Landlord in English Agrarian Development*. London: Macmillan, 1983.

Marvell, Andrew. *The Poems and Letters of Andrew Marvell*. Ed. H. M. Margoliouth. Revised by Pierre Legouis with E. E. Duncan-Jones. Oxford: Clarendon P, 1971.

A Maske presented on Candlemas nighte at Cole-overton by the Earle of Essex, the Lorde Willobie, Sr Tho. Beaumont, &c. In Rudolf Brotanek, *Die Englischen Maskenspiele*. Vienna and Leipzig, 1902. 328–37.

Massinger, Philip. *The Plays and Poems of Philip Massinger*. Ed. Philip Edwards and Colin Gibson. 5 vols. Oxford: Clarendon P, 1976.

————. "Two Poems of Philip Massinger." [Ed.] Percy Simpson. *The Athenaeum*. 8 September 1906, 273–74.

Massinger, Philip, and Thomas Dekker. *The Virgin Martyr*. In *The Dramatic Works of Thomas Dekker*. Ed. Fredson Bowers, 3: 365–480.

Massinger, Philip, John Webster, and John Ford, with John Fletcher. *The Fair Maid of the Inn*. Glover and Walter 9: 143–219.

Masten, Jeffrey A. "Beaumont and/or Fletcher: Collaboration and the Interpretation of Renaissance Drama." *English Literary History* 59 (1992): 337–56.

Masters, Robert. *The History of the College of Corpus Christi in the University of Cambridge*. 2 vols. London, 1753.

Matthews, Brander. *With My Friends: Tales Told in Partnership, with an Introductory Essay on the Art and Mystery of Collaboration*. London: Longmans, 1891.

Maxwell, Baldwin. *Studies in Beaumont, Fletcher, and Massinger*. Chapel Hill: U of North Carolina P, 1939.

Mayhew, Graham. *Tudor Rye*. Falmer: Centre for Continuing Education, U of Sussex, 1987.

Melville, Herman. "Barrington Isle and the Buccaneers." *Putnam's Monthly Magazine* 3 (April 1854): 346–47.

Middleton, Thomas. *A Game at Chess*. Ed. J. W. Harper. London: Ernest Benn, 1966.

Miles, Rosalind. *Ben Jonson: His Life and Work*. London: RKP, 1986.

Milton, John. *A Masque presented at Ludlow Castle*. In *John Milton: Complete Shorter Poems*. Ed. John Carey. 168–229. London: Longman, 1968.

————. *Works*. Ed. Frank A. Patterson. 18 vols. New York: Columbia UP, 1931–38.

Miner, Earl. "The Wild Man through the Looking Glass." In Dudley and Novak, eds., 87–114.

Montrose, Louis Adrian. " 'Eliza, Queene of Shepheardes,' and the Pastoral of Power." *English Literary Renaissance* 10 (1980): 153–82.

More, Thomas. *Utopia*. Trans. Paul Turner. Harmondsworth: Penguin, 1961.

Morley, Thomas. *Cantvs Madrigales. The Triumphs of Oriana, to 5 and 6 voices: composed by diuers seuerall aucthors*. London, 1601.

Moryson, Fynes. *Itinerary*. London, 1617.

Murray, John Tucker. *English Dramatic Companies, 1558–1642*. 2 vols. London: Constable, 1910.

Neal, Daniel. *The History of the Puritans or Protestant Non-Conformists, from the Reformation under King Henry VIII to the Act of Toleration under King William and Queen Mary*. 2nd ed. 2 vols. London, 1754.

Neill, Edward D. *The English Colonization of America During the Seventeenth Century*. London, 1871.

————. *History of the Virginia Company of London*. Albany, NY, 1869.

Newdigate, Bernard H. *Michael Drayton and his Circle*. Oxford: Shakespeare Head P, 1941.

Nichols, John. *The History and Antiquities of the County of Leicester*. 4 vols. London, 1795–1815.

————. *The Progresses, Processions, and Magnificent Festivities of King James the First*. 4 vols. London, 1828.

Nicoll, Allardyce. *Stuart Masques and the Renaissance Stage*. London: Harrap, 1937.

Nicoll, John. *An Houre Glass of Indian News or A True and tragicall discourse, shewing the most lamentable miseries, and distressed Calamities indured by 67 Englishmen, which were sent for a supply to the planting in Guiana in the yeare. 1605. Who not finding the saide place, were for want of victuall, left ashore in Saint Lucia, an Island of Caniballs, or Men-eaters in the West-Indyes*. London, 1607. Ed. Rev. C. Jesse. *Caribbean Quarterly* 12.1 (March 1966): 46–67.

Norbrook, David. "Panegyric of the Monarch and its Social Context under Elizabeth I and James I." D. Phil. thesis. University of Oxford, 1978.

————. *Poetry and Politics in the English Renaissance*. London: RKP, 1984.

————. "The Reformation of the Masque." In Lindley, ed., 94–110.

————" 'What cares these roarers for the name of king?': language and utopia in *The Tempest*." In McMullan and Hope, eds., 21–54.

Norbrook, David, with Henry Woudhuysen, eds. *Penguin Book of Renaissance Verse*. Harmondsworth: Penguin, 1992.

Oliphant, E. H. C. *The Plays of Beaumont and Fletcher: An Attempt to Determine their Respective Shares and the Shares of Others*. New Haven: Yale UP, 1927.

Orgel, Stephen. *The Illusion of Power: Political Theater in the English Renaissance*. Berkeley: U of California P, 1975.

————. *The Jonsonian Masque*. Cambridge, MA: Harvard UP, 1965.

————. "Prospero's Wife." *Representations* 8 (1985): 1–13.

Orgel, Stephen, and Roy Strong. *Inigo Jones: The Theatre of the Stuart Court*. 2 vols. London: Sotheby Parke Bernet; Berkeley: U of California P, 1973.

Osgood, Herbert L. *The American Colonies in the Seventeenth Century*. Vol. 1, *The Proprietary Province in its Earliest Form; The Corporate Colonies of New England*. 1904; New York: Columbia UP, 1930.

Parker, L. A. "The Agrarian Revolution at Cotesbach 1501–1612." *Transactions of the Leicestershire Archaeological Society* 24 (1948): 41–77.

Parliament, Houses of. *Journals of the House of Commons*. Vol. 1: 1547–1628. London, 1803.

Patterson, Annabel. *Censorship and Interpretation: The Conditions of Writing and Reading in Early Modern England*. Madison: U of Wisconsin P, 1984.

————. *Pastoral and Ideology: Virgil to Valéry*. Berkeley: U of California P, 1988.

————. *Shakespeare and the Popular Voice*. Oxford: Blackwell, 1989.

Pearl, Sarah. "Sounding to present occasions: Jonson's masques of 1620–25." In Lindley, ed., 60–77.

Pearse, Nancy Cotton. *John Fletcher's Chastity Plays: Mirrors of Modesty.* Lewisburg: Bucknell UP, 1973.

Peckard, Peter. *Memoirs of the Life of Mr. Nicholas Ferrar.* Cambridge, MA, 1790.

Pestell, Thomas. *The Poems of Thomas Pestell.* Ed. Hannah Buchan. Oxford: Blackwell, 1940.

Pettet, E. C. "*Coriolanus* and the Midlands Insurrection of 1607." *Shakespeare Survey* 3 (1950): 34–42.

A pleasant conceited historie, called The taming of a shrew. London, 1594.

Plutarch. *The Lives of the Noble Grecians and Romanes compared together by that Grave Learned Philosopher and Historiographer Plutarke of Chœronea. Translated out of Greeke into French by James Amyot . . . and out of French into English by Thomas North.* London, 1579.

Pollard, A. W., and G. R. Redgrave. *A Short-Title Catalogue of Books Printed in England, Scotland, & Ireland and of English Books Printed Abroad, 1475–1640.* 2nd ed. Revised by W. A. Jackson, F. S. Ferguson, and Katherine F. Pantzer. 2 vols. London: Bibliographical Society, 1986.

Potter, Lois. "Topicality or politics? *The Two Noble Kinsmen,* 1613–1634." In McMullan and Hope, eds., 77–91.

Purchas, Samuel. *Hakluytus Postumus: or Purchas His Pilgrimes: Contayning a History of the World in Sea Voyages and Lande Travells by Englishmen and others.* 20 vols. Glasgow: James Maclehose and Sons, 1905–1907.

————. *Virginia's Verger; Or a Discourse shewing the benefits which may grow to this Kingdome from American English Plantations, and specially those of Virginia and Summer Ilands.* In Purchas 19: 218–67.

Puttenham, George. *The Arte of English Poesie.* Ed. Gladys Doidge Willcock and Alice Walker. Cambridge: Cambridge UP, 1936.

Quarles, Francis. *The Complete Works in Prose and Verse of Francis Quarles.* Ed. Alexander B. Grosart. 3 vols. London, 1880.

Quinn, David B., ed. *New American World: A Documentary History of North America to 1612.* 5 vols. New York: Hector Bye, 1979.

Reed, John Curtis. "Humphrey Moseley, publisher." *Oxford Bibliographical Society: Proceedings and Papers* 2.1 (1928): 57–142.

Riggs, David. *Ben Jonson: A Life.* Cambridge, MA: Harvard UP, 1987.

Ristine, Frank Humphrey. *English Tragicomedy: Its Origin and History.* New York: Columbia UP, 1910.

Rowland, R. C. "The Plays of John Fletcher: A Critical Study." D. Phil. dissertation. University of Oxford, 1955.

Russell, P. E. "A Stuart Hispanist: James Mabbe." *Bulletin of Hispanic Studies* 30 (1953): 75–84.

Sandys, E[dward] S[eton]. *History of the Family of Sandys.* Vol. 1. Barrow-in-Furness, 1930.

Sandys, George. *The Humanist as Traveler: George Sandys's 'Relation of a Journey begun An. Dom. 1610.'* Ed. Jonathan Haynes. London: Associated University Presses, 1986.

Savage, James E. "The Date of Beaumont and Fletcher's *Cupid's Revenge*." *ELH* 15 (1948): 286–94.

———. "The 'gaping wounds' in the text of *Philaster*." *Philological Quarterly* 28 (1949): 443–58.

Schwartz, Murray M., and Coppélia Kahn, eds. *Representing Shakespeare: New Psychoanalytic Essays*. Baltimore: Johns Hopkins UP, 1980.

Sedgwick, Eve Kosofsky. *Between Men: English Literature and Male Homosocial Desire*. New York: Columbia UP, 1985.

Shakespeare, William. *The Complete Works*. Gen. Eds. Stanley Wells and Gary Taylor. Oxford: Clarendon P, 1986.

———. *Antony and Cleopatra*. Wells and Taylor, 1127–66.

———. *Coriolanus*. Ed. Philip Brockbank. London: Methuen, 1976.

———. *Coriolanus*. Wells and Taylor, 1199–1239.

———. *The First Part of King Henry the Fourth*. Ed. A. R. Humphreys. London: Methuen, 1960.

———. *King Henry VIII*. Ed. R. A. Foakes. Arden edition. London: Methuen, 1957; "reprinted with minor corrections 1964."

———. *Measure for Measure*. Wells and Taylor, 893–924.

———. *A Midsummer Night's Dream*. Ed. Harold F. Brooks. London: Methuen, 1979.

———. *A Midsummer Night's Dream*. Wells and Taylor, 351–76.

———. *Othello*. Wells and Taylor, 925–64.

———. *Pericles*. Ed. F. D. Hoeniger. London: Methuen, 1963.

———. *Pericles*. Wells and Taylor, 1167–98.

———. *The Taming of the Shrew*. Ed. Brian Morris. London: Methuen, 1981.

———. *The Taming of the Shrew*. Ed. H. J. Oliver. Oxford: Oxford UP, 1984.

———. *The Taming of the Shrew*. Wells and Taylor, 29–61.

———. *The Tempest*. Ed. Stephen Orgel. Oxford: Oxford UP, 1987.

———. *The Tempest*. Wells and Taylor, 1315–40.

———. *The Tragedy of King Lear*. Wells and Taylor, 1063–98.

Shakespeare, William, and John Fletcher. *The Two Noble Kinsmen*. Ed. Eugene M. Waith. Oxford: Oxford UP, 1989.

———. *The Two Noble Kinsmen*. Ed. Fredson Bowers. Bowers 7: 145–298.

———. *The Two Noble Kinsmen*. Ed. Richard Proudfoot. London: Arnold, 1970.

———. *The Two Noble Kinsmen*. Wells and Taylor, 1379–1414.

Sharpe, Kevin, ed. *Faction and Parliament: Essays on Early Stuart History*. Oxford: Clarendon P, 1978.

Shepherd, Simon. *Amazons and Warrior Women: Varieties of Feminism in Seventeenth Century Drama*. Brighton: Harvester, 1981.

———. *The Women's Sharp Revenge: Five Women's Pamphlets from the Renaissance*. London: Fourth Estate, 1985.

Sidney, Sir Philip. *An Apology for Poetry*. Ed. Geoffrey Shepherd. Manchester: Manchester UP, 1973.

———. *The Countess of Pembroke's Arcadia (The Old Arcadia)*. Ed. Katherine Duncan-Jones. Oxford: Oxford UP, 1985.

Skura, Meredith Anne. "Discourse and the Individual: The Case of Colonialism in *The Tempest*," *Shakespeare Quarterly* 40 (1989): 42–69.

[Spencer, Terence John Bew, and Stanley Wells, eds.] *A Book of Masques in Honour of Allardyce Nicoll.* Cambridge: Cambridge UP, 1967.

Spenser, Edmund. *The Faerie Queene Book Five.* Ed. Ray Heffner. *The Works of Edmund Spenser: A Variorum Edition.* Ed. Edwin Greenlaw et al. Baltimore: Johns Hopkins UP, 1936.

Spinrad, Phoebe S. "James Shirley: Decadent or Realist?" *English Language Notes* 25.4 (June 1988): 24–32.

Stallybrass, Peter, and Allon White. *The Politics and Poetics of Transgression.* London: Methuen, 1986.

Stillinger, Jack. *Multiple Authorship and the Myth of Solitary Genius.* New York: Oxford UP, 1991.

Stith, Rev. William. *History of the First Discovery and Settlement of Virginia.* Williamsburg, VA, 1747.

Stoudt, John Baer. *Nicolas Martiau: The Adventurous Huguenot, the military engineer and the earliest American ancestor of George Washington.* Morristown, PA: Morristown P, 1932.

Stow, John. *Annales, or A Generall Chronicle of England.* London, 1600.

———. *Annales, or A Generall Chronicle of England.* Augmented by Edmund Howes. London, 1631.

Strachey, William. *A true reportory of the wracke, and redemption of Sir Thomas Gates Knight; upon, and from the Ilands of the Bermudas: his comming to Virginia, and the estate of that Colonie then, and after, under the government of the Lord La Warre, July 15. 1610.* Purchas 19: 5–72.

Strong, Roy. "The Popular Celebration of the Accession Day of Queen Elizabeth I." *Journal of the Warburg and Courtauld Institutes* 21 (1958): 86–103.

———. "Queen Elizabeth I as Oriana." *Studies in the Renaissance* 6 (1959): 251–60.

Strype, John. *Annals of the Reformation.* London, 1728.

———. *Life and Acts of the Most Reverend Father in God, John Whitgift, D. D.* 4 vols. London, 1718.

Taunton, Nina. "Did John Fletcher the Playwright Go to University?" *Notes and Queries* 235. 2 (June 1990): 170–72.

Teissedou, Jean-Pierre. "*The Prophetess* de John Fletcher (1579–1625): Puissance de la magie ou magie de la puissance?" In *La Magie et ses Langages,* ed. Margaret Jones-Davies. Lille: U de Lille, 1980.

Thorndike, Ashley H. *The Influence of Beaumont and Fletcher on Shakspere.* Worcester, MA: Oliver Wood, 1901.

Todorov, Tzvetan. *The Conquest of America: The Question of the Other.* Trans. Richard Howard. New York: Harper, 1984.

———. *Mikhail Bakhtin: The Dialogical Principle.* Trans. Wlad Godzich. Minneapolis: U of Minnesota P, 1984.

Tomlinson, Sophie. " 'She that plays the King': Henrietta Maria and the threat of the actress in Caroline culture." In McMullan and Hope, eds., 189–207.

Tricomi, Albert. *Anticourt Drama in England, 1603–1642*. Charlottesville: UP of Virginia, 1989.

Tymms, Samuel, ed. *The East Anglian*. Vol. 3. London, 1869.

Vaughan, Alden T., and Virginia Mason Vaughan. *Shakespeare's Caliban: A Cultural History*. Cambridge: Cambridge UP, 1991.

Vautor, Thomas. *The First Set: beeing Songs of diuers Ayres and Natures*. London, 1619.

Venn, John, and J. A. Venn, eds. *Alumni Cantabrigienses: A Biographical list of all known students, graduates, and holders of office at the University of Cambridge, from the earliest times to 1900*. Cambridge: Cambridge UP, 1922.

Waith, Eugene M. "Mad Lovers, Vainglorious Soldiers." *Research Opportunities in Renaissance Drama* 27 (1984): 13–19.

———. *The Pattern of Tragicomedy in Beaumont and Fletcher*. New Haven: Yale UP, 1952.

Wallis, Lawrence B. *Fletcher, Beaumont & Company: Entertainers to the Jacobean Gentry*. Morningside Heights, NY: King's Crown P, 1947.

Wells, Stanley, and Gary Taylor, eds. *The Complete Works*. See under Shakespeare, William.

Whitaker, Alexander. *Good newes from Virginia. Sent to the counsell and company of Virginia*. London, 1613.

White, Hayden. *Tropics of Discourse: Essays in Cultural Criticism*. Baltimore: Johns Hopkins UP, 1978.

Wickham, Glynne. " 'The Two Noble Kinsmen' or 'A Midsummer Night's Dream, Part II'?" In *Elizabethan Theatre*, 7. Ed. G. R. Hibbard. London: Macmillan, 1980. 167–96.

Wilbraham, Sir Roger. "The Journal of Sir Roger Wilbraham . . . For the Years 1593–1616." In *The Camden Miscellany*. Vol. 10. Ed. Harold Spencer Scott. London, 1902. 3–129.

Wilkinson, Robert. *Lots Wife. A Sermon preached at Pavles Crosse*. London, 1607.

———. *The Merchant Royall. A Sermon preached at White-Hall before the Kings Maiestie, at the Nuptials of the Right Honourable the Lord Hay and his Lady, vpon the Twelfe day last being Ianuar. 6. 1607*. London, 1607.

———. *A Paire of Sermons svccessively preacht to a paire of Peereless and succeeding Princes. The Former as an Ante-Fvnerall to the late Prince Henry, Anno Dom. 1612. October 25. The first day of his last and fatall sicknesse. The Latter preacht this present yeere 1614. Ianuar. 16. To the now liuing Prince Charles, as a preseruer of his life, and life to his Soule*. London, 1614.

———. *A Sermon preached at North-Hampton the 21. of Iune last past, before the Lord Lieutenant of the County, and the rest of the Commissioners there assembled vpon occasion of the late Rebellion and Riots in those parts committed*. London, 1607.

[Wilmot, J.]. *Valentinian: A Tragedy. As 'tis Alter'd by the late Earl of Rochester*. London, 1685.

Wilson, Arthur. *The History of Great Britain*. London, 1653.

Wilson, Edward M. "Did John Fletcher read Spanish?" *Philological Quarterly* 27 (1948): 187–90.

Wodenoth, Arthur. *A Short Collection of the Most Remarkable Passages from the originall to the dissolution of the Virginia Company.* London, 1651.

Womack, Peter. *Ben Jonson.* Oxford: Blackwell, 1986.

Wotton, Sir Henry. *The Life and Letters of Sir Henry Wotton.* Ed. Logan Pearsall Smith. 2 vols. Oxford: Clarendon P, 1907.

Wright, Louis Booker, ed. *The Elizabethans' America: A Collection of Early Reports by Englishmen on the New World.* London: Arnold, 1965.

Yoch, James J. "The Renaissance Dramatization of Temperance: the Italian Revival of Tragicomedy and *The Faithful Shepherdess.*" In Maguire, ed., 114–38.

Yoklavich, John. "Donne and the Countess of Huntingdon." *Philological Quarterly* 43 (1964): 283–88.

Zagorin, Perez. *The Court and the Country: The Beginnings of the English Revolution.* London: RKP, 1969.

INDEX

absolutism, 35, 132, 260, 262
Adams, Simon, 200
agency, xii, 35
Aléman, Matheo, 257
Alice, dowager countess of Derby, 17, 54, 64, 70, 194–95, 280, 290 n
Archer, Gabriel, 211
Aristophanes, 157–59, 162, 165–66, 175
Ashby-de-la-Zouche, xi, 15–18, 21, 22, 24, 25, 29–32, 35, 47, 54, 63, 110, 132, 194, 200, 204, 239, 255
Aston, Sir Walter, 15, 16, 57, 60, 62, 63, 64
Aubrey, John, 140

Bacon, Francis, 236
Baker, Sir Richard, 9
Bakhtin, Mikhail, 155, 298 n
Beaumont, Francis, ix, xi, xii, 11, 12, 15, 21, 33, 35, 37, 60, 63, 64, 72, 110, 114, 134, 143, 152; *The Knight of the Burning Pestle,* 259, 260, 261; *Masque of the Inner Temple and Gray's Inn,* 15, 32, 100–102, 213, 221; "Salmacis and Hermaphroditus," 16
Beaumont, Francis, and John Fletcher: *The Captain,* 143, 310; *The Coxcomb,* 160–61; *Cupid's Revenge,* 57, 94, 143; *A King and No King,* 143; *Love's Cure,* 135, 150–54, 156, 300–301 nn; *Love's Pilgrimage,* 259; *The Maid's Tragedy,* 86, 92–94, 143, 174; *The Noble Gentleman,* 135, 259; *Philaster,* 110–15, 143, 194; *The Scornful Lady,* 79; *The Woman Hater,* 12, 13, 14, 57, 86, 88–92, 143, 161, 260, 277–78 n, 294 n
Beaumont, Henry (Francis's brother), 11
Beaumont, Sir John (Francis's brother), 11, 16, 63, 64, 71, 72
Beaumont, Sir Thomas, 15, 18, 29, 33, 65, 72, 203–4
Bellan, Le Sieur de, 224, 227, 230
Bentley, G. E., 132, 142, 153
Berkenhead, Sir John, 140, 146, 147
Blackfriars theater, 35
Blewitt, Benjamin, 205, 206
Bodley, Sir Josias, 44
Book of Sports, The, 120–26, 188–89
Bowers, Fredson, 148–49
Bridgewater, earl of, 195–96
Bristol, 8
Brome, Richard, 16
Brown, Paul, 212, 223
Browne, William, 56
Buc, Sir George, Master of the Revels, 87, 88, 93, 94
Buckingham, duke of, 34, 200
Burre, Walter, 261
Burrows, William, 72

Cadiz, 258
Calvinism, 7, 8, 66, 68
Cambridge, 1, 4, 5, 8, 11
Campion, Thomas, 100
carnival, 80, 122, 123, 127, 131, 162
Castlehaven, earl of, 195–96
Catholicism, 4, 8, 96
Cave, Sir Thomas, 24, 26
Cecil, Lord Treasurer, 10, 12, 56, 89

Cervantes Saavedra, Miguel de, 169, 258–61
Chambers, E. K., 137, 153
Chapman, George, 17, 60, 61, 62, 100, 105, 106, 213–15, 217, 221; *The Memorable Maske of the Middle Temple and Lyncolns Inne*, 105, 213–15, 218
Charles I, king of England, 64
Chesterfield, earl of. *See* Stanhope, Philip
Cinque Ports, ix, 6, 7
Clare, Janet, 94, 113
Cokayne, Sir Aston, 143–44
Coke, Sir Edward, 46
Coleorton, 16, 29, 30, 31, 32, 35, 72, 156, 160, 194, 283 n
Coleridge, Samuel Taylor, 137, 146
collaboration, x, xi, xii, 12, 21, 32, 87, 88, 92, 95, 132–55, 260, 262, 295 n, 300–301 nn
Collinson, Patrick, 1, 2, 4
Corpus Christi College, Cambridge (Bene't College), 4, 5, 11
Cotesbach, 41, 42, 65, 82
Cotton, Charles, 143
Cotton, Sir Robert, 65
country, 21, 24, 30, 34, 35, 55, 70, 83, 110–31, 187–91, 194, 297 n
Coventry, 37
Cranbrook, 1, 2, 4, 5, 6, 7, 8, 14, 17
Crashaw, William, 207, 208
Cumberland, countess of, 34

Daborne, Robert, 133, 141
Daniel, Samuel, 56
Danvers, Sir John, 202
Davenant, William, 241
Davies, Lady Eleanor, 196
Davies, Sir John, 9
Dekker, Thomas, 33, 141
Devereux family, 41, 42
Devereux, Lady Frances, 30
Devereux, Robert, earl of Essex, 12, 42, 258

Digges, Sir Dudley, 201, 202
Digges, Leonard, 257
Dollimore, Jonathan, 53, 149–53
Donne, John, 27, 28, 63
Drayton, Michael, 16, 56, 57, 62, 63, 70, 71, 99
Dryden, John, 241
Dyce, Alexander, 106

Edwards, Philip, 221
Elizabeth (née Stuart), queen of Bohemia, 15, 26, 32, 56, 99, 112, 194, 200, 213, 215
Elizabeth I, queen of England, 2, 5, 7, 9, 10, 23, 32, 67, 103, 186, 192–96, 199
Essex, earl of. *See* Devereux, Robert
Exeter, earl of, 48

feminocentrism, 32, 35, 196
Ferrar, John, 202, 205
Ferrar, Nicholas, 202
festivity, 42, 58, 67, 120–31
Field, Nathan, 60, 105, 133, 134, 141, 215–16
Finkelpearl, Philip, 36, 57, 60, 67, 70, 111
Fletcher (née Baker), Mary (step-mother), 9
Fletcher (née Holland), Elizabeth (mother), 5, 8
Fletcher, Giles senior (uncle), 1, 2, 8, 11–13, 20, 56
Fletcher, Giles junior (cousin), 56
Fletcher, John: birth, ix, 1, 5, 6, 7; at Cambridge, 11; childhood, 6–11; patronage, xi, xii, 1–36; possible authorship of Coleorton masque, 30, 32, 35; response to Midlands revolts, 54–84; verse-letter to fifth countess of Huntingdon, 17–22, 27–29, 72, 114; work as negotiation between country and London, 24, 35; work with Beaumont, 12, 14, 87–99. Works: *Bonduca*, 95, 294 n; *The Chances*, 259; *The Faith-*

ful Shepherdess, ix, 15, 17, 34, 55–
70, 94, 183, 185, 190–96, 221,
261, 289 n; *The Humorous Lieutenant,* 172–74; *The Island Princess,*
198, 222, 224–35, 254, 259; *The
Lovers' Progress,* 142; *Monsieur
Thomas,* 123–24; *The Night-
Walker,* 76; *The Pilgrim,* 176–81,
183, 185, 191–92, 194, 259;
Rule a Wife And Have a Wife, 207,
259; *Valentinian,* 95–98, 170–72;
A Wife for a Month, 174–75; *The
Wild-Goose Chase,* 134, 162, 164–
65, 167–70, 182–83, 235, 259,
260; *Wit Without Money,* 71–84,
123, 260, 292; *The Woman's Prize,*
123–25, 143, 157–60, 162–66,
175–76, 181, 260; *Women Pleased,*
85, 126–31, 156, 166, 178, 185,
235, 260
Fletcher, John, and Nathan Field,
Four Plays, 103, 106, 198, 215–22
Fletcher, John, Nathan Field, and
Philip Massinger: *The Knight of
Malta,* 142; *The Queen of Corinth,*
142, 144, 259
Fletcher, John, and Philip Massinger:
Beggars' Bush, 106–8, 114, 127,
144, 259, 295–96 nn; *The Custom
of the Country,* 142, 259; *The Double
Marriage,* 142, 144, 182, 259; *The
Elder Brother,* 144; *The False One,*
142, 144; *The Little French Lawyer,*
142, 144; *The Prophetess,* 183–96,
259, 303 n; *The Sea Voyage,* 182,
198, 235–54, 260, 310 n; *The
Spanish Curate,* 144; *The Tragedy of
Sir John Van Olden Barnavelt,* 87,
88, 132, 143, 172; *A Very Woman,*
142, 144
Fletcher, John, Philip Massinger,
Ben Jonson, and George Chap-
man, *The Bloody Brother,* 142, 144
Fletcher, John, and William Rowley,
The Maid in the Mill, 115–18, 122
Fletcher, Nathaniel (brother), 11, 12

Fletcher, Phineas (cousin), 2, 8, 11,
20, 56
Fletcher, Richard, junior (father), 1,
4–8, 10, 11
Fletcher, Richard, senior (grand-
father), 1, 2, 5, 8
Foakes, R. A., 147–48
Ford, John, 141
Foucault, Michel, 152, 154, 223,
261
Foxe, John, 1, 2, 94, 130
Frederick, elector palatine, 15, 32,
56, 99, 100, 112, 200, 213, 215
Fuller, Thomas, 9, 10, 85, 87, 88,
92, 132, 136

Gates, Sir Thomas, 209
Genesis, 165
Goodwin, Ralph, 18, 21
Goodyer, Sir Henry, 27
Gossett, Suzanne, 215
Grace-Dieu, 15, 16, 71, 72
Gray's Inn, 12, 100
Greenblatt, Stephen, 244–45
Greville, Fulke, 56
Grindal, Archbishop, 5
Guyana, 203, 211, 244

Hakluyt, Richard, 244
Hall, Joseph, 236–40, 253
Hamor, Ralph, 207
Harington, Sir John, 8, 9, 10
Hastings, Catherine (née Dudley),
countess of Huntingdon, 203
Hastings, Captain Edward, 203
Hastings, Elizabeth (née Stanley),
countess of Huntingdon, xi, 16,
17, 18, 25, 26, 27, 35, 63, 64,
70, 114, 194, 212, 255, 257
Hastings, George, fourth earl of
Huntingdon, 25, 26
Hastings, Henry, fifth earl of Hun-
tingdon, x, xi, 14, 15, 17, 21–27,
30, 34, 35, 37–48, 51–52, 71,
132, 200, 203–6, 212, 236, 255
Hastings, Sir William, 15

Healey, John, 236, 237
Helgerson, Richard, 70, 292
Henrietta Maria, queen of England, x, 196, 261, 292
Henry, Prince, 26, 56, 62, 64, 96, 99, 100, 102, 213
Henslowe, Philip, 133, 141, 142
Hensman, Bertha, 141, 142
Hickman, Andrew, 215
Hildersham, Arthur, 24
Hobbes, Thomas, 199
Holles, Sir John, 26
Hope, Jonathan, 134
Hoy, Cyrus, 59, 134, 143–45, 148, 152, 154
Humfrye, Sir Thomas, 45
Huntingdon, earl and countess of. *See* Hastings
Hutchinson, Lucy, 122

India, 25
Inner Temple, 15, 32, 100
Islington, 5

James I, king of England, 12, 22, 23, 24, 25, 30, 32, 37, 42, 51, 56, 63, 67, 70, 89, 96, 99, 100, 103, 104, 106, 108, 113, 114, 118–22, 193–94, 199–203, 208, 213–15, 218, 227
James, Henry, ix
Jehangir Khan, Great Mogul of India, 25
Jones, Inigo, 101, 133
Jonson, Ben, 13, 14, 15, 16, 33, 56, 60, 100, 122, 130, 133, 134, 149, 213, 215, 250, 257. Works: *Hot Anger Soon Cold*, 133; *Love Restored*, 121; *Robert II, or the Scot's Tragedy*, 133; *Sejanus*, 64, 133, 146; *Volpone*, 16; *Workes*, 133

Kent, 1, 2, 6, 9
King's Company, ix, 13, 33, 34, 36, 126
Koestenbaum, Wayne, 138–40, 149

Lambeth Articles, 8
Lang, Andrew, 138
Langbaine, Gerard, 136–37
Langdale, Abram, 2
Lanyer, Æmilia, 34
Leicester, 37, 42, 43, 44, 47, 64, 67
Leicestershire, 15, 24, 30, 36, 41, 42, 44, 47, 54, 71
"local" reading, xi, 35, 36
Lollards, 7
London, 8, 9, 13, 32, 35, 36, 37, 41, 44, 45, 47, 55, 70, 72, 79, 82, 119, 255

Mabbe, James, 257–58
McLuskie, Kathleen, 141, 145, 146, 164, 175
Malcolm, Noel, 199, 200, 202
Marcus, Leah, 35, 36, 120, 121, 122
Marlowe, Christopher, 11
Marprelate, 9, 120
Marston, John, 17, 54, 194
Martiau, Nicholas, 205–6, 213
Martin, John, 40, 41, 42
Mary, queen of England, 2
Mary, queen of Scots, 8, 17
masque, 21, 31, 32, 33, 35, 156
Masque of Truth, 100
Massinger, Philip, x, 14, 15, 32, 33, 87, 133, 134, 143–45, 152, 153, 172, 182, 185, 239, 241, 279 n; *The Duke of Milan*, 14, 33; *The Guardian*, 106
Massinger, Philip, and Nathan Field, *The Fatal Dowry*, 144
Massinger, Philip, and Thomas Dekker, *The Virgin Martyr*, 144, 184
Massinger, Philip, John Webster, John Ford, and John Fletcher, *The Fair Maid of the Inn*, 144, 259
Masten, Jeffrey, 154
Matthews, Brander, 137–38, 140
Mayhew, Graham, 6, 7
Melville, Herman, 75
Mermaid Inn, 15, 16

Middleton, Thomas, 17, 72; *A Game at Chess,* 34, 85
Midlands revolts, 37–84, 283–87 nn
Mildmay, Sir Anthony, 43
Mildmay, Sir Walter, 23, 65
Milton, John, 194–96, 236
Montagu, Sir Edward, 43
Montrose, Louis Adrian, 57
More, Sir Thomas, 236, 237, 255
Morley, Thomas, 193
morris dance, 29, 58, 106, 125, 127, 151
Mulcaster, Richard, 13, 17
Mullaney, Steven, 35

Nansimahum, 203
Netherlands, 6, 44
New Historicism, 59
Newton, 41, 43
Nicoll, John, 198, 211, 241, 242, 244–45
Norbrook, David, 56, 196
Northampton, 37, 44, 48
Northamptonshire, 15, 36, 42, 43, 48, 54

Oxford, University of, 5, 11, 15, 36
Oxfordshire, 40, 43, 47, 53, 61

pageants, 33
Parker, Archbishop, 4, 5
Parry, Sir Thomas, 43
pastoral, 55–70, 78, 120, 126
patronage, 1–36, 212–13, 279 n, 282 n
Patterson, Annabel, 48, 49, 52, 53, 54, 261
Pearce, Edward, 13, 14
Pembroke, Henry Herbert, earl of, 14, 34, 212, 236
Pembroke College, Oxford (Broadgates Hall), 11
Pepys, Samuel, 240
Pestell, Thomas, 28, 30, 64, 194
Philippines, 224
Plato, 236, 257, 261

Plutarch, 52
Pocahontas, 222–24, 228, 242
Privy Council, 42, 44, 45, 201
Protestantism, xi, 1, 2, 4–7, 11, 12, 20–22, 26, 28, 32, 35, 56, 65, 71, 72, 96, 99, 100, 102, 103, 113, 114, 129, 195, 200, 213–14, 219, 255, 258
Purchas, Samuel, 199, 209–11, 222
Puritanism, 1, 4, 5, 7, 25, 29, 32, 120, 125, 129–31, 236
Puttenham, George, 56–57

Quarles, George, 43
Quarles, John, 41, 42, 72, 82
Queen's College, Cambridge, 11
Queen's Revels, Children of, 13

Raleigh, Sir Walter, 203
republicanism, 169, 200
Revelation, Book of, 130–31
Reynolds, John ("Captain Pouch"), 44, 47
Rich, Sir Nathaniel, 199, 200
Ridley, Nicholas, 2
Rochester, earl of, 135
Roe, Sir Thomas, 25–26, 28, 200, 201
Rolfe, John, 222–24, 227, 228, 233, 242
Rowley, William, 115, 141
Rye, ix, x, 6, 7, 8

Sackville, Sir Edward, 202
St. Paul's, Children of, 13, 14, 17
Sandys, Sir Edwin, 65, 199–206
Sandys, George, 200, 203, 242
Sandys, Sir Samuel, 202
Sedgwick, Eve Kosofsky, 139
Shakespeare, William, ix, 13, 34, 35, 36, 95, 134, 137, 143, 146, 183, 212, 241, 262; *Antony and Cleopatra,* 53; *Coriolanus,* xi, 52, 53, 54, 55; *King Lear,* 112; *Macbeth,* 142; *Measure for Measure,* 89, 254; *A Midsummer Night's Dream,*

Shakespeare, William (*cont.*)
 60–61, 65, 173, 290 n; *Othello*,
 163, 301 n; *Pericles* (with Wilkins),
 173, 185, 250, 254, 288 n; *The*
 Taming of the Shrew, 157–58, 162–
 64, 182; *The Tempest*, 77, 107,
 182, 185, 190–92, 195, 197–99,
 211–12, 221, 224–25, 232, 236,
 240–41, 247, 252; *Timon of*
 Athens (with Middleton), 142; *The*
 Winter's Tale, 254
Shakespeare, William, and John
 Fletcher: *Cardenio*, 259, 312 n;
 Henry VIII, ix, 102–4, 106, 108,
 123, 147–48, 218; *The Two Noble*
 Kinsmen, ix, 105–6, 122, 190,
 215, 261, 297 n
Shelton, Thomas, 258
Sherley, Sir Thomas, 42
Shirley, James, x
Sidney, Sir Philip, 14, 32, 33, 56,
 59, 258
Skipwith, Sir William, 15, 17, 24,
 44, 62, 64
Skura, Meredith, 208
Smith, Sir Thomas, 202, 204, 205
Southampton, earl of, 12, 200, 202–
 4, 212, 258
Spain, 18, 21, 113, 114, 257–62
Spenser, Edmund, 31, 32, 33, 56,
 57–58, 60–61, 66, 195, 240, 254
"Spenserian" poets, 2, 8, 23, 56, 57,
 95, 100, 288–89 nn
Staller, Thomas, 5
Stanhope, Katherine, 14, 15
Stanhope, Philip, earl of Chesterfield,
 14
Star Chamber, 41, 72, 118, 120
Stillinger, Jack, 154
Strachey, William, 198, 241–45
Stratford-upon-Avon, ix
Sussex, ix, 6, 36

Tenterden, 6
Thirty Years War, 99, 112

Todorov, Tzvetan, 246
Tourneur, Cyril, 141
Townsend, Sir Robert, 64
Tragedy of the Plantation of Virginia,
 A, 242
tragicomedy, x, 55, 58, 59, 60, 70,
 84, 90, 105, 260
Tresham, Thomas, 40, 42, 71
Trinity College, Cambridge, 4

Udall, Nicholas, 13
unease, x, 54, 58, 65, 79, 84, 87,
 90, 92, 131, 151, 156, 182, 196,
 199–200, 231, 242, 256, 257,
 260, 261, 262

Vautor, Thomas, 193
Virginia, 105, 199–214, 222, 224,
 229, 239
Virginia Company, 28, 198–209,
 213–15, 242

Wade, Christopher, 1, 2, 8
Waith, Eugene, 262
Walkley, Thomas, 110, 112, 113
Warwickshire, 42, 43
Washington, George, 205
Weald, 2, 6, 7, 14
Webster, John, 141
Welham, 45, 46
Whitaker, Alexander, 207
Whitehall, 35, 113
White Mountain, battle of, 113
Whitgift, Archbishop, 8
Wilde, Oscar, 138
Wilkinson, Robert, 48–55, 62, 65,
 84
Wilson, Arthur, 194
Wilson, Thomas, 258
Wither, George, 56
Worcester, 8, 11
Worcestershire, 43
Wotton, Sir Henry, 12

Yoch, James, 67